Civil Rights and the Presidency

Civil Rights and the Presidency

Race and Gender in
American Politics
1960–1972

HUGH DAVIS GRAHAM

New York   Oxford
OXFORD UNIVERSITY PRESS
1992

Oxford University Press

Oxford   New York   Toronto
Delhi   Bombay   Calcutta   Madras   Karachi
Petaling Jaya   Singapore   Hong Kong   Tokyo
Nairobi   Dar es Salaam   Cape Town
Melbourne   Auckland

and associated companies in
Berlin   Ibadan

Copyright © 1992 Hugh Davis Graham.
This book is an abridgement of
The Civil Rights Era: Origins and Development of National Policy,
Copyright © 1990 by Hugh Davis Graham.

Published by Oxford University Press, Inc.,
200 Madison Avenue, New York, New York 10016

Oxford is a registered trademark of Oxford University Press

Library of Congress Cataloging-in-Publication Data
Graham, Hugh Davis.
Civil rights and the presidency / Hugh Davis Graham.
—Abridged ed. p. cm.
ISBN 0-19-506649-9.—ISBN 0-19-507322-3 (pbk.)
1. Civil rights—United States—History—20th century.
2. Affirmative action programs—Government policy—
United States—History—20th century.
3. United States—Politics and government—1945–
I. Title.
JC599.U5G685 1992 323.1'73—dc20 91-18773

2 4 6 8 9 7 5 3 1

Printed in the United States of America
on acid-free paper

Contents

Civil Rights and the Presidency

Introduction

Social Movements and National Policy: The Transformation of the American Administrative State

This is a story about a rare event in America: a radical shift in national social policy. Its precondition was a broader social revolution, the black civil rights movement that surged up from the South, followed by the nationwide rebirth of the feminist movement.[1] The social movements took hold and spread at the grass roots, but the policy revolution that responded to them was made in Washington. This is therefore a study of national policy elites, their behavior and motives, their options and decisions, and the consequences of those decisions. The combined weight of their achievements, most notably the civil rights laws of 1964, 1965, 1968, and 1972, together with supporting court decisions and administrative enforcement, broke the back of the system of racial segregation and destroyed the legal basis for denying minorities and women full access to education, employment, and professions, and the opportunities of the private marketplace and the public arena.

The broader impact of these laws on American society, however, could not readily be discerned by contemporary citizens. The "rights revolution" of 1960-72 provided the cutting edge for a profound shift in the way Americans related to their government that extended far beyond the arena of race and gender policy. During the civil rights era the American administrative state reached out and embraced workaday relationships between its citizens and both public and private institutions in a way that had never before been contemplated—except, perhaps, in temporary wartime emergencies, and in the largely failed "first" Reconstruction.

The story's main focus, federal policy in civil rights during 1960-72, was originally conceived, like most studies of civil rights, as centering almost exclusively on racial policy. But the evidence and the logic of civil rights theory demanded the inclusion of gender as well as racial policy. The historical experience of group discrimination, the politics of group protest in the 1960s, the race-sex analogy in policy debate, and the inclusion of sex with race in the statutory protections of the Civil Rights Act of 1964, all required that the black and feminist movements and their policy consequences be considered together. Other groups of course shared the burden of historical discrimination, and civil rights theory would extend as well to Hispanics, Asians, and other minorities. But the nature of group protest and policy debate during the 1960s ordained that such groups would play a relatively modest role, at least through 1972.

Not surprisingly, the issues of black civil rights dominate the early drama. But the policy revolution of 1960-72 involved a dual transformation that in many ways confounded the traditional race-sex analogy. By equating the victim status of women and oppressed minorities, the analogy held that discrimination against blacks and women flowed from similar causes (oppression by white males) and required similar remedies (coalitions for government reform, as in the Civil Rights Act of 1964). The movement for black civil rights was originally driven by liberalism's classic theory of individual rights and nondiscrimination. Through its successes during the mid-1960s, however, the black freedom movement evoked new theories of compensatory justice and group rights. In doing so it generated new internal divisions within the civil rights coalition. By the late 1960s the surging "second-wave" feminist movement, by invoking principles of egalitarianism that were at once radical and classic, provided a revealing counterpoint to the black agenda, which was moving away from the NAACP's historic model of a "color-blind" Constitution. Increasingly, following the breakthrough Civil Rights Act of 1964, feminists demanded a "sex-blind" Constitution to achieve equal rights. Black leaders, however, having at long last won the victory of color-blindness in the decade between *Brown v. Board of Education* and the Civil Rights Act of 1964, feared increasingly that a color-blind Constitution would freeze the inequities of past discrimination.

The choice of the period 1960-72, like all such decisions about periodization, requires some defense. One can easily nominate plausible earlier events for a starting point, and historians are cursed by causal hindsight with a vast universe of plausible origins. Suffice it here simply to claim that the challenge of the sit-ins in the South and the election of John F. Kennedy as President in 1960 catapulted the civil rights issue into the forefront of national consciousness. It did this with an escalating logic and moral force that for the first time (since the first Reconstruction) compelled all three branches of the federal government to confront and attempt to remedy the brutal legacy of discrimination. This effort began cautiously with John F. Kennedy's executive order in the spring of 1961, which injected into public discourse the ambiguous phrase, "affirmative action." The momentum of reform escalated after the Birmingham violence into Kennedy's civil rights bill of the summer of 1963. Following Kennedy's assassination in November 1963, Lyndon Johnson broke the southern and conservative resistance with the Civil Rights Act of 1964 and, following the Selma march, the Voting Rights Act of 1965. Johnson completed his Great Society reforms in civil rights with the somewhat surprising Open Housing Act of 1968.

Thereafter both the Johnson and Nixon administrations and the Congress continued to struggle with the unresolved problems of civil rights enforcement for both blacks and women until 1972, when Congress sent the Equal Rights Amendment to the states with astounding majorities, and Richard Nixon signed the Equal Employment Opportunity Act of 1972. Nixon confirmed the "Second Reconstruction" in much the same way that Eisenhower had confirmed the New Deal—not by embracing it, but by accommodating to it on the margins in a way that guaranteed its legitimacy and secured its permanence in the federal establishment. After 1972, as one major study confirmed, congressional interest in further debate over the fundamental assumptions and structures of the new civil rights laws and their enforcement mechanisms (as distinct from congressional interest in adding new groups, such as language minorities and the handicapped, to the protected-class model) dropped "virtually to zero."[2]

The post-Watergate administrations of presidents Ford and Carter would grapple with Congress and respond to court decisions over policies of applying the new protections and claims, and of extending the umbrella of newly protected classes to include such groups as Hispanics and language minorities, the physically and mentally disabled, institutionalized persons, the elderly, children, and the unborn. In the 1980s the Reagan administration would attempt to mount a counterrevolution, only to find in Congress, in the federal courts, and in the vast administrative apparatus of the permanent government formidable barriers to dramatic change. Thus the events of the 1960s shattered the old mold, and by 1972 the fundamental attributes of the new order were set in place.

History and Civil Rights Policy: The Dual Reconstruction of 1960-72

Contemporary accounts of the civil rights movement and reforms of the 1960s, and the first wave of historical accounts during the 1970s, emphasized dramatic events like the protests at Birmingham and Selma and their causal link to the breakthrough laws of 1964 and 1965. Policy analysis similarly emphasized the formulation and enactment phases of the policy cycle, but devoted little attention to the obscure and complex phase of implementation.[3] This book broadens the basis of historical analysis to include the full policy cycle, with special attention to reconstructing from the archives the crucial process of policy implementation. At the same time, however, this study also narrows the lens to focus more intensively on decisions and events that in the longer view have demonstrated an abiding importance—and have often generated a lasting controversy—that was not acccorded them at the time. Controversies that dominated the headlines of 1960-72 have since faded in importance, many of them the welcome casualties of success: the major battles over desegregating Jim Crow school systems, over segregation in public facilities and accommodations, over the right of blacks to cast ballots in the South, and over the impunity with which white terrorists plied their trade. These controversies dominated the first phase of the reform era and their focus was the South. They generally involved positive-sum rights, such as equal access to the voting booth, to the public schools, to parks and hotels and restaurants, rights that all citizens could claim and the polity could accommodate without denying the rights of others.

Beneath these claims, however, were conflicts that more closely approximated a zero-sum game. Beginning in the late 1960s, in a social environment heated by urban violence, federal enforcement agencies began to apply group remedies to speed the redistribution of jobs and income to designated minorities. When the new preferential policies were challenged in court by whites as discriminatory themselves, the federal courts generally approved them as necessary to compensate the protected classes from the lingering effects of past discrimination. The collision of competing individual and group claims to jobs and contracts, to appointments and promotions, and to higher education and professional schools, was accelerated by rising federal efforts to rectify the "underutilization" of minorities. Opponents raised the cry of "reverse discrimination." The issue of racial quotas first arose during the great national debate over the Civil Rights Act of 1964, and the apparent illogic and illiberalism of fighting discrimination with counter-discrimination produced a national consensus in 1963-64 that embedded a ban on such practices in the heart of the new law—or so it was thought at the time. But these issues were raised again in the late Johnson years and passed unresolved into the first Nixon administration. They came to dominate the civil rights controversies after 1972 when reverse discrimination suits like *Bakke* and *Weber* split the Supreme Court, much as they divided the entire country.

The reforms of the civil rights era raised these more difficult controversies over equal results and compensatory justice in the process of resolving the problems of equal treatment. With hingsight we can seek the origins of these persistent and troubling issues in the policy deliberations of national elites who grappled with them, solving some, exacerbating others. The story begins in 1960, when the sit-in tactic of civil disobedience reinvigorated the black protest movement and forced the issue of racial equality into presidential politics. Kennedy's narrow victory and weak congressional base led to an executive strategy of civil rights enforcement that centered on the complicated and somewhat perplexing executive order of 1961. Its unlikely and unhappy architect was Vice President Lyndon Johnson. It summoned from the obscure, statutory boilerplate of the Wagner Act of 1935 an enigmatic phrase, "affirmative action," whose ambiguous meaning would be haltingly defined in a long thread of controversy that would tie the Kennedy era to our own in ways the New Frontiersmen could not have contemplated.

Kennedy's circumspect beginning thus launched the modern presidency toward a triumph of classic anti-discrimination that would redeem the failures of the first Reconstruction. Lyndon Johnson would fulfill the fallen Kennedy's legacy, and sign into law the watershed Civil Rights Act of 1964. But at the peak of its triumph, in 1965, the liberal core doctrine of nondiscrimination confronted liberalism's paradox of history: the timeless principles of republican liberty, as they are discovered and proclaimed, are perforce applied only to the present and future. This works well with most positive-sum rights, such as nondiscrimination in hotels and restaurants, parks and schools, and the voting booth. But in the more nearly zero-sum world of economic opportunity, of jobs and promotions, history has left a legacy of deep scars on excluded groups. "Freedom is not enough," Lyndon Johnson told the graduating class at Howard University in June 1965. "You do not wipe away the scars of centuries by saying: Now you are free to go where you want, do as you desire, choose the leaders you please," he explained. "You do not take a person who for years has been hobbled by chains and liberate him, bring him to the starting line and then say, 'You are free to compete with all the others,' and still justly believe that you have been completely fair."[4]

"We seek not just freedom but opportunity," Johnson said, "not just equality as a right and a theory but equality as a fact and as a result." He thus seemed to proclaim, beyond the procedural goal of equal treatment as a necessary but insufficient precondition, a more ambitious and elusive substantive goal—"the next and more profound stage of the battle for civil rights." Once he reached the White House, Lyndon Johnson confronted his battles for civil rights honestly, carried them aggressively to the Congress and the public, fought them courageously, and won most of them. This was the triumphal first phase of the civil rights era. But the Phase II battle that Johnson launched in Congress in 1966 outlived his administration. It lasted through the first four years of Richard Nixon's administration and culminated in the Equal Employment Opportunity Act and Title IX of the education amendments of 1972, and in congressional passage of the Equal Rights Amendment. The forces that drove Phase II were broader, newer, and more complex than liberalism's vintage crusade against discrimination, which had shattered the defenses of segregation in 1964-65. Otherwise the momentum of Phase II should not have survived the catharsis of ghetto riots, Black Power, political assassination, and hard-hat backlash that convulsed the nation during the late 1960s and early 1970s. Such forces and their consequences yield their secrets only through the perspective of time and through the archival documents that chart the evolution of public policy.

Civil Rights as Harbinger of the New Social Regulation

Thus the presidency dominates this volume. The massive paper trail of its inner deliberations, masked behind its public rhetoric, constitutes the core of the evidence. Congress in its independent legislative role often anticipated and outflanked the President—especially during the Nixon administration, when Congress was controlled by the opposition party. Similarly the federal judiciary, despite the shift in 1969 from the Warren to the Burger Court, asserted an expanding role in shaping social policy. Indeed the judicial rulings of the civil rights era show a striking continuity in empowering the executive agencies and their custodians. The courts extended the reach and reinforced the authority of a new regime of social regulation that was being constructed largely without blueprint or even conscious awareness. In an unplanned yet seemingly symbiotic relationship, the civil rights movement, first led by blacks and then joined by women, formed the expanding edge of the new American administrative state. The civil rights movement of blacks and women provided the cutting edge of political demand and also the new model of remedy for the new social regulation. By the late 1960s, the black and feminist thrust had been joined by a broader aggregation of parallel but uncoordinated interests, including environmental, consumer, and antiwar forces, that accelerated the evolution of the new social regulation through the 1960s and beyond.

This vast and largely undirected process centered in the executive branch, where the commanding heights of federal policy are theoretically controlled by the White House. In implementing social policy, however, the well-entrenched executive establishment in the "subpresidency" has enjoyed formidable advantages in distributing the budget and designing the rules of the game. While presidents and congresses come and go, the federal agencies abide. Through administrative law and regulation, the bureaucracy defines the precise meaning of broad statutory provisions that Congress could not realistically tailor to the shifts and nuances of America's workaday life. This then is a story not only of presidents and powerful White House aides, of prominent cabinet secretaries and attorneys general and their loyalist lieutenants among the President's battalion of senior but temporary "Schedule-C" political appointees. It is also a story of the "permanent government" of the career civil servants in the semi-independent mission agencies and their sub-baronies in departments like Labor, HEW, Defense. It is the story of novel sub-agencies like the clumsily named and yet extraordinarily important Office of Federal Contract Compliance Programs (OFCC) in the Department of Labor, and especially of the era's fragile infant among regulatory boards, the Equal Employment Opportunity Commission (EEOC).

Telling such a story necessarily involves such arcane bureaucratic entities and statutory constructions as Title 7 coverage, "pattern or practice" suits, bona fide occupational qualifications, Section 5 preclearance, cease-and-desist authority. At its heart lie such crucial statutory obscurities as Title 7's controversial Section 703(j), which meant a ban on racial quotas, and wonderfully bureaucratic nomenclature like "Revised Order No. 4," which when decoded meant including women in requirements for minority proportionality in job distribution. Such gray contrivances of statutory law and the bureaucratic imagination lack the graphic and emotional appeal of the murders of civil rights workers in Mississippi or the ghetto riots in Watts and Detroit. But in the long run of policy continuity and its aggregated impact they are probably more important.

Black Civil Rights and Women's Liberation as Social Movements

In 1960, black protest stood alone in the postwar era as a modern social movement gathering force at the grass roots. Since the bus boycott in Montgomery, Alabama, in 1955–56 had catapulted the young Rev. Martin Luther King, Jr., to national prominence, the black civil rights movement had remained "*The* Movement." By 1966, however, women were mobilizing nationally, and the escalation of American intervention in Vietnam was generating an aggressive antiwar movement. By 1972, the proliferation of social movements demanding change included Hispanics, American Indians, college students, gays and lesbians, consumer advocates, and a wide variety of environmental-protection groups.[5] But the dominant constituencies in the civil rights movement of the 1960s remained blacks and women. Together in 1960 they counted 110 million Americans, or approximately 57 percent of the U.S. population.

The first generation of scholarship on the mobilization of blacks and feminists in the 1960s emphasized their historic similarities. Writing in 1977, historian William Chafe in *Women and Equality* found strong commonalities in the historical experience of blacks and women. Both were oppressed groups which had shared, literally for centuries, modes of physical, economic, and psychological subservience under the social control of white males. Both groups were marked by immutable, physical differences that set them apart from white males, and as a consequence they had been systematically excluded from society's power relationships, especially political authority and control of property. Abolitionist women themselves perceived this and were embittered when the feminist declaration at Seneca Falls was betrayed in 1868 by the addition through the Fourteenth amendment of a novel constitutional reference to "male" rights. On the eve of the modern civil rights movement, Gunnar Myrdal added to *The American Dilemma* a special appendix on women, entitled "A Parallel to the Negro Problem," that reinforced the analogy between race and sex discrimination.[6] Chafe found common experiences of modern collective protest for blacks and women in the liberating dislocations of World War II and the postwar contradictions between the democratic creed and discriminatory practice. For women, the black civil rights movement itself was a catalytic precipitating event, and in their respective mobilizations, both blacks and women had invented effective new tactics of protest that generated group solidarity. For blacks, the bonding experience flowed from the act of civil disobedience, especially the sit-ins; for women, an equivalent experience was found in feminist consciousness-raising groups.

During the 1960s and subsequently, leaders of black rights organizations kept a polite distance from the feminist movement. This restrained solidarity reflected both muted resentment at feminist competition for the energy and resources of civil rights reform, and fear that controversy over the ERA or abortion rights might slow the drive for racial equality. But feminist leaders embraced the race-sex analogy from the beginning. The National Organization for Women was founded in 1966 in the midst of a feminist campaign to force the fledgling EEOC to take sex discrimination as seriously as race discrimination and to apply the same remedies. True to the historical pattern, the blacks remained in the vanguard and the women continued to play catch-up. The women's Nineteenth amendment was the black's Fifteenth; their crusade for the ERA echoed the black's Fourteenth; their eleventh-hour inclusion in the great Civil Rights Act of 1964 came from a surprising tactical coup on the House floor that is replete with its own ironies of strange and expedient political alliance.[7] The sovereign principle that drove modern feminism also lay at the heart of the NAACP's model, which was classic liberalism's demand for the equal treatment of individuals irrespective of their ascribed status or immutable attributes.

Yet race and gender are by no means commensurate as physical and cultural attributes, and profound differences have characterized the social circumstances and historical experiences of blacks and women in America. Chief among them is women's intimate cohabitation with "the oppressor." The nuptial and family bond denied women the shared physical and geographic space that had historically nourished the group cohesion of racial and ethnic minorities. It thereby allowed the intervening variable, socio-economic class, to confound the American feminist movement in ways and degrees that were never experienced by black protest. Both social movements felt the internal divisions of class tension. Black intellectuals had long complained that the tiny black bourgeoisie aped the white power structure. But historic poverty had greatly flattened the black class pyramid, and the shared poverty of most blacks buttressed black cohesion in the face of racial oppression. For women, however, the social distribution of women almost perfectly mirrored the sharper class pyramid of the larger society. The result was frustrated or fractured feminist cohesion. The literature on woman suffrage provides a depressing but sobering reminder of these persistent class (and also racial) divisions among American women.[8]

In the 20th century the post-enfranchisement experience of both groups with voting reveals how differently class distinctions affected voting behavior. Historically, class divisions have been relatively inconsequential among blacks, who have tended to vote as a racial bloc irrespective of differences in income and education. Enfranchised blacks for three generations voted for the party of Lincoln. But during the 1930s these loyalties were dislodged by Franklin Roosevelt's New Deal, and by the 1960s the black vote had become massively Democratic. Among women, however, the political impact of femaleness remained virtually undetectable. American women, like men, have historically voted their class, their religion, their region—but not their sex.[9]

When the decade of the 1960s began, the status of black civil rights and that of women's rights differed sharply. The black civil rights movement was a smoldering volcano that appeared to be highly regionalized. In the northern and western states, all of which for generations had banned racial discrimination in civic life and in public facilities and accommodations, and most of which, since World War II, had created state commissions to prohibit discrimination in private employment as well, the fault line of racial oppression was assumed to start in Washington. From there it curved sharply south-westward, through the vast southern black belt and into Texas. The nation's racial problem seemed to be a southern problem.

The feminist movement in 1960, on the other hand, was not only invisible, it was implausible. Most of the American states, far from banning legal distinctions based on gender differences, to the contrary enforced a special set of labor laws that applied only to women. Dating from the era of Progressive reform, these laws required different treatment for women precisely because they were not men. Women, being generally smaller and weaker than men and being potential or actual mothers as well, were therefore protected from such dangers as heavy labor, longer hours, jobs requiring travel and hazardous activity, workplaces lacking proper rest facilities. No state commission against discrimination in 1960 was charged with enforcing equal treatment for women.

Under these circumstances, from the perspective of 1960, the eruption of the southern sit-ins in February of that year was not surprising. The national explosion of second-wave feminism that followed shortly thereafter, on the other hand, was astonishing.

CHAPTER 1

America in 1960:
Blacks and Women on the Eve of
Social Revolution

The Paradox of Social Movements

When we compare the social conditions of blacks and women in the United
States in 1960 we find a paradox. Both groups, not surprisingly, score well
below their respective reference groups, whites and men, on such basic indicators of well-being as income and education. Blacks and women differed markedly, however, in their ability to close the gap on their counterpart groups.
Most of the gaps separating the conditions of blacks and whites had been
closing since the end of the Depression. But many of the socio-economic gaps
separating the attainments of women and men had been *widening,* especially
since World War II. Logic would suggest that under these conditions, blacks
would react positively to their improving social status, while resentment would
grow among women. But in the social reality of America in 1960, we find
instead the opposite pattern. Therein lies the paradox. The evidence of group
resentment in 1960 pointed to an incipient eruption on the part of black
Americans, particularly in the South, while among American women there was
scant public evidence of widespread discontent. How do we describe and account for this, and what does it tell us about the sequence of events that
produced a revolution in public policy affecting both blacks and women during
the next dozen years?

Twelve million of the nation's 19 million blacks in 1960 lived in the southern
states, where an elaborate system of biracial caste had segregated the region's
schools, job, places of commerce, and social institutions for as long as living
memory. In 1954 the U.S. Supreme Court had ruled, in *Brown v. Board of
Education,* that racially segregated schools were unconstitutional. Yet by 1960
only 1 percent of southern black schoolchildren were attending school with
whites. The promise of the *Brown* decision had been quickened during 1955–56
by the success of the boycott against segregated seating in buses in Montgomery,
Alabama, led by Dr. Martin Luther King, Jr. But the momentum of the Montgomery movement then seemed to dissipate. President Dwight D. Eisenhower had

been unwilling to endorse desegregation as a moral imperative for the nation, and the initial moderation of southern political leaders had shifted by the late 1950s toward open defiance. By 1960 the South's blacks were still subjected to the daily humiliations of a Jim Crow system that had not fundamentally changed since the era of World War I. Blacks were required by state laws and local ordinances to sit in the back of the bus, drink from the "Colored" water fountains, attend Negro schools and colleges. Blacks were prohibited by public law and commercial policy from sitting at lunch counters in the five-and-dime stores or trying on clothes in the department stores. For black Americans in the South it was a challenge even to find a place downtown to urinate.[1]

For the 40 percent of blacks living outside the South, the economic and social incentives for leaving the South had generally been rewarded by higher incomes and an escape from Jim Crowism. The median annual income of black families in Arkansas in 1960, for example, was $1,305 (in constant 1988 dollars, $5,202). In Michigan, however it was $3,670 ($14,630 in 1988 dollars). The mean family income for *all* American blacks in 1960 was $3,233 ($12,888 in 1988 dollars). But for whites in the U.S. the median family income in 1960 was $5,835 ($23,261 in 1988 dollars). This meant that America's blacks since 1940 had gained 16 percentage points on whites in narrowing the racial earnings gap. It also meant that black families in Michigan were more prosperous (by a margin of 15 percent) than white families in Arkansas. Nonetheless, the family income of black Americans by 1960 had risen to only 55 percent of white family income.[2]

The same story of huge racial disparities despite considerable postwar gap-closing applied to education. Between 1940 and 1960 the percentage of white males completing high school in the U.S. jumped from 12.8 percent to 22.2 percent—an increase of 74 percent. The corresponding improvement for blacks showed a *314 percent* gain in high school completion rates. But this great leap forward started with only 3.8 percent of blacks completing high school in 1940, and by 1960 it still left 88 percent of America's black males with less than a high school education. Similarly, white life expectancy had increased from 64.2 years in 1940 to 70.6 years in 1960, while the average lifespan for blacks had grown during the same period from 53.1 to 63.6 years. Thus the longevity of blacks had increased by 20 percent while white longevity had increased by only 10 percent. Yet whites on average still lived seven years longer than blacks. Between 1940 and 1960, infant mortality had been cut by 49 percent for whites and 53 percent for blacks. Yet by 1960 black babies still died twice as frequently as white babies.

Furthermore, not all indicators showed narrowing racial gaps. The black-white gap in unemployment, which had been negligible (employment was low for both groups) at the end of World War II, had steadily worsened for blacks. By 1960 black unemployment was twice the white rate: 10.2 percent for blacks and 4.9 percent for whites. Black arrest rates had climbed from twice the white rate in 1940 to five times the white rate in 1960, and the black percentage of the U.S. prison population had grown during the same period from 26 percent to 38 percent.[3]

Looking back from the perspective of the 1990s, we recognize these early symptoms of an urban pathology that would explode in ghetto riots in the late 1960s. But at the dawn of the 1960s the social indicators holding promise for most Americans were those that reflected growth and opportunity in income and education. And in these the main patterns seemed persistent: black rates of improvement for the post-Depression generation typically exceeded the white rates, and both showed growing opportunity in the great postwar surge of American affluence. As conservative commentators in 1960 pointed out, most evidence and trends showed that black Americans were better off than ever before. American Negroes continued to gain on whites, the editors of the *Wall Street Journal* observed, and they were much better off than blacks in Africa.[4]

Yet, paradoxically, black dissatisfaction seemed to grow almost inversely with the relative gains. During the late 1950s, political sociologists had begun to talk about "revolutions of rising expectations." They were referring primarily to the social and anticolonial revolutions in the underdeveloped world during the postwar era, especially in former European colonies like India, Kenya, Indonesia, and Algeria. But the thesis of relative deprivation seemed to apply to mass-based protest generally, wherever it occurred. It held that social mobilizations are driven less by objective conditions of deprivation, such as profound poverty, than by perceptions of unfairness coupled with a quickening pace of change that heightened expectations. For social analysts in 1960 the most dramatic and recent revolutionary upheaval in the western hemisphere had occurred not in prostrate Haiti, where there was little hope, but instead in Cuba, which in the mid-fifties had boasted the second-highest rate of economic growth in all of Latin America.[5]

American Women in 1960

In contrast to the circumstances of black Americans in 1960, for whom the narrowing of racial gaps since the Depression had coincided with rising protest, American women had experienced a widening of many gender gaps while manifesting little tangible evidence of discontent. Public opinion polling, which was a mature and vigorous enterprise by 1960, nonetheless shed little light on the perceptions of either blacks or women in the United States. Paul Sheatsley, a pioneer in surveying racial attitudes, explained the pollsters' inattention to black attitudes: "It never occurred to us when we wrote the questions in the Forties and Fifties to ask them of blacks because [Gunnar] Myrdal's dilemma was a white dilemma and it was white attitudes that demanded study."[6] Similarly, questions on feminist issues were rarely asked prior to the middle 1960s.[7] When a Gallup poll in 1962 asked a sample of American women whether they felt themselves victims of discrimination, two out of three said no.[8]

In view of the sudden mobilization of the modern feminist movement in the middle 1960s, it is customary to identify as a major catalytic event the publication in 1963 of journalist Betty Friedan's *The Feminine Mystique*, which sold more than a million copies.[9] Friedan's book was a *cri de coeur* that indicted the

American social structure generally, and the purveyors of public taste in the mass media in particular, for confining women's proper role to the kitchen, the bedroom, and the nursery of middle-class suburbia. She addressed women who shared her own frustrations, well-educated white women whose professional and career aspirations were blocked by sex discrimination and role stereotyping. Her special target was the women's magazines (for which she had frequently written)—*The Woman's Home Companion, McCall's, The Ladies' Home Journal, Redbook*—and the cult of female domesticity they relentlessly invoked. Their pages paraphrased "ad nauseam," Friedan wrote, the Freudian theories promulgated by best-selling books like *Modern Women: The Lost Sex* (1947). Its authors, psychoanalyst Marynia Farnham and sociologist Ferdinand Lundberg, saw feminism as symptomatic of a "deep illness"; they traced its roots to penis envy and regarded the independent woman as "a contradiction in terms."[10]

In 1955, Adlai Stevenson, the champion of liberal Democrats and the party's nominee for President in 1952 and 1956, told the commencement assembly at Smith College that modern woman's participation in politics should come through her role as wife and mother. "Women, especially educated women," Stevenson said, "have a unique opportunity to influence us, man and boy."

> This assignment for you, as wives and mothers, you can do in the living room with a baby in your lap or in the kitchen with a can opener in your hand. If you're clever, maybe you can even practice your saving arts on that unsuspecting man while he's watching television. I think there is much you can do about our crisis in the humble role of housewife. I could wish you no better vocation than that.[11]

Stevenson, a national leader of great urbanity and sophistication, was voicing sentiments widely shared by both sexes in the postwar era. The editors of *The Woman's Home Companion* published Stevenson's address verbatim in the September 1955 issue.

Stevenson assured the Smith graduates that "whether we talk of Africa, Islam, or Asia, women 'never had it so good' as you." Perhaps so. But when the comparison was with the previous achievements of American women, not with women in third-world countries, the status of U.S. women relative to men in 1960 in many ways had worsened since the 1920s. In education, the proportion of women attending college in comparison with men had dropped from 47 percent in 1920 to 36 percent in 1960. Moreover, by the mid-fifties almost two-thirds of undergradute women were dropping out of college, most of them to marry. In 1920, women held 15 percent of the doctoral degrees and 26 percent of the full-time positions on college faculties, but by 1960 the female share of doctorates had declined to 10 percent and faculty posts to 22 percent. Only 8 percent of medical school students and 5 percent of law students in 1960 were women.[12]

While the declining participation of women in professional and career pursuits reinforced the cult of female domesticity that was celebrated by magazines like *The Ladies' Home Journal,* the growing participation of women in the labor force seemed to contradict it. During the 1950s, women joined the workforce at a rate four times that of men. By 1964, 40 percent of all women over sixteen were in the paid workforce, compared with 25 percent in 1940. Unlike the pre-1940 pattern, when most women workers were young, single, and transient in the labor force, a majority of the new female workers were married, many of them re-entering the job market after child-raising to provide a second income.[13] Although the new women workers were increasingly well educated—over 53 percent of female college graduates held jobs in 1962, in contrast to 36 percent of those with only a high school diploma—they crowded into the bottom of the job market. The surge of women into the labor market increased their family income but placed a downward pressure on average women's earnings. The ironical result was that the ratio of women's earnings to men's, which had begun to narrow with the flood of women into the factory and office during World War II, peaked in 1956 at 63.9 cents on the dollar. It then began a long downward slide, through the 1960s and into the 1970s, driven by the low wages of pink-collar jobs (the ratio bottomed in 1973 at 56.6 percent). Black women, who unlike white women had long participated heavily in the workforce, mostly as farm laborers and domestic servants, suffered the double jeopardy of race *and* gender discrimination. They earned only 25.9 percent of white male earnings in 1948, and by 1960 this ratio had climbed to only 28.2 percent. (Black men's earnings during the same period crept from 58.5 percent to 59.6 percent of white male earnings.)[14]

Sex Segregation in the Job Market

The pink-collar workforce was channeled into low-wage, noncareer-ladder jobs by an inherited mesh of institutional and cultural forces that most Americans in 1960 took for granted as part of the natural social order. Practices that appear bizarre to the eyes of the 1990s were so routine in 1960 that they were neither challenged nor particularly noticed. Women looking for job openings in the classified ads would find them segregated by sex in the daily newspapers. In the January 3, Sunday edition of the *New York Times* in 1960, for example, the job openings were published in sex-segregated sections, with 14 pages listing help-wanted ads for males and 8 pages listing jobs for females. The *Times'* sex-segregated listings were typical of the national press. The dominant category of jobs offered under Help Wanted—Female fell into the file clerk/steno-typist/secretary bloc. The next largest bloc described jobs for the general-purpose administrative assistant called a "Girl Friday." The men's section carried the male equivalent of the low-paying female jobs—"mail boy," driver, guard, building custodian, bank teller. But here, additionally, were the jobs with futures, separating the white-collar world of men from the pink-collar world of women: accountancy, auditor, draftsman, management, production, exports.

The newspapers listed no third, sexually neutral column of jobs that might be performed by either men or women.

Pink-collar jobs customarily paid weekly wages, not annual salaries. Jobs like clerk-typist and receptionist/switchboard operator typically paid $70 per week in 1960—the equivalent of $14,500 in 1988 dollars. Legal stenographers and airline stewardesses ("Company will train brite, attractive gals") offered $100 per week, and an experienced "Gal Friday" earned $115. The magisterial *New York Times* did not advertise for newspaper reporters, but of the 100 signed news articles published in the *Times* that Sunday morning in 1960, only three carried the by-lines of women reporters.[15] The jobs listed under Help Wanted—Male included high-salaried career positions like marketing and administrative vice president, production manager, research director, jobs that paid in the $15,000-$30,000 range ($60,000-$120,000 in 1988 dollars). The lexicon of the job market carried its male equivalent of Gal Friday and stewardess—boilerman, repairman, draftsman, delivery man, messenger boy. Employers seeking to fill salaried positions as executives, engineers, bond and trust officers, patent attorneys, and similar presumptively men's jobs placed their ads exclusively in the male columns. In the sex-segregated job market, even bra-girdle sales managers and corset buyers were listed under Help Wanted—Male.

The world of sex roles in 1960, as viewed through the prism of the *New York Times* that first Sunday in January, was not entirely devoid of challenge, however. The Soviet launch of *Sputnik* in 1957 had called attention to the crucial role of brainpower in the Cold War, and this had prompted a scattering of comments by editorial writers and presidents of women's colleges about the significantly greater participation by Soviet women in science, engineering, and medicine. This theme was addressed in the *Magazine* section that January 3 by Marya Mannes, a staff writer for *The Reporter* magazine, in an essay titled "Female Intelligence: Who Wants It?"

Mannes echoed the recent complaint of Smith College president Thomas Mendenhall that because a majority of college women were dropping out of school to get married and raise families, few were left to pursue advanced study for professional and scientific careers. Were women capable, Mannes asked, of the kind of abstract intelligence that can analyze, innovate, and create, the mind of the scientist and artist? Perhaps women did not equal men "to the degree of genius," she answered, conceding that "the long history of man has produced no female Bachs or Shakespeares or Leonardos or Galileos." Madame Curie, Mannes agreed, "is in lonely company." Nevertheless, she said, "women in every time have given to the mainstream of the arts, letters and sciences."[16] In 1959 a visiting delegation of Russian professional women had expressed amazement, Mannes reported, at finding so few American women in science or the professions in the U.S. Yet such comments from foreign visitors or women's college presidents, she observed, "are met by a massive wave of indifference emanating from women even more than from men." Why? The aspiration to professional achievement is unpopular with women, Mannes answered, *because* it is unpopular with men. "[T]he average American male is uneasy in the presence of markedly intelligent women," she said. If that kind of intelligence is "a deterrent to love, then it is voluntarily restricted or denied by women themselves."

Mannes' article produced a storm of letters to the *Times*. The majority of those printed by the newspaper came from women who attacked "Miss Mannes" (like most American newspapers, the *Times* identified the marital status of women in their courtesy titles) for libeling American men and women alike. She was accused of taking her social cues from the Russians. Her call for community-supported day-care facilities, wrote a woman from Hartford, Connecticut (who signed both her maiden name and her married name), "smacks of the Red Chinese commune system." The most telling criticism was that Mannes was blind to woman's primal mission. "If she does not realize the enormous importance of this business of giving birth to a child—rather than a serious article—and lovingly shaping this growth until he is fully mature," wrote a New York woman, "then Miss Mannes does not have the vaguest idea of what life is all about."[17]

In 1960, Marya Mannes was ahead of her time, even in cosmopolitan New York. The state of New York had led the nation in government efforts to ensure nondiscrimination in jobs and career opportunities. But nondiscrimination in the 1940s and 1950s had basically meant enforcing fair employment practices for Negroes and Jews, not women. New York had created the State Commission Against Discrimination (SCAD) in 1945. The first such state agency in the nation, it became a model for the urban-industrial states of the North and West. By 1960 there were two dozen such state-level commissions, and a score of municipal equivalents as well.[18] As religious-based discrimination faded in American life, these agencies, in states like Massachusetts, New Jersey, Illinois, Wisconsin, and California, concentrated almost exclusively on racial discrimination. In 1960, *none* included jurisdiction over sex discrimination.

In the summer of 1960 the chairman of New York's SCAD, a black insurance official named Elmer A. Carter, was interviewed on NBC-TV's "Direct Line" show about fair employment trends. The League of Women Voters had submitted a question asking whether the New York commission had any plans to add sex discrimination to its charge. His fair-employment agency had "enough headaches," Carter replied, without adding sex discrimination to its jurisdiction. "I hope the Legislature never gives us that power," he said.[19] Carter's stance was a common one in 1960, and it reflected a sober assessment of political and cultural realities: anti-discrimination meant anti-*racism*. Civil rights meant *black* civil rights. "The Movement" meant the Negro protest movement (the work "black," used as both noun and adjective, did not begin to displace the term "Negro" until the middle 1960s). The only other social movement of major consequence in the United States in 1960 was anti-communism, and it was alive and thriving. The word "sexism" did not exist in the public vocabulary in 1960. The concept that it described was neither new nor entirely dormant, for a shrunken sorority of American feminists had kept the flame alive. But there was no significant women's movement in 1960 in the United States—or anywhere else, for that matter.

Black Civil Rights as a Social Movement

Prior to the emergence of the black civil rights movement in the late 1950s, scholars had generally viewed social movements unsympathetically. They were associated with extremist groups and crowd psychology, like fascist brown-shirts and ethnic insurgencies in Europe. In America the history of social movements was dominated by radical agrarians, labor syndicalists and anarchists, religious fundamentalists, and vigilante groups like the White Caps and the Ku Klux Klan.[20] The effusion of reformist movements in the 1960s—first black civil rights, then the feminist, antiwar, environmental, consumer-protection and other movements—led social scientists to broaden their theories and to attempt, through historical and cross-national comparisons, to construct models that would account for their behavior, especially in relation to government policy.[21]

Historically, social movements have spanned the political spectrum and are difficult to define. But they commonly share four characteristics: (1) spontaneous and collective insurgency, (2) a group consciousness rooted in a sense of shared injustice, (3) a structure organized to mobilize group resources, and (4) a belief system or ideology that provides a vision of the future.[22] Social movements have occupied a volatile middle area of the continuum of collective social development. At one end of the continuum are forms of collective behavior that tend to be short-lived or episodic and often violent, like peasant rebellions, worker insurgencies, regional episodes of vigilantism, or racial lynchings and ethnic attacks. Given enough continuity and time, however, social movements can stabilize and evolve toward the other end of the continuum into mature interest groups, like the United Mine Workers or the National Right to Life Committee.[23] The original feminist movement of the 19th century, for example, followed this path. Beginning with the radical feminism that spun out of the abolitionist movement, "first-wave" feminism was shouldered aside by the racial issues of Reconstruction. Frustrated by rejection and torn by internal discord, the 19th-century feminist movement transformed its radical challenge into a more accommodationist and in many ways more conservative blend of non-threatening "social feminism" that stressed civic reform, moral uplift, and women's special capacity for nurture. By the turn of the century the feminists had narrowed their focus to a drive for woman suffrage. Following ratification of the Nineteenth amendment in 1920, the suffragist movement essentially matured into the League of Women Voters.[24]

Black America, on the other hand, during the first half of the 20th century had not produced an enduring social movement. The National Association for the Advancement of Colored People (NAACP), founded in New York in 1910 by a biracial coalition of northern progressives, was from the beginning an elite organization within its middle-class constituency. A federation of state and local chapters committed to classic liberal doctrine and funded mainly through membership dues, the NAACP quickly became the nation's mainline lobbying organization for black civil rights. Marcus Garvey's Harlem-based Universal Negro Improvement Association of the 1920s, on the other hand, was spontaneous and mass-based. But the Garvey movement could not deliver on inflated promises within a hostile national environment, and it quickly disappeared in the Depression. Until the 1950s the American black majority in the South was too effectively intimidated by the monopoly power of white segregationist regimes to launch a social movement. The *Brown* decision of 1954, however, provided a source of moral and constitutional legitimacy that outranked the local sanctions of Jim Crow. In this new social environment, the bus boy boycott in Montgomery, Alabama, produced both a spontaneous movement and a charismatic leader.[25]

The Montgomery Bus Boycott and Martin Luther King, Jr.

King's movement in Montgomery, which he did not begin but was early called to lead, impressively fulfilled all four of the basic criteria for emerging social movements. A spontaneous revolt against Jim Crowism that was triggered by the humiliation of segregated buses, it was rooted in the black church, organized by the Montgomery Improvement Association (MIA), and driven by a vision of the "Beloved Community" of Christian brotherhood. A crucial catalytic element, however, was missing. This was a symbolic form of collective action that captured the mind's eye as well as the public's imagination. Collective protest performs three functions for successful social movements. First, it dramatizes injustice through focused anger and shared victimhood. Second, it mobilizes the constituency for direct action. Third, it steels the resolve of the members through the annealing fires of group psychology. Labor unions, for example, had sealed their solidarity through the strike, and prohibitionists had turned to saloon-smashing. Later, when the manipulation of symbolic politics was better understood by a generation raised with television, anti-war protesters would burn draft cards, and the physically disabled would picket in wheelchairs. The Montgomery movement captured public sympathy with its moral vision, and King provided a commanding leader. But the MIA lacked a riveting, visual image that symbolized its claim to justice.

In the late 1950s the psychology of consciousness-raising and the mobilizing power of political symbols were not yet familiar to King and his lieutenants. When Rosa Parks in 1955 ignored the busdriver's order to give up her seat to a white passenger in Montgomery, her act of civil disobedience carried great symbolic power. Although her protest was by no means entirely spontaneous, in time she became a folk hero of the movement. In 1955, however, Parks was quickly ejected from the bus by the authorities, and no cameras captured her gesture of defiance. The ensuing bus boycott was effective in unifying Montgomery's black community and in battering the budget of the transit system. But the nonriding of buses was an inherently unphotogenic non-event.

A boycott that protested an immoral law, it was not itself illegal. It thus provided a bonding experience to nurture solidarity, but did not contribute an act of civil disobedience that forced the hand of authorities. Lacking a mechanism for producing martyrs, a customer boycott could attract but not long retain the attention of the mass media.

Ironically, Montgomery's city fathers had, through their intransigence, inadvertently cooperated with the black boycott by drawing national attention to it as a racial contest of wills.[26] Similar black boycotts against segregated bus seating had occurred earlier, for example, in Baton Rouge, Mobile, Tallahassee, and Jackson, Mississippi. But in these towns, moderate civic leaders had negotiated compromises that ended local crises and prevented the spread of the boycott tactic. In Montgomery the boycott was sustained long enough for the MIA to win its bus desegregation suit in federal court. In the aftermath of this victory, King founded the Southern Christian Leadership Conference (SCLC), won substantial financial backing from philanthropic foundations, and in 1958 published *Stride Toward Freedom: The Montgomery Story*.[27] Despite King's growing status as an international celebrity, however, the SCLC remained poorly organized and programmatically weak. By 1960 the King-led movement had claimed the moral high ground with its message of the Beloved Community—white and black together, seeking to overcome a legacy of racial division that had crippled both communities. But King and his cohort of southern black clergymen had been unable to devise a program that captured the energy of this vision and hurled it against the foundations of segregation.[28] His lost momentum had created a vacuum that the sit-ins would spontaneously fill, bringing with them a new generation of young foot soldiers whose protest was fueled by the volatile chemistry of idealism and anger.

The Sit-ins and the Student Nonviolent Coordinating Committee

The student sit-in in Greensboro, North Carolina, on February 1, 1960, ignited a firestorm that spread throughout the South. Like the bus boycott in Montgomery in 1955, the Greensboro sit-in was not the first attempt of its kind. Between 1957 and January 1960, sixteen southern towns experienced sit-ins of a sort. But none had combined just the right mix of elements to spark social combustion. Even the highly organized protests in Nashville, Tennessee, in the fall of 1959, led by a young black minister and Vanderbilt divinity student, James Lawson, failed to trigger a chain reaction. Well schooled by Lawson in the tactics of nonviolent resistance, the Nashville group had stayed in the targeted restaurants and lunch counters only long enough to demonstrate refusal of service. They then withdrew to discuss strategies and tactics in a workshop environment, thereby removing the provocation that drew public attention.[29]

In Greensboro, however, the four black freshmen from North Carolina A&T University sat unserved at the Woolworth lunch counter that Monday, and stayed until closing time. The next day they returned, reinforced by two dozen of their fellow students. By Wednesday the demonstrators filled almost all of Woolworth's 66 seats, and the lunch counter became a money-loser. On Thursday they were joined by a sprinkling of supporting young whites, and by Friday they numbered more than 300—not including an accompaniment of police officers and news reporters that was becoming standard for such news-worthy and photogenic events. The next week the sit-ins spread through North Carolina to Durham, Winstom-Salem, Raleigh, and Charlotte. By the end of February the sit-ins had spread to cities in neighboring Virginia, South Caro-lina, and Tennessee, and also to Florida, Alabama, and Texas. By March the sit-in protesters were increasingly attracting white harassment, and in Deep South towns like Birmingham and Orangeburg, South Carolina, they were subjected to violent attacks. By mid-April the demonstrations had spread to 85 cities throughout the southern and border states, and more than 2,000 protesters had been arrested. Within a year, more than 150 cities and towns had been affected, arrests had exceeded 4,000, and as estimated 70,000 demonstrators had participated in the protest surrounding the sit-ins.[30]

In retrospect, the sit-ins seem ideally scripted to set the new tone of protest and activism for the 1960s. First and most noticeably, they engaged fresh new battalions of black youth throughout the South. Like the Montgomery move-ment, the sit-ins were black-initiated and black-led. But unlike the Montgom-ery movement, which had a firm structure and local leadership but lacked sustained momentum, the sit-in movement lacked both structure and clear leadership, yet spread like a contagion. The new activists were drawn from a cadre of 200,000 college students whose degrees offered entry into the black middle class. The sons and daughters of a black lumpen-bourgeoisie whose middle-class status had always been tenuous in segregated America, they were seized by the sudden new possibilities of achieving liberalism's vision of a color-blind and upwardly mobile society. Thus while the challenge to Jim Crow posed by nonviolent civil disobedience was indeed radical, the integrationist values of the student protesters were conservative and even patriotic. The four freshmen in Greensboro carefully kept the receipts from their purchases of Woolworth sundries in order to show the white waitress that they were paying customers who had already been served at a counter a few feet away. They demanded equal treatment—nothing more, nothing less. "All I want," ex-plained a student leader in Charlotte, "is to come in and place my order and be served and leave a tip if I feel like it."[31]

Lacking coherence, and spontaneous youth movement found an organizing force in fifty-five-year-old Ella Baker, a veteran of New York's NAACP who had been recruited in 1957 to help organize the SCLC headquarters in Atlanta. In early April 1960, Baker with King's backing invited student representatives from southern black colleges to attend a planning conference in mid-month at the campus of her alma mater, Shaw University, in Raleigh, North Carolina. Baker, who had soured on SCLC as too cautious and too King-centered, and who resented the condescension toward women she found in the SCLC leadership, was surprised by the response. Almost 200 students attended, most of them from 56 black colleges and high schools in 12 southern states (although the three-day conference included 19 white delegates from northern campuses).[32]

The delegates rejected the role of youth auxiliaries to SCLC or the NAACP, and instead formed an independent organization that they awkwardly called the Temporary Student Nonviolent Coordinating Committee. In a political compromise, SNCC elected as chairman a native of Mississippi, Marion Barry, who had grown up in Memphis and was active in the Nashville group as a student at Fisk. The SNCC headquarters was set up at Atlanta University (where SNCC dropped the modifier "Temporary"), and at a large conference in October SNCC gave notice that it would press the old-guard black leadership to escalate nonviolent protest. Thereafter the senior leadership of King and SCLC, already at odds with the NAACP over turf and fund-raising, would find it increasingly difficult to control the impatient youth movement.[33]

The sit-in explosion of 1960 was primarily a phenomenon of Rim South communities like Nashville, Tallahassee, Houston, and the cities of the Carolina piedmont, where the barracks of the new foot soldiers were the dormitories of Fisk, Florida A&M, Texas Southern, North Carolina A&T, and similar black colleges. The sit-ins had found some success in opening lunch counters and restaurants in cities like Nashville, where the demonstrators were highly organized and disciplined, and where the city's political establishment and the state's political environment were moderate.[34] But the tactical advantage of the early sit-ins, which was to generate publicity and focus pressure on vulnerable businesses with a substantial black trade, confronted strategic disadvantages in the Deep South. There the Jim Crow laws were mandated by hard-line segregationist legislators. Statewide political trends were hardening in resistance to desegregation, as white politicians like Governor Orval Faubus of Arkansas learned that segregationist appeals were rewarded at the polls. Finally, business leaders in Deep South communities, who in private might prefer desegregation to chaos, were too vulnerable to segregationist counterpressures to risk desegregating one-at-a-time in violation of state segregation laws. As a result the sit-ins were far more effective as a mobilizing tool than as an instrument of desegregation.[35]

Atlanta, however, was a major exception in the Deep South. A commercial metropolis that claimed to be "Too Busy To Hate," Atlanta contained a strong network of black institutions. These included the church-based black establishment symbolized by the Rev. Martin Luther King, Sr. ("Daddy" King to black Atlantans) and the Ebenezer Baptist Church; the headquarters of SCLC and Martin Luther King, Jr.; and a dense nest of black college campuses—Clark, Morris Brown, Morehouse, and Spelman colleges, and Interdenominational Theological Center, and the professional schools of Atlanta University. Atlanta's dominant daily newspaper, the *Constitution,* enjoyed a reputation for racial moderation that found national acclaim through the Pulitzer Prize awarded in 1959 to editor Ralph McGill of the *Atlanta Constitution* for opposing racial segregation. Moreover, the city's business establishment valued Atlanta's reputation for New South moderation, and the city's Democratic mayor, William B. Hartsfield, was beholden to black votes for his survival.[36]

Despite these relative advantages for black prospects in Atlanta, prestigious black colleges like Morehouse and Spelman were sending their graduates into an economic future that seemed to have no place for them. Black graduates who scanned the classified pages of the *Atlanta Constitution* in 1960 would find no entry-level jobs that led into the ranks of the middle class. Under "Help Wanted, Male, Colored," the *Constitution* on the first Sunday in 1960 offered Atlanta's black men only *three* jobs: one carwasher, one custodian, and one broiler cook (that job turned out to be in Harrisburg, Pennsylvania).[37] Under "Help Wanted, Female, Colored," there were more opportunities: six openings for maids, several dry cleaning jobs for shirt operators/wool pressers, one salad girl, and one child care girl. White females looking for work in Atlanta would at least find job listings for waitresses, salesladies, or secretaries (frequently the ads specified that applicants be unmarried and 25–35 years of age). But for such jobs no blacks need apply.

Small wonder, then, that when the fall 1960 semester brought thousands of black college students back to their campuses in Atlanta, they did not quietly resume their studies. Instead they regrouped their forces and renewed their sit-in assault, this time against Atlanta's major department store, Rich's. A reluctant Martin Luther King, Jr., was persuaded to join them. He could scarcely remain aloof and retain his credibility as a moral exemplar. On October 19, King was arrested with thirty-five other protesters at Rich's. But he received a special sentence: four months at hard labor in a rural Georgia prison. King's offense for this draconian sentence was a misdemeanor—the technical violation of an earlier probation for driving with an expired license. From that unlikely spot King became the center of the symbolic politics of presidential electioneering, as the campaigns of Vice President Richard Nixon and Senator John F. Kennedy raced neck-and-neck to the wire.[38]

CHAPTER 2

The Kennedy Presidency and Black Civil Rights
1960–1962

The Presidential Election of 1960 and the Civil Rights Legacy

On October 26, 1960, Senator John F. Kennedy placed a telephone call to Coretta Scott King to pledge his support for the early release of her husband. Kennedy's call appears in retrosepct to have been a master stroke of campaign strategy, especially in view of the senator's tiny margin of victory over Vice President Nixon in November—a plurality of 112, 803 votes out of almost 69 million cast. The election was so close that many groups could make plausible claims to have provided the deciding votes—Catholics, organized labor, Irish, Poles, even southern white Democrats. But in the election post-mortems, a crucial margin of black electoral clout seems to have hinged on Kennedy's dramatic and yet risky gesture by telephone. Nixon wrote in his memoir of 1962, *Six Crises,* that "this one unfortunate incident in the heat of the campaign seemed to dissipate much of the support I had among Negro voters because of my record."[1] Nixon biographer Stephen Ambrose agrees: "The episode hurt Nixon badly."[2]

Actually there were two Kennedy phone calls. The call that sprung King from jail was placed by Senator Kennedy's brother and campaign manager, Robert, to Oscar Mitchell, the DeKalb County (Georgia) judge who had sentenced King to hard labor in a rural prison. Further pressure on Judge Mitchell was applied in Georgia by prominent state Democrats. The most notable of these was Mayor Hartsfield in Atlanta, who lobbied openly for King's release, but pressure was also applied behind the scenes by Governor Ernest Vandiver. Within the Kennedy campaign, the phone-call intervention had been urged by Kennedy's chief aide on civil rights issues, Harris Wofford, a white liberal who had served for three years as an attorney for the U.S. Commission on Civil Rights. Working on civil rights issues with Louis Martin, a veteran black party professional, and with Kennedy's brother-in-law Sargent Shriver, Wofford symbolized a campaign staff that was young, well financed, and politically effective. The October phone calls to King climaxed a campaign in which the issue that held the greatest potential for shattering Kennedy's coalition was instead transformed into a margin of victory. But the slimness of that margin, and the vagueness of the campaign debate over the meaning of civil equality, denied the new President the congressional support needed to attack the problem of segregation that the sit-ins had raised.

The presidential election of 1960 combined traditional and novel elements in a way that dramatized the new ingredients and exaggerated their influence. These included two procedural innovations that were closely related: (1) the prominence of television and the corresponding advantage of "telegenic" candidates and (2) the displacement of the party conventions by the state primaries in the nominating process. Added to this were two substantive innovations: (1) the Roman Catholicism of the Democratic nominee and (2) the new salience of racial policy in presidential contests. In all four areas, Senator Kennedy received most of the attention. On television, his was the fresh face, boyishly handsome, voicing appeals to youthful idealism in the distinctive accents of Boston and Harvard. An outsider to the established club of party leaders, Kennedy had to win the nomination by beating his rivals in the spring primaries; armed with the momentum of this popular mandate, Kennedy could demand its confirmation at the Democratic national convention in Los Angeles in July. As the Catholic contender, Kennedy had to prove his independence from church dogma and ecclesiastical hierarchy. And as the Democratic nominee in the year of the sit-ins, Kennedy had the most to lose from a North-South split over the racial issue.

Of the new substantive issues, the religious debate would prove ephemeral. On the whole, the electorate addressed it in a mature and clarifying debate. Kennedy dealt with the issue candidly, Nixon handled it responsibly, and the campaign eventually defused its distorting and destructive potential. On election day Kennedy seems to have gained slightly more votes than he lost on the religious question.[3] The matter of racial policy, on the other hand, was an issue that potentially reached to the heart of the country's political nerve system. It was, indeed, the Achilles' heel of the Roosevelt coalition, which the Democratic nominee must hold together in order to win.

Racial Politics and the New Deal Coalition

During the 1930s and 1940s, when New Deal liberalism mainly meant economic redistribution and relief programs for America's have-nots, public opinion polls showed that southerners identified themselves as liberals at a rate *higher* than that of any other region in the country.[4] This was sensible, since the South was the poorest region of the country. Roosevelt's New Deal liberalism had committed the national government to intervene in the marketplace to maximize growth and employment. It meant reforms like Social Security, TVA, farm security programs, liberal credit and trade policies, wartime sacrifice to crush the fascist powers, and cold war opposition to international communism. Southern Democrats in Congress had helped build this liberal legacy, and within its economic and international tradition, southern whites could remain loyal to the political house of their fathers—the Democratic party of Roosevelt, Wilson, Jackson, and Jefferson. By the late 1950s, however, the *Brown* decision and the rise of black protest in the South were threatening to split the Roosevelt coalition by shifting the core meaning of liberalism from economic redistribution to social reform, especially in race relations.

In assessing the presidential contest of 1960, it is important not to project back upon that election the partisan polarization that followed the 1960s, and thus exaggerate the pace and extent of racial concern in the mass electorate. Prior to the 1960s, the race issue cut across party lines. Survey researchers during the 1950s were surprised (and dismayed) to discover the ideological inconsistency of American voters.[5] Public opinion seemed philosophically incoherent about liberal-conservative distinctions. Neither major party was seen as more closely associated than the other with racial reform in civil rights policy. Indeed, the Republican party in Congress, as the party of Lincoln and Emancipation, had always been more hospitable to racial liberalism than the Democrats, whose southern racial conservatives dominated the standing committees of Congress, especially in the Senate. In the 85th Congress, which in 1957 passed the first civil rights bill since the Reconstruction, two-thirds of the Senate's racial liberals (42 of 63, according to one study) were Republicans.[6]

The dominant constituencies in the Democratic party in 1960 lay on the left of the Roosevelt coalition: organized labor, urban ethnics, racial minorities, the intellectual and academic establishment. In these constituencies, voters tended to be liberal on both economic and social issues. On civil rights reform, for example, all of these Democratic groups supported desegregation of the South. The party's major ideological anomaly was the historically "Solid" (meaning white and Democratic) South, where the economic liberalism of an impoverished region was accompanied by the social conservatism of rural and small-town Protestants. The Democratic party's challenge of 1960 was how to mobilize its liberal constituencies without alienating the Solid South. The problem of southern white conservatism within a liberal national party was not novel— Truman was almost defeated by it in 1948. But the rising crisis over desegregation was increasing regional and ideological tensions within the party.

Nationally, the Republican party had been dethroned by the Crash and the Depression, and in 1960, Democrats in the national electorate still greatly outnumbered Republicans. Public opinion surveys throughout the 1950s showed a familiar pattern of party identification: almost half of the respondents identified themselves as Democrats, barely a third said they were Republican, and 10 percent claimed to be independent.[7] As the majority party since 1932, the Democrats normally won presidential elections when citizens voted their party affiliations.[8] With the unbeatable Eisenhower no longer on the Republican ticket, a "normal" election in 1960 should once again return a Democrat to the White House. As the racial issue grew, however, the loyalties of southern white Democrats weakened. In a close contest the defection of enough southern states could break up the Roosevelt coalition and reduce it to a presidential minority. This had never happened and, despite the revolt of southern "Dixiecrats" against Truman in 1948, Truman's victory had confirmed the majority muscle of the Roosevelt coalition. The ensuing Republican victories of the hero of World War II, General Dwight Eisenhower, were so one-sided that although in 1952 "Ike" won the 57 electoral votes of Florida, Tennessee, Texas, and Virginia, and in 1956 he carried these four again and added Louisiana, he would have won both elections with no southern votes at all. But with Eisenhower off the ballot, the southern vote promised to be crucial in 1960.[9]

The Republicans, being a minority party, enjoyed greater internal coherence than the polyglot coalition of Democrats. Demographically, Republicans were primarily a party of the suburbs—disproportionately white-Protestant, with above-average levels of education and income. Geographically, the core of Republican strength lay in the conservative heartland of the mid-western plains and the Rocky Mountain states. This was the Grand Old Party of senators Robert Taft of Ohio and Everett McKinley Dirksen of Illinois. To add to this base, Eisenhower had made promising inroads in the states of the Rim South. But the moderate-to-liberal Republican establishment of the Northeast remained to be propitiated. This was the party of Thomas E. Dewey, the New York governor who had lost to both Roosevelt and Truman, and of New Englanders like Senator Prescott Bush of Connecticut (George Bush's father). It was Ivy League and patrician, generally conservative on economic issues like taxation and government regulation of business, but relatively liberal on social issues like civil rights and civil liberties. These preferences, however, were generally the *opposite* of the political preferences of southern whites. It thus is not surprising that the presidential aspirations of Republican Governor Nelson Rockefeller of New York found little support in the South. In 1960, liberal Republicanism was represented most prominently among presidential aspirants by Rockefeller and by President Eisenhower's Ambassador to the United Nations, Henry Cabot Lodge, Jr., who had lost his Senate seat in Massachusetts to John Kennedy in 1952.

As a sitting Vice President, Richard Nixon faced no serious threat to his nomination to succeed Eisenhower. But Nixon's incumbency in the administration left him little room to promise new policies in pursuit of votes. It was thus left for Kennedy to play the aggressor role, sorting through the political issues in search of a winning combination, while avoiding risks that might alienate voter blocs. Kennedy's only recourse was to run the gauntlet of presidential primaries and then carry the challenge to the incumbent party in November. In the process Kennedy accelerated the development of a two-stage process that has since become standard doctrine for presidential aspirants in both parties. To political consultants and speechwriters, the two-stage, out-and-back approach was essential to any hope of victory. To political candidates, on the other hand, it suggested opportunistic, finger-in-the-wind politics, and hence was unmentionable.[10]

The first step was designed for the primary contests. It required shifting the candidate's pitch away from the political center of the national electorate toward the party's center of gravity. This generally meant a leftward shift for

Democratic hopefuls and a rightward shift for Republicans. The goal was to win the nomination from the party faithful, whose political zeal moved them to vote in party primaries and to elect delegates to the national nominating conventions. This level of party activism tended to locate such voters further from the political center than the average American voter. Then, with the nomination in hand, the candidate's second step was to shift back toward the center to win the votes of the centrist majority who elected presidents. This spring-to-fall, candidate-to-nominee transformation was somewhat less pronounced in 1960 than it was later to become. In the partisan alignments of the New Deal era, the parties were more ideologically balanced internally than they would be after 1960, and thus their respective minority blocs—the conservative Democrats and the liberal Republicans—held stronger bargaining positions for moderating candidate views. The spring-to-fall shift was also generally greater for challenging candidates, like Kennedy, who enjoyed more freedom to bid for votes by promising new policies, than it was for incumbents like Nixon.[11]

Kennedy versus Nixon

Prior to 1960, John F. Kennedy had demonstrated little in the way of liberal credentials. Kennedy's congressional career had emphasized international affairs with a tone of Catholic anti-communism. He was considered an outsider by party liberals, whose loyalties were tied to the traditions carried by Eleanor Roosevelt and Adlai Stevenson. As a leading student of Kennedy's civil rights record observed, "Kennedy himself knew few Negroes and had no reputation as a civil rights advocate."[12] But as a candidate for the presidential nomination, Kennedy in the spring of 1960 moved leftward to challenge a leading rival with more imposing liberal credentials, Senator Hubert Humphrey of Minnesota. Kennedy responded to the sit-ins by praising them: "It is in the American tradition to stand up for one's rights," he said, "even if the new way is to sit down."[13]

Kennedy's superior campaign organization and youthful appeal drove Humphrey from the primaries; in July, Kennedy won a first-ballot victory from the Democratic convention in Los Angeles. There the platform committee drafted the most liberal civil rights plank in the party's history. It approved the sit-ins, called for a timetable for school desegregation, and demanded equal access to "voting booths, schoolrooms, jobs, housing, and public facilities." The civil rights plank even summoned Congress to create a permanent "Fair Employment Practice Commission."[14] Kennedy then stunned his liberal supporters by selecting as his vice-presidential running mate the Senate majority leader from Texas, Lyndon Baines Johnson.

Unlike Kennedy, and certainly unlike Johnson, Richard Nixon in his years of government service had accumulated a moderately substantial set of civil rights credentials. As Eisenhower's Vice-President, he had chaired the president's watchdog committee on fair employment in government contracts.[15] An honorary member of the NAACP in California since the 1940s, Nixon had been praised by Martin Luther King for helping pass the Civil Rights Act of

1957, and in private correspondence King wrote that he found Nixon reasonable, persuasive, and sincere.[16] The NAACP's executive director, Roy Wilkins, applauded Nixon for supporting reforms in the Senate that would allow smaller majorities to stop filibusters.[17] According to Ambrose, Nixon was "consistent in his denunciations of Jim Crow as much so as any of his rivals for national leadership and much more so than most."[18]

Because he was virtually assured of his party's nomination for the presidency, Nixon concentrated on unifying his party. At the Chicago convention in July, he accepted most of the liberal civil rights plank proposed by Governor Rockefeller, which placed the Republicans almost on a par with the Democrats by endorsing the Supreme Court's school desegregation decision and by calling on Congress to create a permanent "committee on equal job opporunity."[19] Nixon also reached out to the northeastern wing of his party by selecting Lodge as his running mate. The Republican ticket looked formidable, with its east-west balance, its legacy of peace and prosperity under Eisenhower, and its experience in presidential administration and international affairs.[20]

In the fall television debates between Nixon and Kennedy, which commanded great public attention, civil rights issues were little discussed. Each nominee concentrated his challenge on his opponent's capacity to lead the cold war most effectively against the Soviet Union and Red China. Kennedy and Nixon in fact differed little on the major issues of foreign and domestic policy, and during the fall both men avoided the kind of platform-plank specificities that might alienate large voter blocs. In such a contest, Nixon's advantages of incumbency were counterbalanced by two disadvantages. First, the blurring of issue differences had placed a premium on style and personality, areas where Kennedy was better endowed. Kennedy carried the glamor of Camelot. Nixon, on the other hand, carried a public image of corner-cutting ambition. Red-baiting had marked his ascent in California politics and in Congress, and Nixon's dark-jowled countenance and the "Tricky Dick" image lent themselves to ridicule in editorial cartoons. The shift in campaign coverage from print to broadcast journalism, and from radio to television, had generally rewarded Kennedy and punished Nixon.

Second, Nixon's claim to moral leadership in the Cold War was weakened by the silence of the Eisenhower-Nixon administration on the nation's leading domestic moral issue: racial segregation in the South. In the wake of the Warren Court's school desegregation decision, Eisenhower in the 1956 election had won approximately 40 percent of the black vote. This included the acknowledged vote of Martin Luther King, Jr., and of "Daddy" King as well. But although President Eisenhower had used federal troops to enforce court-ordered integration in Little Rock in 1957, he had refused to endorse the *Brown* decision as morally correct. Then in the early 1960s the sit-ins had turned up the heat on the moral issue.[21]

This presented both a problem and an opportunity for the two nominees. For Nixon, the opportunity was to accelerate the defection of white southerners from the Roosevelt coalition. But this carried a danger of alienating black voters in key electoral states like California, Illinois, and Ohio, where the black vote had been crucial to Truman's defeat of Dewey in 1948. For Kennedy, the opportunity was to win a close election the way Truman had done, while holding southern white defections to a minimum. To achieve this Kennedy had shrewdly insisted on Johnson as his running mate, and Johnson was tireless in barnstorming the South on behalf of party loyalty. Senator Kennedy's courting of the southern barons of Congress over the years had paid off in a network of cordial party relationships, and in 1960 even segregationist governors like Ernest Vandiver of Georgia and John Patterson of Alabama worked diligently to support their party's national ticket. Two incidents during the fall campaign illustrate both the volatile quality of the race issue for both candidates and the greater handicap it seemed to place on Nixon.

When Governor Vandiver charged in September that Nixon was a card-carrying member of the NAACP, which was generally despised by white south-erners, Nixon avoided the issue, and his campaign staff attempted to bury it. An assistant press secretary issued a statement explaining that Nixon had merely been made an honorary member of the NAACP by a chapter in Califor-nia. "He has not contributed any money or effort to the operations of the NAACP," the aide insisted. "He is not now an active member and never has been."[22] Roy Wilkins, executive director of the NAACP, complained that Nixon's support in the South seemed based on anti-Negro and anti-Catholic elements—an emerging coalition against which "Kennedy and Johnson looked like shining liberals."[23]

Although Kennedy, far more than Nixon, spoke in eloquent generalities during the campaign about the problems of ghetto dwellers in education, health, and employment, his political instincts showed a similar nervousness when the race issue sharpened. When news reporters began asking about the King-centered telephone calls in late October, Kennedy at first ducked the questions and then downplayed his call's importance. Robert Kennedy feared that his brother's call to Mrs. King might be viewed by white southerners as pandering to the black vote, and thus result in the possible loss of three south-ern states. Yet Nixon could not exploit the opening. He remained paralyzed, unwilling on the one hand to raise Kennedy's symbolic bid for the black vote, but also unwilling to risk the appearance of approving the abuses of heavy-handed southern officials like Judge Mitchell.[24] Despite Nixon's extensive cam-paigning throughout the South and his generally more conservative posture on state rights, polls showed that southern whites generally failed to distinguish between the two candidates on civil rights issues. Nixon's waffling on the NAACP issue alienated many blacks, while his silence on the King incident denied him compensating gains among segregationist whites. Kennedy on the other hand managed to have the best of it both ways. His cautious moderation on civil rights issues avoided alienating most southern white Democrats, and the southern newspapers paid relatively little attention to the King phone-call incident. Meanwhile Kennedy's campaign staff moved aggressively to exploit among black voters the telephone gesture to King. Black churches across the nation were flooded with two million pamphlets that contrasted Kennedy's compassionate outreach to "No Comment Nixon." Black parishioners were reminded that the Kennedy phone call had convinced the Rev. Martin Luther King, Sr., to switch his support from Nixon to Kennedy.[25]

Kennedy's balancing act paid off on election day. Approximately three-fourths of America's black votes were cast for the Democratic ticket—up from 60 percent in 1956. Yet among white voters in the South, a majority cast their ballots for the Democratic party as well—as they had done for more than a century. It was the last time they would do so. But in 1960 the Kennedy-Johnson ticket, by carrying a swath of southern states that included the Carolinas, Georgia, Louisiana, and Texas, and also by winning close votes in key industrial states like New Jersey, Pennsylvania, Michigan, and Illinois, won an electoral majority of 303 to 219. The black vote was crucial in carrying Texas and South Carolina for Kennedy, and in winning Pennsylvania and Illinois as well.

Kennedy won so narrowly that he was denied the winning candidate's customary "coattail" effect of strengthening his party cohort in Congress. Indeed, in an extraordinary reversal of pattern, the Democrats in 1960 lost 21 seats in the House and two in the Senate. Kennedy's campaign has emphasized the attributes of new-era politics—youth, telegenic vitality, wit and charm, idealism, and a challenge to outmoded traditions of religious and racial bigotry. But the basic political alignments and strategies of 1960 were of New Deal vintage. Like Roosevelt and Truman, Kennedy had held together the Democrats' volatile coalition of blacks, ethnic minorities, southern whites, urban Catholics, and rural and small-town Protestants. The margin of victory, however, was narrowing and the inner tensions were rising.

Congressional Stalemate and Executive Authority

The coattail-less election of 1960 transformed a nominee who had pledged the presidency to a moral commitment against racial oppression, into a President-elect who promptly lapsed into a four-month silence on the civil rights issue. In the newly elected 87th Congress, the Democrats' large partisan majorities in the House (263 Dem.; 174 Rep.) and Senate (64 Dem.; 36 Rep.) were deceptive, because the southern Democrats often voted in an informal, conservative coalition with the Republicans. President Kennedy thus lacked a program majority in Congress. Like Franklin Roosevelt before him, Kennedy felt compelled to defer to the powerful southern committee chairmen, who were able to hold the new administration's civil rights initiatives hostage to such higher Kennedy priorities as defense, tax, and trade legislation.[26] Even Harris Wofford advised Kennedy to avoid embroiling his first 100 days in a congressional battle over civil rights bills that almost certainly would be lost.[27]

Following his inauguration on January 22, 1961, Kennedy sent Congress sixteen messages spelling out his legislative priorities. But civil rights was not among them. When liberals in the Senate launched their biannual attempt to weaken Rule 22 on cloture, which defined the number of votes needed to stop a filibuster, Kennedy ducked the fight, and the conservative coalition of Republicans and southern Democrats defeated the change. Kennedy did throw the weight of the White House behind a successful attempt to "pack" the Rules Committee, which controlled the fate of bills already reported out of House committees and waiting for floor votes. Pushed by Speaker Sam Rayburn and the Democratic leadership, the proposal would weaken the grip of the committee's powerful chairman, Howard W. Smith of Virginia, by adding new members who would be less subservient to "Judge" Smith's conservative majority. But Kennedy's legislative agenda and his interest in weakening the Rules Committee roadblock had little to do with civil rights policy.

Having ruled out any significant presidential requests to Congress for civil rights legislation, Kennedy attempted to fill the vacuum, which was embarrassing and appeared hypocritical, by taking initiatives in three areas of executive discretion. One area, the traditional reward system to patronage and senior appointments, drew its force from symbolic politics. During his first year in office Kennedy appointed NAACP attorney Thurgood Marshall to the Second Circuit Court of Appeals in New York, where he would gain judicial seasoning and lead the list of candidates in the speculation over the first Negro appointment to the Supreme Court. To groom another such black "first," Kennedy appointed Robert C. Weaver, a career civil servant with a doctorate in economics from Harvard, to head the Housing and Home Finance Agency. Weaver's name was most frequently mentioned as head of a potential cabinet-level department of urban affairs. Given the historic reluctance of Democratic presidents to appoint minorities to high-ranking government posts, Kennedy's appointments represented a substantial increase.

Kennedy's second area of executive discretion was more aggressive enforcement of existing presidential authority over the government's civil rights policies. To preside over the Justice Department as the nation's chief law-enforcement officer, Kennedy appointed as Attorney General his younger brother, Robert. Unlike the President and the Vice President, the 35-year-old "Bobby" was a lawyer, although he had never tried a case in court. The appointment was controversial. But Robert Kennedy's reputation for arrogance was accompanied by the acknowledgment even from his critics that through his personal force and his recruitment of able lieutenants, he had greatly energized the Justice Department. The Attorney General invigorated the department's Civil Rights Division by increasing the number of staff attorneys and by appointing Washington lawyer Burke Marshall to direct it. During the first year under Robert Kennedy's leadership the Justice Department faced down opposition to court-ordered integration in New Orleans public schools and a the University of Georgia. Justice lawyers also filed charges to stop the attempts of the rural South's courthouse power elite, in black-majority counties like Haywood and Fayette in Tennessee, to prevent blacks from registering to vote by firing them, denying them credit, terminating their farm leases, evicting them from tenant quarters, and canceling their licenses and bonds.[28]

Robert Kennedy's efforts to enforce the rulings and orders of the federal courts, while more vigorous and creative than his predecessors under Eisenhower, were limited by the political and constitutional constraints of the federal system. American schools and police forces were constitutionally the responsibility of state and local governments and officials, not federal agencies. The tradition of American federalism had shielded a long history of abuses, like the official intimidation of black voters in the South's "Black Belt" counties. But federalism also prohibited the creation of a national police force, or a centralized ministry of education, or a nationalized voter-registration system. The events of 1961–63 would be played out against a long tradition of local primacy in these matters.

Federal efforts to defend the rights of blacks merely to ride integrated buses without being molested, or to enter public schools and colleges as students, would ensnarl the Justice Department and the Kennedy administration in episodes of southern resistance and communal mayhem that were often tinged with political farce. The major episodes began with the Freedom Rides sponsored by the Congress of Racial Equality (CORE) during the summer of 1961, which disintegrated in mob violence in Alabama. The triggering event the following year was the admission of a black Air Force veteran, James Meredith, to the law school at the University of Mississippi in September 1962—an event that sent 500 federal marshals and 5000 army troops to Oxford, Mississippi, and resulted in 160 injured marshals and two civilian deaths. A year later attention shifted to the charade staged by Governor George C. Wallace of Alabama, in September 1963, to block integration at the schoolhouse door.[29]

In all of these encounters, the Kennedy administration seemed caught up in a Greek drama, captive of a script that sustained tragedy and farce, but that permitted no decisive act to break free from the moral and political dilemma. The administration seemed trapped in the middle, reacting to the initiatives of others. The issue of racial fairness and equal citizenship was not likely to find resolution until the Congress joined the federal courts and the presidency in grappling with the institutional causes and structural roots of racial dualism. Yet between the Kennedy inauguration and the summer of 1963, Congress remained paralyzed by its own Madisonian maze of internal checks and balances, and the presidency remained largely neutralized by an insufficiency both of political will and of popular demand that the Congress act decisively. The convergence of political will and popular demand would not be forthcoming until a tidal wave of black protest surged up from the South, drawing its power from its own creative drama, and building momentum from sit-ins to freedom rides to the violent streets of Birmingham—all of it on prime television time. In the meantime, in an attempt to recapture some initiative and independence of action in civil rights policy, John F. Kennedy, like Franklin Roosevelt under somewhat similar circumstances in 1941, turned to a third presidential strategy: the executive order. And in doing so Kennedy turned to an unlikely architect and enforcer of civil rights policy: Vice President Lyndon Johnson.

Lyndon Johnson and the Origins of Executive Order 10925

During the presidential campaign in 1960, Senator Kennedy had promised that one of his first acts as President would be to issue, with a "stroke of the pen," an executive order to ban racial discrimination in federally assisted housing. Once elected President, however, Kennedy quickly learned from his own advisers and appointees that such an order would raise serious constitutional issues and administrative problems. Kennedy also learned—quietly—from Lawrence O'Brien's office of congressional liaison in the White House and from Democratic leaders in Congress that many northern Democrats, who were comfortable attacking southern racism in areas like hotel and restaurant segregation and job discrimination, were distressed at the prospect of running for re-election in 1962 while defending their President's nationwide ban on discrimination in housing.

It was a paradox of race relations in the United States that the South's Jim Crow laws, which rigidly separated the races in schools and jobs, parks and restrooms, hotels and restaurants, did not extend to housing. But in the North these patterns were reversed: racial distinctions were impermissible in the northern schools, workplaces, and public facilities, but de facto desegregation was the rule in northern residential neighborhoods.[30] The combination of constitutional reservations, technical problems, and political caution persuaded Kennedy to withhold his promised penstroke until after the the fall 1962 congressional elections. By a process of elimination, Kennedy's executive-order options were narrowed to the one campaign pledge about civil rights policy that he could redeem without roiling his fragile coalition of allies in Congress. Kennedy had promised that he would reorganize the "do-nothing" Committee on Government Contracts that Eisenhower had appointed and Nixon had chaired.[31]

Nixon's chairmanship of Ike's contracts committee meant that the government's fight against job discrimination in the Kennedy administration could be led by no lesser office than the vice presidency. The country's most visible equal-employment problems in taxpayer-supported jobs were with the major defense plants in the South, where employers had long deferred to local segregation laws and to Jim Crow union practices. Defense contractors in the South, like Lockheed's hugh aircraft plant near Atlanta or the shipyards at Norfolk, had built close relationships with the region's political leaders, men like Senator Richard Russell of Georiga, chairman of the Senate Armed Forces Committee and mentor to Lyndon Johnson since New Deal days. But Lyndon Johnson's ability to persuade such men was legendary. He spoke a language of status and power they understood, and his arguments were couched in a Texas drawl. Johnson's biographers have disagreed profoundly over the depth and principled quality of his Hill Country populism.[32] But virtually all who knew him conceded that, like Huey Long, he seemed oddly free of the racial prejudice that was a hallmark of his native region.[33] George Reedy, an Irishman who grew up with robust ethnic hostilities in the Chicago area, and whose long tenure on Johnson's Senate and vice-presidential staff made him resent Johnson's capacity for crudeness and cruelty, was puzzled by the Texan's racial fair-mindedness. "Strangely enough, Mr. Johnson is one of the least prejudiced or biased or intolerant or bigoted men I have ever met," Reedy observed. "I don't believe there is any racial prejudice in him whatsoever."[34]

For Vice President Johnson, however, such an appointment to head the government's fair-employment committee was fraught with peril. Johnson well knew and feared the miseries of the vice presidency. Historically the office had seemed to institutionalize either impotent sycophancy or, rarely but more dangerously, disloyalty fed by frustration and ambition. Johnson's fellow Texan, John Nance Garner, had despised both his vice presidency and his President, Franklin Roosevelt (it was Garner who evaluated the vice presidency as "not worth a pitcher of warm spit"). Unlike Nixon, Johnson was not a lawyer, and he lacked training and experience not only in the areas of contract and labor law but also in the broader field of executive administration. His unique experience as Senate majority leader during the 1950s fell precisely in the crucial area where Kennedy most needed help, in the legislative politics of the Hill. But despite the suprisingly cordial relationship that President Kennedy and Vice President Johnson maintained, the White House offered Johnson no substantial role in shaping presidential policy, and Johnson, though miserable in the limbo of the vice presidency, never publicly complained.[35]

Johnson, like Nixon, saw his vice presidency as a springboard to the White House. In this standard scenario, loyal service to John Kennedy would lead to Johnson's re-election as Kennedy's running-mate in 1964, and then to his own presidential nomination in 1968. Elected President in his own right in 1968 (at the age of 60) and re-elected in 1972, he would then retire in honor to Texas in 1977, where he would build his presidential library and entertain world leaders at the LBJ Ranch on the Pedernales. Such projections were not uncommon among Washington politicians, and their speculation was accompanied by much wood-knocking. Over the generations, Potomac Fever had spawned hundreds of such visions, most of them far more fantastic than Johnson's not unreasonable anticipations.

In 1961, Johnson's new national office had freed him from the more parochial requirements of representing Texas. This had included a ritual defense of segregation that he participated in with other southern politicians during the 1950s, which had made him distrusted if not despised by liberals.[36] A master of consensus politics on the Hill, Johnson's instinct for wellsprings of compromise was like a divining rod, and in 1961 it pointed violently away from the controversial specter of FEPC—the Fair Employment Practice Committee that Roosevelt had created by executive order during World War II, which the conservative coalition in Congress had killed at the war's end, and which white southerners had learned to despise. Johnson feared the whiplash of the racial issue, which could destroy his presidential ambitions. Caught in the middle of left-right warfare as head of a new quasi-FEPC, Johnson could expect to be attacked in the North for failing to end job discrimination, and attacked in the South for even trying. He was pleased that Kennedy had asked him to chair the National Space Council, which would channel major space investments into the South. But he tried desperately to avoid chairing the President's new fair-employment committee. Kennedy, however, was unyielding: Johnson was the Vice President, and he was a southerner, and he *had* to head the administration's new committee on equal employment opportunity (EEO).[37] Soon after the 1960 election, Kennedy asked Johnson to recommend what the administration's new fair-employment operation should look like and what it should do.

The President's Committee on Equal Employment Opportunity

Between December 1960 and early march 1961, Johnson and his staff struggled to define the structure and duties of the Kennedy administration's new enforcement instrument for fair employment. The chief designer of the executive order was Abe Fortas, a Memphis lawyer and Johnson adviser from New Deal days. A major role also was played by Nicholas Katzenbach, the deputy attorney general who represented both the professional continuity of the Justice Department and the political interests of the Kennedy loyalists. Also involved were two Texans who joined Johnson's vice-presidential staff: aide Bill Moyers, a divinity student whom Kennedy would later tap as Sargent Shriver's deputy at the Peace Corps, and Hobart Taylor, Jr., the Houston-raised son of a black political ally of Johnson, whose training and career as a lawyer had taken him to Michigan. The new Labor Secretary, Arthur Goldberg, was also involved because the Labor Department would provide most of the operation's administrative support—as it had done for the contracts committee that Nixon had chaired under Eisenhower. Finally, Johnson's general-purpose press aide, George Reedy, was kept busy checking with all political interests likely to be affected, so that Johnson, in his typical quest for consensus, would not be blind-sided by an interest he had not considered or an important party he had not consulted.

Quests for political consensus tend to minimize risk and gravitate toward centrist positions. Johnson's working group on the executive order for civil rights, and ultimately the President and his chief advisers, were no exception. They considered but eventually rejected most radical departures or controversial models, such as Roosevelt's FEPC, or the state fair-employment commissions like New York's State Commission Against Discrimination (SCAD), with their statutory authority, their annual budget appropriations, and their authority to issue cease-and-desist orders to halt employer discrimination. Commissions or agencies with these powers required a statutory basis with annual legislative appropriations, and any such proposals were expected to go nowhere in the 87th Congress. As a result, Johnson's planning group recommended that the new executive order should combine Eisenhower's two obscure EEO committees (one for government contracts and one for federal jobs) into one committee, and repackage it with a broader membership and with modest new authority.

The executive order would cover all employers with government contracts, and it would add new jurisdiction over labor unions. A Democratic administration could scarcely get away with excluding organized labor from fair-employment responsibility. This meant that the committee that President Kennedy's order would create, and that Vice President Johnson would chair, would police job discrimination in companies and unions that worked on contracts or subcontracts to build the U.S. government's offices and military bases, tanks and bombers, or to sell it gasoline or toilet paper. This alone covered the pace-setting core of the country's manufacturing economy. By 1960 the U.S. government's size and its defense commitments had grown so large that federal contracts reached down through a vast network of subcontractors and suppliers to fund the paychecks of approximately 15 million workers.

The new committee's jurisdiction would *not,* however, include federal grants-in-aid. The Kennedy administration would not risk upsetting Congress by imposing through executive order a policing operation on the popular grants-in-aid programs. These grants were the heart of Congress's discretionary reward system, and control over them was jealously guarded. They helped state and local governments pay for land-grant universities, community colleges, hospitals, highways, airports, libraries, parks and conservation programs, urban renewal and similar local projects. Local economies relied on their stimulus. Members of Congress got re-elected by claiming credit for them. They were popular with local constituencies because historically they had helped pay for local needs while *not* imposing strict guidelines from Washington about what these local needs should be and how they should be met.

None of the predecessor committees under Truman or Eisenhower had covered grants-in-aid, and given Kennedy's precarious relationship with Congress, the new administration was not about to launch its anti-discrimination operation by ordering the colleges and hospitals and highway departments in the cities and states to start reporting to the federal government on their local hiring practices. The Kennedy administration christened this new endeavor with a new title, the President's Committee on Equal Employment Opportunity, that was as bureaucratically awkward and unmemorable as its predecessor committees (even the acronym, the PCEEO, was unpronounceable). President Kennedy launched his committee with great fanfar at a White House press conference on March 7.[38] The fanfare was novel, and therefore important. Kennedy signed Executive Order 10925 on March 6, and the following day he summoned the press to the White House to announce that "through this vastly strengthened machinery I have dedicated my administration to the cause of equal opportunity in employment by the government or its contractors." "I have no doubt," Kennedy said, "the the vigorous enforcement of this order will mean the end of such discrimination."[39] What was most auspicious about Executive Order 10925 and the PCEEO it created was the concerted effort to place the full prestige of the presidency behind the moral imperative of nondiscrimination.

In contrast to Kennedy's White House kickoff, the presidential decrees of previous administrations had been low-profile to the point of invisibility. The contract compliance orders of Truman and Eisenhower had been brief and technical. Indeed they had been almost apologetic or defensive, typically signed without ceremony and printed in the *Federal Register* with no accompanying statement, then quietly promulgated with a cautious presidential eye cocked toward an unenthusiastic or hostile Congress. President Eisenhower had never disguised his reservations about federal regulation of private choice, including hiring practices. Few American citizens had ever heard of the government's

EEO committees. Moreover, the committees' ability to threaten contract cancellation had never actually led to a cancelled contract or to a debarred contractor. The press and television paid them no heed. Presidents were content that their EEO committees worked quietly and stayed out of the newspapers.

Against this background, Kennedy's full press conference of March 7 marked a new departure. From the White House he launched a heavily staged public relations effort. Creating the Johnson committee and promoting his executive order with such fanfare was the first major shot in the campaign that was to climax so spectacularly in the historic Civil Rights Act of 1964.

The Origins of "Affirmative Action"

Executive Order 10925 is historically noteworthy for a second reason. It contained a vague and almost casual reference to "affirmative action." The term traced its lineage at least as far back as the New Deal's Wagner Act of 1935. There it was used to emphasize the positive obligation of the National Labor Relations Board (NLRB) to redress unfair labor practices. The NLRB was authorized to order the offending party "to cease and desist from such unfair labor practice, and to take such affirmative action, including reinstatement of employees with or without back pay, as will effectuate the policies of this Act."[40] The Wagner Act thus seemed to link affirmative action to obligations that extended beyond the duty to cease offending. Employers could be required, for example, not only to stop firing workers who joined unions but also to reinstate them and award them back pay. Appropriate affirmative action in this analogy would therefore extend from negative aspects of relief and remedy, such as cease-and-desist orders, to include positive aspects like reinstatement and back pay.

At the end of World War II the concept of affirmative action was extended from the federal arena in the Wagner Act, where it affirmed an obligation to protect organized labor against union-busting tactics, to the level of state and municipal governments, where it was linked to nondiscrimination in employment. In 1945 the state government of New York, seeking to guarantee a fair-employment environment for service veterans returning to the civilian workforce, created SCAD as the first state-level FEPC. Using the NLRB as a model, New York's pioneering "Law Against Discrimination" incorporated large hunks of the Wagner Act language, including the relief clause that linked the commission's cease-and-desist authority to "affirmative action" for victims of discriminatory acts.[41]

Thus from the beginning the concept of affirmative action was somewhat vague and open-ended. On the one hand it was closely linked to the specific requirements of the quasi-judicial process. These typically included administrative hearings, a finding of fact identifying a victim of a discriminatory act with intent to harm, a cease-and-desist order, and "make-whole" relief that might include rehiring and back pay. In the history of the state FEPCs since World War II, this was the only practical or legal meaning the phrase could claim. On the other hand, it held at least the potential for a broader interpretation in the future, perhaps to imply special efforts by government to compensate for a history of anti-union activity by employers, or to compensate somehow for a history of discrimination against minorities.

Although in the long run this aspect of Kennedy's order proved to be of great significance, in hindsight it is laced with the irony of unintended consequences. Like all its predecessors, and the state FEPC laws as well, Kennedy's order was grounded in the historic model of criminal and civil jurisprudence in Anglo-American law. In this traditional, tort-based model, the defendant was regarded as innocent until proven guilty, and the burden of proof fell on the plaintiff and the prosecution. Also, like its predecessors and like the state fair employment laws as well, Kennedy's order made no attempt to define the harmful discrimination it proscribed. Invidious discrimination was defined by convention as an intentional denial to minorities, prompted by prejudiced motives, of rights and opportunities freely accorded to non-minorities. Denying a Jew admission to medical school because of his religion was a violation of the anti-discrimination laws. Proof of discrimination required plaintiffs to produce convincing evidence of intent after the alleged discriminatory act had occurred, even though this often required complainants to adduce proof that was uniquely possessed by the powerful organizations whose motives and behavior were the subject of the complaint.[42]

Given the dominance of the Anglo-American model in nondiscrimination law, with innocence assumed absent proof of guilt, the type of activity left available for "affirmative action" was constricted in time and variety. Kennedy's executive order, like Roosevelt's FEPC, lacked statutory authorization. It thus lacked also the entire legislative rationale that empowered regulatory agencies like the NLRB and the state EEO commissions to issue cease-and-desist orders and require make-whole relief such as back pay. Kennedy's PCEEO was an executive response to the problems dramatized by the sit-ins in political circumstances that blocked an effective congressional solution. Its cutting edge was the threat to withhold or withdraw federal dollars from discriminators. The meaning of affirmative action in Executive Order 10925 was to require that government employers and private contracts provide wide public notice of all employment and promotional opportunities, more aggressive recruitment in hiring and appointments, and special encouragement for minorities to seek advancement. When Johnson sent Kennedy his draft order for the President's approval and signature, the Vice President proposed that the standard nondiscrimination clause in government contracts "be revised to impose not merely the negative obligation of avoiding discrimination but the affirmative duty to employ applicants and to treat employees on the job on the basis of their qualifications and not because of race, creed, color or national origin."[43] Thus the commitment to the unspecified positive efforts of affirmative action was linked to the classic goal of nondiscrimination. "The contractor will not discriminate against any employee or applicant for employment because of race, creed, color, or national origin," Kennedy's executive order decreed. "The contractor will take affirmative action to ensure that applicants are employed, and that employees are treated during employment, *without regard* to their race, creed, color, or national origin [emphasis added]."[44]

The Problems and Lessons of Lockheed-Marietta

Three days before President Kennedy signed his executive order on job discrimination, the Pentagon announced the nation's first billion-dollar procurement for a single military system. It was a ten-year contract negotiated with Lockheed Aircraft Corporation to build the giant C-141 jet transport. The plane would be built at Lockheed's sprawling plant at Marietta, Georgia, near Atlanta, where one roof covered 76 acres of plant and four and a half miles of corridors. Lockheed's plant was constructed with federal funds on federally owned land adjacent to an airbase. There Lockheed had built the sturdy C-130 Hercules, and its $100 million payroll was the largest in Georgia. Lockheed's headquarters was in Burbank, California, but the company's strategic move into Georgia had been nurtured by Georgia's two senior members of Congress, Senator Richard Russell and Representative Carl Vinson, each the chairman of his chamber's Committee on Armed Forces.

In 1961 the Marietta workforce of 10,500 was still segregated by race, and its 450 black workers were confined largely to low-paying unskilled jobs.[45] The population of the metropolitan Atlanta area in 1960 was 23 percent black. But fewer than 5 percent of Lockheed's employees at the Marietta plant were black. The few semi-skilled workers among Lockheed's black workers were segregated in an all-black local of the International Association of Machinists (IAM). This effectively excluded them from training for higher-paid skilled jobs, because the apprenticeship programs were controlled by the IAM's all-white local.[46] The IAM itself had been organized in Atlanta in 1888 and had barred Negro membership from the beginning. The formal race bar was removed by the international union in 1948, but IAM locals throughout the country, and particularly in the South, continued to practice racial segregation. At Lockheed-Marietta in 1961, the washrooms and drinking fountains bore "White" and "Colored" signs, as did the cafeterias.

On April 7, the day Kennedy's executive order officially took effect, the NAACP's labor secretary, Herbert Hill, submitted to Lyndon Johnson's new committee thirty-two affadavits of complaint from black workers at Lockheed-Marietta. Hill, who was white, had a reputation for militancy. He had filed previous complaints against Lockheed with Vice President Nixon's committee, but had gained little visibility and no successful outcome. This time Hill picked a moment of high visibility and professed commitment from the new Kennedy administration, and he extracted from a spokesman for the PCEEO a public pledge to cancel the contract of *any* employer who refused to comply with the President's new ban on discrimination.[47]

In response to Hill's complaints about Lockheed-Marietta, the PCEEO's staff director flew to Burbank to negotiate with Lockheed's president, Courtlandt S. Gross. Within organized labor, parallel pressure on the Marietta unions to desegregate was applied from Washington by AFL-CIO's president, George Meany, and by its vice president Walter Reuther, both of whom were members of Johnson's committee. The loose federal structure of the AFL-CIO, which had been the key to merging organized labor's craft and industrial unions in 1955, prevented national officers like Meany and Reuther from ordering local unions to change their rules and procedures. But labor's international leadership, with the exception of the skilled craft unions in the construction trades, was firm in its opposition to racial discrimination, and AFL-CIO pressure on Marietta's District 33, and especially its all-white machinist local, was intense.

As a result, the black machinist local at Marietta voted on April 23 to integrate. When the white local made no move to accept the black machinists, IAM president A.J. Hayes ordered the district locals desegregated anyway. Supporting pressure also came from a new and previously unlikely quarter: the Pentagon. Defense Secretary Robert S. McNamara had brought Adam Yarmolinsky over from the White House as a special assistant whose trouble-shooting portfolio included civil rights. Yarmolinsky, one of Kennedy's top talent hunters and a fellow Harvard alumnus, enjoyed the support of the White House as well as the strong backing of McNamara and his deputy secretary, Roswell Gilpatrick. The result was the creation of a powerful new source of policy and staff support for the Johnson committee's challenge.

In response to these pressures, in early June, Lockheed-Marietta removed all the "White" and "Colored" signs from the washrooms. To ease the social awkwardness of integrated water fountains, the company replaced them with paper-cup taps (which according to the *New York Times* required 63,000 paper cups a day). The Marietta management handled the problem of cafeteria desegregation with a similar sensitivity to the social customs of a southern workforce that was 95 percent white: they abandoned Jim Crow cafeterias in favor of mobile, stand-up canteens. Lockheed's president then flew to Marietta and began long-range employment netogiations with the PCEEO staff over accelerated hiring, upgrading, and access to apprenticeships for blacks. So far it looked easy.[48]

The suddenness of the apparent turnaround at Lockheed-Marietta in the summer of 1961 suggested several immediate lessons. One was that aggressive pressure by the NAACP appeared to be crucial in accelerating the momentum of Kennedy's executive order. Herbert Hill became adept at exploiting press coverage of the new committee's compliance efforts. He labeled as merely "peripheral" Lockheed's dismantling of the Jim Crow signs at Marietta. He demanded immediate and substantial payoff in new black jobs, and he soon broadened his attack to include segregated Western Electric plants in Winston-Salem, Greensboro, and Dallas. Hill's barrage of complaints acted as a goad to the new committee, at once accelerating its enforcement vigor, while at the same time endowing the PCEEO with a certain patina of judicial even-handedness in refereeing the difficult transition from Jim Crow to nondiscrimination. In the metaphor of precinct psychology, Hill's bad cop could play nicely to the committee's good cop.[49]

A second lesson was suggested by the surprising ease with which such major national firms were willing to abandon their traditional deference to the South's biracial system, especially if the stakes and visibility were high and their competition was obliged to act similarly. Lockheed seemed particularly amenable to such pressures. With 90 percent of the company's business coming from the air force, and with employment at Marietta down by almost half since the peak of the mid-fifties, Lockheed wished to please its government sponsors. The Lockheeds of American industry were so financially beholden to government contracts that they had no intention of fighting the committee, especially in light of the damaging publicity that surrounded such charges. Indeed they often welcomed such pressure as an occasion to legitimate breaking down traditional job barriers, which had artificially constrained their labor supply, inhibited management flexibility, and elevated labor costs.

Nevertheless, by 1962 criticism of the Johnson committee was increasing. Herbert Hill was the most persistent. But the PCEEO was a natural lightning rod for liberal critics. Headed by "Cornpone" Lyndon Johnson, the committee was a Who's Who of cabinet officers and the power elite of corporate America. But its tiny staff of forty worked with a budget that was smaller than that of the government's Bureau of Coal Research. It symbolized to critics on the left a Kennedy Band-Aid, hopelessly overmatched by the magnitude of the problems confronting America, a painful reminder of the need for comprehensive civil rights legislation that the President would not even request.

The Strengths and Weaknesses of Executive Enforcement of Civil Rights

Reflecting these divisions, the PCEEO was itself divided. A hawkish faction, led by Attorney General Robert Kennedy, found the committee's investigations too prolonged and its settlements too timid. A dovish faction, led by Atlanta attorney Robert Troutman, pushed a voluntary compliance program called "Plans for Progress," which contained no real teeth and seemed to produce only paper gains. Johnson was caught in the middle, and as the pace of black protest increased against a background of congressional stalemate, the Attorney General began to attack Lyndon Johnson at committee meetings, humiliating him in front of his senior staff.[50]

Later critics would dismiss the PCEEO as a paper tiger that never cancelled a contract. This was technically correct. But it failed to acknowledge the limited options and leverage available to the committee, and also the importance of the enforcement precedents it forged. Most major contractors readily negotiated agreements through the committee's conciliation process. That failing, however, the committee generally proved willing to roll out its sanctions, which included referring noncooperating firms to the Justice Department. During the summer of 1962, Attorney General Kennedy used this leverage to win desegregation agreements for major southern operations of several recalcitrant firms. These included Tennessee Coal and Iron in Birmingham, and oil refineries in Louisiana and Texas run by Continental Oil and Cities Service.[51] At the other end of the spectrum of contractors, where second-tier subcontracting firms were many and small, the PCEEO moved with reasonable firmness to demonstrate Lyndon Johnson's claim that "We Mean Business." When blacks complained of racial discrimination at five Comet Rice Mills plants in Texas, Arkansas, and Louisiana, and also at Danly Machine Specialties of Cicero, Illinois, the committee staff investigated the complaints. When the companies continued to deny the discrimination that Johnson's committee staff had documented, the PCEEO announced publicly that the companies were barred from further contract work. In response to this bad publicity, both companies quickly conceded. The important sanction was the threat of contract denial, not its frequency. For companies that lived on government contracts, to be officially found no longer "in compliance" with contracting regulations, including EEO requirements, invited future failure in the bidding process. During Lyndon Johnson's unhappy yet hard-working chairmanship, the committee began to explore the new terrain that defined the meaning of being "in compliance."[51]

One of the PCEEO's first steps was to ask the twenty-seven major federal agencies for a racial nose-count of their employees. This request ironically produced confusion and resistance, since keeping job applications or employee records by race had been widely prohibited during the 1950s as a progressive safeguard against racial discrimination. Labor secretary Arthur Goldberg, whose credentials as a liberal Democrat were unassailable, told a House committee in 1961 that he was "shocked" to learn that a Labor Department official had classified job applications by race.[52] But the Johnson committee directed the federal agencies to improve the "underutilization" of blacks and minorities and to report their progress in hiring and promotions. By the summer of 1962, the data in PCEEO reports revealed that proportionally, blacks were slightly *over*represented in federal civilian employment. Blacks represented 11.7 percent of the nation's population, but the federal government's 282,600 black workers represented 13 percent of the U.S. government's civilian labor force. When black job-holders exceeded the level of proportional representation, a phenomenon that occurred early in labor-intensive service agencies like the General Services and Veterans administrations and the Department of Health, Education and Welfare, the Johnson committee shifted its enforcement scrutiny to the *quality* of minority employment. The PCEEO emphasized the concentration of minorities in the lower-paid job ranks, and their scarcity in the smaller, technical agencies like the Federal Aviation Administration and the National Aeronautic and Space Administration.[53]

By 1963 the PCEEO reported that it was processing twice as many complaints as its predecessor committees under Eisenhower, and that it was requiring a much higher rate of "corrective action," which generally meant committee directives to employers to hire or promote or grant a petitioned transfer. The PCEEO's 1963 report showed corrective-action requirements in 44 percent of sustained complaints, which was considerably higher than the 20 percent average of the Eisenhower committees and the similar 20-year average of New York's EEO commission. But in relation to the magnitude of the black unemployment rate alone, which was still more than twice the white rate (10.2

percent to 5 percent), such victories seemed tiny. From 2.2 million federal civilian employees and 15.5 million contract employees, the PCEEO received only 4,810 complaints in 1963. Johnson's committee, however superior the batting average of its compliance staff, nonetheless required only 1,673 corrective actions. Meanwhile 700,000 black workers remained unemployed in the United States. And little damage had been done to the foundations of the biracial caste system in the South.

Interagency committees like the PCEEO are useful for communication and for seeking political consensus and advice. But as instruments of policy implementation they are inherently weak because they spread responsibility and dilute authority. Given these limitations, the achievements of the Johnson committee were substantial, and the humiliation that the frustrated Robert Kennedy visited upon Lyndon Johnson was politically petty and mutually damaging. Nonetheless it is clear in hindsight, and evidence was accumulating even by the early 1960s, that the complaint process alone was not likely to produce either the breakthrough so long sought by liberal champions of a national FEPC, or the bureaucratic nightmare that congressional conservatives so long had feared. Indeed, congressional conservatives seemed to have little to fear at all from the Kennedy administration's legislative proposals. Having asked for so little and won even less in civil rights legislation from the 87th Congress, Kennedy welcomed the 88th Congress in early 1963 in a similar spirit of caution. On February 28 he proposed only modest amendments to existing voting-rights laws, and asked for a four-year extension of the Civil Rights Commission, whose authorization was scheduled to expire in late 1963.

Moreover, while Kennedy continued to temporize over black civil rights, internal pressures were building in the hitherto dormant area of women's rights. By 1963 the increasing attention to civil rights and equal employment opportunity had fueled the planning of a group of Democratic women who had been deliberating in relative obscurity on a presidential commission appointed by Kennedy in 1961 and asked to report in 1963. Through accidents of timing, the report of the President's Commission on the Status of Women coincided with passage of the Equal Pay Act of 1963, and also with the publication of Betty Friedan's *The Feminine Mystique*. Together they quickened the pace of the feminist dialogue, accelerating it toward a convergence in 1964 with the forces of reform in black civil rights. Yet the convergence, when it came, seemed more like a political collision. In equal-rights theory, the parallel dialogues over black rights and women's rights should have been driven by a common logic of nondiscrimination and converging toward similar goals of equal treatment for all citizens. Yet the national discourses over black rights and women's rights were curiously disconnected. Indeed, the campaigns against race discrimination and sex discrimination seemed to deflect each other, like electrical forces carrying a similar charge.

CHAPTER 3

The Separate Civil Rights Bills of 1963 for Women and Blacks

The Irony of Equal Rights in 1963

Looking backward from the perspective of the Civil Rights Act of 1964, the forces opposing discrimination by race and sex appear to have converged during 1963 on their path of legislative theory. In the eleven-month period prior to the assassination of President Kennedy on November 22, the Kennedy administration sponsored two equal-rights bills, one primarily for blacks and one for women. Both bills eventually became law.

During the first half of 1963, the administration introduced an equal-pay bill for women, one that had died in the previous Congress. On June 10, 1963, Kennedy signed the Equal Pay Act of 1963 in the presence of several congresswomen, representatives of national women's organizations, and leading proponents of the bill in his administration. Foremost among the last was Esther Peterson, an assistant secretary in the Labor Department who also served as director of the Women's Bureau. A veteran lobbyist for organized labor, Peterson skillfully led a coalition that had been fighting for a federal equal pay law for 18 years.[1]

The following week, in response to the racial violence in Birmingham surrounding the demonstrations led by Martin Luther King, Kennedy abandoned his earlier caution in civil rights proposals and asked Congress for a law that would destroy the foundation of racial segregation in the South. By early November, with the administration's approval, Congress had strengthened the original Kennedy bill by banning discrimination in private employment because of race, religion, or national origin. Then, early in 1964, Congress added sex discrimination to the employment practices prohibited by the civil rights bill. By the spring of 1964, two major streams of anti-discrimination, both seeking equal rights, one for blacks and the other for women, were speeding toward convergence in law under the signature of President Lyndon Johnson.[2]

Beneath the surface similarities of the campaigns, however, were significant differences. The tough new civil rights bill that Kennedy sent to Congress in the wake of the Birmingham violence was targeted against the heart of the nation's race problem: the biracial caste system of segregation in the South. The Equal Pay bill, on the other hand, was directed against a practice—paying women lower wages than men for doing the *same* work—that was no longer widespread and that depressed women's earnings far less than the wholesale exclusion of women from high-paying jobs. By 1960 the practice of racial segregation in the American South, and the edifice of white supremacy upon which it was based, was widely rejected in national and world opinion. But the global practice of assigning women different rights from men had not been so rejected. Indeed, the tradition of dual gender standards had not been seriously examined or even acknowledged by the American public since the ratification of woman suffrage in 1920. In 1960, race discrimination was regarded as a serious national problem for the United States, but its pathology and solution were seen as regional. Sex discrimination, even when acknowledged as a national problem, was not generally regarded a serious matter.

What was most striking about the differences between the main civil rights campaigns on behalf of blacks and women in 1963 is the centrality and coherence of the drive for racial reform on the one hand, and the marginality of the drive for women's rights on the other. The black-focused civil rights bill reflected a century of consistent liberal doctrine. Its bedrock assumption was that the Constitution was color-blind. Consequently there could be no compromise with Jim Crowism, no exceptions in statute or jurisprudence where race might remain in the law as a legitimate source of exclusion from public life and commerce. For women, however, the proposition that the Constitution should also be *sex*-blind was an abstract notion that had received political lip-service but had never commanded more than a tiny minority of active supporters in American public life. The women's organizations and groups that supported Kennedy-Johnson administration, and the women who found positions of leadership within its ranks, were overwhelmingly opposed to the Equal Rights Amendment (ERA). Most of these groups and organizations had opposed the ERA since its introduction in Congress in 1923. The profound differences over the constitutional mandate between the racial and gender reformers of 1963 were rooted not only in inherent distinctions between race and sex as innate human characteristics but also in the social interplay of a third variable that had never been immutable: economic class.[3]

The Janus Face of Sex Discrimination

Historically, the issue of gender equality in America has been far more complicated by the cross pressures of economic class than has the issue of racial equality. The American black community, to be sure, has always reflected internal class conflicts between the black bourgeoisie and the impoverished mass of African-Americans. But three centuries of racial oppression had cemented the dominance of racial over class concerns for black Americans. Throughout American history, when poor blacks on the farm or in the factory had threatened to make common cause with poor whites, the landowners and industrialists who opposed such populist coalitions had shattered the class solidarity by appealing to the racial prejudice of whites. The primacy of racial over class subordination for American blacks was a brute fact of survival. It has been symbolized in 20th-century America by the pre-eminence among black protest organizations of the NAACP. As an elite-led organization of the black middle class, the NAACP has nonetheless consistently fought racial discrimination without making basic class distinctions. Despite the NAACP's bourgeois membership base, its great campaigns were fought to vindicate the rights of ordinary black citizens—the Scottsboro Boys, the victims of lynchings in the South, the black schoolchildren in Topeka and Little Rock.

In American women's history, however, and probably for all of women's history, the reverse has been more often the case. Class-based concerns, not gender solidarity, have shaped the decisions of American women about private associations like their churches and clubs, schools and colleges, and also about public issues like political party affiliations, votes for candidates, and attitudes toward taxes, public expenditures, and foreign policy. Because the institutions of marriage and the family dictated a distribution of women throughout the social class structure that paralleled the male distribution, women, unlike blacks, have lived intimately with "the oppressor" and hence they have shared his class identification. As a result the politics of female equality has reflected that division.[4] In the 20th century this class division within the American women's movement has persisted, and in the period between the ratification of woman suffrage in 1920 and the passage of the Civil Rights Act of 1964, it largely neutralized the feminist impulse. The suffragist coalition celebrated the ratification of the Nineteenth amendment by splitting into two warring factions that mirrored the frustrating divisions of gender and class. The dominant National American Women's Suffrage Association, having led the coalition that won the franchise, was succeeded by the League of Women Voters, which thereafter concentrated on civic-minded voter education.[5]

Meanwhile the progressive women associated with the trade-union movement pursued special protective legislation for women and children. They rooted their arguments in gender differences. Because women were smaller and weaker than men, they said, special laws were needed to protect women, as wives and mothers, from the sweatshop working conditions of industrializing America. Consequently, the progressive reformers persuaded state legislatures to pass laws that set maximum hours for women (typically 48 hours per week) and that excluded them from jobs requiring heavy lifting (typically 35 pounds or more). Protective laws commonly excluded women from physically dangerous jobs like mining and foundry work, and from morally dangerous jobs like night work or traveling sales positions. The statutes often required employers to provide women workers with special facilities for rest and feminine hygiene. The progressive reformers had designed similar measures (without the gender-based rationale), such as maximum-hour and minimum-wage requirements, to protect the health and well-being of working men. These laws, however, were struck down by the conservative federal courts. The most famous case was

Lochner v. New York in 1905, wherein the Supreme Court ruled that maximum-hour restrictions violated the worker's freedom of contract, as guaranteed by the Fourteenth amendment. But in 1908 in *Muller v. Oregon* the U.S. Supreme Court held that similar laws were permissible for women because the female's delicate nature and maternal role required society's special protection. The trade-union movement regarded such protective laws as important liberal victories in an age of industrial exploitation. Liberal reformers, like Eleanor and Franklin Roosevelt, who cut their teeth on such battles, developed powerful instincts to protect such hard-won gains.[6]

In 1920 the protectionists found new voice and leverage in the creation of the Women's Bureau in the Department of Labor. When the National Women's party (NWP), led by the militant suffragist Alice Paul, dedicated itself in 1923 to crusading for the ERA, the stage was set for four decades of intramural feminist conflict. But throughout these years the anti-ERA, protectionist wing held dominance. Its dominant personality was Eleanor Roosevelt. The leadership included such Democratic veterans of trade-union liberalism as Mary Anderson, who headed the Women's Bureau from its founding in 1920 through 1944; Frances Perkins, Franklin Roosevelt's secretary of Labor; and Esther Peterson, a labor lobbyist with roots in the Amalgamated Clothing Workers Union. Its achievements were anchored in the New Deal's triumphs for organized labor, most notably the Wagner Act of 1935 and the Fair Labor Standards Act of 1938. But the liberal legacy also included the enactment of protective legislation in most states.[7]

By 1940, forty-three states and the District of Columbia had enacted protective laws for women. When ERA supporters mounted a major drive at the close of World War II to capitalize on national gratitude for women's support of the war effort, the Women's Bureau countered by rallying in opposition a veritable Who's Who of liberal organizations. At its peak this coalition, organized as the National Committee to Defeat the UnEqual Rights Amendment, linked forty-three organizations, including the American Civil Liberties Union, the AFL, the CIO, the American Association of University Women, the YWCA, the National Consumer's League, the national councils of Catholic and Jewish women, and the League of Women Voters. It also included Americans for Democratic Action, the Democratic party's inner club of liberal activists and guardians of the ideological canon.[8]

Opposing this liberal-labor coalition in the women's movement were the upper-class women who supported the ERA. Led by the small but aggressive NWP under the irrepressible Alice Paul, the ERA coalition included the professional and club women of the National Federation of Business and Professional Women's Clubs, the General Federation of Women's Clubs, the National Association of Women Lawyers, and the National Education Association. Politically, the ERA supporters tended to be Republicans or conservative southern Democrats. Being highly educated and generally affluent, the ERA women embraced a brand of radical egalitarianism that emphasized procedural freedom over substantive equality. In demanding equal freedom to compete with men in professional life and financial transactions, the NWP championed a vision of equal opportunity that was libertarian. It thus attracted the support of such bastions of conservatism and otherwise unlikely feminist allies as the National Association of Manufacturers, the U.S. Chamber of Commerce, and the American Retail Association. By the 1960s, liberal critics called the NWP women the "tennis-shoe ladies." The image of little old ladies in tennis shoes categorized them as archaic right-wingers, and reinforced the psychological barrier the liberal Democrats had erected against the ERA.[9]

The Kennedy Administration and the Equal Pay Act of 1963

The feminist dichotomy with its curious twists of alliances persisted into the Kennedy administration.[10] Because the ERA appealed to well-educated women who resented their exclusion from the executive suites of business and the professional worlds of medicine and law, the ERA had become a natural Republican issue. It was also a relatively safe Republican issue, since Congress historically had either ignored the ERA or considered it only in combination with a special exemption for women's protective laws, a provision that would effectively nullify the amendment. Republican platforms had ritually endorsed the ERA since 1940. The Democratics had followed suit without fanfare or much enthusiasm in 1944. But the postwar drive for the ERA had galvanized the Women's Bureau coalition, and by 1960 the party's labor coalition under Esther Peterson's guidance had succeeded in deleting the ERA endorsement from the Democratic platform.[11]

This invited Republican exploitation, and in the presidential election of 1960 the task fell to vice-presidential candidate Henry Cabot Lodge. He reminded voters that the Democratic party contained the main source of opposition to Negro rights, and that the Kennedy-Johnson platform had abandoned their party's previous commitment to equal rights for women. In mid-October 1960, Lodge joined Kennedy in a campaign appearance at New York's Waldorf-Astoria Hotel, where they were guests of the National Council of Women in the United States. Speaking before 1000 delegates of the federation, which claimed a combined membership of 4 million, the candidates had been asked to address the conference theme of "American Women—the Nation's Greatest Untapped Resource." Lodge did so. As Eisenhower's ambassador to the United Nations, he asserted that more women ought to receive ranking positions in the foreign service. "Certainly," he said, "there should be no discrimination at all on account of sex."[12] Kennedy, however, ignored the conference theme, and used the occasion to attack the Eisenhower administration's policies toward Africa. In 1960, it was still politically possible for a presidential candidate to sidestep entirely the issue of women's rights.

Once in office, Kennedy moved to defuse the potentially dangerous question of women's rights by appointing a special commission to study the matter. On December 14, 1961, Kennedy issued an executive order establishing the President's Commission on the Status of Women. Nominally chaired by the infirm Eleanor Roosevelt (who died the following year), the commission was directed by Esther Peterson. During the 1940s the study-commission device had been pressed by Mary Anderson and the Women's Bureau, and during the 1950s it was urged by Brooklyn congressman Emanuel Celler, a pro-labor Democrat who chaired the House Judiciary Committee. The goal of the liberal Democrats was to blunt drives for the ERA and contain the damage from the feminist split. Kennedy's status-of-women commission, whose final report and recommendations were not expected until late 1963, was broadly based (including gender, with 11 men and 15 women). But it was dominated by trade-union veterans like Peterson herself, and while the panel's internal debate showed a rising challenge to protectionist dogmas from some younger members with professional backgrounds, the commission would not embarrass the President by fighting over the ERA.

In the meantime, Peterson won the backing of Labor secretary Goldberg and the White House to press Congress for an equal pay law. The trade-union movement had supported the principle of equal pay for the same work since the era of World War I, when the large-scale movement of women into the industrial labor force threatened to depress wages for male family heads. World War II had produced a similar set of circumstances, with women flooding into the workforce to replace men who left for military service. When demobilization at the war's end sent almost ten million servicemen back toward the civilian economy, organized labor sought a federal equal-pay bill. The labor movement supported equal pay for equal work as a matter of liberal principle. But as a practical matter, labor also wanted to prevent the peacetime competition between the war-swollen female workforce (which had jumped from 25 percent of all workers in 1940 to 36 percent in 1945) and the returning veterans from driving down industrial wages for all workers.

In response to these conditions, the Women's Bureau coalition of trade unionists and protectionist feminists had introduced equal-pay bills every year since 1945, but without success. Their efforts had been blocked in the House primarily by the opposition of Representative Graham Barden of North Carolina, chairman of the House Education and Labor Committee. But in 1961 the committee chairmanship had shifted to Harlem's Adam Clayton Powell, who supported the equal-pay measure. The driving force behind the equal-pay bill in the House was Representative Edith Green of Oregon, and in the Senate it was Pat McNamara of Michigan—both Democrats with strong ties to organized labor.

The equal-pay bill generated little controversy and drew little organized opposition. Few critics wanted to argue against the principle of paying people the same wages to do the same work. But outside of Peterson's Women's Bureau coalition, there was little enthusiasm for the bill. Republicans, southern Democrats, and business interests like the U.S. Chamber of Commerce worried that the bill would create another expensive and intrusive bureaucracy in the Labor Department that would attempt to manipulate the pay policies of private employers. Conservative critics objected less to the principle of equal pay than to the prospect of administrative enforcement by government bureaucrats issuing cease-and-desist orders to businesses.[13] Moreover, Peterson and her allies had failed to produce enough evidence of widespread abuse or economic harm to convince officials at the Budget Bureau and the Council of Economic Advisers that the law was needed, or that its need was strong enough to warrant the administration's investment of scarce political capital in bargaining with Congress. Labor economist W. Willard Wirtz, who replaced Goldberg as Kennedy's Labor secretary in September 1962, thought the bill was unnecessary.[14]

Nonetheless Peterson persisted, and she was a skillful and persuasive lobbyist. She argued that the bill gave the Kennedy administration its only symbol of effective reform on behalf of women. The equal-pay bill was consistent with the Women's Bureau's historic, trade-unionist policy of "specific bills for specific ills"—which meant legislative proposals tailored to correct identified problems, rather than divisive panaceas like the ERA. The bill would reward the support of organized labor, while the ERA threatened to destroy overnight the entire structure of protective laws that the trade-union movement had fought to build for three generations.[15]

Peterson was also a political pragmatist. When the House and the Senate passed different versions of the equal pay bill in 1962, which died when the differences were too great to resolve in conference committee, Peterson made the necessary compromises. Early in 1963, she sought bipartisan support by accepting the recommendations of New York congressman Charles Goodell, a Republican leader on the House Education and Labor Committee. The Goodell approach transformed the bill from a broad grant of new authority to the Labor Department—including cease-and-desist power, which the independent National Labor Relations Board possessed but the Labor Department did not—to an amendment to the established Fair Labor Standards Act (FLSA) of 1938. In this form the new law would rely on existing Labor Department mechanisms for enforcement. Like the FLSA, its coverage would *exclude* business, executive, and professional employees, who were either self-employed or were paid salaries rather than hourly wages, and thus were not covered by the labor-standards regulations. It would also exclude most low-paid women in agriculture and domestic service. The original FLSA, as a political price of enactment in 1938, had excluded both the high-status groups and the low-status groups. Professionals and executives wanted to avoid government controls on their salaries, and farm workers and maids were too politically weak to get themselves included. Nevertheless, the Equal Pay Act would cover most of the nation's 25 million working women, and in 1963 they constituted 34 percent of all American workers. Implicitly it would recognize the right of women to hold employment on the same basis as men, while not directly threatening state protective laws that were based on the opposite assumption.

As a result, the various congressional complaints of 1961–62 about the equal-pay bill, which were never strongly voiced in the first place, were met and satisfied in 1963. First the House and then the Senate passed the bill in May, and President Kennedy signed it into law in early June. Supporters of the Equal Pay Act have pointed out that although the law did not address a major dysfunction in the economic and social system, it led to the correction of equal-work pay inequities in the economy, such as patterns of higher pay for male schoolteachers. During the law's first ten years it required employers to award $84 million in back pay to 171,000 women.[16] It also acted as a bridge to ease the difficult psychological transition, especially among Democratic women and trade-union liberals, from the protectionist tradition to the equal rights tradition.

Nonetheless, the brute problem for American working women in 1963 was not equal pay for equal work. That was a serious problem for the generation of Rosie the Riveter, and especially for her non-unionized colleagues in the early postwar era. By the early 1960s, however, the progressive process of sex separation in the workplace, as symbolized by the ubiquitous segregation of men and women's jobs in the classified ads, had meant not that women are doing the same jobs as men for less pay. Rather, it meant that women were flooding into the labor market to take lower-paying jobs that men didn't want. Under those circumstances, the threat to sex-discriminating employers of equal pay for equal work was almost no threat at all. In the workaday routine of the American economy, virtually all employers were sex discriminators—and quite legally so. *Race* discrimination in employment, however, was banned in half the states, and in 1963 momentum was building to nationalize the racial ban in a comprehensive civil rights act.

The Kennedy Strategy and the Birmingham Breakthrough

In *John F. Kennedy and the Second Reconstruction,* historian Carl Brauer cites President Kennedy's civil rights speech of June 11, 1963, as marking "the beginning of what can truly be called the Second Reconstruction, a coherent effort by all three branches of the government to secure blacks their full rights."[17] The turmoil in Birmingham that began in April, turning quickly to violence and leading to Kennedy's June speech, had been a planned confrontation. The segregationist forces were led by the city's notorious police commissioner, Eugene T. ("Bull") Connor, who vowed to "keep the niggers in their place."[18] Connor's image as Birmingham's chief redneck seemed too archetypical to be credible, like a character from Central Casting; armed with poilce dogs and fire hoses and cattle prods and spoiling for a fight, "Bull" Connor as a symbol of racist intransigence had become a staple of the national news weeklies.

Less apparent at the time was the calculated nature of the black challenge in Birmingham. On the heels of the previous fall's failed protest campaign in Albany, Georgia, where the polite discipline of Police Chief Laurie Pritchett had defeated demonstrators led by Martin Luther King, Jr., the Southern Christian Leadership Conference had repaired to Savannah for a three-day review of strategy. A postmortem on strategic collapse, it called into question the core of King's Christian optimism. What emerged was "Project C"—for Confrontation. To implement Project C, King accepted an invitation in the spring of 1963 to come to Birmingham and lead the protest against Connor's undisciplined defenders of white supremacy. By provoking a crisis that promised a flow of blood on the national television networks, King's "nonviolent" protest would force President Kennedy's hand.[19]

The crackle of black protest and violence that spread regionally and then northward in the wake of Birmingham convinced the Kennedy White House that its cautious legislative proposals of the previous February were inadequate. The Birmingham violence threatened nationwide turmoil. But the post-Birmingham climate of national indignation offered hope by inviting a bolder reach of presidential leadership. It offered relief from the frustrations of the first two Kennedy years, when federal protections were mocked by the bloody reception given the Freedom Riders in Alabama in 1961, and then again in 1962, when Kennedy's cautious and fitful moves during the crisis at Ole Miss had produced bloodshed without a commensurate clarification of federal policy and authority.[20] But in the spring of 1963 Kennedy needed a fitting occasion to announce his new post-Birmingham initiatives.

The occasion was ironically provided by Alabama's governor, George C. Wallace. In response to a federal court order of May 5 to desegregate the University of Alabama, Wallace stage-managed a histrionic posture of defiance. "I draw the line in the dust and toss the gauntlet before the feet of tyranny," Wallace declared, "and I say, Segregation now! Segregation tomorrow! Segregation forever!" This time, however, unlike the Ole Miss crisis in 1962 with Governor Ross Barnett, the President and the Attorney General launched a coordinated series of threats and negotiations. On June 11, Wallace was forced to capitulate. Thus the victory in Tuscaloosa gave Kennedy a fitting occasion to address the nation on the intensifying civil rights crisis.

Speaking on national television that evening from the White House, Kennedy spoke simply and eloquently. "We are confronted primarily with a moral issue," he said, "as old as the scripture and . . . as clear as the American Constitution." The moral crisis was sharpened by the painful events in Birmingham and the "fires of frustration and discord [that] are burning in every city, North and South."[21] It's resolution should not be regarded as a sectional or a partisan issue, Kennedy insisted. On the latter assertion he was indubitably correct, because only Republican support could overcome the certain filibuster of southern Democratic senators in the face of a strong civil rights bill. But Kennedy's denial that the racial crisis was sectional, while statesmanlike, was also politically disingenuous—as was clear from the legislative remedies he proposed and the sectional nature of the bipartisan coalition in Congress that would be necessary to approve the remedies. The symbol of crisis was Birmingham and "Bull" Connor's police dogs and fire hoses on national television, even more than George Wallace's charade in the schoolhouse door. The civil rights problem was exploding intolerably as a *southern* problem. Accordingly, the remedies that Kennedy proposed were regional in their impact. They centered on a radical proposal for Congress to outlaw racial segregation "in facilities which are open to the public hotels, restaurants, theaters, retail stores, and similar establishments." There was no mention of job discrimination, which was a national problem.

When the Birmingham crisis first broke into the headlines in mid-April, the Attorney General had summoned the key White House aides and senior Justice Department staff to plan a new political strategy and to construct a legislative proposal to seize the moment.[22] Assistant Attorney General Norbert Schlei, who was appointed chief draftsman for the new bill, recalled the decision-making process at the initial planning session: "We started with our existing [February] package of voting and Civil Rights Commission, something had to be done about public accommodations, something had to be done about [desegregating] education." "It would be nice, we thought, to do something about employment," Schlei added. "But that was very difficult, that was widely believed to have little or no chance."[23]

Also initially rejected by the White House was a provision for withholding federal aid funds from programs where discrimination was found. This power was avoided in the executive authority of Vice President Johnson's EEO committee. As a legislative proposition, moreover, such a proposal conjured up the nettlesome Powell amendment. Since the middle 1950s Harlem congressman Adam Clayton Powell had sought to amend federal grant-in-aid bills by banning any expenditures for segregated programs. Because such a provision could halt virtually all federal aid programs through the southern and border states, it was politically inconceivable that a majority of Congress would vote for such a measure. As a result the Powell amendment became a Judas-kiss. It tended to endanger or doom liberal bills by requiring federally enforced desegregation of all activities they affected. The Kennedy administration had already been twice bloodied by the Powell amendment in the failed quest for federal aid to education. The polarizing effect of the amendment frustrated the congressional leadership and played into the hands of opponents. A vote against it appeared to be a vote for segregation. Yet a vote for it usually sank liberal bills by adding centrist votes to the conservative opposition. So the legislative planners in the White House and at Justice wanted to stay well clear of such known congressional shoals as the Powell amendment and a national FEPC.

During the administration's reassessment of legislative strategy of late May and early June, Robert Kennedy took the lead in pressing for the risky initiative in public accommodations, supported by his deputy attorney general, Nicholas Katzenbach, and Burke Marshall, assistant attorney general in charge of the Civil Rights Division. Senior presidential aides Ted Sorensen, Lawrence O'Brien, and Kenneth O'Donnell worried that the administration would be unable to overcome a Senate filibuster against such a frontal assault on segregation. Throughout the intensive review of April–May, Vice President Johnson remained excluded, as usual, from the inner circle of Kennedy's policy advisers. As a result of the policy review the President decided to propose a single, omnibus bill that concentrated on desegregating public accommodations and included less controversial measures to aid desegregating school districts and speed black voter registration. Thus all of the bill's major targets were southern. Congress would be asked to give permanent statutory authority to the PCEEO, but *not* to create a new FEPC. Instead, the President would express his general support for pending fair employment legislation that had been introduced into Congress by others, but that in the past had never stood any serious chance of passing.[24]

President Kennedy's moving television address to the nation of June 11 on the moral crisis in civil rights appealed early to American patriotism. "When

Americans are sent to Vietnam or West Berlin," he said, "we do not ask for whites only." It also appealed to a national sense of fairness, including an admixture of white guilt. "The Negro baby born in America today," Kennedy said, "regardless of the section of the Nation in which he is born, has about one-half as much chance of completing high school as a white baby born in the same place on the same day, one-third as much chance of becoming a professional man, twice as much chance of becoming unemployed, about one-seventh as much chance of earning $10,000 a year, a life expectancy which is 7 years shorter, and the prospects of earning only half as much."[25] Kennedy's references to becoming a "professional man" and to the goal of earning an annual salary of $10,000 sound quaint to present-day ears, but no President since Lincoln had addressed the nation in such forthright moral terms about American race relations. The next task would be to propose legislation to Congress.

Public Accommodations and the Universal Powell Amendment

On June 19 the President sent Congress his detailed omnibus bill on civil rights. Its controversial centerpiece was the title on public accommodations, which in the parlance of legislative shorthand soon came to be known as Title 2. In his accompanying message, Kennedy sought to take the edge off the novelty and indeed the radicalism of this federal intervention in local customer choice by pointing out that thirty states and the District of Columbia had already enacted such laws, thereby covering two-thirds of the country as well as two-thirds of its population. But Kennedy's footnoted list of precedents included no southern state except the border state of Maryland.[26] Everyone understood that the heart of the bill was aimed at the segregated South of George Wallace and "Bull" Connor.

To enforce Title 2, Kennedy called for lawsuits by the Attorney General in response to citizen complaints. To justify constitutionally such a novel extension of federal control over local lunch-counter patronage, Kennedy cited the Fourteenth amendment—the guardian of equal protection against state violation of racial equality. But Kennedy drew most of his justification from the dim moral grandeur of the Constitution's interstate commerce clause. This carried a practical political advantage: the Senate leadership could refer the bill for hearings not only to the Judiciary Committee, where chairman James Eastland of Mississippi was expert at bottling up civil rights bills, but also to the Senate Commerce Committee. Chaired by the politically more hospitable Warren Magnuson of Washington, the Commerce Committee could provide the bill safe passage around Eastland's roadblock. The administration's commerce-clause rationale, however, was irksome to Republicans, whose support would be critical to cutting off a Senate filibuster. The Fourteenth amendment was a *Republican* amendment, after all. Moreover, congressional Republicans had come to despise the commerce rationale as constitutionally trite and dangerously elastic, especially since Franklin Roosevelt had successfully used it to justify most of his expansive New Deal regulation of business. To Republicans, the commerce formula amounted to a regulatory carte blanche, designed to entangle in Washington's insatiable regulatory bureaucracy even the most humble, mom-and-pop store for selling a soapbar made in another state.

There was little in the remainder of Kennedy's civil rights message that offered major cause for concern over potential Republican opposition. School desegregation was a political threat primarily to southern Democrats. Southern Republicans typically represented mountain or suburban districts where few blacks resided, and northern Republicans had little to fear from the administration's bill so long as it concentrated on the South's segregated stores and schools. For this reason the administration's surprising proposal in Title 6 for a single, comprehensive congressional ban on federal funding of racially discriminatory programs found a receptive audience on the Hill, at least among nonsoutherners.

The little-noticed Title 6 represented a policy reversal by the White House staff and the legislative advisers from Justice, who had originally feared that any enforcement proposal to cut off federal aid would be anathema on the Hill. These fears, however, had proved unfounded. Instead, to the surprise of Norbert Schlei and his colleagues on the drafting team, "we began to get some very interesting playback . . . all the legislators—Democrats as well as Republicans—wanted to have a Powell amendment type of feature in the bill, that turned out to be Title 6. They said, 'Please, let's get that behind us. Now, that comes up on every bill.' " So the prospect of getting forever rid of Powell's Judas kiss appealed to both sides of the aisle. It appealed to Democrats frustrated by having their liberal legislation torpedoed. To Republicans it offered the threat of withholding federal funds as an economy measure. The serendipitous result, said Schlei, was "a practically unanimous recommendation of all the legislators that we make the Powell amendment controversy obsolete forever by having a sort of universal Powell amendment."[27]

It is one of the great ironies of the civil rights era that such a casual, bipartisan consensus should form around Title 6. It was prompted by Democratic irritation over the theatrics of Congressman Powell, and by Republican belief that the GOP tradition of fiscal prudence required them to support mechanisms for budget cutoff, especially since it seemed targeted exclusively against the racial discrimination of southern Democratic regimes. In the history of the modern administrative state, the armament of social regulation by Washington agencies, so traditionally loathed by Republicans, perhaps owed more to this fleeting moment of unexamined acquiescence in Title 6 than to all the other titles in the landmark civil rights bill combined. This would have been true even had Kennedy included an explicit title on job discrimination—which he carefully excluded.

The Fair Employment Dilemma

Kennedy's failure to include an FEPC proposal disappointed the black civil rights organizations and angered the national labor leadership. The National

Urban League's analysis of the omnibus bill regretted the omission of FEPC, but judged Kennedy's omnibus proposal over-all a "strong and good bill."[28] Organized labor's response, however, was surprisingly harsh. Publicly the AFL-CIO offered its customary strong support, but privately the leadership lashed out at the White House for failing to include FEPC. Both the CIO and even the old AFL before the merger had supported FEPC, and the reasons involved self-interest as well as social justice. Andrew J. Biemiller, the AFL-CIO's director of legislation, sent labor's critique of Kennedy's omnibus bill to Kenneth O'Donnell. It complained that "unions are being universally blamed, often unfairly, for job discrimination. This has resulted in very strained relations between Negroes and the labor movement."[29] Thus "unions, as well as the Negro and the country as a whole, need an FEPC." It was employers, Biemiller said, not labor, who opposed FEPC and who deserved much of the blame for job discrimination. The leverage provided by a national FEPC could help the AFL-CIO leadership force nondiscrimination policies on refractory locals who were shielded by the federation's decentralized structure. As George Meany told the Senate Labor and Public Welfare Committee in July, "We need the power of the federal government to do what we are not fully able to do [by ourselves]."[30]

As for Title 6 on withholding federal funds, the AFL-CIO's severe analysis of the Kennedy bill failed even to notice it. In the public statements and the internal correspondence of the NAACP, the National Urban League, and the civil rights coalition's coordinating organization, the Leadership Conference on Civil Rights, Title 6 was merely acknowledged in passing.[31] The NAACP sensed the title's Powell-amendment potential in desegregating southern schools, but by habit the NAACP looked mainly to judicial orders for enforcement.[32] The Urban League thought the President had full constitutional powers to withhold federal funds without needing to ask Congress for statutory authority. The Urban League therefore regarded Kennedy's Title 6 request as further evidence of "the moderate nature of the President's civil rights bill."[33] In the suddenly hopeful atmosphere of June 1963, most attention was focused on the controversial Title 2, which would desegregate the system that Bull Connor was defending. Only later would attention shift to job discrimination, with its nationwide implications. Almost no attention was paid to Title 6, the sleeper that in time would become by far the most powerful weapon of them all—and in the process would tear at the heart of the labor–civil rights alliance.

Lacking an FEPC proposal, Kennedy's new civil rights bill nevertheless had to address the persistent problem of employment discrimination in *some* fashion. Having decided not to propose a national FEPC for fear of losing the entire package, the administration sought to strike a delicate balance that would not alienate the Democrats' core constituency of nonsouthern liberals. On June 19, Kennedy asked Congress once again to pass his tax-cut, aid-to-education, and job-training measures. These included not only his embarrassingly battered bill for federal aid to education, but also such familiar programs as manpower development and training, youth employment, vocational education, work-study, adult education, and public welfare work-relief and training—none of them especially novel or designed specifically for minorities.[34] Kennedy had asked Willard Wirtz whether a three- to four-year "crash" program of these standard Democratic items would produce a breakthrough in black employment.[35] Wirtz replied that the crucial problem was not training and education but rather the sluggish economy, for which the administration had proposed the Keynesian, pump-priming tax cut. "I am forced," Wirtz said, "to the disheartening conclusion that in the present state of the economy it would be a mistake to hold out the hope that setting up a 'crash' program for Negroes would mean their being employed. It isn't true with whites, and it would be less true with respect to non-whites."[36] Kennedy agreed, and focused his fair employment efforts on Lyndon Johnson's existing committee.

Rejecting a national FEPC, Kennedy on June 19 asked Congress to give the PCEEO, under the continued chairmanship of the Vice President, a permanent statutory basis. This would give the committee a statutory mission and congressionally approved budget, but would not materially affect its present structure, duties, and enforcement powers. Kennedy affirmed to Congress that "I renew my support of pending Federal Fair Employment Practices legislation, applicable to both employers and unions." But he declined to make this part of his own omnibus bill. Kennedy renewed his pledge to issue the long-postponed executive order extending PCEEO coverage to construction jobs supported by federal grants. But his willingness to lead stopped well shy of FEPC. Instead, he implicitly invited Congress to reach further if it could summon the will to try and muster the consensus necessary to overcome a certain Senate filibuster.

The House-First Strategy: H.R. 7152

In the summer of 1963 the administration's top legislative strategists were chiefly concerned about the Senate. There a filibuster seemed inevitable if the civil rights bill had any real teeth, and Minority Leader Everett Dirksen clearly held the keys to cloture. But Dirksen had already declared his opposition to the heart of the bill, Title 2 on public accommodations. For most Republicans, Title 2 appeared to give federal authorities too much control over the free operations of the marketplace. The Senate majority leader, Mike Mansfield of Montana, feared that no such bill could pass the Senate under a Democratic President. But Mansfield agreed that success hinged on getting 67 votes for cloture, and Dirksen would hold the key to shutting off the southern filibuster.[37]

The House, permitting no filibusters, offered a more promising legislative environment. In that chamber the South's customary dominance of committee chairmanships did not include the crucial Judiciary Committee. There chairman "Manny" Celler supported equal rights for Negroes with as much vigor as he opposed the Equal Rights Amendment for women. A bill reported out of Celler's Judiciary Committee would still need to clear Judge Smith's Rules Committee, where the Virginian would surely attempt to block it. But the House leadership under Speaker Sam Rayburn of Texas had "packed" the obstructionist Rules Committee in 1961, and it was doubtful that Smith and his fellow conservatives on the committee could keep a bill of such importance from being considered by the full House. Once the bill reached the House floor, the administration would need a bloc of approximately 65 votes from Republican liberals and moderates to overcome the defection of southern Democrats.

Where might the Republican votes come from and who might deliver them? The liberal House Republicans, like John Lindsay of Manhattan, wanted a strong bill, but they were a tiny minority. The intensely partisan House minority leader, Charles Halleck, seemed an unlikely source, and both Halleck and minority whip Gerald Ford had strongly conservative voting records. So the crucial Republican dealer turned out to be William McCulloch, a man not generally known to the public.

A respected, moderately conservative congressman from Piqua, Ohio (near Dayton), McCulloch was the senior Republican on the 35-member House Judiciary Committee, to which the administration's omnibus bill H.R. 7152 had been routinely referred. McCulloch had supported the moderate civil rights bills of 1957 and 1959–60, but he was known to have felt betrayed in both efforts by the Democratic congressional leadership, when commitments made to the Republican leadership in the House were subsequently bartered away by Senate majority leader Lyndon Johnson in order to avoid filibusters. So Katzenbach urged Robert Kennedy to sound out McCulloch "before he is committed to a position publicly and we should get to work on him immediately." The Attorney General dispatched Burke Marshall, a proven negotiator, to Piqua, Ohio, where Marshall and McCulloch hammered out an agreement.

In return for his support, McCulloch demanded two iron-clad pledges from the administration. First, President Kennedy would not allow the Senate's Democratic leadership to gut the House-passed bill by compromising provisions that had been hammered out in the House. To guard against this, the administration would give McCulloch the sole power to approve any changes that it would accept in the Senate. Second, the Kennedy administration would give the Republicans equal credit for passing the bipartisan bill. These were stiff terms, but McCulloch seemed to be in a position to command a high price. Robert Kennedy pledged not to agree to any changes without McCulloch's approval. "Robert Kennedy," Burke Marshall explained, became "the lawyer for Bill McCulloch."[38]

"Committee Fillibuster" in the Senate

The outlook in the Senate was clouded by not only the prospect of filibuster but also the southern domination of the Senate's committee structure. Both circumstances suggested a House-first strategy, through which a moderately strong bill might offer bargaining chips with which to negotiate for Dirksen's support for cloture in the Senate. Meanwhile the civil rights coalition could build up a a groundswell of national support for a bill aimed primarily at the dramatic southern abuses, with the ironical cooperation of the South's Bull Connors.

The hearings in the Senate Commerce Committee dealt only with Title 2 of the administration's bill, the public accommodations section. The committee was a sympathetic forum for Title 2. Its seventeen members included only five Republicans, none of them from the states of the former Confederacy. The committee's twelve Democrats included only two southern senators. One of these was former Dixiecrat Strom Thurmond of South Carolina (then still a Democrat). But Thurmond's defense of segregation was balanced by the liberalism of the other southerner, Ralph Yarborough of Texas. In eleven days of hearings the Commerce Committee heard 79 witnesses, including half of the nation's governors. Opposition spokesmen were given full voice, as eight southern governors (including George Wallace of Alabama and Ross Barnett of Mississippi) were joined in opposition to the bill by three southern attorneys general, plus the segregationist journalist James J. Kilpatrick of the *Richmond News-Leader* and the arch-conservative nonsouthern publisher, William Loeb of the Manchester (New Hampshire) *Union Leader.*

The opponents of the civil rights bill based their case less on a defense of Jim Crow per se than on the hoary rhetoric of neoConfederate state rights, the mythic memories of Black Reconstruction, the specter of federal tyranny as a betrayal of the Founders, and a plea for gradualism and voluntarism. But those too-familiar pleas were mocked by the televised visions of Birmingham. August witnessed the massive and dignified March on Washington for Jobs and Freedom, highlighted at the Lincoln Memorial by King's moving sermon, "I Have a Dream." The heart of King's dream was that black Americans could "one day live in a nation where they will not be judged by the color of their skin but by the content of their character."[39] Arrayed against this dream, the state rights and property rights arguments that the conservatives advanced in Senate testimony were potentially powerful. But they rang hollow in the manifest absence of state responsibilities and the palpable presence of state brutality. The conservatives seemed implicitly to defend the constitutional rights of "Bull" Connor. They were politely heard, and utterly overwhelmed by the weight of the moral argument. The best state-rights defense against a federal Title 2 was equivalent state efforts at reforming the humiliating abuses of the biracial caste system in public commerce, and in this the southern conservatives manifestly failed.

In the parallel hearings before the Judiciary Committee, the Attorney General's chief antagonist was neither chairman Eastland of Mississippi nor the committee's ranking Republican, Everett Dirksen of Illinois. Eastland's style of chairmanship was judicial, leaving the adversary role to other senators. Dirksen, as the Senate minority leader, was expected to cast a critical eye on bills proposed by Democratic presidents. He performed with theatrical relish as leader of the opposition, in the tradition of midwestern conservatism associated with the Senate's Republican leader during the Truman and Eisenhower presidencies, Robert A. Taft of Ohio. Dirksen had long excelled at needling Senate Democrats for their inability to unite behind civil rights measures. But when Kennedy seized the nettle in June 1963 by sending Congress a public accommodations bill, Dirksen had replied that he was generally comfortable with everything in the bill *except* Title 2, which he said would extend government control to the private domain of merchant and customer choice. But because the public accommodations title of the bill had been sent to the Commerce Committee, where Dirksen was not a member, Dirksen's role in the Judiciary Committee hearings was largely passive. Instead, Robert Kennedy received his interrogation from the committee's second-ranking Democrat, Sam Ervin of North Carolina. Dirksen was content merely to watch the Democrats draw blood from one another over civil rights, as they were long in the habit of doing.

Ervin's frequent protestation that he was just a "poor old country lawyer" was confirmed by his folksy, piedmont demeanor, but belied by his Harvard Law credentials and his experience as a justice on North Carolina's Supreme Court.[40] A younger generation would subsequently recall Ervin as the learned constitutional scourge of Nixon and Watergate. But like the other, and mostly lesser, southern defenders of the South's biracial caste system, Ervin ultimately repaired to the weak reed of state-rights gradualism. The hoary doctrine was constitutionally defensible in theory in 1963, but it was not politically defensible in practice.

From his privileged chair among the committee majority, and fortified by chairman Eastland and the elaborate protocols of senatorial courtesy, Ervin conducted what journalists soon called a "committee filibuster." As the Judiciary hearings, going nowhere, dragged on into August and September, bringing the long-suffering Attorney General with them, Ervin hammered away at the threat of federal tyranny, appealing grandiloquently and at great length to Magna Carta and the Founders and Daniel Webster. Ervin argued with dissembling self-deprecation—"in my feeble way"—less for state rights than for separation of powers, and especially for constitutional restraints and legislative resistance to executive law-making. His instincts for bureaucratic empire-building were acute, and Ervin followed them, like a divining rod, toward Title 6 on fund cut-off. This he linked to a House-proposed provision (not part of Kennedy's omnibus bill) on fair employment, complaining that the "discrimination" that the House bill banned was never even defined in the proposed law. Thus the definitions of what behavior was deemed illegal would perforce be left to the considerable discretion of the President and his agents, who would also apparently determine the punishments. Violators would not be told precisely what behavior was prohibited, Ervin warned, and hence would be held accountable to a kind of floating bill of attainder, with both the crime and the punishment to be decided, *post hoc,* by federal bureaucrats.

A decade later, during the Watergate hearings, Ervin would distinguish himself with the same arguments, and Americans confronted with shocking presidential and executive abuses would resonate to Ervin's indictment. But in 1963, Ervin had no smoking gun. So he was forced to imagine one. And in relentlessly pressing this logic, he was reduced to the *arguendum ad horrendum.* He claimed that the omnibus bill would cover, under its equal employment provisions for federal contracts, the ordinary American housewife and her maid. By hiring a domestic servant and paying social security taxes on her wages, Ervin warned, the American housewife would thereby become a federal contractor! As Kennedy wearily but politely observed, "Senator, I just do not think that makes any sense."[41] And in the political context of the summer of 1963, it didn't.

Origins of Title 7: From the FEPC to the EEOC

Throughout the prolonged hearings in the Senate Judiciary's "committee filibuster," Ervin found it hard going to pin the Attorney General down by demonstrating the horrors that could be expected to follow passage of the administration's omnibus bill. There were several reasons for this. First, Robert Kennedy was too adept at deflecting Ervin's *ad horrendum* logic by returning attention to the simple moral purpose of the bill, which was to eliminate the unfair discrimination against blacks that was so massively demonstrable, especially in the South. Also, Ervin had to reply principally on hyperbolic imagination because he could find so few genuine examples of federal tyranny in the field. Ironically, this was partly because he and his like-minded predecessors had successfully thwarted all attempts at creating a statutory FEPC whose outrages he could document. Also—although Ervin would not concede this—the state and local FEPCs had been, by and large, models of responsible restraint in wielding their cease-and-desist authority. Furthermore, Lyndon Johnson's EEO committee had similarly avoided any heavy-handed abuse of its more limited jurisdiction and circumscribed authority. Finally, the administration bill that Kennedy defended proposed no new federal FEPC, but only a statutory recognition of the Vice President's EEO committee.

The omnibus bill's lack of a fair-employment title was politically helpful to the Attorney General. But it was distressing to the civil rights coalition. The well-organized civil rights community—the NAACP, the Urban League, CORE, Dr. King's SCLC, together with such white-led liberal groups as the ACLU, the Anti-Defamation League, the ADA, and the AFL-CIO, most of them cooperating under the umbrella of the Leadership Conference—was long accustomed to this combination of presidential timidity and congressional resistance, and they had done their homework well. Necessity had forced the civil rights lobby to become practiced manipulators of the pluralistic system of American democracy, and early in the Kennedy regime they had seized an effective opportunity to forge an instrument to serve their purposes.

When Harlem's Adam Clayton Powell became chairman of the House Labor and Education Committee in 1961, he established a special subcommittee on labor and charged it with a singular mission. Powell appointed Congressman James Roosevelt of California (son of Franklin and Eleanor Roosevelt) to chair the new subcommittee, and dispatched it on a transcontinental tour of hearings to inquire into the condition of equal employment opportunity across the land.[42] Although the civil rights spotlight during the early 1960s was focused almost exclusively on the South, the tour of Roosevelt's subcommittee was confined to the upper, nonsouthern tier of the United States. Powell and Roosevelt wanted to demonstrate that racial discrimination in employment was not a peculiarly southern problem, and that even states with vigorous FEP laws and commissions were in need of a strong federal statute and an agency to enforce it. So they held their subcommittee hearings during the fall of 1961 in Chicago, Los Angeles, and New York and consolidated them back in Washington in January 1962. Not surprisingly, the Roosevelt subcommittee's list of witnesses was loaded in favor of their proposed federal commission, as was the membership of the subcommittee and its parent committee as well. [43]

The Roosevelt subcommittee concentrated its hearings on employment areas that the state FEPCs found difficult to reach, such as waiters and bartenders and hotel bellmen in Los Angeles, and nonsalaried commission salesmen in New York. It sought from witnesses like New York's Will Maslow, executive director of the American Jewish Congress and a veteran of Franklin Roosevelt's original FEPC, knowledgeable advice about the strengths and weaknesses of the state FEPCs, and the advantages and disadvantages of a NLRB model for a federal FEPC. Such informed testimony educated the subcommittee and its public on the functional and legal distinctions between the quasi-judicial, administrative agencies like the state commissions on the one hand, and on the other such federal enforcement instruments as the Vice President's interagency committee. A chief and troublesome distinction was that state FEPCs, like the major regulatory commissions on which they were modeled (FTC, NLRB), ultimately enforced their cease-and-desist orders through the courts. A national FEPC could similarly use the courts to enforce cease-and-desist orders against discriminating private employers. But the doctrine of separation of powers would prevent a national FEPC from suing other federal agencies in court. A national FEPC could not impose its requirements on the Pentagon or the Department of Health, Education and Welfare—whose contracts and grants-in-aid offered employment-standards leverage on a third of the American workforce. An alternative source of leverage was the President's constitutional authority over procurement. This was, however, a murky area of executive power, and Congress was reluctant to farm out discretionary authority to federal bureaucrats in such a sensitive area as civil rights enforcement.

From H.R. 405 to Title 7

By 1963, the Roosevelt subcommittee had served its purpose, and the full Powell committee had refined its own fair-employment bill and entered it into the House hopper as H.R. 405. Under normal circumstances, such liberal proposals from the Labor and Education Committee stood little chance of surviving both the Rules gauntlet and the floor votes. The committee's aid-to-education bills, for example, had been ritually slaughtered on the House floor during 1961–63. But the televised brutality of Birmingham had changed the national mood, at least for civil rights. In 1962 subcommittee chairman Roosevelt had persuaded Labor secretary Arthur Goldberg to testify, implicitly for the administration as well as for his department, that he supported the subcommittee's EEO bill "in principle." Roosevelt had resisted the frequent efforts of the more zealous civil rights spokesmen to arm the proposed new federal EEO commission with the powers of both prosecutor and judge. He was constantly looking over his shoulder at the hostile Rules Committee, and he wearied of complaints from angry civil rights activists that his committee's emerging proposal was too timid.

On June 6, 1963, the Roosevelt subcommittee completed ten days of final testimony on H.R. 405, and the full committee reported the bill out on July 22. On its face, H.R. 405 created nothing resembling the "Star Chamber Employment Bureau" that southern critics had denounced. The bill declared it an unlawful practice for an employer, labor union, or employment agency "to fail or refuse to hire or to discharge any individual, or otherwise to discriminate against any individual with respect to his compensation, terms, conditions, or privileges of employment, because of such individual's race, religion, color, national origin, or ancestry."[44] There was no mention of sex discrimination. The Roosevelt subcommittee had briefly considered the question, but spokesmen for organized labor had opposed including sex discrimination, and no women sat on the Roosevelt panel. The proposed enforcing instrument was a five-member Equal Employment Opportunity Commission. This had the advantage of replacing the controversial acronym FEPC with a new and more neutral one, EEOC. The commission's six proposed "powers" testified to its conciliatory spirit: the EEOC would cooperate with similar state and local agencies, pay the expenses of witnesses, offer technical assistance, assist employers in conciliation upon request, make technical studies, and create an advisory and conciliation council. Nothing very frightening there.

The EEOC proposed by H.R. 405 was modeled on the state FEPCs. It thus would be similarly armed with the authority, after an investigation and a finding of probable cause—and also only after the failure of conciliation—to order offending respondents "to cease and desist from such unlawful employment practice and to make such affirmative action, including reinstatement or hiring of employees, with or without back pay . . . as will effectuate the policies of the Act." The language was familiar to civil rights veterans. It traced its lineage through a generation of failed congressional proposals, all the way back to New York's anti-discrimination law of 1945. The proposed EEOC would be empowered to compel witnesses, take testimony under oath, investigate complaints, enter and inspect premises and records, and require employers to maintain stipulated records and make periodic reports. As for jurisdiction over federal employees and government contractors, H.R. 405 recognized the inappropriateness of endowing such a quasi-judicial, administrative agency with court-enforceable authority over other federal agencies. So the bill yielded this authority to presidential discretion.

H.R. 405, however, was no part of the administration's bill. Moreover, Roosevelt's special subcommittee had always been a sideshow in relation to the real powers of Congress. Jurisdiction over civil rights matters was jealously guarded in the House by the Judiciary Committee, which had held summer-long hearings on 168 civil rights bills that members had filed with the committee. Chairman Celler was a veteran New Deal liberal who had appointed himself chairman of his own special subcommittee, and had stacked it with six fellow Democratic liberals (including the lone, populistic southern Democrat, Jack Brooks of Texas). McCulloch was senior among the subcommittee's four Republicans, all of them regarded as moderates or conservatives. By August 5, Celler's Subcommittee No. 5 had completed 22 days of public hearings on the administration's omnibus bill, a process that produced 1,742 pages of printed testimony. Celler then took the committee into closed "markup" sessions, where the real horse-trading could begin, shielded from public scrutiny.

Congress broke for the Labor Day recess on the heels of the March on Washington for Jobs and Freedom on August 28. That evening President Kennedy received the civil rights leaders in the White House, where he rattled off the political arithmetic of the Congress and discouraged demands for an FEPC-style commission. Kennedy's listeners included Martin Luther King, Jr., A. Philip Randolph, Roy Wilkins, Whitney Young, Walter Reuther, and also Lyndon Johnson. Kennedy reminded the group of the strategic advice of Congressman McCulloch: "If I wanted to beat your bill, I would put FEPC in. And I would vote for it, and we would never pass it in the House."[45]

Celler would not reconvene his subcommittee for serious markup until September 10, when the President's tax bill had been safely voted out of the Ways and Means Committee. In a confidential letter to Celler of August 13, Katzenbach had spelled out the administration's cautious negotiating strategy on H.R. 7152, concentrating on the bill's voting and public accommodations titles. Katzenbach had been leery of the bill's draft language on school desegregation (in Title 4) because it included the problematical term "racial imbalance." The language was intended to help justify some forms of federal financial assistance to northern school districts with de facto segregation. But to Katzenbach it carried the risk of sparking a controversy over "quotas, bussing children across town, etc. These are not intended to be endorsed by the act."[46] Katzenbach's six-page letter to Celler devoted only two sentences to job discrimination proposals, and then only to confirm that the administration's bill would grant statutory authority and budget authorization to the Vice President's EEO committee, but would otherwise leave the PCEEO's role unchanged.

Celler, however, would ignore the administration's cautious strategy and Katzenbach's letter, for he had long entertained a private strategy of his own. Soon he would spring this on an angered Robert Kennedy and a dismayed William McCulloch, and threaten to unglue the entire package. The results of this imbroglio would fashion the basic shape of the Civil Rights Act of 1964.

CHAPTER 4

Lyndon Johnson and the Civil Rights Act of 1964

Running the Double Gauntlet in House Judiciary

The Kennedy administration's House-first strategy for the omnibus civil rights bill faced six known obstacles: (1) Celler's Subcommittee No. 5; (2) the full 35-man (and 35-lawyer) House Judiciary Committee; (3) Judge Smith's Rules Committee; (4) the full House; (5) the penultimate hurdle—cloture against the inevitable Senate filibuster; (6) the Senate–House conference committee. Obstacle 6 was potentially treacherous because the conference agreement, if there was one, would have to be ratified by each chamber. In the volatile atmosphere following the Birmingham violence, any misstep could be fatal for the bill, and potentially disastrous for the administration and the nation's race relations. The House-first strategy meant that many of the major substantive decisions would be made in the closed markup sessions of the House Judiciary Committee. There Chairman Celler had a private strategy that he did not entirely share with the White House.[1]

Celler's legislative strategy was not inherently unreasonable. It had twice worked for him in previous civil rights hearings, in 1957 and again in 1959. On both occasions he had begun by emerging with a strong civil rights bill from a subcommittee he had stacked with liberal Democrats. Then he had traded off concessions to the more conservative Republicans in the full Judiciary Committee, in order to report out a moderately strong bill that centered on voting rights and commanded sufficient bipartisan support to pass the House. In the Senate, majority leader Lyndon Johnson weakened to bills enough to convince Richard Russell, dean of the southern senators, that the bill was not threatening enough to justify a full filibuster. The final compromise was then presented to President Eisenhower as a statesmanlike achievement by the Democratic-controlled Congress. In 1963, however, senior House Republicans like William McCulloch were determined not to be thrice used and ultimately betrayed by these Democratic bargaining tactics, and especially by what they regarded as a sell-out in the Senate. They were unwilling, without further guarantees, to support tough enforcement provisions under a Democratic President who could so easily blame them if the bill failed.

On September 10, the House Ways and Means Committee approved Kennedy's tax cut bill, as did the full House on September 30, thereby removing the fear that committee progress on the civil rights bill might endanger the tax cut. So Celler began serious (and closed) markup sessions as soon as the tax cut was safely out of committee. Then on September 15, a bomb blew up the Sixteenth Street Baptist Church in Birmingham, killing four small black girls and injuring twenty other children, and sparking protest riots in which two more children died. On the last day of September, the Civil Rights Commission called for federal guarantees of uniform national voting standards, including the use of federal voter registrars where necessary. The commission also endorsed a national FEPC statute that would cover private businesses and would be enforced by the Labor Department.[2]

In response to these pressures, Celler began markup in an initially bipartisan spirit. This was suggested early in the markup when the subcommittee agreed to an amendment by McCulloch that signified a powerful if rather quiet bipartisan consensus, at least in the North. McCulloch moved to strike from the administration's title on school desegregation a proposal to extend financial aid and technical assistance to school districts that attempted "to adjust racial imbalance."[3] This was code for northern de facto school segregation, and the nonsouthern congressmen wanted to strip from the bill a potential nonsouthern application. Its removal left the bill's school desegregation title applying to southern de jure segregation only. Southern congressmen denounced the maneuver as hypocritical because it made the bill essentially a one-region attack on a national problem. In their own hypocritical way, the southerners were quite right. But, heavily outnumbered on the subcommittee, they were ignored.

That accomplished, Celler then began to override the subcommittee's four-man Republican minority. In rapid succession, the subcommittee's seven-Democrat majority rammed through a brace of strengthening amendments that reflected virtually the full demands of the Leadership Conference on Civil Rights.[4] Chief among them was an amendment by Peter Rodino (D-N.J.) that replaced the administration's modest upgrading of Lyndon Johnson's committee with the full EEOC provision of H.R. 405, including cease-and-desist authority. By October 2, Celler's subcommittee had radically transformed the bill. The public accommodations section was expanded to cover all state-licensed activities. Vice President Johnson's PCEEO was now to be replaced by a national FEPC—or more precisely, an EEOC that was a quasi-judicial administrative agency with both prosecutorial and cease-and-desist power. Finally, the subcommittee gave the Attorney General broad discretionary authority to bring suit if in his judgment the rights of any individual were being infringed from any source in any U.S. jurisdiction.

McCulloch, furious, felt betrayed again—just as in 1957 and 1959. "It's a pail of garbage," snapped the normally mild-mannered ranking minority member.[5] But the Leadership Conference was ecstatic. Southern Democratic congressmen were initially angry at being railroaded in subcommittee by their liberal colleagues. But they quickly warmed to the prospect of first voting *for* Celler's liberal Democratic *coup de main* in the Judiciary Committee, then joining the Republicans to sink it on the House floor. To the more conservative southerners and Republicans, Celler's liberal new package carried the enticing earmarks of a super-Powell amendment.

Liberals Are "in love with death"

Robert Kennedy did not conceal his contempt for "professional liberals."[6] He associated the Eleanor Roosevelt–Adlai Stevenson wing of the Democratic party, where he and his brother had rarely felt welcomed, with a Kamikaze purity. To Bobby such liberals had a "sort of death wish, really wanting to go down in flames." "Action or success make them suspicious," Kennedy said. "They like it much better to have a cause than to have a course of action that's been successful."[7] To Burke Marshall, Celler's subcommittee that September "ran away and closed out this impossible bill," which McCulloch confirmed would never pass the House. So in mid-October the White House mounted a salvage operation, demanding that Celler meet with Katzenbach, Marshall, and McCulloch to fashion a substitute bill acceptable to the Republican minority. Meanwhile, Speaker John McCormack was meeting with Katzenbach and House Republican leader Charles Halleck, asking the Republican leadership to help bail out the Democrats. In return McCulloch demanded that the Attorney General make an "iron-clad oath" before the full Judiciary Committee.

Robert Kennedy's testimony, delivered in executive session on October 15 and 16, was a tour de force. He attacked the subcommittee's expanded definition of public accommodations as both overreaching and vulnerable to changes in state law. He even attacked the subcommittee's expansion of the powers of his own office, warning that it would involve the Justice Department and the federal courts in police functions that had historically been exercised by local officials and would risk the creation of a national police force. Its language was so broad, Kennedy said, that it would extend federal power to "claimed violations of constitutional rights involving church-state relations; economic questions such as allegedly confiscatory rate-making or the constitutional requirement of just compensation in land acquisition cases; the propriety of incarceration in a mental hospital; searches and seizures; and controversies involving freedom of speech, freedom of worship, or of the press." In the name of civil rights, it would endanger the delicate Madisonian balance that had historically protected civil liberties.[8]

Coup and Counter-coup in Fair Employment

In ticking off his objections to the subcommittee revisions, Kennedy had brushed quickly by the revised fair employment title. This seemed to indicate that the administration had no fundamental problem with the substitution of H.R. 405 for the administration's original proposal to give statutory status to the Vice President's EEO committee. But the Republican minority had such a problem. In February 1962, when the Powell committee had originally reported out its EEOC bill (which few students of Congress thought had any chance to pass), a bloc of seven moderate Republicans on Powell's committee had demanded one basic change as the price of their support. Led by Robert P. Griffin of Michigan, they insisted that the proposed new EEOC, *unlike* the state FEPCs, must be *denied* the quasi-judicial power to hold hearings and issue cease-and-desist orders. Instead of in effect holding a trial and declaring a judgment, then, the federal EEOC would be empowered only to investigate and prosecute. This would leave the judicial decisions about guilt and remedy to a federal district court.[9]

Griffin and his Republican colleagues argued that the American Bar Association's longstanding principles of American jurisprudence required that final determinations be made by the courts rather than by an investigative, prosecuting agency. Regulatory agencies should not be both prosecutor and judge, they said. This position reflected the great battle over administrative reform of the 1940s, when a coalition of Republicans and southern Democrats attacked the regulatory abuses they associated with the New Deal.[10] Their prime target had been the NLRB, and their chief instrument had been Howard Smith's special House investigating committee (Roosevelt's wartime FEPC had drawn Smith's special ire because it lacked even the statutory authority that the Wagner Act had conferred on the NLRB). The Smith committee charged pro-labor bias by the NLRB and its hearing examiners, and the investigation's disclosures drew attacks on the labor board not only from the American business community and the American Bar Association, but also from the AFL, which complained of heavy-handed bias by the NLRB in favor of the rival CIO. The chief result under a Republican Congress was the Administrative Procedures Act of 1946, which sought to "judicialize" the procedures of the quasi-judicial regulatory agencies. This in turn had been followed by the Taft-Hartley Act of 1947, which sought to counterbalance the pro-labor tilt of the Wagner Act.

The Administrative Procedures Act rested on the principle of Madisonian separation of the police function of investigation and prosecution, on the one hand, and the judicial function of rendering judgments and determining relief and penalities, on the other. Its administrative reforms added court-like procedural safeguards to the regulatory process. This shift toward a trial model, with lawyerly challenges over rules of evidence, burden of proof, and rights of appeal, emphasized judicial fairness over administrative efficiency.[11] The Republicans on the House Education and Labor Committee had long defended this conservative tradition of administrative reform. They pointed out that their *prosecutorial* model was the standard method through which the Labor department enforced the wage-and-hour provisions of the Fair Labor Standards Act, the unfair labor practices provisions of the Landrum-Griffin Act, as well as the new provisions of the Equal Pay Act for women. Griffin and his colleagues had expressed a common Republican complaint against NLRB-type administrative tribunals, which was that despite the limited reforms of the Administrative Procedures Act of 1946, they "have acquired a well-deserved reputation for ignoring the rules of evidence." What they meant was that in practice, the federal appeals courts so rarely overturned the decisions of such administrative tribunals that the normal burden of proof was reversed, and the accused on appeal found that "he must bear the burden of proving his freedom from guilt."[12]

In addition to this appeal to judicial principle, the Republicans in 1962 had added a practical argument against giving judge-like authority to fair-employment commissions. This was that in the experience of the state FEPCs since their beginnings in New York in 1945, the cease-and-desist orders and accompanying court enforcement almost never had to be used. In support of this assertion they appended the following summary of state FEPC activity through the end of 1961:

State	Cases	Hearings	Cease and Desist Order	Court Action
California	1,014	2	2	2
Colorado	251	4	3	1
Connecticut	900	4	3	3
Massachusetts	3,559	2	2	0
Michigan	1,459	8	6	4
Minnesota	184	1	1	1
New Jersey	1,735	2	2	2
New York	7,497	18	6	5
Ohio	985	2	1	0
Oregon	286	0	0	0
Pennsylvania	1,238	19	0	0
Rhode Island	286	0	0	0
Total	19,394	62	26	18

This was, at first glance, a rather odd supporting argument. It seemed to confirm that the state FEPC model worked quite well—or at least that it functioned without any abuse of cease-and-desist authority. In fewer than 0.3 percent of the cases had formal hearings been necessary. In only 0.1 percent had cease-and-desist orders been issued. Even less frequently had such judgments been adjudicated in state courts—only 18 out of a total of 19,394! But the Republicans argued that the state FEP commissions required courts to enforce their cease-and-desist orders anyway. As an investigating agency a federal EEOC might function as a prosecutor but *not* also as a judge. This was the Republicans price for supporting the fair employment bill in 1962, and that year they had prevailed.

The Powell committee's Democrats, however, were unhappy with that compromise. In 1962, when the hapless House Education and Labor Committee could never seem to get an important bill past the Rules Committee, perhaps it wasn't worth fighting about. But in the post-Birmingham atmosphere of 1963, the committee's Democrats sensed a new political opening. So on July 11 they reversed the 1962 decision by a straight partisan vote of 13-7. When the committee reported out H.R. 405 on July 22, the Democratic majority had returned the proposed EEOC to the original quasi-judicial model based on the NLRB. So when Celler's Subcommittee No. 5 in October incorporated H.R. 405 as the new Title 7 of H.R. 7152, back came the EEOC's judicial role with cease-and-desist orders. Then came the White House salvage operation, which allowed the Republicans to counterattack under the leadership of McCulloch and Halleck. Out again went the quasi-judicial model; in again came the prosecutorial model—like a yo-yo.[13] Such a prosecutorial EEOC would neither decide cases nor issue orders. Instead it would seek relief in federal district court, and then in a trial *de novo* rather than an appeals-level review of a commission decision. The *New York Times'* Anthony Lewis, who was close to the Kennedys, reported that the administration preferred the Powell committee's quasi-judicial model in H.R. 405.[14] But as Burke Marshall was fond of recalling, Robert Kennedy was Mr. McCulloch's lawyer and press agent. So the administration kept its promise to McCulloch and supported the Republican position.

The House Leadership Compromise of 1963

The showdown in the Judiciary Committee came on October 29. On the first ballot, over a motion to approve Celler's subcommittee bill, most of the southern conservatives joined the northern liberals and voted "aye," in hopes of sending to the House an ultra-liberal bill they could then defeat on the floor. But the administration's centrist coalition held and the motion failed 15 to 19. Then a motion to substitute the Kennedy-McCulloch compromise bill was carried 20-14, and H.R. 7152 was reported out to the House.

The House leadership compromise of 1963 represented a strategic victory for the Kennedy brothers, although one purchased at the cost of considerable resentment on the part of the civil rights forces allied under the umbrella of the Leadership Conference. Most attention was focused on the public accommodations section, in which the compromise dropped the sweeping inclusion of all state-licensed establishments and accepted McCulloch's exclusion of personal service establishments (e.g., barber shops and shoeshine parlors) and retail shops without eating facilities. Moderate conservatives like McCulloch wanted to shield mom-and-pop operations from the bureaucratic demands of the regulatory colossus—reasoning that such margins of freedom left breathing room to civil society, but did not compromise the effectiveness of the reforms. To liberals, however, the attack on racial segregation was a moral imperative that made compromise suspect. The public accommodations title was easily the bill's most controversial provision, and arguably its most radically transforming one for the South.[15] But the NAACP's chief Washington lobbyist, Clarence Mitchell, called the compromise a "sell-out" (during Judiciary's tense negotiations in closed session, Mitchell pointed out that "Everybody in there is a white man").[16] But the compromise kept the bill alive, and the EEOC title made it far stronger than the original Kennedy proposal of June 19. With the exception of the new EEOC title, the remaining elements of the House leadership compromise did not reflect major changes. The school desegregation title retained its exclusion of northern de facto segregation, and Title 6 on fund cut-off remained essentially the same potentially powerful weapon, while attracting very little legislative or public attention.

During the summer of 1963 most attention was fixed on the civil rights bill's provision to desegregate southern hotels and stores and restaurants. But by mid-fall the novelty had somewhat worn off the edge of Title 2, and increasing attention was turned to the omnibus bill's new fair-employment provision in Title 7. The compromise bill now contained, in by far its most complicated and lengthy title, a federal FEPC newly christened as the EEOC. It provided for a five-member commission with powers over most private employers to receive complaints and investigate charges of discrimination, including authority to subpoena witnesses and require record-keeping and periodic reporting. The compromise had stripped the agency of cease-and-desist authority. This in turn had stripped away much of the structural apparatus of quasi-judicial agencies that typified the proposed EEOC's administrative models—the NLRB, the Federal Trade Commission, and the state FEPCs. But the EEOC was not stripped of its prosecutorial role. The compromise bill's EEOC could still file civil suits against employers in federal district court for injunctive relief against future violations, including reinstatement and the potential recovery of back pay for victims.

These distinctions, however, were not understood by the public at large. Both the national media and the congressional debate had done a poor job of identifying and explaining them. Half the states possessed their own FEP agencies, most of them modeled on the respected New York initiative of 1945. They offered a variety of powers, coverage, and structure from which an educational comparison might well have been derived.[17] The states lacking FEP agencies offered an implicit control group, dominated by southern states wherein political debate had long ago consigned the FEPC to an opprobrium unworthy of serious discussion. All the more reason, then, for the enlightenment of informed national debate. But such enlightenment largely failed by default. The explorations of the congressional hearings, floor debate, and media coverage, which had illuminated the complexities of governmental regulations of customer policies in hotels and restaurants, found no parallel in the arcane world of quasi-judicial agencies. The consequences of this failed dialogue would risk a resolution that fell between two stools, thereby badly confusing the relationship between ends and means in fair employment.

In November of 1963, however, H.R. 7152 still had a long way to go. Only three weeks after the Judiciary Committee had cleared the compromise civil rights bill, John Kennedy was assassinated in Dallas. His martyrdom would fuel the drive that King's forces had launched from Birmingham. Five days following Kennedy's death, President Lyndon Johnson told a joint session of Congress: "We have talked long enough in this country about civil rights. It is now time to write the next chapter and to write it in books of law." No eulogy, Johnson said, "could more eloquently honor President Kennedy's memory" than the "earliest possible passage of the civil rights bill for which he fought so long."[18]

Judge Smith, the House Rules Committee, and the Irony of Sex Anti-discrimination

In the early fall of 1963 the House Rules Committee had refused to allow the House Education and Labor Committee's H.R. 405 to proceed to the House floor, much as it had regularly and rather easily bottled up such FEP legislation in the past. But once the Judiciary Committee had transformed H.R. 405 into a "Republicanized" Title 7 in the omnibus civil rights bill, Judge Smith and his conservative colleagues on Rules faced an administration-backed compromise that they could delay but stood little chance of stopping. A bipartisan majority for H.R. 7152 was building even on Chairman Smith's bastion in Rules, and further delaying tactics (such as the chairman disappearing into his apple orchard in Virginia) would risk the humiliation of having his committee formally take the bill away from him. So on December 19, Smith grudgingly scheduled the Rules hearings for ten days between January 9 and 30, 1964.[19]

The hearings, as it turned out, were anticlimactic. This was partly because Kennedy's martyrdom and Johnson's pledge to redeem Kennedy's civil rights promise had set a newly expectant tone to the debate. This left the conservative coalition far less free than in the past to savage the bill in Rules. More important, because Celler and McCulloch were united behind the compromise, they could count on a majority on Rules, and this postponed to the House floor any decisive battles over major amendments. The result on Rules was a sort of low and folksy theater, with Smith needling Celler for having railroaded his bill through Judiciary in closed session, then failing to produce the printed testimony of Celler's sole witness, the Attorney General. Celler's excuses were weak on both counts. But in such a contest of political muscle, that was irrelevant.

The Rules hearings featured the exchange of elaborate rhetorical courtesies between the combatants, and occasioned much guffawing from observers. Most discussion centered on integrating public accommodations, as it had throughout the summer and fall of 1963. William Colmer of Mississippi worried: the barbers he knew told him "that they're not equipped or trained to cut the hair of the opposite race." Smith expressed dismay at the new plight of a hypothetical podiatrist whose office might be in a hotel: "If I were cutting corns," the octenagarian committee chairman said, "I would want to know whose feet I would have to be monkeying around with. I would want to know whether they smelled good or bad."[20] Smith later had second thoughts about the taste of that remark, and had it expunged from the record. During the Rules hearing Celler and McCulloch faced down all hostile amendments that were offered and accepted several minor technical amendments. On January

30, to no one's great surprise, the resolution granting a rule for H.R. 7152 carried by a comfortable margin, 11 to 4.

Once the bill was before the full House, however, Howard Smith sprang his one-word surprise. On February 8 he interrupted debate and moved to add one word, "sex," to the list of classes protected by Title 7.[21] "This bill is so imperfect," he said, "what harm will this little amendment do?" Despite the professions of surprise that Smith's one-word bombshell prompted in the media, his proposal of gender protection was not unexpected by the administration. Southern congressmen as early as 1950 had sought to defeat an FEPC bill by adding women to the protected classes. The "friendly" amendment was well understood as unfriendly in intent, and in 1950 it had been rejected by the House. Deputy Attorney General Katzenbach, in his capacity as chief shepherd of H.R. 7152, had warned supporters against the maneuver, and the administration had relied especially on the strong support of Representative Edith Green of Oregon to deflect its mischief. Like most supporters of the civil rights bill, including the liberals represented by the Leadership Conference and the Women's Bureau coalition as well, Green believed that discrimination against blacks was much more severe than against women. She feared that adding sex as a protected category would only defeat the civil rights bill.[22] Otherwise why were southern congressmen pushing it? During the early floor debate, the House leadership had rather easily beaten back several attempts by Democrat John Dowdy of Texas to add sex discrimination bans to several titles of the bill. But Dowdy lacked Smith's unique credentials, and Smith shrewdly confined his amendment barring sex discrimination to Title 7.

Smith indubitably wished to sink the civil rights bill. But surprisingly, the courtly Virginian was also sincere in his unlikely feminist egalitarianism. He had been a congressional sponsor of the Equal Rights Amendment since as far back as 1945—almost as far back as he had been a scourge of FEPC. Ever since then he had maintained loose political ties with the National Women's party and Alice Paul. When Paul founded the NWP in 1913 to add bite to the suffrage movement, the radical, elitist, all-female party had appealed to southern progressives by arguing that women's suffrage would essentially double the vote of the white middle and upper class. With similar logic, in their four-decade, fruitless battle for the ERA, Alice Paul and her aging and dwindling band of NWP colleagues had argued that any equal-employment law that protected blacks must also include women. Otherwise white women would lack an advantage granted to black men.[23] When the President's Commission on the Status of Women, after troubled debate, recommended against the ERA in its final report of October 1963, the National Women's party pressed Judge Smith to sponsor its egalitarian amendment to Title 7.[24] On December 16, the NWP's annual convention unanimously resolved that protection against sex discrimination should be added to the civil rights bill. Otherwise, the resolution observed, the bill would not offer "to a *White woman*, a *Woman of the Christian Religion*, or a *Woman of United States Origin* the protection it would afford to Negroes."[25]

On the House floor, opposition to the Smith amendment was led by Celler and Edith Green. But Green was isolated in her opposition by the other women members. Martha W. Griffiths of Michigan, who was the first woman to join the powerful Ways and Means Committee, led the bipartisan and ideologically strange fight for the Smith amendment.[26] She declared that "a vote against this amendment today by a white man is a vote against his wife, or his widow, or his daughter, or his sister."[27] "It would be incredible to me that white men would be willing to place white women at such a disadvantage," Griffiths said. Under the bill as reported, "you are going to have white men in one bracket, you are going to try to take colored men and colored women and give them equal employment rights, and down at the bottom of the list is going to be a white woman with no rights at all." In response to the nervous ripples of male laughter that occasionally stirred through the House during the debate, Representative Katherine St. George, a genteel Republican from upstate New York, hurled defiance in the teeth of her male colleagues: "We outlast you. We outlive you. We nag you to death. So why should we want special privileges?" "We want this crumb of equality," she said, "to correct something that goes back, frankly, to the dark ages." Her Republican colleague, Catherine May of Washington, echoed the sentiments of the NWP: "I hope we won't overlook the white native-born American woman of Christian religion."[28] In their rather lame and chiefly tactical arguments against Smith's ban on sex discrimination, northern liberals like Green and Celler could only plead that the amendment's timing was "inopportune," while offering against it only the tired argument that it threatened women's protective legislation.

The long congressional battle over the civil rights bill had created many unusual political coalitions, but the brief and decisive row over the Smith amendment created even more ironical pairings than had the left-right coalition in Judiciary the previous October. Emanuel Celler and Edith Green battled the unlikely combination of Howard Smith and Martha Griffiths. Alice Paul got her posthumous revenge on Eleanor Roosevelt. Esther Peterson, who had won her battles in 1963 for the Equal Pay Act and for a successful conclusion of President Kennedy's status-of-women commission despite the division over the ERA, now found herself in the uncomfortable position of leading the Women's Bureau's effort to exclude women from the equal-employment protections of the civil rights bill. The sudden emergence of the gender issue was forcing a realignment in the traditional coalitions. Younger Democratic women were beginning to defect from the protectionist ranks, attracted by egalitarian arguments that women should be able to seek and hold employment on the same basis as men. To women like Maguerite Rawalt, a lawyer who defended the ERA while sitting on the President's Commission on the Status of Women, the gender-based protectionist laws won by Eleanor Roosevelt's generation seemed ill-suited to modern circumstances. On the other hand leading Republican women, who traditionally had supported the ERA and resisted government regulation of business, found less to fear from Title 7 than their conservative male colleagues if the EEOC it created would protect women's rights also.

Republicans and southern Democrats in Congress had frequently combined in a conservative coalition, but such solidarity in defense of radical feminism was a novelty. After only two hours of debate, Smith's amendment passed on a teller vote of 168 to 133, with most of the senior, white, male, conservative southern Democrats apparently voting for it. By February 10, a total of 124 amendments to H.R. 7152 had been offered, and thirty-four had either been accepted by the Celler-McCulloch leadership or had passed on floor votes. Most of these were technical adjustments, although the left-right, egalitarian-chivalric vote for "the ladies" had been followed by a voice vote to permit bona fide fraternal and religious organizations to employ "their own kind," and also by a vote of 137 to 92 to deny protection to atheists and communists. Having failed to overburden the entire bill with sex-protection clauses, Congressman Dowdy tried to do the same thing with a blanket amendment to add age as a protected class. But this too was defeated, by a standing vote, 94 to 123. The black civil rights coalition, which had generally steered clear of the floor fight over sex discrimination, more actively resisted complicating Title 7 by adding age as a protected category. Unlike race and sex, age was a universal rather than an immutable category, and thus presented unique problems in EEO policy (as in child labor and retirement law), as the few state FEPCs that included age were discovering.

On February 10 the exhausted House, trying to adjourn before the Lincoln holiday, voted to approve H.R. 7152 by the decisive margin of 290 to 110. Favoring the bill was a bipartisan phalanx of 152 Democrats and 138 Republicans. Opposing were 96 Democrats and 34 Republicans, with 86 of the Democrats and ten of the Republicans representing the states of the former Confederacy. Clearly the civil rights bill was aimed mainly at the benighted South, which was both abundantly culpable and politically vulnerable. So the bill's measures to protect voting rights and to desegregate schools and public accommodations had all been carefully regionalized by the bipartisan coalition. This had not been done, however, for the bill's fair employment provisions in Title 7. As the bill moved to the Senate, major attention shifted to the the employer community, which feared bureaucratic intrusion on its traditional freedom to hire and promote and fire on merit. This traditionally Republican group would look primarily to the Senate minority leader, Everett Dirksen, to protect their interests. His price for supporting cloture was expected to hinge on the potential reach of Title 7 beyond the South, to affect the behavior of private employers whose interests the Republican party had traditionally defended.

The Courting of Senator Dirksen

Early in January 1964, while the Rules Committee was gearing up to review H.R. 7152, Lyndon Johnson made his pact with Robert Kennedy. "I'll do on the Bill just what you think is best to do on the Bill," Johnson told the Attorney General. "We'll follow what you say we should do on the Bill. We won't do anything that you don't want to do on the legislation. And I'll do everything you want me to do in order to obtain the passage of the legislation."[29] Kennedy agreed that Johnson's pledge to him was "rather extraordinary . . . our relationship was so sensitive at the time that I think that he probably did it to pacify me."[30] Both men understood that their ambition and their obligation to the murdered president required them to submerge their enmity and get the civil rights bill through the Senate. "Where are you going to get the votes?" Johnson asked his Attorney General. "The person who you're going to get the votes from," Kennedy said, "was Everett Dirksen."[31]

Political columnists in early 1964 were speculating that Johnson, in the bargaining process, might allow the Senate conservatives to strip away the most controversial provisions of the House bill, as he had done as Senate majority leader in 1957. In early February, Johnson was asked at a press conference whether he expected a filibuster and whether, in order to get it passed in the Senate, "the bill will have to be substantially trimmed." Johnson replied with a laconic smile that the answer was "yes" to the first question and "no" to the second.[32] Burke Marshall emphasized the Johnson administration's united front against the suspicions of early cave-in, insisting on the record that Title 7 "was not put in there as a trade-off" to bargain for cloture. But hard bargaining for Senate cloture dominated the next three months, and necessarily involved some trade-offs in response to Dirksen's artful probes.

Johnson's refusal to bargain away major elements of the civil rights bill, and his deference to the strategic leadership of his Attorney General, narrowed the maneuvering room available to Dirksen. Bargaining space was further reduced by special circumstances in the Senate that winter and spring. These ranged from such specific constraints as Robert Kennedy's iron-clad oath of 1963 to McCulloch to the newly impatient national mood of the post-Birmingham era.[33] The latter was nicely captured in a typical Dirksenian flourish by the minority leader's "Sermon on the Mount" of May 19. Announcing that the Senate leadership had reached a bipartisan compromise, Dirksen summoned Victor Hugo: no army was stronger than "an idea whose time has come."[34]

The forces converging on a civil rights consensus in 1964 included a delicate balance between carrot and stick. The positive incentives included vigorous moral suasion by the nation's prestigious religious leaders, the constitutional blessings of the dominant legal establishment, and both the martyrdom of President Kennedy and the impatient victimhood of black America— especially Martin Luther King's God-fearing southern legions. On the negative side stood the rising tension and national anger flowing from continued southern intransigence and violence that ranged from Bull Connor's defiance in Birmingham in 1963 to the murder the following year of three young civil rights workers in Mississippi after their disappearance on June 21. Beneath this lay a muted anxiety over the potential for retaliatory black violence. In March, Martin Luther King had warned that if the filibuster lasted more than a month, he and his followers would "engage in a direct action program here in Washington and around the country." In April, when the Brooklyn CORE chapter threatened to paralyze the opening of the New York World's Fair with a massive "stall-in" traffic jam, it was restrained with great difficulty by James Farmer and the worried civil rights leadership.[35] Ghetto rioting did indeed explode that year, in Harlem in July, thus heralding the extraordinarily destructive string of mostly northern and increasingly violent "long hot summers" that would trigger white backlash and would escalate through 1968. The Harlem riot, however, occurred *after* the Congress approved the civil rights bill.

In Congress, the civil rights coalition was aided by an unusual combination: the superior organization of the Senate liberals on the one hand, and on the other the fatal strategic blunder of Senator Russell's southern bloc. To fill the vacuum posed by the aloof, statesman-like posture of majority leader Mike Mansfield, the majority whip, Hubert H. Humphrey (D-Minn.) teamed up with the liberal Republican whip, Thomas Kuchel of California, to organize a crack battalion of disciplined anti-filibuster teams to combat the cadres of experienced southerners. Humphrey channeled his boundless energy toward an uncharacteristic path of patience, moderation, tolerant understanding, and bargaining flexibility. In order to win Republican support against the southern filibuster, Humphrey said, "I would have kissed Dirksen's ass on the Capitol steps."[36]

Unlike Humphrey and the Senate liberals, the southerners remained rigid in their opposition and followed Russell's standfast script to their strategic doom. They persisted stubbornly in their record-breaking filibuster, generally refusing to exercise their great bargaining power in amendment maneuvers until it was too late. The Republican leadership, on the other hand, had far less room to maneuver than the Johnson administration feared. Sitting on a national volcano, they could not risk appearing to combine with the southerners to kill the bill. Moreover, the Lincoln tradition was genuine. So Dirksen did what he had to do, and what he loved doing, playing coyly with the intrigues of backroom negotiation and floor posturing, whittling down the areas of disagreement toward a compromise that would allow him to blunt the bill's most objectionable features and, in the tradition of Lincoln, save the Republic.[37]

The Senate debate of 1964 was unusual in that it occurred entirely on the Senate floor rather than in committee. Normally, a House-passed civil rights bill would be referred directly to the Senate Judiciary Committee. H.R. 7152 had been reported out by the House Judiciary Committee the previous October after closed negotiations and hence had not received the customary open hearings by a substantive committee. Furthermore, the addition of gender to Title 7, which was a radical modification by any measure, had never received any committee hearings at all.

But the Eastland-led Senate Judiciary Committee had a jaded past. Humphrey pointed out that during the previous decade only *one* of 121 civil rights bills had ever emerged from Eastland's lair—and even that one had been a fluke. Indeed, Eastland's committee had already held eleven days of hearings on the original bill during the previous summer, but had heard only one witness, Attorney General Robert Kennedy. On the other hand, the bill's controversial section on public accommodations had received extensive hearings in 1963 in the Senate Commerce Committee.

For these reasons Senate liberals defended a bypass of the Judiciary Committee. They observed that H.R. 7152 had already received 83 days of congressional hearings in six committees, involving 280 witnesses and 6,438 pages of printed testimony. After arguing the procedural question through much of March, the Senate on March 26 rejected a motion to refer the bill to Judiciary by a vote of 34-50. Then on March 30 the Senate began an extraordinary ten-week process of debating and amending on the Senate floor, as a committee of the whole, the most detailed and important civil rights bill of the century. The debate was dominated by Dirksen's intricate dance of negotiations and culminated in the crucial Senate leadership compromise of 1964.

The Senate Leadership Compromise of 1964

Before the Senate could turn to the hard negotiations over the kind of zero-sum dilemmas that might be posed by Title 7's concern for the minority distribution of jobs, the Senate felt compelled to first review the moral debate. These exchanges on the floor centered on the more obvious and almost exclusively southern, positive-sum questions of racial fairness. They were starkly posed, in the nationally televised new format ushered in by the sit-ins of 1960, by the massive southern denial of the right to vote, to eat in restaurants and sleep in hotels, and to go to neighborhood public schools irrespective of one's race. This early South-centered debate was reinforced frequently by news stories that dramatized the South's racial unfairness, such as the early spring's southern foray by Mrs. Malcolm Peabody of Boston. The Boston Brahmin, 72-year-old mother of Massachusetts' governor Endicott Peabody, got herself thrown into jail in St. Augustine, Florida, for trying to dine with Negroes at a segregated motel. As the *New York Times* editorially explained in response to Mrs. Peabody's raid, "the real test of the Dirksen program will be in its proposals for changes in the provisions forbidding racial bias in access to hotels, restaurants and other places of public accommodations."[38] Such attacks invariably provoked southern charges of northern hypocrisy, as when Eastland accused Javits of demanding massive busing to desegregate southern schools, while New York City alone contained at least 165 all-Negro schools. Javits volunteered that the number of predominantly Negro schools in New York was probably closer to 900, but he denied that the city's de facto racial school separation amounted to de jure racial school segregation. Eastland replied that this procedural distinction without a substantive difference continued to elude him, but the colloquy was wearily familiar.

By the spring of 1964, however, this stale scenario would no longer suffice. The senators were long in the habit of rehearsing the same old rhetoric, but something fundamental had changed in the atmosphere of expectations. Javits' self-righteousness had long galled the southerners. But Eastland could no longer bring himself to announce, as he had done so confidently and so incredibly in 1950 during the debate over the House-passed FEPC bill, that "In all the hearings which are talked about, there will not be found a scintilla of proof that there is discrimination in Mississippi or any other state in the deep South. I deny most emphatically that there is discrimination in my state based on race or color."[39] Indeed, the public humiliation wrought by the Jim Crow system was so palpable by 1964 that southern politicians in Washington no longer seemed to have real heart for its defense. Even Senator Dirksen, who had warned since the previous summer that he opposed Title 2's infringement on business freedom, sought a graceful way out of the impasse. So in his negotiations with the Justice Department team and the Senate leadership, Dirksen found a reasonable compromise that would permit him to yield to the moral imperative of Title 2 while still constraining federal intrusion in commerce.

The formula that Dirksen agreed to was devised primarily to limit the EEOC in Title 7 cases. It would allow the Attorney General but not the commission to file anti-discrimination suits, and to do so only where the Justice Department could document a "pattern or practice" of systematic discrimination. By preventing third-party suits filed by groups like the NAACP, such an arrangement could avoid a sea of litigation against businesses while still providing for targeted enforcement by federal authorities. On the other hand, Dirksen well knew that the Justice Department was a relatively small, elite cabinet agency, in comparison with the more typical and large program-running departments like HEW or Defense, and so prided itself on enforcement through key case selection rather than through massive litigation. As a result the Justice Department posed a smaller threat of potential harassment to employers than would a new mission agency like the EEOC, which reminded Dirksen and his more conservative colleagues uncomfortably of its crusading early model: the NLRB. To Dirksen, desegregation of public accommodations had essentially nothing to do with northern constituencies like Illinois in any event. So Dirksen protested Title 2's potential abuses until the Senate's penultimate act. Then Dirksen— like Lord Byron's Julia, whispering "I will ne'er consent"—consented.

During the five weeks following the first of April, Dirksen floated dozens of trial amendments, most of which further refined, moderated, clarified, or restricted the reach of federal enforcement power over private enterprises and citizens. He proposed amendments that would variously delay and stagger implementation, restrict record-keeping requirements, require confidentiality of proceedings, exempt educational institutions, curtail the EEOC's power of subpoena, and require that only individually aggrieved complainants rather than third parties could bring suit (and then only in the districts wherein they resided). Dirksen further sought to restrict the new EEOC's budget, which called for $2.5 million in the first year and $10 million the second. He was reminded, unpleasantly as ever, of the fledgling NLRB, which had jumped from a budget of $659,000 and a staff of 180 in 1936 to a budget of $21 million and a staff of 2,056 by 1963.[40]

Some of Dirksen's more substantive amendments, however, would eventually lead to major litigation. Their debate on the Senate floor would provide a legislative history that would fuel later charges that the courts were ignoring and even reversing the intent of Congress. One of these was the stipulation in Title 6 that federal funds could be cut off only from the specific program against which the complaint of discrimination was lodged, and not from the entire institution.[41] Another was the addition of the word "intentionally" to Section 703(g) of Title 7, to make it clear that discrimination could not be legitimately inferred from statistical distributions in employment patterns. Still another of Dirksen's amendments protected differences in compensation or conditions of employment that resulted from bona fide seniority or merit systems, and that were not based on intention to discriminate on account of race, color, religion, sex, or national origin. Dirksen also reinforced Congressman McCulloch's original ban on racial balance as an enforcement criterion by extending it from Title 4 on school desegregation to include Title 7 and job distribution.

During the first two weeks in May, Dirksen met five times in his Senate office suite for culminating negotiations with Mansfield, Humphrey, Kuchel, and the Justice team of Kennedy, Katzenbach, and Marshall, plus key staff aides and occasionally other senators. By May 13 the essential elements of the compromise that would lead to cloture had been determined. The package of 70-odd amendments required a completely rewritten substitute bill for H.R. 7152. But the significant changes in fundamental approach boiled down to only two. Here Dirksen had insisted on his bottom price. Yet the minority leader's two final demands only narrowed the role of the EEOC. They did *not* include the stipulations that later became so controversial in the courts: the narrow definition of fund cut-off in Title 6; or, in Title 7, the ban on racial quotas, the requirement that discrimination be intentional, and the protection of bona fide seniority and merit systems. This was because Dirksen did not have to exert his unique leverage in order to win agreement in these areas.

Outside the South, the congressional consensus on the meaning of antidiscrimination was unambiguous. Nondiscrimination meant just what it said— *no* person should be discriminated against because of his or her race, sex, religion, or ethnic origin. The consensus was weaker on sex discrimination; that debate, only tentatively begun in the House in response to the Smith amendment, would not be nationally joined until the Civil Rights Act was implemented. But in the classic understanding of discrimination, which meant unequal treatment on account of race, religion, or national origin, the consensus held that all Americans possessed the same rights. Thus minority preferences of any kind would violate civil equality.[42] As Humphrey and the Senate leadership took pains to reiterate in floor debate, the amendments of the compromise package only clarified and codified the original intention of the administration and the congressional leadership.

Dirksen's two basic changes, however, extended beyond this consensus. The goal of both was to reduce the authority of the EEOC, which congressional Republicans regarded as a potential bureaucratic monster, like the early and runaway NLRB. First, Dirksen would require the EEOC to defer to state and local FEP agencies where they existed (as in Dirksen's Illinois). Second, and more important, Dirksen would strip the EEOC of its prosecutorial role.

The first change was designed to reduce the impact of the new law on the North and West, although this was not an acknowledged goal. The civil rights bill was, after all, targeted primarily against the intransigent South. This alone made it politically possible in 1964, because the southern senators could not sustain a filibuster without their Republican allies, and the latter would not join a last-stand defense of the state-based rights of Bull Connor. The second charge, however, seemed to reflect a growing awareness outside the South that while Jim Crow schools and segregated restaurants and black disfranchisement were essentially southern problems, job discrimination was indeed a national phenomenon. When the *New York Times* editorially endorsed the Dirksen compromise as both a sound bargain and yet another congressional lesson that the perfect was the enemy of the good, the *Times* conceded that job discrimination had become "a national, not a Southern, problem."[43] Thus Dirksen's two key changes reflected a nonsouthern and bipartisan consensus that the new law should mainly reform the wicked South, and a fear that the bill's two job discrimination titles, 6 and 7, might impinge heavily upon their nonsouthern congressional constituencies. Hence the EEOC enforcers must be carefully constrained.

Dirksen justified both changes by a higher principle. The first was the Republican (and conservative Democratic) principle that in government-business relations, local primacy must prevail over Washington-knows-best. Responsible fair employment "starts back home," Dirksen said. His amendment requiring EEOC defernce to state FEPCs would reward the local initiative that the state FEPCs represented, he argued, and would greatly reduce the administrative burden on the new federal agency. Dirksen's protection for FEPC states, however, together with the Senate's further reinforcement of McCulloch's earlier House exclusion of de facto segregation or racial balance in the North, drew Richard Russell's complaint that the "bill now has been stripped of any pretense . . . [and] stands as a purely sectional bill."[44] While Russell's charge was not entirely true, the point was telling, and the political value of Dirksen's compromise was clear.

The principle that underpinned Dirksen's second major change, which stripped from the EEOC the power to bring suit, was drawn from the regulatory reform tradition that had produced the Administrative Procedures Act of 1946, and had earlier led Congressman Griffin and his House colleagues to strip away the proposed EEOC's judicial functions. Dirksen wanted to make the EEOC "largely a voluntary agency."[45] He feared that a national EEOC with prosecuting or judge-like authority would be captured by the liberal and minority constituencies that had created the agency, much as the early NLRB had been captured by labor interests. Such an agency might harass employers by imposing minority quotas in hiring and promotions. In Dirksen's home state, evidence of just such a trend was picked up in mid-March by Arthur Krock's syndicated column in the *New York Times*. The story at Motorola sent alarms through the employer community across the land.

Cease and Desist at Motorola

In the fall of 1963 a 28-year-old black man named Leon Myart, who had dropped out of high school and enlisted for a tour in the army, applied to the Motorola Corporation in Chicago for an assembly line job checking for flaws in television sets. He took the company's standard multiple-choice, 28-question general ability test, and his performance led Motorola to reject him. Myart then complained of racial discrimination to the Illinois Fair Employment Practice Commission, which appointed a black attorney, Robert E. Bryant, as hearing examiner. Bryant held a hearing on Myart's case on January 27, and on March 5 he declared against Motorola. Byrant ruled that the test itself was unfair to "culturally deprived and disadvantaged groups" because it did not take into account "inequalities and differences in environment."[46] Bryant then ordered Motorola to hire Myart and to cease giving the test. The hearing examiner's unprecedented cease-and-desist order on testing was attacked and appealed to the full Illinois commission by Motorola, whose outcry was soon joined by the 1400-firm Employers Association of Chicago, the Illinois Manufacturing Association, and the *Chicago Tribune*. In New York, Arthur Krock took up the case in his *Times* column of March 13. Krock warned that Title 7 of the pending civil rights bill threatened "to project the rationale of the Illinois F.E.P.C. ruling throughout the free enterprise system of the United States." "Then a Federal bureaucracy would be legislated into senior partnership with private business," Krock said, "with the power to dictate the standards by which employers reach their judgments of the capabilities of applicants for jobs, and the quality of performance after employment, whenever the issue of 'discrimination' is raised."[47]

The Motorola case quickly became a cause célèbre among conservative critics of the proposed EEOC. Senator John Tower (R-Tex.) placed the decision and the order of the hearing examiner in the *Congressional Record* and used it to attack the civil rights bill. On June 13, Tower won passage on the Senate floor of an amendment, which ultimately became Section 703(h) of Title 7, stipulating that it would be an unlawful employment practice for an employer "to give and act upon the results of any professionally developed ability test" unless it was "designed, intended, or used to discriminate because of race, color, religion, sex, or national origin."[48] Humphrey agreed to Tower's amendment, which the leadership had found to be "in accord with the intent and purpose" of Title 7. The Tower amendment's equation of design, intent, and use reflected the law's traditional standard that proof of discrimination required evidence of intent to harm and that statistical imbalances or disproportional distributions would not suffice.[49]

Denouement on the Senate Floor

In the spring of 1964 the national debate over racial quotas was focused on the Senate floor during the intense six-week courtship of Everett Dirksen by the Democratic leadership and the Motorola case brought this concern to a fine pitch.[50] In response, the civil rights bill's sponsors repeatedly clarified their determination to ban discrimination against *any* citizen on account of his or her race, color, religion, national origin, or sex. Humphrey thus defended the House-passed version of Title 7 in the March debate:

Contrary to the allegations of some opponents of this title, there is nothing in it that will give any power to the Commission or to any court to require hiring, firing, or promotion of employees in order to meet the racial "quota" or to achieve a certain racial balance.

That bugaboo has been brought up a dozen times; but it is nonexistent. In fact, the very opposite is true. Title 7 prohibits discrimination. In effect, it says that race, religion and national origin are not to be used as the basis for hiring and firing. Title 7 is designed to encourage hiring on the basis of ability and qualifications, not race or religion.[51]

In April the floor managers for Title 7, Joseph S. Clark (D-Pa.) and Clifford P. Case (R-N.J.), submitted a joint memorandum to the Senate that responded directly to the complaints of Russell and his southern colleagues that the discrimination that was prohibited was nowhere defined. "The concept of discrimination . . . is clear and simple and has no hidden meanings," Clark and Case explained. "To discriminate means to make a distinction, to make a difference in treatment or favor . . . which is based on any five of the forbidden criteria: race, color, religion, sex, and national origin."

There is no requirement in Title 7 that an employer maintain a racial balance in his work force. On the contrary, any deliberate attempt to maintain a racial balance, whatever such a balance may be, would involve a violation of Title 7 because maintaining such a balance would require an employer to hire or refuse to hire on the basis of race. It must be emphasized that discrimination is prohibited to any individual.[52]

As for the Motorola case, which raised the specter of biased public bureaucrats dictating employee choice, Clark and Case reassured the Senate:

There is no requirement in Title 7 that employers abandon bona fide qualification tests where, because of differences in background and education, members of some groups are able to perform better on these tests than members of other groups. An employer may set his qualifications as high as he likes, he may test to determine which applicants have these qualifications, and he may hire, assign, and promote on the basis of test performance.[53]

By June, when Humphrey was presenting and defending the Senate's compromise with Dirksen, he explained that Section 703(j) on racial balance was added to "state the point expressly" and as "clearly and accurately" as the power of language would permit what the leadership had maintained all along about the bill's intent and meaning: "Title 7 does not require an employer to achieve any sort of racial balance in his work force by giving preferential treatment to any individual or group."[54] The *New York Times* similarly reassured its readers that the "misrepresentations by opponents of the civil rights legislation are at their wildest in discussing this title." "It would not, as has been suggested, require anyone to establish racial quotas," the *Times* editorially insisted. "To the contrary, such quotas would be forbidden as a racial test. The bill does not require employers or unions to drop any standard for hiring or promotion or membership—except the discriminatory standard of race or religion."[55] Humphrey reiterated his assurances with regard to the new amendment in Section 706(g), which required a showing of discriminatory intent: "This is a clarifying change. Since the title bars only discrimination because of race, color, religion, sex, or national origin it would seem already to require intent, and, thus, the proposed change does not involve any substantive change in the title." "The express requirement of intent is designed to make it wholly clear," Humphrey explained; "that inadvertent or accidental discriminations will not violate the title or result in entry of court orders. It means simply that the respondent must have intended to discriminate."[56]

With that understanding, the leadership compromise was honorably sealed. On June 10 the Senate voted 71-29 to close off the record-shattering southern filibuster that had consumed, according to Russell's calculation, 82 working days, 63,000 pages in the *Congressional Record,* and ten million words. On June 17 the Senate approved substituting the leadership compromise bill for H.R. 7152 by a vote of 76 to 18. Two days later it voted 73 to 27 to pass the bill. Republican Barry Goldwater, the Arizona conservative and leading candidate for his party's presidential nomination in 1964, ominously joined the southerners in voting against it. The bill then returned to the House, where Halleck and McCulloch, who had kept in close touch with Robert Kennedy's team at Justice throughout the negotiations, blessed the Dirksen compromise as consistent with their original grand bargain. The House leadership avoided the customary conference committee and agreed to the Senate amendments on July 2 by a roll-call vote of 289 to 126. That same day President Johnson signed the bill into law.

The Civil Rights Act of 1964 was by any measure a spectacular accomplishment. It easily ranked, as historian Allen Matusow proclaimed, in "the great liberal achievement of the decade."[57] Its most radical provision, Title 2, would destroy Jim Crow in public accommodations with amazing speed and with virtually self-executing finality. By shattering southern defenses that had heretofore seemed impregnable, it paved the way for the Voting Rights Act of 1965, which would enfranchise not only the mass of southern blacks but, ironically, even greater numbers of southern whites. In its uniquely contradictory way the Voting Rights Act would permanently transform the classic gridlock of southern politics that V.O. Key so brilliantly described in 1949.[58] Lyndon Johnson, who had been both a manipulator and a captive of that warped system, watched its race-centered politics polarize the southern electorate during the presidential race of 1964. He then set out to destroy the black disfranchisement that had corrupted democracy in his native South.

CHAPTER 5

The Watershed of 1965: From the Voting Rights Act to "Black Power"

"Freedom Summer" and the Election of 1964

Lyndon Johnson preached and practiced the politics of coalition and consensus, and from the perspective of the White House in July of 1964, his logic seemed unassailable. On July 2 he signed the Civil Rights Act in a triumphant White House ceremony. Two weeks later the Republican national convention gathered in San Francisco and for President nominated Senator Barry Goldwater of Arizona, who had voted against the Civil Rights Act. In late August the Democrats would meet in Atlantic City to affirm Johnson's own nomination and to confirm his choice of running-mate. Goldwater's threat on the right was welcome, since the Arizonan's aggressive conservatism yielded to Johnson most of the middle ground. But a more immediate threat had formed within Johnson's camp on his left: the Mississippi Freedom Democratic party, newly created by civil rights workers in Mississippi, was sending to Atlantic City an integrated delegation (4 of the 68 delegates were white) to claim the seats of Mississippi's regular, all-white Democrats.

The Freedom party members were not in a mood for the bargaining and compromise of coalition politics. Mississippi's leading civil rights leader, Medgar Evers, had been slain by a sniper the previous summer. In late June 1964, civil rights workers James Chaney, Andrew Goodman, and Michael Schwerner had been arrested and then disappeared near Philadelphia, Mississippi, and their mutilated bodies were not found until August.[1] Similar danger threatened more than 900 summer volunteers, most of them white students from prestigious nonsouthern universities, who had come to Mississippi to register voters and teach in freedom schools. Led by Robert Moses of SNCC and David Dennis of CORE, and coordinated under an organizational umbrella called COFO (Council of Federated Organizations), the volunteers experienced 1000 arrests, 35 shooting incidents, 30 bombings of homes, churches, and meeting houses, and 80 beatings.[2]

COFO's leaders demanded federal protection for civil rights workers, hoping for the kind of massive intervention that President Kennedy had sent to Ole Miss in 1962. Johnson, who like the Kennedy brothers wanted to avoid the entanglements of such occupations, sent emissaries to remind the COFO workers that the FBI was limited to investigation and was not a national police force. Johnson wanted to avoid racial turmoil and keep his party unified through the August convention; then he hoped to defeat Goldwater by a margin so large that his "Great Society" legislation would sail through the 89th Congress in 1965. In addition to Medicare, federal aid to schools and colleges, the war on poverty, and conservation and environmental protection laws, the Great Society package would include a new voting-rights law with sharp teeth.

Desperate to avoid a nasty credentials fight on national television in Atlantic City, Johnson offered Hubert Humphrey the vice presidency and directed Humphrey to persuade the Mississippi delegation to accept a compromise. In its final form the Johnson-Humphrey compromise offered the Freedom party two at-large voting seats (one black and one white, to symbolize Mississippi's integrated political future). The remaining 66 delegates would be given honorary nonvoting seats with other delegations and, most important (but still somewhat vague), new nondiscrimination requirements would bind all future Democratic delegations. The Freedom party delegates were urged to accept the compromise by powerful persuaders—Humphrey, Bayard Rustin, Martin Luther King, James Farmer, Walter Reuther, even the Freedom party's attorney, Joseph Rauh. But the Freedom delegates rejected the compromise.

Freedom Summer was a radicalizing experience. Many of the white volunteers returned to their northern campuses to lead major sectors of the decade's youth rebellion—Mario Savio in the Free Speech Movement at Berkeley, Staughton and Alice Lynd in the antiwar movement, Jo Freeman in the feminist movement. Black activists in SNCC formed a future Who's Who of radical separatist and black nationalist leaders—Stokely Carmichael, James Forman, Cleveland Sellers.[3] At Atlantic City, Johnson strong-armed the compromise through the convention anyway, and avoided a party split. But as the President and his party headed down the campaign home-stretch under the Democratic banners of coalition politics, liberal reform, and racial integration, the grassroots leaders of the black poor, most notably the rural chapters of SNCC in the South and the northern urban chapters of CORE, were headed in the opposite direction.

If the black activist leaders of SNCC and CORE were headed toward a radical break on the left with the coalition politics of Kennedy-Johnson liberalism, the Goldwater Republicans on the right were breaking with their own party's more moderate traditions. The centrist tradition of post-Hoover Republicanism, which had balanced center-right opposition to the welfare-statism of the New Deal with center-left support for civil rights, appeared to collapse overnight in 1964. The ground for the Republican rightward shift, however, had been prepared in 1958 by the Democrats' congressional sweep, especially in the Senate. That year voter reactions against Eisenhower's second recession and the Soviet *Sputnik* had defeated eleven Republican senators, ten of them racial liberals. All but one were replaced by northern liberal Democrats. In the congressional elections of 1958 through 1964 the GOP lost 32 of its 42 racial liberals in the Senate, and the ranks of liberal Democrats in the Senate jumped from 21 to 45. In 1957 the Republican Senate delegation had been more liberal on civil rights issues than its Democratic counterpart; after 1964 it was the other way around. Republicans in the House, never as liberal as their Senate colleagues in the first place, were headed in the same direction.[4]

Goldwater was a conservative but not a segregationist. In his 1960 autobiography, *The Conscience of a Conservative,* Goldwater wrote that "it is both wise and just for negro children to attend the same schools as whites, and to deny them this opportunity carries with it strong implications of inferiority."[5] He voted against the Civil Rights Act as a states rights conservative who opposed federal controls over areas of traditional state responsibility, like education and voting requirements. Goldwater pointed out that with the exception of the war-hero Eisenhower, Republicans always lost when they offered only a pale imitation of the Democrats' New Dealism. In a 1962 book, *Why Not Victory?,* he called for military power to confront Soviet and Chinese communism. The voters wanted "A Choice, Not an Echo," Goldwater said. A Republican candidate who was a genuine conservative would bring to the polls a "hidden" conservative majority. To Goldwater Republicans, justice was defined in terms of liberty: "Extremism in defense of liberty is no vice," Goldwater declared in his acceptance speech at San Francisco, and "moderation in pursuit of justice is no virtue."

By staking out his appeal so far to the right, Goldwater vacated the center and Johnson promptly claimed it. Goldwater's suggestion that participation in Social Security might be made voluntary, Johnson said, threatened the retirement security of all Americans. Johnson voiced his fear that a Goldwater presidency might send American boys to fight in Asian wars. The Democratic party sponsored national television ads that featured a little girl being vaporized by nuclear explosions. Johnson, having won the support of the leaders of the NAACP, the Urban League, SCLC, and the Leadership Conference (but not SNCC or CORE) for a moratorium on civil rights demonstrations during the election campaign, generally kept the racial issue out of the campaign, and Goldwater did likewise. In mid-October, Johnson flew to New Orleans to give his fellow southerners a "real Democratic speech" about programs to meet the economic needs of Americans of all races, rather than the old, divisive cry at election time of "Negro, Negro, Negro!" By then, polls showed that the "hidden" conservatives had not materialized, and Goldwater appeared to be leading the GOP toward electoral disaster.

On November 3, Johnson crushed Goldwater with a stunning margin of 16 million votes. Johnson carried forty-four states and the District of Columbia to Goldwater's six states, and in the process the Democrats achieved a net gain of thirty-eight seats in the House and two in the Senate. But Goldwater carried the five Deep South states of Alabama, Georiga, Louisiana, Mississippi, and South Carolina. In the process Goldwater's coattails added five new Republican representatives in Alabama and one each in Georgia and Mississippi—in all instances these were the states' first Republicans elected to Congress since Reconstruction.

The displacement of northern Republican congressmen by liberal Democrats, coupled with the new infusion of conservative Republicans from the South, reinforced the new element of party polarization in civil rights policy that the presidential nominees symbolized. Black Americans, who had given 40 percent of their votes to Eisenhower in 1956 and 25 percent to Nixon in 1960, voted 9 to 1 for the Democrats in 1964. But in much of the South they remained massively disfranchised, while in the Deep South most whites were suddenly voting Republican.[6] These tea leaves were not difficult to read: the vote of southern blacks had provided the margin of victory for Johnson in such Rim South states as Arkansas, Florida, Tennessee, Virginia, and probably North Carolina as well. When Johnson sought re-election in 1968, he would not likely face an opponent as vulnerable as Goldwater. To Johnson the continued disfranchisement of southern blacks was morally deplorable, and the prospect of so many nonvoting Democrats was politically intolerable. So immediately following his victory on November 3, Johnson directed Nicholas Katzenbach, who had replaced Robert Kennedy as Attorney General the previous September, to draft "the next civil rights bill—legislation to secure, once and for all, equal voting rights."[7]

No federal voting rights law, however, had effectively produced black ballots since the Reconstruction.[8] But the selective memory of Reconstruction was part of the problem. To conservatives, the legacy of "Black Reconstruction" was corruption: elected politicians in Washington would manipulate the local franchise to remain in power. Republicans had done it after the Civil War, when Negroes voted Republican; Democrats would do it in the "Second Reconstruction," now that blacks had switched their allegiance. Congressional conservatives distrusted New-Dealish, administrative models of centralized regulation, where bureaucrats beholden to the party in power would enforce the law selectively to favor loyal constituencies. To avoid this the conservative coalition in Congress whenever possible substituted judicial models of enforcement that required court-like due process.

Such a model had governed the voting-rights provisions of 1957, 1960, and 1964, provisions which required blacks who claimed racial disfranchisement to sue their local election officials in federal trial courts. This was an expensive, time-consuming, and inefficient process, and in addition it exposed black citizens and their legal representatives to harassment and economic reprisals. The voting (and nonvoting) patterns of the 1964 election had demonstrated the bankruptcy of this good-faith approach in the face of so much blatant bad faith. Even Katzenbach, who respected the tradition of constitutional restraints on national power in a federal system, concluded that the national government would have to go beyond "the tortuous, often ineffective pace of litigation."[9]

Accordingly, on December 18, 1964, Katzenbach recommended to Johnson three ranked alternatives for enfranchising southern blacks. His first preference was a constitutional amendment that would prohibit *all* states from imposing *any* voter qualifications beyond age, a short period of residency (60 to 90 days), conviction of a felony, or confinement in a mental institution. To Katzenbach, this was the most effective way to eliminate the typical southern literacy tests and their accompanying subjective requirements for "understand-ing" various constitutional provisions, vouchers of testament to "good moral character," and the like. The Twenty-fourth amendment, which banned the poll tax in federal elections, had passed Congress in 1962 and was ratified in January 1964. But the amendment affected elections only for federal offices, and in any event the poll tax was far more a symbolic than a practical barrier to the franchise. Katzenbach regarded a constitutional amendment as the "most drastic" alternative. It was slow and cumbersome, vulnerable to "opposition from sources genuinely concerned about federal interference with a fundamen-tal matter traditionally left to the States," and vulnerable even after congres-sional approval to blockage by as few as 13 states.[10]

The Attorney General's second choice was legislation to create a new fed-eral commission that would appoint federal registrars for federal elections only. Such an approach, however, risked a two-pronged Republican attack. Republi-can conservatives would raise a state rights objection to its potential for "fed-eral dictatorial control of the electoral process." Republican moderates and liberals would complain that it would still not enfranchise blacks in state and local elections where their political powerlessness was greatest. Katzenbach's third choice was legislation granting an existing federal agency "the power to assume direct control of registration for voting in both federal and state elec-tions in any area where the percentage of potential Negro registrants actually registered is low." This approach promised the quickest payoff. It had been recommended by the Civil Rights Commission in its first report on voting in 1959, and it had been proposed by President Kennedy as part of his omnibus civil rights bill in 1963. But it had been rejected then because McCulloch and other Republicans opposed it, and Katzenbach himself doubted the constitu-tionality of a statutory takeover by the national government of state and local election procedures.

Martin Luther King and the Crisis at Selma

While Katzenbach's proposals were circulating in the Justice Department and the White House, Martin Luther King returned from his triumph at Oslo, where he had been awarded the Nobel Peace Prize in December 1964, to launch his carefully planned voting-rights offensive in Selma. In his Pulitzer Prize-winning biography of King, *Bearing the Cross,* David Garrow has de-scribed the internal debate within King's SCLC that led to the climax at Selma.[11] The strategic paradox was the realization by King and his lieutenants that nonviolent protest would fail unless it triggered violent repression. Perferably this should occur on prime-time national television, leading to blood-shed and matyrdom, and generating thereby a wave of revulsion that would carry Congress and the Johnson administration before it. What this revised strategy of nonviolent protest lacked in philosophical consistency it gained in political leverage. King had failed miserably in his major desegregation cam-paign in Albany, Georgia, in 1961 and 1962. There police chief Laurie Pritchett had politely arrested and jailed all civil disobeyers, thereby providing little martyrdom and small inducement for television news cameras. But not so in Birmingham in 1963, where Bull Connor played the perfect foil, and the chief result was the Civil Rights Act of 1964. King needed a similarly inhospitable environment to dramatize the need for radical federal intervention to enfranchise southern blacks, and he found it in Selma.[12]

King picked Selma because it promised to provide three crucial ingredients. The first was a convincing demonstration of blatant racial disfranchisement. In 1960 the population of Dallas County, Alabama, of which Selma was the county seat, was 57.6 percent black. But of its registered voters only 2.1 percent were listed as Negroes. Of Selma's voting-age population, 9,542 of 14,000 whites were registered, but only 335 of its 15,115 blacks. The second ingredient was a demonstration of the ineffectiveness of the traditional federal reforms of 1957, 1960, and 1964, operating as glacially as they did through litigation. Despite a sustained black voting drive in Selma between May 1962 and August 1964, blacks were successful with only 93 of 795 attempts to register. During the same period, 945 of 1,232 whites were registered. This was a racial differential in new registrations of 11 percent to 76 percent. Then, in February of 1964, the all-white county government had further stiffened the already draconian registration requirements by curtailing registration to only *two* days per month, while lengthening the process by requiring responses to 68 questions about constitutional provisions and government procedures.

Alabama's registration requirements were the most comprehensive and stringent in the nation, followed closely by Mississippi (although Alabama's registration of 23 percent of eligible blacks in 1964 far surpassed Mississippi's 6.7 percent).[13] Alabama's model was devised by the state's supreme court. Its requirements included the ability to read and write in the English language any article of the U.S. Constitution, to understand and interpret constitutional passages correctly, and to produce a sponsoring voucher from already registered voters that testified to the applicant's "good moral character." Attorney General Robert Kennedy had filed a voting-rights suit against Dallas County as early as April 1961, and the local federal district court had imposed a permanent injunction on the registrar in November 1963. But such protracted and expensive efforts placed few black names on the voter lists. Furthermore, the NAACP, whose chapters provided legal backing for voter challenges in most southern states, had been outlawed by the legislature in Alabama and was preoccupied with defensive lawsuits.

Finally, to arouse national support as he had done in the Birmingham protests, King needed defiant southern officials, like Connor, to play their role. He found such inadvertent allies not only in Governor George Wallace, but most superbly in Dallas County's corpulent sheriff, James Clark—who appeared as if on cue from Central Casting, his racial animosity worsened by an uncontrolled temper, his deputies armed with electric cattle prods, his lapel sporting a "Never!" button.[14] The result was violence and death. A young Selma black, Jimmie Lee Jackson, was gut-shot by a state trooper on February 18 (he died on the 26th). A Unitarian clergyman from Boston, the Rev. James J.

Reeb, was clubbed on the head by local whites on March 9 (he died on the 11th). The bloodletting culminated on March 7, "Bloody Sunday," when 500 demonstrators who were marching toward Montgomery were charged on the Edmund Pettus Bridge by Governor Wallace's state troopers, leaving forty injured in the chaos, with the news networks' television cameras whirring. King's protest against such a demonstrable civic outrage was at once physically dangerous, philosphically somewhat disingenuous, and politically brilliant. The nation was enraged.[15]

The Justice Department and the Voting Rights Bill of 1965

The Democratic majorities in the new 89th Congress were so large that there was little doubt that the administration's new voting-rights bill would pass in some form. The margin of Democrats over Republicans in the House was 295-140, the largest since 1936. In the Senate, the modest net Democratic gain of two seats yielded a ratio of 68 Democrats to 32 Republicans, the largest plurality since 1940. More important in the Senate was the re-election in 1964 of 13 Democrats from the bumper class of 1958—liberals like Philip Hart, Edmund Muskie, and Eugene McCarthy, whom the Goldwater Republicans had hungrily targeted. The conservative coalition in Congress was weakened by the displacement of conservative Republicans by liberal Democrats in nonsouthern districts and, ironically, by the Goldwater-Republican replacement of so many senior southern Democrats from the Deep South. Emanuel Celler's liberal hold was tightened on the House Judiciary Committee, and Judge Smith's weakened grip on the Rules Committee could only delay the inevitable. In the Senate the conservative coalition was so weakened that on Eastland's Judiciary Committee the conservative cohort was now outnumbered by a dominant bloc of nine liberals. In the spring of 1965 the new Congress awaited Lyndon Johnson's pleasure.

The Selma crisis of February and March accelerated the Justice Department's already hurried efforts to draft a bill radical enough to be effective quickly, yet still reasonably respectful of the traditions of the due process and federalism that had made all its predecessors both passable and yet largely ineffective. Katzenbach's favored constitutional amendment was by definition the most constitutionally sound approach. Yet it was also the slowest and most uncertain. Johnson rejected it. Also rejected was Katzenbach's second alternative: the new federal commission to register voters for federal elections only. By leaving unaffected the state and local elections, where black political voice and power were most severely blunted, this approach would invite a resurgence of disfranchisement once the federal heat was off. It would also require the awkward maintenance of a dual system of voter lists in the states and localities wherein it applied. Moreover, President Johnson was leery of creating yet another quasi-independent, bipartisan federal regulatory commission, especially if its task of fair and full enfranchisement would be needed only temporarily to redress a historic wrong. What Johnson wanted was both radical and yet short-lived: a one-shot quick-fix that by permanently enfranchising southern blacks would provide them with the one essential tool wherewith to protect themselves—like everybody else.

This left the third alternative, a law giving an existing agency the power to register voters for state and local as well as federal elections in areas of substantial disfranchisement. It promised to be fast and effective. But it might not be constitutional. A new formula would have to be devised that would achieve five objectives: (1) apply to all elections, (2) identify the target political subdivisions without violating the constitution, (3) suspend the literacy tests and related devices and freeze the electoral governance machinery therein, (4) provide for federal voter registration in the covered areas, and (5) provide an escape mechanism for a return to normal federal-state relations once the offending practices had been purged. Literacy tests and similar subjective devices were at the heart of the problem. Yet they found historic precedent in constitutional law and in naturalization requirements. As voting requirements, reading and writing the English language were widely used outside the South—in 1964 literacy tests were used in Alaska, Arizona, California, Connecticut, Hawaii, Idaho, Maine, Massachusetts, New Hampshire, New York, Oregon, Washington, and Wyoming. The trick for winning a voting-rights bill that would be passable, effective, and constitutional would be to link literacy tests to massive racial disfranchisement, and to do so through a triggering formula that was automatic.

In drawing up a bill for the President, Katzenbach was chiefly assisted by Solicitor General Archibald Cox and lawyers in the Civil Rights Division. The crucial yet thorniest item in the Justice Department draft was the "trigger" provision to identify the disfranchising jurisdictions. Through a two-part formula, the Attorney General would determine whether a literacy test or similar device was used as a voter qualification in the presidential election of 1964, and the director of the Census would determine whether less than 50 percent of the voting-age population in that jurisdiction was registered or voted in the 1964 election. If a voting jurisdiction was positive for both tests, this would automatically suspend all literacy test devices, and the Attorney General would be authorized to send federal examiners to the area to compel the registration of qualified applicants for all elections.[16] The automatic triggering device, described in section four of the bill, was on its face a racially neutral formula, yet in practice it identified most of the offending voting districts.

Even more novel was the "preclearance" provision in section five of the administration's bill. This was added by enforcement-minded lawyers in the Civil Rights Division (CRD), who had cut their teeth doing combat with local southern officials during the era of "Massive Resistance." They had dealt with the most defiant Deep South officials, and their distrust was palpable. They added section five to block attempts by local officials to sabotage the Voting Rights Act by constantly changing their election laws. The preclearance provision provided that if any covered state or subdivision subsequently sought to make *any* change in its election laws or procedures, it would have to obtain the *prior* approval either of the Attorney General or of a federal court. The sour experiences of the CRD lawyers not only with Black Belt election officials, but also with segregationist federal judges in some district courts in the South, prompted them to add the extraordinary proposal that judicial preclearance could not be approved by federal judges in the South itself. Instead, preclearance authority would be given *only* to a federal three-judge district court in the District of Columbia—by long reputation one of the most liberal benches in the land.

Under the preclearance provision, covered jurisdictions seeking merely to replace ballot boxes with voting machines would be unable to do so unless they obtained a prior court judgment that their proposed change "does not have the purpose and *will not have the effect* [emphasis added] of denying or abridging the right to vote on account of race or color." Some provision for preclearance was a sensible precaution, since almost a hundred of the South's 1,109 counties (most of them in Mississippi and Alabama) had produced such abysmal records of black disfranchisement that the Justice Department monitored them regularly. But section five was a sleeper provision that in time would create a substantial monitoring bureaucracy in the Justice Department and generate a flood of resentment and litigation.[17] Archibald Cox warned Katzenbach that section five's disruption of normal federal relationships was "exceedingly dangerous" and "probably unconstitutional."[18]

There simply wasn't time, however, to draft a carefully crafted bill and iron out all the wrinkles. The violence in Selma had ignited the nation's indignation against the Deep South's political repression of blacks. President Johnson demanded the "goddamnedest, toughest, voting-rights bill" his staff could devise.[19] Johnson had agreed with Martin Luther King, when King conferred at the White House on February 9 (freshly bailed out the Alabama jailhouse), that the voting law should rest on an automatic formula rather than on litigation, and that the hated literacy tests in such areas must be suspended. Most important, the two main operative provisions of the voting-rights law, sections four and five, would be temporary, and the covered jurisdictions would be provided with a bail-out provision. The color-blind norms of the law, as a statute enforcing the Fifteenth amendment, would be permanent. But sections four and five were emergency provisions, designed to break the back of racist disfranchisement in approximately one hundred counties in seven southern states.

Congress was hungry to act, and the Warren Court had given early indications that the boldest reforms of the Great Society were constitutionally acceptable. On December 14, 1964, a unanimous Supreme Court in *Heart of Atlanta Motel v. U.S.* upheld the public accommodations section of the Civil Rights Act of 1964 in record time.[20] Then on March 8, 1965, the Supreme Court gave further indication of its hostility toward the South's traditional battery of voting restrictions by unanimously ruling unconstitutional Louisiana's "understanding clause," by overturning a lower federal court's ruling against a similar Justice Department suit in Mississippi, and by agreeing to review a lower court ruling that approved poll taxes for state and local elections in Virginia.[21]

Thus committed, Johnson journeyed to Capitol Hill on March 15 to address a joint session of Congress on voting rights—it was the first such personal appearance by a President on a domestic issue since 1946. There Johnson delivered his forceful "We Shall Overcome" address on the Negroes' right to vote. "Every device of which human ingenuity is capable has been used to deny this right," he said, and "It is wrong—deadly wrong." "Their cause must be our cause too," Johnson pledged. "Because it is not just Negroes, but really it is all of us, who must overcome the crippling legacy of bigotry and injustice. And we *shall* overcome."[22] Two days later the administration's hastily assembled bill, which was still in the process of spirited debate within Justice, was dispatched to the Hill.

The 89th Congress and the Voting Rights Act of 1965

The political challenge for the Johnson administration was to move quickly, steering a middle course between Senate liberals who sought a stronger bill and House efforts by the conservative coalition to substitute a weaker bill. Thus the circumstances of 1964 were essentially reversed in the 89th Congress: with neither Eastland's Judiciary Committee nor a southern filibuster putting up their once formidable obstacles, the administration could avoid the delay of a House-first strategy and push the bill simultaneously through both chambers.

Under the bipartisan leadership of Majority Leader Mansfield and Minority Leader Dirksen, the administration's bill (S. 1564) was sent to the Judiciary Committee on March 18, but with tight instructions to report it back by April 9. In Judiciary, Eastland's conservatives were outmanned by the bloc of nine liberals. So the liberals added a ban on the poll tax in state and local elections and narrowed section four's triggering threshhold from 50 percent of black *and* white eligible voters to 25 percent of voting-age *racial minorities*. But they exempted from the triggering formula all political subdivisions that according to the 1960 census had a nonwhite voting-age population of less than 20 percent. This provision would exclude the vast majority of the nation's political subdivisions from the bill, most of them in the North and West. The Mansfield-Dirksen leadership, however, shared Katzenbach's fear that a poll tax ban by statute was unconstitutional and would endanger the entire bill. So they refused to accept it, and on May 11 in a narrow 45-49 roll-call vote on the Senate floor they defeated an attempt led by Edward Kennedy to retain it. The leadership provided instead for the Attorney General to test the constitutionality of the poll tax in court. On May 25 the Senate voted 70-30 to break a desultory southern filibuster, and the following day the Senate passed the bill by a 77-19 roll-call vote and sent it to the House.

In the House the administration's bill, H.R. 6400, was sent to Celler's Judiciary Committee. Like its Senate counterpart, the House Judiciary Committee was dominated by liberals who viewed the poll tax ban as a litmus test of commitment to civil rights. So Celler's committee amended the bill by adding the poll tax ban that the full Senate had narrowly dropped. Then the Rules Committee delayed the bill for the month of June. But when H.R 6400 reached the floor of the House on July 9, Congressman McCulloch and House minority leader

Gerald Ford offered a substitute bill. It would delete both the poll tax ban *and* the administration's automatic trigger as both unconstitutional and unnecessary. Like the Senate bill, the McCulloch-Ford substitute would direct the Attorney General to bring suit against poll tax states. To replace the triggering formula, it would cover potentially *all* political subdivisions in the nation by authorizing the appointment of voting examiners when the Attorney General received twenty-five or more "meritorious" complaints of voter discrimination.

The McCulloch-Ford substitute was an attractive alternative for conservatives and moderates who believed that Congress had no power to ban state and local poll taxes as election requirements, and who also regarded the state-based automatic trigger as a crude and disingenuous device for attacking a problem that was highly specific to individual political subdivisions. Moreover, McCulloch's county-by-county approach seemed superior because it would necessarily include the southern states of Arkansas, Florida, Tennessee, and Texas, all of which were not covered by the administration's trigger because they lacked literacy tests. Also, the Republican substitute would render irrelevant the trigger's idiosyncratic inclusion (owing to American Indian voting patterns) of three counties in Arizona and one county in Idaho. But when southern House Democrats, led by former governor William Tuck of Virginia, rallied to the Republican substitute as less "objectionable" than H.R. 6400, many northern Republicans in the shadow of Selma grew fearful of voting with the southerners. On July 8, the McCulloch-Ford substitute was defeated in a 166-215 teller vote. The following day, H.R. 6400 was passed, 333-85, by a roll-call vote.

The ensuing Senate-House conference committee, however, could not find agreement on the poll tax ban, which the House had embraced and the Senate had rejected. The southern states had originally adopted the poll tax around the turn of the century as part of their disfranchising armament. It was directed chiefly against blacks but decimated the voting ranks of low-income whites as well.[23] By 1965, however, all but four of the eleven states had dropped the levies. In Alabama and Mississippi, the poll tax was a minor adjunct to the literacy test battery; in Texas and Virginia, which historically had disfranchised blacks and poor whites almost equally, no disfranchising effect against blacks could be traced to the poll tax by the 1960s.

Although the poll tax question by 1965 was largely irrelevant to racial disfranchisement, it provided a rallying symbol for liberals to stand up for "tougher" civil rights enforcement. In the conference committee in July of 1965, however, the administration and the Senate conferees stood firm against the poll tax ban, and the Leadership Conference privately conceded that the poll tax question was not worth endangering the bill. So the House conferees yielded to the Senate on the poll tax, and in the August 2 conference report the Senate conferees returned the favor by dropping Senate provisions geared to specific racial percentages. Despite all the fencing and posturing over the poll tax, Congress added only a largely redundant provision for the Attorney General to challenge the tax in court—a path that he was already pursuing. Congress also authorized the federal courts as well as the Attorney General to suspend tests and appoint examiners in voting-rights suits brought by the Attorney General. Finally, the conference accepted the Senate's "American flag" amendment, which senators Robert Kennedy and Jacob Javits had proposed to enfranchise Puerto Ricans living in New York who were illiterate in English, but who could demonstrate completion of at least the sixth grade in a school "under the American flag" where classes were taught in a language other than English. By and large, in the 1965 conference committee on voting rights the two houses cancelled out each other's distinctive changes and gave the administration essentially what it had asked for in the first place.

On August 3 the House adopted the conference report by a thumping vote of 328-74, with 37 southern Democrats voting for the bill. Most of the latter, like Charles Weltner of Atlanta, who had also voted for the Civil Rights Act of 1964, represented urban areas where the black vote was substantial. The Senate approved the report the following day by a similar margin (79-18; including 6 southern Democrats in support), and President Johnson made a special gesture by traveling to the Capitol on August 6 to sign the bill into law.

President Johnson's Howard Commencement Address: "Equality as a Fact and as a Result"

On June 4, with the Senate having just passed the voting-rights bill and with success in the House a virtual certainty, the confident President delivered a historic address before an audience of 14,000 persons attending the graduation ceremonies at Howard University. In a speech suggested by Bill Moyers and written by Labor assistant secretary Daniel Patrick Moynihan and White House aide Richard Goodwin,[24] Johnson celebrated the imminent passage of the Voting Rights Act as the latest in a long line of victories, in which freedom was only a beginning:

> But freedom is not enough. You do not wipe away the scars of centuries by saying: Now you are free to go where you want, do as you desire, choose the leaders you please.
>
> You do not take a person who for years has been hobbled by chains and liberate him, bring him up to the starting line of a race and then say, "You are free to compete with all the others," and still justly believe you have been completely fair.[25]

It was not enough just to open the gates of opportunity, Johnson said, because "All our citizens must have the ability to walk through the gates." Then the President proclaimed "the next and more profound stage of the battle for civil rights. We seek not just freedom but opportunity—not just equity but human ability—not just equality as a right and a theory but equality as a fact and as a result."

When Johnson announced that "equality of opportunity is essential, but not enough," he was voicing without change the liberal prose of two gifted intellectuals he had inherited from Kennedy. But the effect was electric on his predominately black audience, which "sat in stunned silence," and then finally "applauded out of shock and self-identification."[26] The *New York Times'* Tom Wicker compared Johnson's speech favorably in historic importance to the Supreme Court decree in *Brown v. Board of Education.* At the time of the President's speech at Howard, Congress was debating and would soon pass a provision in the Voting Rights Act (section four) authorizing federal courts in voting suits brought by the Attorney General to suspend literacy tests and similar devices if they were used "with the effect" of discriminating, even if this was not their intent. The preclearance provision of the bill's section five would also authorize the Attorney General to disallow any electoral changes in affected areas if in his judgment the proposed changes would "have the effect" of racial discrimination. This language hinted at a radical shift in civil rights law, born of anger and impatience, from procedural to substantive criteria, from intent to effect, from equal opportunity as a right to equality as a fact and as a result. But gathering momentum much faster in the summer of 1965 was the anger and impatience of urban blacks outside the South, whose grim lives were little affected by public accommodation and voting-rights laws.

The Watts Riot, "Black Power," and White Backlash: 1965–1966

Five days after the President triumphantly signed the Voting Rights Act, a spectacular riot led by young black males exploded in the depressed Watts section of Los Angeles. A fifty-square mile slum where 98 percent of the population was black, two-thirds of the quarter-million residents were on welfare, and unemployment among adult males was 34 percent, Watts was patrolled by a district police force of which 200 of the 205 officers were white.[27] The riot was set off on August 11, 1965, when white officers arrested a black man for drunken driving. In six days of arson and looting, more than 7000 rioters faced the Los Angeles police force and 14,000 national guardsmen; 34 were killed, 864 were treated in hospitals for injuries, 4000 were arrested, and damage from fire and vandalism was estimated at $45 million.

In retrospect, the Watts riot marked a fateful watershed for the Johnson administration and the Great Society. In the euphoria of signing the Voting Rights Act, Johnson could legitimately bask in the knowledge that the momentum of the Great Society was producing a cornucopia of achievement for 1965: the Voting Rights Act, Medicare, federal aid to education, urban mass transit, the new Department of Housing and Urban Development, clean air and water pollution programs, immigration reform, national endowments for the arts and the humanities. Johnson's popularity ratings were soaring, and the media had grown respectful of the political genius of the former "cornpone" Vice President. Johnson had achieved a White House intimacy with Martin Luther King, Roy Wilkins, and Whitney Young, and he even seemed to enjoy a surprising rapport with the university-based community of intellectuals with whom he had always been uncomfortable. In his Howard speech, the President announced that he would convene a White House conference on civil rights and invite the nation's leading scholars and experts, civil rights leaders, and top government officials. Its theme, "To Fulfill These Rights," echoed the promise of the Declaration of Independence and was also meant to signify the fulfillment of the 1947 report of President Truman's Committee on Civil Rights: *To Secure These Rights*.

Within a year, however, the euphoria and consensus were shattered. In July, Johnson committed the country to a major combat role in Vietnam. Then in August, the racial explosion in Watts seemed to mock the recent victory for black voting rights in the South. By the following spring, black nationalist sentiment was radicalizing SNCC and CORE, deflecting them from their interracial and nonviolent origins toward racial separatism. In May of 1966, Stokeley Carmichael ousted John Lewis as head of SNCC. In June, when a shotgun felled James Meredith on his one-man protest march in Mississippi, Carmichael and Floyd McKissick, the like-minded new head of CORE, challenged King's leadership and nonviolent principles. Journalists were captivated by Carmichael's rallying cry of "Black Power!"[28] Within a year of the explosion in Watts, the stereotypical image of black America in the national media had been transformed—from nonviolent victims of Klan terrorism, to looting rioters crying "Burn, baby, burn." SNCC and CORE splintered into anarchy.

By the summer of 1966, King had moved his base of operations to Chicago to dramatize the nationwide problems of slum housing, joblessness, and police brutality. Moving into a slum apartment on Chicago's West Side, he found the black ghetto gang-ridden, angry yet dispirited, racially hostile, and selfdestructive. Its brittle culture lacked the bedrock of religious faith and peasant strength that had disciplined his southern legions in Christian nonviolence. King's foray in Chicago was a near fiasco. Mayor Richard Daly ran an efficient machine that provided few clear targets. Freedom marches into white ethnic neighborhoods like Marquette and Cicero drew racist jeers from hostile Poles, Germans, Italians, and Lithuanians that stunned even the famous veteran of the Birmingham jail.[29]

White Americans were shocked by the Watts riot and resented the surge of black separatist rhetoric from the leaders of SNCC and CORE. A Harris poll of mid-1966 showed that 75 percent of white voters believed the Negroes were moving too fast—up sharply from 50 percent in 1964. The congressional elections of 1966 were looming against the backdrop of a collapsed consensus. The administration's new civil rights bill, which was centered on an openhousing proposal, was rejected by Congress in 1966. In the November elections the GOP capitalized on the white backlash by recapturing from the Democrats eight governorships, three Senate seats, and forty-seven House seats. As the *Congressionally Quarterly* observed, "The pro-civil rights coalition which had operated so effectively in previous years—Republicans and Northern Democrats in Congress and civil rights, labor, and church groups outside Congress—fell apart in 1966."[30]

The split in the civil rights coalition, against a background of black separatism and white backlash, had a paralyzing effect within Congress. But, paradoxically, it energized the Johnson administration. The wave of urban violence increased the sense of urgency in mission departments like Justice, Labor, and HEW, and especially in the fledgling new regulatory agency, the EEOC. The administration was anxious to reward civil rights organizations like the NAACP and the Urban League, whose leaders worked through the system and retained a faith in its coalition-based politics and democratic processes. The open-accommodations and voting-rights provisions of the civil rights laws of 1964–65 were rapidly desegregating the South's parks, hotels, restaurants, and voting booths. More difficult, as King was learning in Chicago, was the problem of securing equal access for minorities to jobs, promotions, skill training, and career education. This was more of a "zero-sum" game, because unlike hotel beds and restaurant seats, public school desks and ballot boxes, the pool of available positions was limited.

Access to coveted jobs, appointments, and admissions was governed by a complex web of tradition and preference, merit and seniority. Much of this legacy of assessing promise and rewarding achievement in the American workplace was praiseworthy and little of it was illegal per se. The Civil Rights Act had created a mechanism to attack discrimination because of race, sex, religion, or national origin. Now the Johnson administration was under pressure to make it work.

CHAPTER 6

The EEOC and the Politics of Gender

That "poor enfeebled thing": The Retail Model of the EEOC

When the EEOC opened for business on July 2, 1965, its deputy general counsel was Richard K. Berg. Berg had joined the new commission from the Justice Department, where he had helped draft Kennedy's omnibus civil rights bill and had subsequently monitored the progress of Title 7 through the Congress. Following the enactment of the Civil Rights Act, Berg published in the *Brooklyn Law Review* an analysis of its evolution and the enforcement implications of the compromises that shaped it.[1] Berg observed that at the heart of Title 7 lay a contradiction between competing models for the EEOC. One model was the standard regulatory model for agencies like the FTC and especially the NLRB. This was the model that Adam Clayton Powell and James Roosevelt had used in the House Education and Labor Committee during 1962–63 to design H.R. 405, and that Celler's Judiciary subcommittee had incorporated into Kennedy's civil rights bill. It envisioned a quasi-judicial body with authority to hear cases, compel witnesses, and issue orders enforceable through the courts. Congress created such agencies to enforce *public* rights. These were rights that the government was obligated to enforce, such as the right of all citizens to be protected from tainted food, unsafe trains, fraudulent securities, or union-busting employers. To enforce public rights, regulatory agencies were given "quasi-judicial" powers that differed among the agencies, but that combined the roles of prosecutor and judge. The goal was to produce administratively efficient regulation with some court-like guarantees of due process, but without bogging down in litigation. Thus the public's rights were policed by the agency, much as local police and traffic courts protected citizens from drunken drivers without waiting for formal complaints. Such complaints were welcome, but not essential.

When in the fall of 1963 the McCulloch compromise in the House stripped away the proposed EEOC's cease-and-desist authority, it still left the commission a prosecutor's role of bringing charges of discrimination against employers and unions. The EEOC could thus protect the public's interest in nondiscriminatory employment. But when the prosecutorial role was stripped away in the Dirksen-engineered Senate compromise of the spring of 1964, it left the EEOC with a core responsibility of enforcing a *private* right to nondiscrimination by responding administratively to individual complaints. Liberals complained that this would reduce the toothless agency to a reactive posture. It would respond to the initiatives of others on a case-by-case, "retail" basis rather than take the initiative to attack broad, "wholesale" patterns of discrimination in large firms, unions, and entire industries. As Berg observed: "the leadership compromise turned the NLRA pattern inside out, and the emphasis is now shifted to the resolution of individual grievances and away from obtaining broad compliance."[2] In his 1966 study of fair employment law, Michael Sovern referred to the EEOC as a "poor enfeebled thing."[3]

The Civil Rights Act had indeed created a modest and circumscribed authority to police an enormous problem in a huge jurisdiction. The EEOC had scarcely moved into its offices when the Watts riot shook the nation. The agency's jurisdiction was scheduled to cover within three years 358,000 firms employing 30.6 million workers, including 16 million members of 52,000 union locals. Yet the budget of $5.2 million that Congress approved for the EEOC in 1966 was smaller than that of the Office of Coal Research. Its staff of 314 was smaller than that of the Federal Crop Insurance Program. The agency was budgeted to process 2000 complaints in its first year. But it received 8,854 complaints. This was partly due to the campaign of the NAACP, led by Herbert Hill, to flood the agency with complaints. Jack Greenberg, head of the NAACP Legal Defense Fund, told the *Wall Street Journal* that Title 7's provisions were "weak, cumbersome, probably unworkable." "We think the best way to get it amended," Greenberg said, "is to show that it doesn't work."[4]

The agency got off to a poor start. By not appointing the five commissioners until June of 1965, President Johnson wasted almost a year of start-up planning. His attention was elsewhere—with problems in Vietnam and the Great Society agenda in Congress. But in choosing a "name" chairman, Franklin D. Roosevelt, Jr., Johnson picked a weak administrator whose chief interest in appointive office was to position himself to return to elective office (he had represented New York's 20th district in Congress from 1949 to 1955 and had been appointed under secretary of Commerce by Kennedy in 1963). As predicted, Roosevelt resigned to run for governor in New York before his first year was out. The disgusted Johnson, unable to persuade other big-name Democrats to chair the shaky new agency, in September of 1966 appointed Stephen N. Shulman, a 33-year-old lawyer-technocrat who was general counsel for the air force. Shulman was highly regarded for his organizational abilities, which the EEOC sorely needed. But he was unknown to the general public and his appointment was read by the civil rights community as a downgrading of the commission.

The EEOC's main problem during its troubled shake-down cruise was role-confusion. Congress had created an agency designed to process individual complaints and then to seek conciliation. But the commission was administratively weak, and its staff, which resented both the burden and the limits of the complaint-processing role, was quickly overwhelmed by the flood of paper and negotiations. The civil rights lobby was offended by the commission's lack of enforcement powers and its case-by-case approach. Caught between an angry constituency and a circumscribed mission, the EEOC floundered. During the first 18 months it received 15,000 complaints. Of these, 6,040 were earmarked for investigation, but the small investigation staff processed only 3,319. By the time the five commissioners had made individual determinations of probable cause, and the agency's five-person conciliation staff had conducted confidential negotiations with the employers, the agency after 21 months could claim only *110* concluded cases.[5]

In a critical review of the EEOC's early performance, the Budget Bureau complained that despite a growing backlog in complaint-processing, the agency was devoting only a third of its budget to its main function of identifying complaints with probable cause and negotiating conciliation agreements with employers. The Budget Bureau report found one potential source of relief, however, in the pattern of complaints. It noted with surprise that a *third* of the EEOC's complaints charged *sex* discrimination.[6] This led the Budget Bureau analysts to suggest that the EEOC's undermanned compliance staff could concentrate on the racial complaints at the expense of the sex-driven complaints. "[L]ess time [could] be devoted to sex cases," the Bureau analysts reasoned, "since the legislative history would indicate that they deserve a lower priority than discrimination because of race or other factors."[7]

The Male World of Antidiscrimination: The Moynihan Report and Playboy Bunny Jokes

From the perspective of the male establishment during the Kennedy-Johnson years, the Budget Bureau analysis was correct. The leaders of liberal reform overwhelmingly were men. Prejudice to them primarily meant racism, and its ancillary meaning was ethno-religious: anti-Semitism, anti-Catholicism. Sex discrimination had a historic meaning—hence the Nineteenth amendment and the Equal Pay Act. But "sexism" as yet had no meaning or place in the lexicon of public discourse. The four-decade intramural war over the ERA had frozen the feminist dialogue in an archaic polarity. In 1964, Howard Smith's part-mischievous "sex" amendment had stolen a march on history. Hitching a ride on the momentum of black civil rights, it was escorted briskly through the race-centered debate without a dialogue of its own. Congress during 1963–64 produced hundreds of hours in hearings and thousands of pages in testimony on racial equality, but there were no committee hearings or reports on gender equality at all.

In 1964 the campaign for black civil rights was driven by a mature social movement. But second-wave feminism did not yet constitute a social movement. In an ironic reversal, the feminist surprise victory of 1964 would force the inner dialogue of consciousness-raising that normally preceded such policy breakthroughs. In the meantime, the men of power had learned to take racism very seriously. But they found it difficult to take women's equality seriously. The major black organizations took no position on the women's rights issues, although privately their leaders had resisted the complications of adding gender or age discrimination to their FEPC campaigns. Organized labor had consistently opposed racial discrimination and supported FEPC laws. But labor's men of power displayed a masculine contempt for the ERA. The correspondence of the AFL-CIO's chief congressional lobbyist, former Wisconsin congressman Andrew J. Biemiller, was peppered with snide and fraternal allusions to the ERA. "[I]f the ladies who are now worrying about [the ERA] did not have this to worry about," Biemiller wrote a colleague in 1960, "they would find something else. Vive le (sex) difference!"[8]

Within the Kennedy-Johnson administration, the white male liberals pressed the campaign for black equality while steering clear of entanglements over women's rights. In 1961, George Reedy had warned Vice President Johnson that adding sex to the PCEEO's jurisdiction would "throw the committee into complete chaos." Sargent Shriver, the director of Johnson's anti-poverty program, told Congress in 1964 that the Job Corps would be all-male in order to concentrate on "primary breadwinners."[9] Hubert Humphrey recommended to Johnson in August 1965 that an executive order to coordinate EEO enforcement should "not cover discrimination on grounds of sex." That would unnecessarily complicate the priority task of attacking racial discrimination, Humphrey said. He had been advised by Labor secretary Wirtz and by John Macy, chairman of the Civil Service Commission, that "the liklihood of adverse political reaction from women's groups is small."[10]

That same summer, 1965, saw the release of the explosive Moynihan Report on the Negro family. A Harvard sociologist appointed by President Kennedy as assistant secretary of Labor for policy planning, Daniel Patrick Moynihan was alarmed over the disorganization of the black family structure. His report, which was unapologetically male-centered, emphasized the weakening of the position of the black male and the encouragement, by government welfare policy as well as by broader economic and social factors, of female-headed families. In a preview memorandum to the White House in January 1965, Moynihan warned that the deteriorating stature and authority of the black male had created a "pathological matriarchal situation which is beginning to feed on itself."[11] The heart of the problem, Moynihan said, "is that the Negro family structure is crumbling." Illegitimacy rates had soared past *one quarter* of all black births (the white rate was 3 percent). The "main reason for this," Moynihan explained, "is the systematic weakening of the position of the Negro male." "By contrast," Moynihan noted, "Negro women have always done and continue to do relatively well." They had higher rates of college graduation and were getting "better jobs, higher salaries, more prestige." "We must not rest until every able-bodied Negro male is working," he said, "[e]ven if we have to displace some females. (In the Department of Labor, after four years of successful effort to increase Negro employees, we found that in non-professional categories 80 percent were women!)" "More can be done about redesigning jobs that are now thought to be women's jobs and turning them into men's jobs," Moynihan added. A "great problem for the Negro male," Moynihan said, was that "his type of job is declining, while the jobs open to the Negro female are expanding."[12]

The subsequent uproar over the Moynihan Report saw its author ostracized by much of the liberal-academic and civil rights community and hounded into resignation. But the liberals were incensed by Moynihan's allegedly patronizing attitude toward American blacks and their culture, not toward women. Liberal critics accused Moynihan of blaming the black victims of white discrimination for their plight.[13] So effective was the intellectual community's ban on critical analysis of minority cultures that public debate was muted for two decades—by which time the ignored pathology had worsened by a factor of two, and impoverished, female-headed families with fatherless children had become the norm in the black underclass. The outcry against Moynihan's report in 1965 merged with the swelling protest over Johnson's Vietnam policy. But it included no significant voice of protest from women's groups over its male-centered policy implications.

Small wonder, then, that in 1965 the American public mind at large, as mirrored in press coverage and political discourse, did not take the new issue of sex discrimination seriously. Indeed, leaders in business and journalism found in it occasion for comic relief. When the *Wall Street Journal* in a special report asked corporate executives how they felt about Title 7, a perplexed airline personnel executive said: "We're not worried about the racial discrimination ban—what's unnerving us is the section on sex." "What are we going to do now," he asked, "when a gal walks into our office, demands a job as an airline pilot and has the credentials to qualify? Or what will we do when some guy comes in and wants to be a stewardess?"[14] An electronics executive in Nashville, whose nonunion firm hired only nimble-fingered women to assemble the delicate electronic components, complained that he would have to "hire the first male midget with unusual dexterity if he shows up." A telephone company official similarly worried about the threat of male operators, although he dismissed as "fantasy" the possibility that some women might want to become linemen.

Even EEOC chairman Franklin Roosevelt instinctively played to this gallery at the commission's kick-off news conference on July 2, 1965. "What about sex?" a reporter asked Roosevelt. "Don't get me started," Roosevelt replied with a laugh. "I'm all for it."[15] Shortly thereafter the *New York Times* ran a major story on the newly discovered "bunny problem." This would arise when a male applied for a job as a Playboy Bunny—or a woman to be an attendant in a male Turkish bathhouse, a man to clerk in a corset shop, a woman to be a tugboat deckhand.[16] The following day the magisterial *New York Times* editorialized that Congress ought to "just abolish sex itself."[17] This was because in light of the new federal policy against sex discrimination, everything was going to have to be neutered—housemaid, handyman, Girl Friday, even the Rockettes. "Bunny problem, indeed!" the *Times* despaired, "This is revolution, chaos. You can't even safely advertise for a wife anymore." It was inconceivable that the *Times* would use such a tone in an editorial over black civil rights. But behind the gleeful play of the bunny joke lay a series of hard questions that Title 7 now raised and that the new EEOC would be expected promptly to address, although virtually no systematic thought had been given to the answers.

The New Feminists and the EEOC: The Question of Race-Sex Analogy

When the EEOC opened for business in the summer of 1965, virtually all signs pointed the commission toward caution in interpreting the new ban on sex discrimination. Staff director Tom Powers assured Secretary Wirtz in September 1965: "The Commission is very much aware of the importance of not becoming known as the 'sex commission.' "[18] This consensus was captured in one of the EEOC's early staff studies by consultant Frances R. Cousens, who had been research director of Michigan's FEPC. She observed that the addition of sex discrimination to Title 7 "was to seriously weaken the Commission. Intergroup relations professionals have long believed that although discrimination according to sex needs consideration, it differes substantially from that based on race, religion, or national origin; to include sex as a provision of Title VII does, in fact, undermine efforts on behalf of minority groups."[19] Cousens complained that from the beginning the EEOC staff was "inundated by complaints about sex discrimination that diverted attention and resources from the more serious allegations by members of racial, religious, and ethnic minorities."

When the EEOC opened its doors for business on July 2, 1965, only one of the five commissioners was female, Aileen C. Hernandez. Born Aileen Clarke in New York City in 1926, daughter of Jamaican immigrants, her Hispanic surname came from a four-year marriage in 1961 to a cutter in the Los Angeles garment industry. A Democrat who had worked as education director for the International Ladies' Garment Workers Union in California, she had joined the staff of the California FEPC in 1962 and was the only EEOC commissioner with state experience in fair employment law. Hernandez complained that a meeting between the commissioners and employers in California was arranged in a private club that barred women. "The message came through clearly that the Commission's priority was race discrimination," she recalled, "and apparently only as it related to Black *men*."[20]

When Johnson announced a White House Conference on Equal Employment Opportunity for August 19–20 to showcase the new agency, only nine of the seventy-five speakers and panelists were women (six of these were on the panel dealing with sex discrimination that Hernandez chaired). Chairman Roosevelt called the question of sex discrimination "terribly complicated" and indicated that the commission would formulate policy slowly on a case-by-case basis.[21]

The EEOC's most obvious problem was to define what Title 7 meant for women's protective laws. Section 708 asserted that state laws that conflicted with Title 7 were now invalid. Its purpose was to supersede segregation laws in the South. The Jim Crow laws were not mentioned per se, but they obviously were overruled by a list in section 703 of acts that were now prohibited. These were: to refuse to hire or to discharge any individual or to limit, segregate, or classify employees in any way which would deprive them of employment opportunities or otherwise adversely affect their status as employees, because of such individual's race, color, religion, sex, or national origin. But what did this require of the EEOC if a woman in Arizona filed a complaint against an employer who refused to hire her because state law prevented her, but not men, from working more than eight hours a day?[22] Was California's 50-pound limit on an employee's lifting a legitimate ceiling for women but not for men, especially in light of higher pay for heavier work? Was the 15-pound limit in Utah legitimate?

These questions were logically compelling, but there was little political pressure to confront them immediately. There was no organized voice to force them onto the public agenda in 1965. They affected the lives of wage-earning women, but the lobbies representing the interests of working women, the Women's Bureau and organized labor, did not want the questions to be raised. Neither did the EEOC, which had received no guidance from Congress and was anxious to avoid the controversy. The same problem of unequal gender rules and practices surfaced almost immediately in another form, however, and this time there was an aroused female constituency. Women's protective legislation had an honorable lineage among liberal reformers, and its different treatment of men and women was designed to benefit women. But the same could not be said for the long tradition of sex-segregated job listings.

The Problem of Jane Crow in the Classified Ads

The omnibus civil rights bill passed by the House in 1964 prohibited job advertisements or referrals "indicating any preference, limitation, specification, or discrimination, based on race, color, religion, sex, or national origin. . . ." Like most of the language of Title 7, this provision was designed with the South's racial caste system in mind, and the single word "sex" had simply been added to the list by Judge Smith's amendment. Its target was the Jim Crow job listings in southern newspapers, like the *Atlanta Constitution*'s "Help Wanted—Colored" ads, that segregated blacks into menial jobs. By 1965, however, many of the South's metropolitan newspapers had dropped the practice, and resistance to abandoning it had been reduced, as with resistance to integrated restaurants, to marginal redoubts in the small-town and rural South.

Most American newspapers, however, continued to publish separate classified advertisements for men and women. On Friday, July 2, 1965, the day the Civil Rights Act of 1964 took effect, the *New York Times* published its customarily segregated job listings for males and females. The only difference between those want-ads and the classified listings of 1960 was the insertion of a special notice, in a small box atop the help-wanted section. The notice explained that in observance of the passage of the Civil Rights Act of 1964, "Qualified job seekers of either sex are invited to consider job opportunities in either the Male of Female help wanted columns. . . ."[23]

The confused nature of the race-sex analogy was little noticed or discussed by Americans in 1965. Its contradictions complicated the application of Title 7, which treated discrimination by race and sex as analogous in most of its provisions, but provided vaguely for some exceptions for distinctions of gender. State FEPCs were enforcing employment rights in half of the American states when Title 7 became law, and 43 states had protective laws for women. But only three states—Hawaii, New York, and Wisconsin—had added a ban on discrimination based on sex.[24] In September 1965 in the pioneer FEPC state of New York, the *Wall Street Journal* ran a special report on another leading EEO state, Wisconsin. The FEP law in progressive Wisconsin had been amended in 1961 to cover sex discrimination. Since then, the *Journal* reported, only 16 complaints had been filed, and only one had required a public hearing.[25] In that short time, a male advantage in schoolteacher salaries in Wisconsin had been removed, the face amount of employee pension benefits had been equalized for the sexes, and a male former medic in the army was ordered admitted to a state vocational school's course on practical nursing. But no one had challenged the single-sex classified advertisements in politically liberal Wisconsin's newspapers.

Because the public debate over sex discrimination remained confused, and was still marked by deep internal divisions among women, Congress had added exceptions clauses to Title 7 in the aftermath of the Smith amendment. The chief exceptions clauses for women excluded them from coverage when sex was "a bona fide occupational qualification for employment" (in the lexicon of government acronyms, this became a "BFOQ"). The BFOQ in theory exempted men as well as women, since it wouldn't do to have restroom attendants of the opposite sex in either restroom. But no committee hearings or report had examined how a BFOQ was defined. For blacks, the ban on racially segregated want-ads was accorded widespread understanding, and the regional practice quickly disappeared. But for women, the ban produced bunny jokes.

Secretary Wirtz urged the EEOC to interpret the BFOQ exception narrowly, and to ban gender as well as racial separatism in job listings. This is "not a provision," Wirtz said, "that permits a general labeling of jobs as 'men's jobs' or 'women's jobs.' "[26] At the White House conference on equal opportunity in August 1965, deputy EEOC counsel Richard Berg announced that the commission was going to put the burden on the employers to make the case for BFOQ exceptions. "If they can't think of any reason not to do it [hire women for jobs traditionally held by men]," Berg warned, "then they'd better do it."[27] Shortly thereafter, in response to an airline stewardess complaint, the EEOC issued its first ruling (the *Wall Street Journal* reported that "the honor went to the ladies"): any labor-management agreement or corporate policy that required dismissing females when they marry would violate Title 7.[28]

Nonetheless, the preponderance of signals the EEOC was receiving emphasized the differences between sex and race, not the similarities. The commission was urged to impose a total ban on special state laws for Negroes and on "colored" job ads. But at the same time great caution was urged on behalf of women's protective legislation. There was no evidence in public opinion of significant support from either sex for a ban on single-sex ads. Furthermore the American Newspaper Publishers Association, which offered no defense of racially segregated want ads, defended the necessity for separate-sex classified ads. The ANPA argued that both their readers and their advertisers preferred the traditional and market-efficient single-sex ads, and that nothing in Title 7 gave the EEOC authority over the publishers of classified advertising. Title 7 controlled the employer placing the ad, the ANPA maintained, not the newspaper publishing it. Whatever the merits of the ANPA's economic and cultural arguments, their legal argument about the limited reach of the EEOC was a serious one. And implicit in their complaints was a powerful political argument—i.e., politicians traditionally accorded great weight to the view of newspaper publishers.

The voice of caution on policing sex discrimination made sense to most of the males who dominated the EEOC as well as the ANPA. But rigorous in dissent was Aileen Hernandez. "It is the advertiser's responsibility to insert in his ad that he does not discriminate and the job is open to males and females," she argued. "If there is a B.F.O.Q. he should come to the EEOC and get a ruling, not make the determination himself."[29] But EEOC General Counsel Charles Duncan—also a black—disagreed. "I have never heard it suggested that the Commission had the power to pass on in advance what was and what was not B.F.O.Q," Duncan replied. "I have never heard it said we could not," Hernandez countered. Staff director Tom Powers warned: "If the Commission lets itself get into the position where it has to pass on every single instance in which any covered employer in the United States believes that Sex is a bona fide occupation[al qualification], you are going to load yourself down with so many questions in the Sex area that you are not going to have time to do anything else of significance."

In response to this debate, Chairman Roosevelt on August 18 announced a flat ban on racially separate want-ads. But he appointed a 17-member advisory committee to study the question of single-sex ads.[30] The commission expected to issue a comprehensive set of guidelines on sex discrimination in November. In October the *Wall Street Journal* carried a special report on the young agency's uncertain "shadow boxing" with the permutations of job discrimination. Summoning a prize-fighting metaphor, the *Journal* predicted that the "youthful pugilist" EEOC would demand preferential treatment for Negroes under the euphemistic guise of affirmative action. But "on behalf of the ladies" the EEOC would only produce "a succession of light jabs against unchivalrous treatment, just enough to qualify as effort though far short of enthusiasm."[31] Shortly thereafter the EEOC ruled that racially segregated local unions, seniority lines, and promotion lists violated Title 7. Then in November the commission announced its guidelines on sex discrimination. Consistent with its stance on race discrimination, the commission led off by ruling several common business practices as illegal acts of sex discrimination. First was a refusal to hire a woman based on "assumptions of the comparative characteristics of women in general," or of "preferences of co-workers," or on "stereotyped characteristics of the sexes." Second, it was impermissible to classify jobs as "light" or "heavy" or "male" or "female," or to maintain separate seniority lists if this were done to affect women adversely. Third, employers could not fail to hire or promote women solely because they were married.[32] So far the race-sex linkage was close.

The race-sex equation was more problematical, however, in policies dealing with state protective laws and classified advertising. Roosevelt noted that there was nothing in the legislative history of Title 7 to indicate that Congress intended to strike down state protective laws. Indeed, Roosevelt said, Emanuel Celler had written him that Congress had no such intention. The EEOC would therefore "consider qualifications set by such state laws or regulations to be bona fide occupational qualifications and not in conflict" with Title 7.[33] The agency hedged, however. State legislatures should review their labor codes to update archaic and irrelevant provisions. In the future the EEOC reserved the right to judge such complaints on a case-by-case basis. Roosevelt gave an example: if a state's restriction on the weight a woman could lift was set "unreasonably low," and thereby excluded her from otherwise desirable benefits, it would not be considered valid. Implicit in this codicil was an assumption that the EEOC possessed the authority to rule against such restrictions.

When it came to classified advertisements segregated by sex, however, Roosevelt acknowledged the commission's belief that "Culture and mores, personal inclinations, and physical limitations will operate to make many job categories primarily of interest to men or women."[34] So the commission would not require unified want ads by gender, as it had done by race. The EEOC would require only that advertisers specify in the ad that the job was open to both males and females and that publishers print a notice on each help-wanted page that their listings were not intended to exclude persons of the opposite sex. Four months later, in response to pressure from the newspaper publishers, the EEOC retreated from even its timid compromise of November. The revised ruling of March 1966 bound advertisers but not publishers to the restrictions on gender preference.[35]

The EEOC and the Revolt of the New Feminists

The EEOC's cautious, compromising approach to gender discrimination during its first year was not inherently unreasonable, given the murkiness of congressional intent. But the agency's waffling on sex discrimination came at a crucial moment of psychological receptiveness among feminist leaders. Angered by the agency's double standard on job discrimination, they broke free of the divisions of the past and coalesced around an emerging feminist agenda that centered on equal treatment. To the new feminists this meant that the Constitution and the Civil Rights Act were sex-blind as well as color-blind. By 1966, second-wave feminism as a social movement was in full tilt. Caught in the middle was the hapless EEOC, whose deference to the different "culture and mores, personal inclinations, and physical limitations" of men and women could scarcely have been better timed to enrage the battalions of professional women who were flocking to Washingtion to take control of their own policy agenda.

When the *New York Times* published its too-clever, bunny-joke editorial on women's equality following the White House EEO conference in August 1965, Esther Peterson wrote a letter of protest to the *Times*. She had battled and bested the ERA battalions for most of her distinguished career. But angered by the cute and condescending *Times* that August, Peterson accused the editors of cultivating a tone of ridicule for women's issues. The *Times'* worries over male Playboy bunnies and Rockettes were misplaced. They should ask instead: "How many jobs are 'women's jobs' merely because they are menial, routine, monotonous and, of course, low-paying?"[36] Peterson's letter reflected a general reversal of her earlier opposition to the Smith amendment. The sharp divisions between the Women's Bureau coalition and the ERA position were blurring. New feminist voices were emerging that increasingly combined Democratic affiliation with equal-rights fervor.

Such a leader was Representative Martha Griffiths of Michigan. In 1964, Griffiths had led the drive that forced the Smith amendment through the House—to the constant tune of masculine guffaws. Riled by such indignities and irritated by the EEOC's downgrading of gender issues, Griffiths lashed out at the EEOC in May 1966 for its backsliding on women's rights. On June 20, Griffiths took the House floor and blasted the EEOC in an attack that consumed six pages of the *Congressional Record*.[37] To document her charge that the EEOC mirrored the media's demeaning practice of concentrating on various odd and hypothetical cases of sex discrimination, she read from the latest *EEOC Newsletter* a discussion of the relative merits of women working as dog wardens and men as house mothers. She accused the EEOC's executive director, Herman Edelsberg, of insisting at his first press conference (when he had replaced Tom Powers the previous fall) that he and his colleagues at the EEOC thought men were "entitled" to have female secretaries, and of explaining to an audience at New York University in April 1966 that the sex provision in Title 7 was a "fluke" that was "conceived out of wedlock."[38]

As the congressional whip who drove the Smith amendment through the House, Griffiths rejected the "whining" excuse of EEOC officials that the sex provision was a "fluke." "Since when is it permissible," she asked, "for an agency charged with the duty of enforcing the law, to allude to the assumed motive of the author of legislation as an excuse for not enforcing the law?" The "shilly-shallying" EEOC, Griffiths said, was "wringing its hands about the sex provision" when its real excuse was that "sex discrimination cases take too much time and thus interfere with the EEOC's 'main' business of eliminating racial discrimination."[39]

In *It Changed My Life,* Betty Friedan recalled how during the EEOC's first tumultous year of interpreting Title 7, Commissioner Richard Graham sought her help in organizing independent woman's groups to lobby the EEOC in the same way the effective black groups had done:

> Richard Graham, a real fighter for women who had emerged on that commission, told me that he personally had gone to see the heads of the League of Women Voters, the American Association of University Women and other women's organizations with national headquarters in Washington, to get them to use pressure to have Title VII enforced on behalf of women. And they had been appalled by the very suggestion. They were not "feminists," they had told him.[40]

An engineering executive from Wisconsin, Graham had been Peace Corps director in Tunisia, and in 1965 was recommended to President Johnson by Bill Moyers (to fill one of the EEOC's two Republican seats) as a Republican of unusual vision. Graham and Hernandez wanted more organized feminist lobbying to strengthen their hand—they needed a feminist NAACP. Friedan heard a similar plea from a young attorney on the EEOC's legal staff, Sonia Pressman, who requested anonymity for fear of losing her job.[41] These insider appeals to the new feminists, asking for an independent source of counterbalancing pressure on the EEOC, reflected the inherent limitations of the status-of-women groups. The women who sat on presidential commissions and interagency committees were a new and thin network of appointed, top-down reformers, not representatives empowered by a grass-roots social movement. It was difficult for them to create independent lobbying groups, because so many of them were either government officials or represented established women's organizations that had traditionally avoided lobbying.[42]

The turning point for the feminist lobby came in June of 1966. First, Representative Griffiths attacked the EEOC on the House floor. Second, word leaked out that Richard Graham's initial one-year term as commissioner was being allowed to expire, although the administration gave no reason and had no replacement in mind. Third, delegations from the state status-of-women commissions gathered in Washingtion for a convention, with Friedan attending officially as a writer and unofficially as a feminist organizer. Out of this fertile sea of discontent the National Organization of Women was conceived.[43] On October 29, when NOW was officially christened, EEOC castoff and proto-feminist Richard Graham became a founding vice president. So too did Aileen Hernandez, who resigned from the EEOC in frustration (in 1970 she would succeed Friedan as NOW's president). For the growing feminist coalition, NOW's gain was the EEOC's loss, because the commission was now stripped of its only two feminist voices—a black woman Democrat and a white male Republican.

Yet the loss of Graham and Hernandez from the EEOC deflected the agency only temporarily from following the logic of the race-sex equation. This was partly because the pattern of individual complaints showed that women workers were upset about unequal treatment. The EEOC's first annual report revealed that 60 percent of the complaints were racial, and *37 percent* charged sex discrimination.[44] Unlike the black complainants, where the dominant charge during the EEOC's first year was over hiring discrimination (23.7 percent), the women complained least of all about hiring. Almost none complained that they were barred from the corporate executive suite or blocked from career success in such professions as law and medicine. Instead, their main complaint was over unequal employee benefits, such as pensions and medical coverage (30 percent), closely followed by discriminatory seniority lines (24 percent). Twelve percent cited the unfair restrictions of state protective laws, especially the limit on their right to earn extra pay through voluntary overtime, like the men. While 37.3 percent of the charges filed by blacks complained about hiring and firing, only 5.6 percent of the women did so.[45]

Additional evidence of the patterns of sex discrimination came from the EEOC's special staff studies. In August 1966 the agency completed a staff study of 18,000 help-wanted ads in 21 newspapers. The study found few violations concerning race, national origin, and religion. But sex-segregated want ads remained common. As a result of the study the commission itself charged 75 advertisers with running unlawful ads (although by law the commission could not identify them until after conciliation). The 21 newspapers that published the ads, however, were not so charged, consistent with the commission's reinterpretation of April. Some of the offending ads specified a preferred race—e.g., a "white attendant" or "Anglo carhops," and these were ruled illegal per se. But most of the offending ads indicated a gender preference— e.g., "Executive sales positions for men," "Lady in charge, northside shop," "Insurance trainee, man age 22 to 25"—and these the EEOC regarded as unredeemed by the requisite BFOQ.

The Belated Feminist Conversion of the EEOC

During the last two years of the Johnson administration, the new evidence of employment discrimination combined with the ground swell of feminist lobbying to drive a recalcitrant EEOC toward enforcement policies that equated race and sex discrimination.[46] In applying Title 7 to the protective laws, for example, the EEOC considered a challenge to California's rather typical limit for women of eight hours a day and 48 hours a week. In August 1966 the commission refused to rule against California's eight-hour limit for women. "The Commission cannot rewrite state laws according to its own views of the public interest," the commissioners explained. Women adversely affected by these laws should bring suit in federal court, the EEOC advised.

Feminist groups counterattacked and found that they could command news attention by challenging relics of state discriminatory laws. They attacked a Texas law against women dancing in tents; a Nebraska law keeping women off juries unless the judge approved of their restrooms; laws in seven southern states making fathers the presumptive legal guardians of their minor children. They attacked a Washington state law preventing a married woman from filing suit in a state court unless her husband joined in the suit and Louisiana's Napoleonic code for granting men most property rights.[47] Many of these laws were crippling residues of the ancient code of *feme covert*. Some were long unenforced, but usefully bizarre to the feminists—such as the Texas law of 1856 that recognized the legal right of a husband to kill his wife's paramour if he caught them in *flagrante dilecto* whereas the wife's equivalent reprise was regarded as murder. In assaulting the special-protection laws in courts and news conferences, the state federations of business and professional women's clubs were especially active in Texas, where communal property laws were brazenly male-dominated, and in Ohio, where historically strong union forces had helped shape a body of industrial law that barred women from nineteen job categories.

In response to the feminist assault, the EEOC called a major hearing for May 2–3, 1967, on the three most controversial issues involving sex discrimination: state protective laws, classified advertising, and different pension benefits for men and women.[48] These hearings were full and gave the EEOC needed breathing room. But they were inconclusive, and they were not soon followed by a commission verdict, as would be expected of a court. Following these hearings, however, the EEOC began to go with the flow of the changing tide of opinion and argument on the major disputed issues of gender discrimination. By 1968 it had managed to reverse virtually all of its earlier cautionary retreats, and in 1969 the commission began to rule almost as aggressively on gender as it had from the beginning on race.[49]

This transition was paralleled by a transformation of the commission membership itself, from one dominated by white males to one dominated by members of the "affected class" groups. By the end of the Johnson administration, EEOC vice-chairman Luther Holcomb, a Dallas minister and Johnson loyalist who feared a runaway commission, was often reduced to a lone dissent against a bloc consisting of two blacks, a Hispanic, and a woman. On the issue of state protective legislation, for example, the EEOC in February 1968 reversed its ruling of August 1966 on the California eight-hour law. In August 1969 the commission found that such protective laws by their very nature "conflict with Title 7 of the Civil Rights Act of 1964 and will not be considered a defense to an otherwise established unlawful employment practice or as a basis for the application of the bona fide occupational qualification exception."[50] On single-sex classified ads, the commission repeated the cycle. On August 6, 1968, it reversed itself and ruled in a 3-2 decision that separate want-ad columns by gender were unlawful per se.[51] Similarly, in a protracted dispute over whether airline stewardesses constituted a BFOQ exception, the EEOC took 27 months before ruling, in February 1968, that flight attendant jobs did not merit BFOQ exceptions.[52] The commission subsequently struck down airline rules barring married stewardesses and limiting stewardess age.

Over all, by the end of the Johnson administration the EEOC seemed settled on a path that would tightly link race and sex in EEO enforcement. At first an adversary to feminist groups, the commission would seek to build a coalition of constituent groups, adding women to blacks, Asians, Hispanics, and American Indians as members of officially protected classes—a "minority" coalition that in the 1970s approached three-fourths of the United States population.[53] When the EEOC opened for business in 1965, its regulatory stance reflected the assumptions about race and gender in public policy that undergirded its founding charter in 1964: the Constitution was color-blind, but not entirely sex-blind. Equal treatment for the races was required, but biological role differences and a legal tradition of special protection complicated the pursuit of equal opportunity for women. By 1968 the EEOC had largely reversed itself on gender equality. Equal treatment replaced the special protection laws, and the BFOQ exceptions were narrowed to accommodate only exotic marginalia, like the Rockettes. Congress had not been clear in its own collective mind about these matters, and the vagueness of its mandate in 1964 left the EEOC ample room to stretch its interpretation—especially under the lash of the newly unified feminists.

At the same time, however, political and economic forces were driving the EEOC's racial policy in an opposite direction. Congress in 1964 could scarcely have been more explicit about its demand for equal treatment and its rejection of racial preferences. But the ghetto explosions lent a new urgency to the nation's social agenda, and the new social regulators at the EEOC found themselves increasingly at loggerheads with their founding charter.

CHAPTER 7

Race, Affirmative Action, and Open Housing 1965–1968

Racial Violence and Group-based Remedies

By the summer of 1967 the EEOC, like the civil rights movement that provided its constituency, was in disarray. The Watts riot of 1965 and the Black Power surge of 1966 had alienated public sympathy. This is turn had produced Republican gains in the 90th Congress. In the summer of 1966, ghetto violence exploded in Chicago, Cleveland, Dayton, San Francisco, Atlanta, Omaha, and dozens of smaller communities. The Johnson administration's civil rights proposal for 1966, which featured an open housing provision and cease-and-desist authority for the EEOC, was defeated in Congress. The EEOC, under attack from feminist groups, was criticized by the Budget Bureau for administrative incompetence, and its budget proposals were slashed in Congress. The agency's complaint backlog was a growing embarrassment. By the spring of 1967 the EEOC was taking 15 months to process a complaint, although Title 7 required that complaints be processed within 60 days. The 60-day time limit had never been realistic, but by the end of 1967 the EEOC's processing time exceeded two years.

In July 1967 a mega-riot erupted in Detroit. It lasted a week and left forty-three dead, 7200 arrested by police and National Guard troops, hundreds injured, 1300 buildings destroyed, 5000 people homeless, and $50 million in property damage.[1] Less spectacular riots broke out in the ghettos of Boston, Cincinnati, Milwaukee, and Newark. The race riots, which rarely occurred in southern cities, seemed to confirm that the reforms of 1964–65 had focused too narrowly (and too self-righteously) on the South. The racial violence of the "long hot summers" produced contradictory reactions from the public and from political leaders. Public policy followed a two-pronged, carrot-and-stick approach: the institutions of law and order must be strengthened to control civil commotion; but government must also address the underlying causes of social unrest.[2] The ghetto violence of 1965–68 intensified the pressures on government to strengthen social control, which meant more community policing and better riot-control training and equipment, and social amelioration, which meant measures to attack the roots of discontent—joblessness, slum housing, poor schools, loss of hope.[3]

In the face of the need for more and better jobs for minorities, the EEOC's frustration deepened at the mismatch of its huge responsibility and its narrow authority. "We are out to kill an elephant," chairman Shulman complained, "with a fly gun."[4] The EEOC's professional staff, which was quarreling over sex-discrimination policy, was unified on racial policy. Aggressive enforcement on both counts meant an expansive interpretation of the EEOC's authority. The agency's staff, dominated not surprisingly by liberals and members of the protected classes, resented the tight restrictions that Title 7 imposed. The EEOC's complaint-response model symbolized to the civil rights community the trivialization of the nation's most pressing domestic and moral concern. To them it rang of the voluntarism of a largely neutered agency. They were stung by the impracticality and moral fecklessness of the case-by-case, retail approach to a historic injustice that demanded wholesale remedies.[5]

If the EEOC was to move beyond the limitations of the complaint model— beyond putting out fires with persuasion, or beyond "mere" passive nondiscrimination toward an affirmative program that attacked broad patterns of discrimination—then four fundamental changes would have to be made, either in the language or the interpretation of the commission's founding law. The first of the four was the most difficult. It would reach to the heart of the EEOC's dilemma by changing the definition of discrimination itself. To move radically beyond the complaint model, the definition of what constituted discrimination would have to be extended beyond the *intent* standard of the common law tradition, which was stipulated by Congress in Title 7, toward a new *effects* standard. This would require a shift in the criteria of discrimination from invidious intent by those accused of wrongdoing, to harmful *impact* upon members of the affected class irrespective of intent.

Civil rights lawyers argued that fair-employment law should be detached from a historic grounding in criminal law, where intent was customarily a matter of evil motivation, and shifted toward the less stringent standards of tort law, where intent was regarded as merely an awareness of foreseeable consequences of one's conduct, and hence less difficult to prove. The need to prove harmful intent placed a heavy burden on plaintiffs, especially when the accused discriminators were employers who controlled the processes and records of employment. To plaintiff lawyers, the standards of proof and penalty in fair-employment law seemed mismatched. The daunting standard of evil intent from the criminal law was paired with the timid penalties of the civil code, often at the punitive level of mere misdemeanors. Like white-collar crime generally, employment discrimination seemed widespread, hard to prove, rarely prosecuted, and lightly punished, while its disadvantaged victims were numerous and suffered serious harm.

Such a shift from harmful intent to unequal results was implicit in the new concept of "institutional racism."[6] By this was meant the patterns of historic preference in institutions and their power structures that had excluded minorities for so long that discriminatory intent was no longer required to maintain majority dominance. Theoretically, institutionalized racism required individual racism to imbed racist bias in organizational norms and procedures. Once established, however, institutional racism could be maintained even in the absence of racial prejudice itself. From this premise it followed that reactive policies of nondiscrimination, as practiced, for example, by the state fair-employment commissions, would not fundamentally change such patterns.

The traditional FEPC model was driven by individual complaints and geared to individual remedies. But institutional racism was defined as a group-based phenomenon that victimized *classes*, not just individuals, through accumulated historical wrongs. Thus remedies to be effective must be group-based. This would require an interventionist and compensatory form of affirmative remedy for protected classes.[7] The implications of such a theoretical redefinition were profound. It challenged the core of Title 7's rationale, which was the traditional concept of individual rights under a color-blind Constitution. If the equal-treatment model was to shift toward an equal-results model, then discrimination would be identified not by intentional acts of harm to individuals, but rather by the unequal effects (or "disparate impact") that institutional racism produced. Acts of racial discrimination need not be proved. Rather, they could be inferred from the maldistribution of jobs, promotions, appointments, and other benefits.

Such an "effects" standard would have to be based on a statistical demonstration of unequal impact in the distribution of jobs and rewards. This statistical test was the second change that a new definition would require. To demonstrate unequal effects, the EEOC would need a comprehensive, national data base with which to document maldistributions. Such an information bank, however, did not exist, either at the EEOC or in the files of the Bureau of Labor Statistics or elsewhere in government. Its absence, ironically, owed much to the successful campaign of the liberal coalition during the 1950s to stop the practice of keeping records by race. In 1955 the Eisenhower administration had been persuaded to disapprove racial identifications in employee records, and the Kennedy administration had reaffirmed this policy as recently as 1962.

Third, assuming the availability of data for a statistical analysis of the distribution of jobs and other benefits by minority category, the EEOC would then need a model of fair distribution against which to compare actual distributions for rendering judgments. Such a model would necessarily be based on some variation of a theory of proportional representation. That is, equal opportunity would be defined as, absent discrimination, an equal chance to represent one's group in the workface relative to the group's size. The proportional model assumed that all racial, ethnic, and cultural groups were equally endowed for employment competition by their history, culture, physical attributes, and vocational interests. Individuals differed widely, and group differences might permit some extraordinary and marginal exceptions to a rule of strict proportionality (Asians in professional basketball, gender BFOQs). But the normal distribution of jobs and other benefits should reflect only population variables. The proportion of blacks or women or other minorities in certain job categories would therefore be expected to equal their proportion in some appropriate labor pool—e.g., the general U.S. population, the regional or local population, the workforce or skill population, the applicant pool.

The proportional model of representation was incompatible with traditional, individually based standards of competitive merit. Its proponents enjoyed an intuitive advantage when they argued that standards of individual merit did not convincingly account for the overrepresentation of blacks and minorities among domestic servants and sanitation workers, or their underrepresentation among firemen, police detectives, or skilled construction craftsmen. On the other hand, the concept of institutional racism could not account for the overrepresentation of Jews in academe or Asians in science, despite long histories of racial and ethnic discrimination against them. The proportional model leveled the peaks of achievement and the valleys of disadvantage with a two-edged sword. It clashed so discordantly with the American work ethic and the immigrant mythos that Congress in 1964 had dismissed it in debate and banned it in statute. Nonetheless, without such a model of proportional representation there could be no measureable benchmark of "underutilization" with which to justify preferential remedies.

Finally, given (1) an "effects" definition of discrimination, (2) a comprehensive data base with which to compare the distribution of rewards and benefits in society, and (3) a proportional model of appropriate distributions, the EEOC would need (4) the authority to require compensatory remedies—specific measures of hiring and promotion sufficient to rectify discrepancies with the model. The remedy for institutional racism would seem to require from government some form of minority preference. "Affirmative action" would therefore shift from special recruitment and training efforts toward racial, ethnic, and gender preferences. The EEOC, however, had been so defanged by the Dirksen compromise of 1964 that it lacked the authority to enforce even the traditional, retail model of discrimination. Or so it appeared in 1965.

The EEOC as a Subversive Bureaucracy

During the racial crisis of 1965–68, as pressures on the EEOC mounted to provide an effective alternative to black violence, the agency found itself increasingly at odds with the legal framework that governed its work. The congressional conservatives of 1964, alarmed by the talk of racial quotas and by the Motorola case, had demanded as the price of passage that such a model of compensatory or preferential affirmative action be prohibited by the statute. The Senate, though sharply divided over the civil rights bill, was virtually unanimous in agreeing that any civil rights act must prohibit the use of group-based, equal-results approaches in civil rights enforcement. As a result, all four steps required for an equal-results transformation faced statutory barriers in Title 7. On the question of discriminatory intent versus harmful effect, Title 7 required that the courts find that a respondent "has intentionally engaged" in an unlawful employment practice. As Hubert Humphrey explained to his Senate colleagues: "The express requirement of intent is designed to make it wholly clear that inadvertent or accidental discriminations will not violate the title or result in entry of court orders. It means simply that the respondent must have intended to discriminate."[8]

As for a proportional model and compensatory remedies in fair-employment law, Title 7 prohibited any requirement of "preferential treatment to any individual or to any group" because of race, color, religion, sex, or national origin, or on account of "an imbalance which may exist" in their numbers or percentages relative to nonminorities. "Title 7 prevents discrimination," Humphrey had assured the Senate in the spring of 1964, trying to dispatch what he called the false "bugaboo" of racial quotas. "It says that race, religion, and national origin are not to be used as the basis for hiring and firing."[9] The EEOC's legal staff, after months of research on Title 7's web of authority and constraints, found no ambiguity in its commands: "By the explicit terms of Section 703(j)," observed a brief in the EEOC's office of legal counsel, "an employer cannot be found in violation of Title 7 simply because his use of minority groups does not mirror their representation in the community." Hence an employer "is not required to redress an imbalance in his work force which is the result of past discrimination." "Under the literal language of Title 7," the analysis concluded, "the only actions required by a covered employer are to post notices, and not to discriminate subsequent to July 2, 1965."[10]

The reference to July 2, 1965, had a dual meaning. That was the date set by Congress in the Civil Rights Act for Title 7 to take effect and the EEOC's authority to begin. But it also represented a grandfathering-in of past discrimination—a historical statute of limitations. Congress wanted to make a clean break with the past, to start with a clean slate, to prevent a sea of charges and litigation that spun endlessly backward into allegations of past wrongdoing. It was partly for this reason that Congress excluded suits for damages in Title 7, and limited relief to hiring, reinstatement, and back pay. The Civil Rights Act had been southern-focused, and suits against the past sins of Jim Crow could consume endless energy and expense. The limit on retroactivity was a device that Congress had periodically used in regulatory and administrative statutes to enforce a forward-looking perspective (and to allay political fears of retroactive punishment). For proponents of an equal-results standard, however, the 1965 cutoff date in the Civil Rights Act had the effect of sealing off the *historical* argument that was crucial to an effects test. "Institutional racism" was a socio-cultural model that required historical incubation. How could past discrimination be documented if history only legally began in 1965? And even if the EEOC could somehow bring off the first three changes—substitute a historically based effects test for the intent standard, demonstrate statistically a "disparate impact," and devise compensatory remedies calculated to make job distribution proportional to minority populations—where would it find the authority to enforce them?

Only a subsequent Congress or the federal courts could fundamentally change Title 7's assignment of functions, duties, and limits for the EEOC. But the EEOC, like all agencies of the "permanent" government, enjoyed certain advantages in the normal politics of bureaucratic aggrandizement over the temporary government of the President and his appointees, and also over Congress. As a regulatory agency, albeit an unusually circumscribed one, the EEOC would be expected to formulate certain rules and regulations to guide the behavior of those within its jurisdiction. It was entirely normal behavior for a government agency to seek leverage and freedom of manuever by broadly interpreting its enabling legislation. This was especially critical (but also potentially dangerous) for a new regulatory agency when the stakes were high and passions were aroused.[11] Few new agencies in American government have been as alienated as the EEOC by the statutory constraints of their creation, and hence few have been as subversive of their founding charter. Most bureaucracies, however, have used broad construction to enhance their power. And so the EEOC, so weakly armed for so mighty a battle, maneuvered internally to deal itself a stronger hand.

From Retail to Wholesale Enforcement: A Southern Strategy

The early EEOC commissioners and staff were neither united nor prescient enough to agree on a master plan of attack that would subvert their restrictive charter. Rather, a rough blueprint emerged during 1965–68 through a trial-and-error process, one that paralleled and was accelerated by the agency's groping for a consensual approach to sex discrimination. A similar dialectic was occurring elsewhere in government, especially in new civil rights sub-agencies like the Office of Civil Rights in HEW and the Office of Federal Contract Compliance Programs (OFCC) in the Labor Department.[12] In a parallel process, clientele groups in the civil rights community were solidifying relationships with the sympathetic new agencies in a time-honored courtship of American government. At the EEOC, the meshing of the civil rights lobby and the new civil rights bureaucracy was accelerated in the summer of 1967 when President Johnson, while Detroit was burning, appointed a young, black, White House staffer, Clifford L. Alexander, Jr., as chairman of the EEOC.

When Shulman announced in March 1967 that he would only continue as EEOC chairman through the completion that July of Roosevelt's initial two-year term, Johnson realized that the time for minority leadership had arrived. The departure of Aileen Hernandez in late 1966 had left Samuel Jackson as the only black commissioner. But Jackson was a Republican. A lawyer and former head of the NAACP chapter in Topeka, Kansas, Jackson was also regarded by the Johnson White House as too closely tied to the politics of the NAACP.[13] When no "name" black Democrats would agree to leave their judgeships or professional practices to risk the crossfire in such a weakly armed agency, Johnson agreed reluctantly to appoint his only black aide. Alexander's credentials were gold-plated: Harvard *cum laude* in 1955, Yale law degree, army veteran, New York law practice (including Harlem youth work), National Security Council staff under Kennedy (a Harvard connection through McGeorge Bundy), White House counsel under Johnson.[14]

Under Alexander's leadership, the EEOC pursued four lines of activity that gradually converged to produce a new strategy. The goal was to substitute an equal-results standard for Congress's equal-treatment rationale. The four areas of policy development were conciliation, data-gathering, hearings, and rule-making. Looking back at this extraordinary turn-around from the perspective of the 1990s, the EEOC's strategic plan looks more coherent than it appeared during the late 1960s to its embattled architects. In the beginning the commission worked dutifully through the Johnson administration to win cease-and-desist power from Congress. When this failed, however, and Congress showed little interest in modifying its basic design of 1964, the EEOC turned increasingly toward the regulatory practice of issuing rules and guidelines. The confrontation with the feminists in setting policy for classified listings, airline stewardesses, and state-protection laws had taught the commission that rule-making can greatly enhance an agency's authority as well as its effectiveness. A corollary benefit of rule-making was that federal courts had historically granted great deference to the expertise of the independent regulatory commissions. As the Warren Court accelerated its intervention in policies as varied as political apportionment, the rights of the accused, school integration, privacy rights, and school prayer, the EEOC looked increasingly toward the courts to grant it the power that Congress had denied. In the process the EEOC developed its own version of the Southern Strategy—a polar opposite of the regional politics of Richard Nixon.

The potential of conciliation was the first policy arena to be tested, and this predated Alexander's arrival. Conciliating complaints was after all the EEOC's clearest assignment. From the beginning the agency had resented this function and starved it of resources. But a huge conciliation settlement in the spring of 1966, in which the EEOC teamed up with the departments of Justice, Labor, and Defense, demonstrated the potential of building precedents by attacking extreme examples of racial discrimination in the South. The settlement involved the giant shipyard at Newport News, Virginia, the largest employer in the state and a major builder of naval warships. Of the shipyard's 22,000 workers, 5000 were black. Like Lockheed-Marietta in the early 1960s, the Newport News shipyard mirrored its southern environment by discriminating systematically against black workers. But also like Lockheed, the shipyard seemed to welcome external pressures to change. As a builder of atomic submarines, its ties to the U.S. military establishment were far too crucial to risk defending the South's Jim Crow traditions. So in 1966 the shipbuilding company agreed to promote 3,890 of its black workers, and also to designate 100 blacks to become supervisors.[15]

The settlement at Newport News came at an opportune time for the EEOC. Hammered by the feminist attacks, the agency needed a victory. But the shipyard victory was deceptive. Newport News had been an easy target. Moreover, the government's big guns were held by contract compliance authorities from the Pentagon and the Labor Department, backed by the Justice Department, operating under Title 6 and President Johnson's Executive Order 11246 of 1965, not by the EEOC and its conciliation popgun under Title 7. The lesson of Newport

News was not that the EEOC would find success through conciliation agreements. This was what Congress had intended in 1964, but the commission itself was developing a more ambitious agenda. Rather, the Newport News settlement taught the EEOC that the South's segregated past carried present consequences that Title 7's cutoff date of 1965 could not erase. The shipyard settlement provided a promising precedent: a racist institutional past was linked by job statistics to disproportional employment patterns, and the remedy required compensatory relief for racial minorities through numerical quotas.

A second component of the EEOC strategy was to maintain a nationwide data bank on jobs and minorities. The EEOC overcame early impediments to minority record-keeping by following the precedents of the PCEEO and the lead of the federal courts, which were requiring racial reporting in school desegregation cases. The goal of the commission's national reporting scheme was to provide a unique *middle* level of employment data. For the first time this would permit comparisons of minority employment patterns between geographic areas and within specific industries. The EEOC's individual complaints already provided *micro*-level data. But they were unsystematic and episodic, and permitted only crude generalizations. The Bureau of Labor Statistics, on the other hand, long had provided *macro*-level data on employment trends, which the Bureau derived from national surveys of approximately 50,000 households. These surveys could reveal, for example, that in 1966 the proportion of whites in managerial jobs in the U.S. was 15 percent and in technical/professional jobs it was 12 percent, whereas for blacks it was only 5 percent for both categories.[16] But individual complaints at the bottom and nationwide surveys at the top could not show what the EEOC needed in the middle. The EEOC needed to demonstrate *industry-specific* patterns, such as the distribution by race, ethnicity, and sex of workers in the electrical and aerospace industry in Los Angeles, or in railroad employment in Cleveland, airlines in Atlanta, or retail trade and medical services in New York. Beginning in 1967, the commission's new minority-employment reports began to provide the answers.

In 1967 the EEOC used Shulman's computer systems to analyze EEO forms from 43,000 American businesses with 26 million employees, and from 52,000 union locals representing 16 million workers. The results showed that blacks disproportionately worked in blue-collar jobs throughout the nation, and especially in the South. In metropolitan Atlanta, for example, blacks were 23 percent of the population but held 33.8 percent of the blue-collar jobs. In New Orleans blacks were 30.7 percent of the population and 44.8 percent of the blue-collar workforce. In Chicago, blacks were 14 percent of the population but held 20.6 percent of the blue-collar jobs.[17] Blacks and Hispanics were blue-collar workers in an economy that was beginning to move away from blue-collar jobs.

The most striking result of the statistical study, however, was its demonstration by area and industry of minority underrepresentation in *white*-collar jobs. These were jobs with a future, most of them in the technical and service enterprises where the economy would grow. In Kansas City, blacks were 11.2

percent of the population but only 2.1 percent of the white-collar workforce; in Cleveland, the black 13 percent of the population held 3.2 percent of the white-collar jobs. Moreover, within those white-collar categories most blacks were either in low-paying clerical and sales positions or they worked as hospital orderlies in growth businesses like health services. In Chicago, for example, where blacks held only 4.7 percent of white-collar jobs, 80 percent of these were low-paying service jobs. In certain industries blacks held only a tiny share of white-collar jobs: 2.8 percent in the aerospace industry in Los Angeles, 1 percent in air travel in Atlanta, 0.7 percent in Cleveland railroads.[18]

A series of regional hearings, the third activity in the EEOC's four-pronged approach, confirmed the pattern seen in the agency's statistical studies. Together they reinforced the agency's hope that the South could supply the ammunition to attack the nationwide problem. The most pressing problem in the South was black access to better blue-collar jobs, including promotion and transfer out of dead-end Jim Crow jobs. Fortunately for the EEOC and its minority constituency, the history of segregation guaranteed that most southern employers would find no effective defense to black challenges. For this reason the racial barriers were rapidly falling throughout the South—accelerated, where necessary, by Justice Department suits. Opportunities for Negroes would expand rapidly in the South because the walls of segregation had excluded them so massively for so long. But the EEOC's toughest assignments lay to the north and west.

The commission's experience with regional hearings reinforced the lesson that the EEOC's most ambitious targets lay outside the South. The first hearing was held in Charlotte, North Carolina, in January 1967. The commission chose the Carolina piedmont to expose the discriminatory labor practices of the area's notorious textile industry. But most of the textile companies, fearing a witch-hunt, refused to testify (the EEOC, unlike most regulatory agencies, lacked the power of subpoena), and the hearings were hostile and unproductive. Privately, EEOC officials conceded that the textile industry was a low-wage, contracting, technically backward sector that scarcely typified the country's employment problems or opportunities.[19]

By 1968 the EEOC had shifted the focus of its hearings to white-collar discrimination in the North and West. In January 1968, Alexander chaired a widely publicized hearing in New York City, where black workers for more than two decades had been protected by the granddaddy of all state FEPCs. The EEOC's annually updated statistics revealed that blacks were 11.5 percent of New York's metropolitan population but held only 5.7 percent of the white-collar jobs. Of the 4,249 New York firms reporting statistics to the EEOC, 1,827 reported no black employees at all, and 1,936 reported no Hispanics. Only 3.5 percent of the 35,819 employees in New York's securities and brokerage businesses were black, and blacks held only 2 percent of white-collar jobs in the city's booming air travel business. Similar hearings in San Francisco and Los Angeles in 1969 produced similar findings of minority underrepresentation in the service and technical jobs where pay was high and the economy was growing.

From Equal Treatment to Equal Results: A Judicial Strategy

The final hurdle was the EEOC's most difficult. This was the move to a statistically based "effects" standard that would ground its affirmative-action remedies in a proportional model of the workforce. By 1968 this had become the EEOC's governing legal strategy. But the agency had prudently kept a low profile on the matter so as not to alarm conservative critics. The commission's supporters in the civil rights coalition justified its quiet rejection of Title 7's intent standard with a kind of higher-law doctrine. The overarching social goal of the Civil Rights Act, they argued, must override specific restrictions in Title 7 that defeat its broader purpose. Commissioner Jackson explained to NAACP members in 1968 that the "EEOC has taken its interpretation of Title 7 a step further than other agencies."[20] The Civil Rights Act banned not only racial discrimination per se, Jackson said, but also employer practices "which prove to have a demonstrable racial effect." "The underlying rationale for this position," he said, "has been that Congress, with its elaborate exploration of the economic plight of the minority worker, sought to establish a comprehensive instrument with which to adjust the needless hardships resulting from the arbitrary operation of personnel practices, as well as purposeful discrimination." "This approach would seem to disregard intent," Jackson conceded, "as crucial to the finding of an unlawful employment practice." The EEOC's *Administrative History* confirmed the strategic switch: "Unlike state FEP agencies which continue to rely on intent, the Commission has begun to rely on the constructive proof of discrimination."[21] By "constructive proof" the agency meant demonstrations of statistical imbalance or disparate impact.

The EEOC's switch to an effects standard, with its implication of group remedies and minority preferences, was at bottom a gamble on intervention by the federal courts. Congress showed no interest in revising its great concordat of 1964. But the federal bench under the Warren Court had shown a growing willingness to reconstruct or disregard congressional intent in the interest of broader social purposes.[22] The challenge for the EEOC would be to use the South's racist history to present sympathetic federal judges with egregious examples of what Lyndon Johnson, in his Howard commencement address of 1965, had described as the unfair footrace between the hardy and the lame. Given the leverage offered by rule-making, which the EEOC had learned from its unsteady performance in the sex-discrimination rulings, and given the judiciary's traditional deference to the expertise of regulatory agencies, two areas of rule-making looked most promising. One was employee testing. The other was seniority.

Congress in the Civil Rights Act had been careful to exempt from the statute standard employee tests and seniority systems. Both practices were widely used and defended in American business and labor relations. But the two practices also tended to freeze-in historical disadvantages and to punish innocent victims of past discrimination. The seniority system, especially in the South, grandfathered-in the pre-1964 white monopoly on the best jobs. When veteran Negro workers subsequently moved into higher-paying job classifications, they sank to the bottom of the job-specific seniority lists.[23] Testing froze the clock somewhat less dramatically, but perhaps more persistently, because it reflected the results of generations of Jim Crow schooling. The EEOC concentrated its early challenges on seniority practices in the South because their unfairness seemed self-evident and their impact was more direct. Because Title 7 prohibited the EEOC from bringing suit, its lawyers filed friend-of-the-court briefs to support minority workers, whose suits against seniority systems and testing practices were typically sponsored by NAACP lawyers or the Justice Department itself. But it was a challenge over testing, not seniority, that eventually won the EEOC the jackpot. In 1968, this stunning victory—the Supreme Court's *Griggs* decision—was still a few years away. What was more pressing for the agenda of the civil rights coalition in 1968 was an unanticipated breakthrough in housing discrimination, coming to a climax against a background of renewed urban rioting in the wake of the murder of Martin Luther King.

The Strange Career of the Open Housing Act of 1968

Given the rejection by Congress in 1966 and 1967 or President Johnson's civil rights proposals, no significant civil rights legislation was expected to pass in 1968. Congress-watchers agreed that by 1968 the coalition of northern Democrats and moderate Republicans, which had been essential to passing the laws of 1964 and 1965, was in disarray.[24] Senator Dirksen continued to oppose empowering federal officials to police the motives of sellers and renters of housing. The House in the 90th Congress was in a more conservative mood. Similarly, the public seemed disinclined to "reward" the Detroit rioters of 1967. Congressmen running for re-election in 1968, mindful of the results of 1966, were wary about issues like open housing and equal employment enforcement, where the southern, Jim Crow focus of the crusade of 1964–65 was lacking. In his civil rights message to Congress on January 24, 1968, Johnson merely reiterated his request of 1967: cease-and-desist authority for the EEOC and an open-housing law, plus two lesser measures—protection of civil rights workers and nondiscrimination in federal and state juries. Congress seemed uninterested. Nevertheless, Congress should pass these bills, Johnson said, "because it is decent and right."[25]

Then in a rapid and surprising sequence of events, the Senate took up the fair-housing bill in early February 1968, voted to shut off a southern filibuster on March 4, and sent the bill to the House. On April 10 the House agreed to accept the entire Senate bill in order to avoid the dangers of a conference, and President Johnson signed the bill into law the following day. It was an astonishing turnaround.

Early in February 1968, Senator Walter Mondale (D-Minn.) revived the administration's open housing bill of 1967 by introducing it as an amendment to a bill to protect civil rights workers, which the administration had requested in early 1967 and the Senate Judiciary Committee had approved in November. Mondale's open-housing amendment was co-sponsored by Republican Edward W. Brooke of Massachusetts, the Senate's only black member, and was supported by the usual bipartisan coalition of liberal northern senators, but not by Dirksen. The amendment produced the expected filibuster on the merits, led by Ervin, and as late as February 19 the *Wall Street Journal* was referring to "the almost certainly doomed bill banning racial discrimination in housing."[26]

On February 20, however, a surprisingly close cloture vote showed the Senate's Republicans to be evenly split over the open-housing bill—although they had twice voted heavily against cloture, at Dirksen's behest, in the open-housing debate of 1966. This reflected an important development in the reputedly more conservative 90th Congress. The gain of 47 seats in 1966 had strengthened the conservative Republican bloc in the House, now newly led by minority leader Gerald Ford of Michigan. But the Republicans' three-seat gain in the Senate had not correspondingly increased that chamber's conservatism. The growth of two-party politics in the South, the liberalism of urban voters generally in the 1960s, and the higher turnover of senators was reversing an historic pattern by turning the Senate into a more liberal chamber than the House. As a consequence, Dirksen's Republican colleagues in the Senate were more willing to support a compromise open-housing bill than were Ford's House Republicans.[27]

The result of these circumstances was another famous, eleventh-hour, Dirksen switch and bipartisan compromise to save the civil rights bill. Dirksen offered an amended version of the bill that would cover an estimated 80 percent of all housing, compared with Mondale's 90 percent. By exempting single-family, owner-occupied housing if it was sold or rented by the owner rather than real estate brokers or agents, Dirksen shielded "Mrs. Murphy's boarding house"—a Republican symbol of rectitude, entrepreneurial independence, and right to privacy from government bureaucrats. The Dirksen compromise's Republican trimming on coverage was modest, and Walter Mondale called the revised bill "a miracle." Dirksen explained his sudden discovery that a federal open housing law wasn't unconstitutional after all by observing modestly: "One would be a strange creature indeed in this world of mutation if in the face of reality, he did not change his mind."[28]

Dirksen was a master at capturing public attention, and in the spring of 1968 he concentrated on the question of coverage and the plight of Mrs. Murphy. But more important than the coverage formula was the enforcement provision. The Johnson administration's original bill had avoided creating a new enforcement agency, like an EEOC for Housing. In 1967 Representative John Conyers of Detroit, a black Democrat, had sponsored such a provision in the House with the backing of the Leadership Conference. But Johnson's congressional nose-counters had early concluded that neither chamber of Congress would accept an administrative policeman for housing discrimination. Instead, the administration's 1967 bill gave enforcement to the secretary of Housing and Urban Development (HUD), armed with a modified version of cease-and-desist authority. But like the House Republicans, Dirksen objected to a coercive model, where an administrative agency in Washington would police America's local housing sales with a cease-and-desist club. So Dirksen's compromise of 1968, echoing the events of 1964, repeated the enforcement mode of Title 7. The right to nondiscrimination in housing would be declared national policy, and housing discrimination would everywhere become a crime. But judges, not Washington bureaucrats, would determine guilt and punish offenders.

The new national right to fair housing would be, like the right to nondiscriminatory employment, more a private than a public right. It would be enforceable primarily by citizen complaints and suits in court. In those suits the 1968 law stipulated that the "burden of proof shall be on the complainant."[29] The HUD secretary, like the EEOC, would receive complaints, hold hearings, and seek compliance through conciliation. Also like Title 7, the Dirksen-compromised housing bill would empower the Attorney General to sue on behalf of citizens where he found a "pattern or practice" of housing discrimination. This compromise made the right to nondiscriminatory housing, like Title 7's fair-employment right, a public right (with tax dollars providing government lawyers to represent the complainants) to the extent that the Attorney General was willing to devote Justice Department resources to suing major offenders.[30]

With Dirksen and the Republicans aligned behind the compromise bill, the Senate on March 4 voted cloture by precisely two-thirds in a 65-32 roll-call vote, and on March 11, following a lively amending process on the floor that concentrated on anti-riot provisions, the Senate passed the bill by a roll-call vote of 71-20. This plunged the House into a debate over whether to vote directly on the Senate bill, which the administration and the House Democratic leadership favored, or to send it to conference, where it might die. Both major Republican presidential candidates in 1968, Nelson Rockefeller and Richard Nixon, urged accepting the Senate version. The procedural debate was shattered when an assassin gunned downed Martin Luther King in Memphis on April 4.

Since early March, when Johnson had surprised the nation by withdrawing from the presidential campaign, King had been working with striking sanitation workers in Memphis. When reports raced through black neighborhoods throughout the nation that King had been murdered by a white man, riots broke out in 130 American cities and towns. The most destructive was in Washington, D.C., closely matched by nearby Baltimore. The Washington riot cost nine lives, and the national toll was 46, all but five of them black. Nationwide, some 2600 fires caused property damage of more than $100 million, and disorders led to 20,000 police arrests and involved 130,000 troops and national guardsmen. In the emotional aftermath of King's murder, the House accepted without amendment the Senate version of the open-housing bill on April 10, by a roll-call vote of 250-172, and thereby avoided a conference committee. Lyndon Johnson, who had pushed the bill for 27 months and had fought for it effectively despite his lame-duck status as President, signed it into law the following day.

The Lessons of 1968

The Open Housing Act of 1968 had been regarded as something of a fluke, an exception to the watershed rule that the Watts riot of 1965 and the Black Power surge of 1966 divided the reforms of 1964–65 from the racial backlash of the late 1960s. At the grass-roots level of public opinion and social movements, the discontinuity between the decade's two halves was obvious and profound. But at the level of political leadership in the presidency and Congress, the discontinuity obscures common elements that link the civil rights laws of 1964, 1965, and 1968. All three reforms were race-centered (the voting-rights and fair-housing laws had no gender focus at all, since unlike racial and ethnic minorities, women did not live and vote in women's neighborhoods). All were grounded in liberalism's command not to discriminate. All bore the stamp of a distinctive Johnson-Dirksen compromise. The Open Housing Act, like the Civil Rights Act, denied coercive authority to the specialized enforcing agency (the EEOC and HUD) and restrained their enforcement budgets.[31] Both laws, like the Voting Rights Act, reserved enforcement teeth to the Justice Department, which was less likely than administrative agencies to be captured by interest groups.

Over-all, the record of the 90th Congress in social policy did not differ sharply from that of the 89th, despite all the references to conservative "backlash" in the news media. In his study of the political impact of the 1960s riots, political scientist James W. Button concluded that despite the rhetoric of backlash, the federal government expanded its redistributionist social programs throughout the Johnson administration.[32] The shift of public opinion against the Great Society's anti-poverty war, Button said, came only after the outbreak of student and anti-war violence in 1968–69 that led into the Nixon administration. Congress in 1968 passed, in addition to the open housing bill, a $5.3 billion National Housing Act that included controversial federal subsidies for low-income ownership, rent supplements, and model cities programs. The Senate in 1968 made its decision to pass the fair-housing law *before* King's assassination and the race riots it sparked. Congress in 1968 was persuaded by the argument of the Johnson White House, and especially by Roy Wilkins and Clarence Mitchell of the NAACP, that failure to pass a fair-housing bill would fuel black nationalist appeals for separatism. It is true that the Open Housing Act was by far the least effective of the three landmark civil rights laws of the Kennedy-Johnson years.[33] But at the level of government, the most important discontinuity in the 1960s is not found in the presidency or the Congress, or even in the federal courts. Rather, it lies in the ironic reversals of the goals and means sought by the organized spokesmen for blacks and women, and translated into administrative policy by enforcement agencies.

The travail of the EEOC provides a window on this obscure, inner world of the bureaucracy in connecting ends to means in social policy. In 1964 and 1965, Congress finally agreed with the liberal coalition that the Constitution was color-blind, and that discrimination because of race was therefore illegal. As a consequence the legal basis of southern segregation was nullified in 1964 and the political defenses of black disfranchisement were destroyed in 1965. But the EEOC, frustrated by the limits of nondiscrimination in an era of racial violence, had switched by 1968 to color-conscious remedies to support an equal-results standard. Because the EEOC lacked both the authority to adopt such a standard and the power to enforce it, the agency's quiet turnaround remained an abstraction. Beyond the clientele-group network that linked the EEOC to the major civil rights organizations, the Leadership Conference, and the state and municipal EEO professionals, the commission's reversal of strategy went largely unnoticed by the public and the media.

On the gender side of the EEO enforcement ledger, however, the trajectory of policy had been in an opposite direction. When the 1960s began, the debate among women still centered on gender differences, as it had for half a century, and the dominant voices defended protectionist policies that hinged on these differences. By 1966 the feminist movement was in full mobilization, and the fight over EEOC policies accelerated the transition from difference-based policies to an equal-treatment standard for women. By 1968 the EEOC had abandoned its early waffling with BFOQs and sex-segregated classified ads, and was requiring equal treatment for women virtually across the board.

Thus by 1968 both black and feminist leaders in the major lobbying organizations had won the EEOC to their view. Because feminist leaders had supported the Negro protest movement and had used the race-sex analogy to win equal priority with blacks in enforcement, the American public tended to equate the liberationist goals and strategies of blacks and women. But the underlying philosophical reversals of both groups, passing like trains in the night, led toward different political strategies. Partisans of an equal-results standard for minorities found no comfort in Title 7 and little sympathy in Congress. The federal courts, however, were moving toward race-conscious remedies in school desegregation, and this line of reasoning offered a path to empowerment for enforcement agencies like the EEOC.

For feminist groups the reverse was true. The federal judiciary's expansion of minority rights for racial and ethnic groups under the Constitution's 5th and 14th amendments was matched by no hint that the judges might find in the same amendments any authority or obligation to require equal rights for women. Congress, on the other hand, showed signs of wavering in its traditional opposition to the Equal Rights Amendment—just as women's groups, Democrats and Republicans alike, were uniting in their demand for it. Conveniently, 1968 offered a bellwether of political trends: a three-way presidential election with no incumbent among the contenders.

CHAPTER 8

The Nixon Presidency:
Domestic Policy and Divided Government

*The Resurrection of Richard Nixon: Realignment for the
"Silent Majority"*

When Richard Nixon re-entered the presidential competition in 1968, he was a two-time loser. After his presidential defeat by Kennedy he returned to California, where in 1962 he ran for governor against the lackluster incumbent, Democrat Edmund "Pat" Brown. Nixon's gubernatorial campaign resurrected the anti-communist themes that had worked for him in California during the congressional races of 1946–50. By the early 1960s, however, the threat of domestic communism stirred little interest among California voters. Nixon's red-baiting revived the unsavory, "Tricky Dick" image of his races against Democrats Jerry Voorhis for a House seat in 1946 and Helen Gahagan Douglas for the Senate in 1950. California voters responded by re-electing Brown with a 300,000-vote majority. Embittered by the results, Nixon emerged from an election-night vigil, exhausted and hung-over, to tell reporters that they would not have "Nixon to kick around anymore, because, gentlemen, this is my last press conference."[1]

The defeat in California removed Nixon from the presidential field in 1964, when he might have reclaimed his party's nomination as the sitting governor of California. Nixon's loss in 1962 thus seemed a disguised blessing; as Goldwater led the Republicans to electoral catastrophe in the fall of 1964, Nixon supported his party dutifully, but kept his distance from Goldwater's more extreme positions. During the years of Johnson's presidency Nixon stumped the country tirelessly on behalf of Republican candidates for Congress and state office. By 1968 he had earned a comeback opportunity. But the political odds were steep: his party had been humiliated in the Goldwater debacle of 1964; Democrats held a 3-to-2 advantage in national voter indentification; and in Congress, Democrats outnumbered Republicans, 64-36 in the Senate and 248-187 in the House.

Yet by 1968 Nixon was convinced that the Democrats' New Deal coalition, which Kennedy had narrowly held together to beat him in 1960, was disintegrating. Nixon's goal was to preside, as President, over a realignment in American politics that would return the Republican party, during the last third of the century, to the position of "normal" majority it had enjoyed during the first third of the century. In the late 1960s the Roosevelt coalition, like American society generally, was fragmenting in confusion. The party's cracks were widening into a fault line that divided the Democratic constituencies on the left—organized labor, black and Hispanic minorities, academics, the literary and artistic avant-garde, anti-war groups—from those on the right. Nixon targeted for defection two large constituencies from the Democrats' center-right: middle-class white Protestants in the South, where the higher-income suburbs were already going Republican, and in the North, the disaffected voters in lower-middle-class ethnic neighborhoods, especially Catholics of eastern European origin.

Nixon and his campaign lieutenants—Wall Street lawyer John Mitchell, Los Angeles public-relations executive H.R. "Bob" Haldeman, Seattle zoning lawyer John Ehrlichman—called these voters the "forgotten Americans." As beneficiaries of New Deal security and postwar prosperity, these middle-class voters believed in the work ethic that validated the American dream. Their memories of the 1950s inspired pride rather than apologies, and they resented the trends of the 1960s—urban rioting, disrespect for the flag, the arrogance of the youthful counterculture, the solicitude of the courts for the rights of criminals. Kevin Phillips, a young political analyst for the Republicans, described these "Middle Americans" with hopeful prophecy in the title of his 1969 book, *The Emerging Republican Majority*.[2] To pollsters Richard Scammon and Ben Wattenberg, they were *The Real Majority*—"unyoung, unpoor, unblack."[3] Most of them had grown up in families with Democratic loyalties. But by the late 1960s the Democratic party seemed to these voters to have adopted as clients the groups that symbolized what was wrong with America—rioting blacks, draft-dodgers, rebellious youth, the able-bodied on the dole. America had not been like this under Eisenhower.

By August 1968, when the Democratic national convention met in Chicago to nominate Vice President Humphrey and his running-mate, Senator Edmund Muskie of Maine, the nation was reeling from a series of shocks and calamities: the Tet Offensive of January, Johnson's withdrawal from the presidential race in March, King's assassination and the burning and looting of the national capital in April, the squalor of the Poor People's March and "Resurrection City" in Washington in May, and Robert Kennedy's assassination in June. From Chicago, television captured the symbols of Democratic turmoil—street violence, public obscenity, Hippies and Yippies, revolutionary blacks. The party of Roosevelt seemed to have lost its bearings, its self-composure, its dignity.[4]

The Election of 1968: Issue Realignment and Divided Government

As the leading Republican presidential candidate in 1968, Richard Nixon was well positioned to profit from the Democrats' self-destruction. Experienced in high office and in world affairs, Nixon enjoyed a weak association with the crusades in Vietnam, in race relations, and in anti-poverty warfare that were bringing down the Johnson administration. Nixon intended to keep his distance from the controversial issues that were splintering the Democratic coalition. During the spring he danced cautiously around the dangerous open housing issue, generally avoiding the topic while the bill was pending in Congress. Then after the assassination of King and the passage of the fair-housing law, Nixon told delegates at the Republican convention in Miami in August that the prudent course had been to "vote for it and get it out of the way . . . to get the civil rights and open housing issues out of our sight so we didn't have a split party over the platform when we came down here to Miami Beach."[5] Nixon knew that the racial issue was dangerous, that if played with too heavy a hand, it could split the coalition of moderates and conservatives on which his presidential ambitions hinged.[6] During the Senate debate over civil rights in 1964, Nixon had called the bill "a step forward if it is administered effectively."[7] In 1966 he warned a meeting of the party faithful in Jackson, Mississippi, that there was "no future in the race issue" for the Republican party.[8]

Yet Nixon owed his nomination in 1968 to southern Republicans who preferred him to northern liberals like governors Nelson Rockefeller of New York and George Romney of Michigan or Senator William Percy of Illinois, and who feared that they could not win with their real favorite, Ronald Reagan.[9] Political commentators reached an early consensus that Nixon's campaign manager, his law partner John Mitchell, had engineered a "Southern Strategy" with Republican Senator Strom Thurmond of South Carolina, and that Nixon had pledged to repay the debt by curbing federal pressures for school desegregation and by appointing southern conservatives to the Supreme Court.

Nixon's Southern Strategy, however, was really a border strategy. His overtures were directed not toward the Deep South that Goldwater had carried, but rather toward the Rim South as symbolic of Middle America. Nixon selected as his running-mate Maryland's governor, Spiro Agnew. A former county executive, Agnew symbolized the upward mobility of ethnic voters from Democratic city machines to suburban Republicanism. More important, Agnew was a caustic critic of rioters and flag-burners. As governor in 1968, Agnew had chastised Maryland's Negro leaders for remaining silent while Baltimore blacks burned and looted their city in the wake of King's assassination. Agnew was Nixon's hitman, as vice-presidential candidates often are; his main target was of course Humphrey and the Democrats, but his chief competition, in bidding for the votes of disaffected blue-collar Democrats, was George Wallace.[10]

In 1964, Wallace's protest candidacy against the Johnson administration had shown surprising strength with ethnic voters in Democratic primaries in Wisconsin, Indiana, and Maryland. In 1968, Wallace formed the American Independent party to carry nationwide his attacks against school busing for racial balance, criminal-coddling judges, draft-dodging students, flag-burning radicals, "pointy-headed" intellectuals. By the mid-summer of 1968, polls showed Wallace winning 20 percent of the vote. "There's not a dime's worth of difference" between the Democrats and the Republicans, Wallace said. Agnew countered by denouncing "phony intellectuals . . . who don't understand what we mean by patriotism and hard work."[11] Wallace was a greater threat to Nixon than to Humphrey, because the Wallace protest appealed especially to disaffected lower-middle-class whites whose traditional ties to the Democratic party were breaking.[12] In the South, Wallace voters had been blasted loose from their loyalty to the party of Roosevelt by the Goldwater campaign of 1964. Goldwater's electoral disaster of 1964 had thus provided a shock that accelerated realignment in the South. In the North, the Wallace voters of 1968 had generally been supporters of Kennedy and Johnson. But they could no longer stomach the Democratic party of Hubert Humphrey.[13]

In 1968, Nixon ran a campaign that was richly financed, measured in pace and tone, and largely issueless. Although his chief interest and claim to expertise lay in foreign affairs, on the most burning issue of the day, the war in Vietnam, Nixon said little. To do otherwise, he explained, might jeopardize the peace negotiations being conducted in Paris. Stressing the dignity of his experience rather than the substantive issues of debate, Nixon appealed in broad terms to the "silent majority" who paid their taxes and did not riot. To Nixon these Middle Americans included middle-class Negroes with a stake in society, and to them he pledged a program of "black capitalism." On civil rights issues he had little to say beyond the customary nostrums—it was a time for moderation and healing, for rejecting the extremes of racial segregation and forced busing, for trying to make the existing laws work rather than adding new ones. Otherwise, as President he would take charge in foreign affairs and let the cabinet preside over domestic programs.[14]

On November 5 Nixon won by a surprisingly small plurality. He received 43.4 percent of the three-party vote as against 42.7 percent for Humphrey and only 13.5 percent for George Wallace. Nixon won handily in the electoral college, with 301 votes to Humphrey's 191 and Wallace's 46. Wallace carried Alabama, Georgia, Louisiana, and Mississippi, while Nixon won most of the Great Plains, the Rocky Mountain states, and the Far West. Nixon enjoyed a half-million-vote margin over Humphrey in the South, although nine out of ten black votes went to Humphrey. Humphrey had rallied the Northeast, but, with the exception of Texas, he had lost the entire "Sunbelt"—a term that would gain currency in the 1970s to characterize the high-growth region stretching from Florida to California. The most telling indicator, however, that something new was happening in American political life was this: Nixon was the first candidate since Zachary Taylor in 1848 to win the presidency while his party failed to carry either the House or the Senate.

The party split between the White House and the Hill meant divided government—a phenomenon that was impossible in Europe's parliamentary systems, and that in the American presidential system had been regarded as an artifact of the immature, antebellum years. Its unexpected reappearance in 1968 raised the danger that partisan warfare could escalate into governmental paralysis. To this potentially troublesome novelty, the election of 1968 added another electoral shift, one whose dimension was obscured by the third-party

Wallace factor. In 1964, Johnson had won with approximately 61 percent of the presidential vote. Four years later Humphrey received 20 percent fewer votes. Thus the combined Nixon-Wallace vote in 1968 arguably represented a conservative majority of 57 percent. Absent the Wallace factor, Nixon's victory in 1968 appears in retrospect to have displaced the Democrats as the "normal" majority of American presidential contests.

Yet Nixon's election was scarcely a substantive mandate. With the Vietnam issue confusing normal voter behavior and with candidate Nixon proposing little more than opposition to crime and inflation, there seemed to be no clear domestic mandate at all. Moreover, Wallace remained the wild card, the potential spoiler in 1972 for Nixon's grand realignment. Wallace relished the spoiler role, and the shadow of his presence would condition Nixon's postures and policies in his first presidential term.

The Nixon White House and Domestic Policy: 1969

Immediately after the November election, Nixon asked Columbia University economist Arthur Burns to direct a series of planning task forces on domestic policy issues.[15] By 1968, task-force planning was a familiar component of presidential transitions. It helped the President-elect sort out priorities among campaign promises, shape the legislative agenda for the administration's first 100 days, and require the executive agencies to respond to the President's policy initiatives.[16] The Nixon campaign, however, was so vague that the Burns-led task forces could avoid volatile issues like civil rights, and concentrate instead on applying the principles of tighter management and orthodox Republican economics to discipline and reshape the organizational sprawl and fiscal disorderliness of the Great Society. A few symbolic and politically vulnerable programs of the Johnson legacy were recommended for the chopping block, like Model Cities and the Job Corps. But the Burns agenda represented no Republican counter-revolution, much as the Eisenhower agenda in 1953 had implied no repudiation of the New Deal. The chief recommendations in the Burns report to Nixon of January 18, such as revenue-sharing and block grants and streamlining the federal executive structure, marked a politically moderate and fiscally prudent program of Republican reform that could be hurt by a fight over social programs with a Democratic Congress.

Having outlined no domestic agenda during the presidential campaign, Nixon abandoned the customary practice in January of assessing the state of the union and announcing a new legislative program. Instead he planned a post-inaugural trip to Europe to try to arrange a face-saving end to the Vietnam war.[17] In his inaugural address on January 20, Nixon asked Americans to "stop shouting at one another" and give him a chance to honor America as peacemaker—a task he pursued by visiting Europe in February and March, and Asia in July and August.[18] By mid-March, however, grumbling was increasing from Republicans in Congress that the new administration had no clear legislative agenda. Nixon's first "Hundred Days" were characterized by globetrotting, not by introducing legislative programs. The White House sent Congress no major domestic proposals until the middle of April, when Nixon, prodded by Bryce Harlow, the head of congressional liaison on the White House staff, sent Congress a slapdash agenda for domestic legislation. Nixon's message to Congress of April 14 explained that his search for peace abroad and executive reorganizations at home had delayed his legislative proposals. He listed program intentions—but provided few details—in crime control, welfare, revenue-sharing, indexing Social Security payments against inflation, and providing new tax-credit incentives for business investment.[19]

Nixon's inattention to the substance of domestic policy was characteristic. As biographer Stephen Ambrose described Nixon's "basic domestic theme" in the launching of his presidency, "style was more important than substance, PR more important than action."[20] The result was an incoherent domestic agenda. Lacking any substantive theory of domestic policy, Nixon possessed no philosophical gyroscope or ideological predisposition with an identifiable core—certainly not the kind of conservative commitment that most Republicans in Congress expected. "Our troops across the nation are grumbling about the administration's 'liberal' direction," Bryce Harlow told the President during his first hundred days.[21] Columnists began to refer with puzzlement to Nixon's "Tory socialism." Nixon as congressman, Vice President, and as gubernatorial candidate had been a consistent red-baiting anti-communist, but as President he argued for détente with the Soviet Union and accommodation with Red China. Nixon as President supported social programs that shocked conservatives—a guaranteed annual income, large-scale federal aid for college students, the creation of the Environmental Protection Agency, and even a federal freeze on prices and wages.[22]

Policy Incoherence in Civil Rights

In civil rights policy, however, the reputation of Nixon's presidency was shaped from the beginning by journalists who emphasized the Southern Strategy. Throughout Nixon's first term the headlines featured his appeals to the politics of racial backlash. Nixon's cabinet was all-white, like Eisenhower's (and, unlike Eisenhower's, all-male as well). Nixon's sole campaign commitment of 1968 in response to the racial crisis had been to encourage "black capitalism," and his sole civil rights initiative during the hundred days was to issue an executive order on March 5 that created an Office of Minority Business Enterprise in the Department of Commerce.[23] The new OMBE, however, had no program budget and no authority. Instead it was directed to "coordinate" the efforts of 116 existing programs in 21 different agencies. Its tiny staff of ten professionals was buried in the Commerce Department. Nixon proposed no transfer of federal programs or agencies (which would have required agreement from Congress) to add muscle to the OMBE efforts, and asked for no new funds from Congress. To the dismay of Leonard Garment, the White House aide who coordinated minority affairs, the creation of the black-oriented

OMBE triggered a turf war with the Small Business Administration, led by a Hispanic, Hilary Sandoval.[24] The bureaucratic in-fighting over minority advantage was reported in the *Wall Street Journal* and further tarnished Nixon's singular, bargain-basement initiative. "Nothing much is happening," deadpanned Clarence Mitchell; "Black capitalism is a shambles," said Whitney Young."[25]

During the spring of 1969, while Nixon was traveling in Europe and the White House was struggling to sort out its domestic agenda, a series of events external to the White House increased the anxieties within the civil rights establishment about the administration's uncertain intentions. During Senate hearings in March over the contract compliance programs, Everett Dirksen threatened to use his influence with the White House to fire EEOC chairman Clifford Alexander, whom an increasingly ill-tempered (and profoundly ill) Dirksen accused of conducting "carnival-like hearings" that symbolized his agency's "punitive harassment" of businessmen.[26] On April 9, Alexander resigned as EEOC chairman, with a parting blast at the Nixon administration for its "crippling lack of support."[27] In early May the Civil Rights Commission released a study by consultant Richard P. Nathan, *Jobs and Civil Rights,* which the commission had funded two years earlier. Although all of Nathan's data predated the Nixon administration, the commission used the occasion of its release to attack the new administration as "seriously deficient" in enforcing the civil rights laws.[28]

In the area of school desegregation, Nixon's initial policies reinforced his image as architect of the Southern Strategy. During his first year in the White House, Nixon shifted the emphasis of federal policy in enforcing school desegregation away from fund cutoff under Title 6 of the Civil Rights Act and back to lawsuit-filing by the Justice Department.[29] At Nixon's insistence, HEW secretary Robert Finch reversed course in the fall of 1969 and asked the federal courts to *delay* desegregation requirements for 33 school districts in Mississippi. The request was rejected by Nixon's own first appointee to the Supreme Court, Chief Justice Warren Burger, who spoke for a unanimous Court. Virtually no observers, inside as well as outside the White House, expected the federal courts to reverse their stiffening requirements for school desegregation. But Nixon's shift from administrative to judicial enforcement in school desegregation was politically calculated to shift the onus of racial busing from the presidency to the courts.[30]

Also during his first year, Nixon nominated a southern conservative to the Supreme Court to replace Justice Abe Fortas, who had resigned under fire for financial improprieties. The nominee, Clement Haynsworth, was a wealthy South Carolinian, chief judge of the Fourth Circuit Court of Appeals, and a jurist whose opinions and scholarly writings had earned wide respect in the legal community. But Haynsworth's conservative rulings in civil rights cases and labor-management disputes drew opposition from the Leadership Conference, and the Democratic Senate, angered by the Republicans' successful attacks on Fortas, rejected Haynsworth in November 1969.[31] This infuriated Nixon, who in January 1970 compounded his problem with the opposition-led

Congress by nominating a federal appeals judge from Florida, G. Harrold Carswell, whose intellectual mediocrity and racist past drew a storm of protest that doomed the nomination.[32] Having fixed his image in the public eye as more sympathetic to the constituency of George Wallace than to that of the late Martin Luther King, Nixon heated up his anti-busing rhetoric during the first term, even to the point of proposing a constitutional amendment to prohibit busing for racial balance in the schools. Small wonder that the image of Nixon in civil rights memory summons the selection of Agnew, the payoff implicit in the Southern Strategy, the nomination of Carswell, the politically cynical proposal to trivialize the Constitution by adding an amendment about school buses.

Nixon's opposition to school busing for racial balance, while explainable as an electoral strategy in an era of backlash, was consistent with the standard Republican doctrine, as codified in the Dirksen compromises of 1964 and 1965, that rights inhered in individuals and not in groups, that nondiscrimination did not permit preferences or quotas for any race, and that the federal courts should not engage in social engineering. While attempting to shift from the presidency to the courts the onus of enforcing school desegregation in the southern and border states, Nixon hoped to protect northern suburban voters—typically Republicans—from judicial attacks on de facto segregation outside the South. As President he largely achieved both goals.

In the South, Nixon's reputation followed his anti-busing posture. Yet the reality was otherwise. During his first term Nixon presided with quiet firmness and surprising success over a sustained effort to ease the path of school desegregation throughout the South.[33] The proportion of black children in the South attending all-black schools plunged from 68 percent in 1968 to only 8 percent in 1972. In the rural and small-town South, where residential segregation was far less pronounced than in northern cities and where school busing to segregated schools was traditional, desegregation could produce rapid integration (at least for the majority of rural whites who could not afford to send their children to the mushrooming, private, church-related academies). Ironically, by the end of Nixon's first term, the southern school systems led the nation in racial integration. Outside the South, however, the Supreme Court, by a narrow margin that was determined by Nixon's Court appointees, ultimately stopped the busing for racial balance before it reached the northern suburbs.[34] By 1974, the proportion of black children attending schools that were 95 percent or more black had declined in the South to 20 percent. But this measure of de facto segregation had *risen* to 50 percent in the northern and western states, where whites were fleeing inner-city school districts.[35]

While the controversies over school desegregation and judicial appointments captured public attention, the Nixon administration was developing two parallel policies to address the nation's racial crisis that were based on contradictory models. One of these was voting rights, and the other, equal-employment rights. Nixon's equal-employment proposal was a Tory-socialist initiative on the left that seemed to contradict Nixon's busing rhetoric and Court appointments on the right. This triggered a job-discrimination debate that centered not on Title 7 and the EEOC, but rather on the obscure Title 6 and, even more obscure, the Labor Department's new Office of Federal Contract Compliance and its Philadelphia Plan. The outcome of Nixon's surprising initiative in equal-employment policy, a revived Philadelphia Plan that featured minority preferences in employment (discussed in the next chapter), would split both parties in Congress and fuel a growing controversary over "reverse discrimination." Ultimately, the storm over the Philadelphia Plan and racial quotas would split Nixon's own party most profoundly. In the 1980s it would lead to a repudiation of Nixon's affirmative-action legacy by the GOP's resentful conservative wing during the presidency of Ronald Reagan.

In debate over voting rights, however, the Nixon administration, unprepared, was reacting to a Democratic initiative in Congress. In response the Nixon White House hammered out a moderately conservative, consensual Republican doctrine that unified the party behind its President. It then encountered a new political environment, however, that included opposition control of both houses of Congress, unanticipated and accelerating interventions in social policy by the federal courts, and in the case of voting-rights policy, a new and strategically placed entrant in Washington's interest-group politics. This was the voting-rights bar. A small but rapidly growing community of civil rights lawyers, Justice Department attorneys, academic specialists, and think-tank experts, the voting-rights bar drew its growth not from disputes over the right to vote, but instead from demands that minorities win elections. As a result of these new conditions, the voting-rights bill that Nixon ultimately signed in 1970 turned the President's original, center-right strategy upon its head.

Extending the Voting Rights Act

The voting-rights issue was raised at the beginning of the Nixon administration by Emanuel Celler, who announced in the first week of the 91st Congress that the House Judiciary Committee would hold hearings on the Voting Rights Act later that spring. Two of the 1965 law's nineteen sections, the statistical trigger in section four and the preclearance provision in section five, were scheduled to expire on August 5, 1970. In 1965 they had represented such a novel intrusion on state and local authority that the Johnson administration and congressional leaders had defended them as five-year emergency measures. Section four, the key to the law's success, suspended literacy test laws in seven southern states (Alabama, Georgia, Louisiana, Mississippi, South Carolina and Virginia, and 39 counties in North Carolina) where the statistical trigger identified non-participation by a majority of voting-age blacks. Section five, a corollary to section four, required the prior permission of appointed federal officials in Washington for any changes in local electoral laws. The unprecedented interference of these two sections with traditional state prerogatives had been justified in the eyes of Congress (and also the Supreme Court, which upheld the Voting Rights Act shortly after is was passed) by historic patterns of black disfranchisement in the South that were no longer tolerable to the national polity.[36] But Congress in 1965 approved this radical short-circuiting on the assumption that normal federal-state relationships would resume at the expiration of the "5-year cooling-off period."[37] As Celler's own committee agreed, "Congress expected that within a 5-year period Negroes would have gained sufficient voting power in the States affected so that special federal protection would not be needed."[38]

The results of the 1965 law had been spectacular. By the summer of 1969, more than 800,000 new black voters had been registered in the covered states.[39] Federal voting examiners had been sent to 64 counties and parishes in five states (Alabama, Georgia, Louisiana, Mississippi, and South Carolina), and as a result black registration increased from 29 percent of the voting-age population to 56 percent. In Mississippi, black registration jumped from 7 percent to 60 percent (while white registration soared to a stunning 92 percent). The Justice Department had filed 19 voting rights suits under the Act and had reviewed 345 proposed changes in election laws, disapproving only ten under section five's preclearance provision. Conservatives cited this record in arguing that the law had performed successfully, and that the two exceptional sections for triggering and preclearance should therefore terminate as the law's proponents had originally planned. Congressional scholar Gary Orfield, a strong supporter of extension, agreed: "Most resistance to the laws was based not on the voting issue but on the drastic changes in state and local powers imposed by the law. . . . [the] grant of veto power over state legislation to an appointed federal official was unprecedented and strongly resented."[40]

The debate over voting-rights renewal in 1969 was awkward for both parties. The Democratic leadership in Congress had to explain why the government should renew two five-year emergency measures which had demonstrably achieved their goal of breaking the back of black disfranchisement in the South. Proponents of extension pointed to evidence of continued southern resistance and warned that when sections four and five expired, the covered jurisdictions would quickly reimpose racially discriminatory voting requirements. They cited a 1968 report of the Civil Rights Commission, *Political Participation,* that described continued harassment of Negroes attempting to register and new attempts to block black office-holding in the Deep South.[41] Several federal court decisions in the late 1960s had documented attempts by white officials in southern Black Belt counties to dilute the impact of black electoral strength. To liberal Democrats it seemed imperative that the Nixon administration not be allowed to confirm its Southern Strategy by dismantling the federal apparatus that had enfranchised the mass of southern blacks, who after all constituted the core of liberal Democratic strength in the South. As a consequence one of the last official acts of Johnson's Attorney General, Ramsey Clark, had been to send the Speaker of the House, on January 15, 1969, a proposal simply to extend the Voting Rights Act of 1965 for five additional years. One week later Celler introduced a straight-extension bill, H.R. 4249, and scheduled Judiciary Committee hearings to begin in May. The civil rights coalition hoped that this early pressure would flush Nixon out on the matter and avoid the delay that tended to work on the side of expiration, especially in light of the omnipresent possibility of Senate filibuster.

The Quest for a Coherent White House Policy

True to its early form, the Nixon administration had no plan. Reacting to Celler's challenge but lacking a policy, Nixon on February 18 directed Attorney General Mitchell to study the matter of voting-rights extension and recommend a policy by March 7. Arthur Burns, the new President's senior counselor for domestic program development, set to work on a proposal that would redeem Nixon's campaign pledge against regional legislation. Burns' goal was to deregionalize the Voting Rights Act by discontinuing the selective triggering and preclearance provisions, which were so offensive to conservatives, and replacing them with a voter-protection formula that would apply equally to all U.S. electoral jurisdictions. One such solution, urged on the administration by Jerris Leonard, the assistant attorney general for civil rights, was to extend section four's ban on literacy tests to cover the entire nation. The ban would thus no longer be regionally selective. Burns rejected that solution, however, on the conservative grounds that state requirements for voter literacy served as rational public purpose and fell within the legitimate and historic purview of state responsibilities in the federal system. Furthermore, such tests had not been shown by evidence to be used discriminatorily in the fourteen *non*southern states that required them.[42]

Instead, Burns called for replacing sections four and five with two new provisions. First, no person who registered to vote in any state during the five-year span of the original Voting Rights Act could subsequently be denied the right to vote because of failure to pass a literacy or similar test. This proviso would apply nationwide. But it was designed to protect newly enfranchised black voters in the South, and thus also to protect Republican lawmakers from attack for breaking the faith. Second, to protect similarly potential *new* registrants in all states from racial discrimination, Burns proposed that completion of the sixth grade or of six months of honorable service in the U.S. armed forces should exempt voter applicants from any literacy or similar test in any state. Illiterates seemed rarely to vote Republican, Burns knew, and he reminded Nixon that by following his sixth-grade strategy instead of a national ban on literacy tests, the administration would redeem its pledges and "avoid paying homage to illiteracy."[43]

Late in May the Justice Department floated a proposal based on Burns' sixth-grade strategy, and Bryce Harlow's nose-counters in legislative liaison sought out the reactions of Republican leaders on the Hill. The results showed a divided Republican minority, but most expressed willingness to support the President. Congressional Republicans knew that opposition to Celler's bill would invite Democratic charges that the Republicans had sold out black voting rights to the Southern Strategy. Moreover, a hard-eyed political logic (not, however, to be acknowledged in public) argued that in the long view

Republicans should benefit from the mass enfranchisement of southern blacks, because the liberal-redistributionist politics of black voters would drive the more conservative southern whites toward the Republican party. By replacing sections four and five with a sixth-grade formula, the Republicans could defend the Voting Rights Act's gains in the South while discarding regional legislation and treating all of the states alike.

The Gaston County Decision and the Voting-Rights Bar

On June 2, however, a Supreme Court decision sharply undercut the rationale behind the sixth-grade formula. In *Gaston County v. United States,* the Warren Court ruled 7-1 that a county in North Carolina could not take advantage of the Voting Rights Act's "bailout" provisions and adopt a racially neutral literacy test similar to those used in states like New York and California. Congress had included the bailout procedure in 1965 as an incentive to good behavior, the reward for which was release from coverage. Jurisdictions in the South could file bailout pleas in federal district court in Washington on the ground that no test had been employed for discriminatory ends in the preceding five years. But when Gaston County, North Carolina, followed this procedure in 1968, its petition was denied by the district court. On June 2, 1969, the Supreme Court agreed. The Warren Court ruled in *Gaston* that although the county's new literacy test was racially neutral on its face, like those used in New York and California, the county's long *history* of segregated schooling made it impossible for even an equally applied literacy test to produce racially fair results. Gaston County's racially segregated schools had "deprived its black residents of equal educational opportunity," Justice John Marshall Harlan wrote for the majority, "which in turn deprived them of an equal chance to pass the literacy test."[44] The implication of *Gaston* was that even were section four to expire in August 1970, voting jurisdictions with a history of legal segregation, whether covered by the 1965 statistical trigger *or not,* might still be barred from adopting literacy tests because their history of segregated schooling made racially neutral applications impossible.

The *Gaston* decision was a fatal blow to Burns' sixth-grade approach. No new sixth-grade law could remove from southern counties like Gaston the burden of their segregationist past. They could not adopt a racially neutral literacy test—as for example had Kings County, New York, which held Emanuel Celler's home borough of Brooklyn—no matter what provisions Congress voted. In the wake of *Gaston* the White House was persuaded by Jerris Leonard's argument: "The only course available to the President consistent with his position against regional legislation is to propose a nationwide ban on literacy tests."[45] "If this were done in a permanent form," Leonard added, "it would permit a revision of Section 5, so that the Act would have no regional application." To the Nixon White House, now robbed by *Gaston* of its sixth-grade formula, Leonard's proposal offered an attractive trade-off: stretch section four's ban on literacy tests to cover the entire nation, but allow its statistical trigger, and therefore also section five, to expire as originally planned. A nation-wide ban on literacy tests would by definition need no statistical trigger. This would make section five redundant, because preclearance from Washington applied only to the electoral jurisdictions identified by section four's trigger.

But here was the rub. Section four had been the master key that unlocked the chains that bound black voters in the South. Section five on the other hand had been only a supplementary precaution, designed not to enfranchise any-body but rather to prevent backsliding. Its goal was to block dirty tricks by racist electoral officials, such as changing the place and hours of voting pre-cincts in order to reduce black voting. Given the dirty-tricks history of many white registrars in the Deep South, section five was seen in 1965 as a prudent precaution. Like the gun in the sheriff's holster, section five's very availability had minimized its use. Since 1965 the Justice Department had received 345 requests to approve changes in voting arrangements in covered jurisdictions, and had objected to only ten. To conservatives, who found section five a standing affront to states' rights principles of local self-government, its expira-tion as a five-year emergency measure was essential. But to liberals who re-garded states' rights federalism as a shield behind which local elites had always exploited vulnerable minorities, section five provided the rationale for a new kind of centralized and permanent form of social regulation—in this case the monitoring of local electoral behavior by Washington officials. Like any new field of government regulation, whether it concerned airwaves or airlines or atomic energy or hospital standards, the breakthrough legislation for voting rights in 1965 had sparked the growth of a network of interested parties and associations. It centered on an expert cadre of civil rights lawyers, government attorneys, and federal judges who held center stage in the newly crowded arena of voting-rights litigation.

As the new head of the Civil Rights Division in Justice, Leonard had inher-ited a professional staff of about forty attorneys, most of whom were perma-nent civil service lawyers hired during the expansionist days of the Johnson administration. They tended to share the liberal views of former Attorney General Ramsey Clark, and many of them had cut their teeth on field work in the South dealing with the most troublesome local officials.[46] They viewed sections four and five as the heart of their enforcement authority. Their ideologi-cal commitment and their practical experience with refractory officials in the South, combined with their career ambitions and agency loyalties, produced not surprisingly an expansionist impulse. Ironically, a staff reorganization di-rected by Mitchell during his first year as attorney general created a new Voting Rights Section within the Civil Rights Division. Mitchell's purpose had been to break up the geographic organization that had accumulated resentments and distrust between southern officials and the Justice Department during the Ken-nedy and Johnson years and replace it with an organization based on function (such as school desegregation, voting rights, protection of civil rights workers). But the practical effect of organizing a voting section, as historian Steven Lawson observed, was to furnish "an unforeseen opportunity for disgruntled attorneys to move into it."[47] Over the years the government's suffrage lawyers had formed close working relationships with their staff counterparts on the congressional judiciary committees, and also with staffs of the civil rights, labor, and religious organizations that lobbied in coordination with the Leadership Conference. This fast-growing group of liberal professionals constituted the nucleus of a new, Washington-centered, public interest group that dominated the voting-rights bar.

On June 26, Mitchell, having five times postponed his testimony before the House Judiciary Committee while the White House struggled to fashion a coherent policy, finally presented his voting-rights proposal before Celler's Subcommittee No. 5. Once before the cameras at the witness table, Mitchell enjoyed exploiting an ironic transposition of roles: the civil rights coalition in Congress was defending the status quo and regional legislation, while the Nixon administration was arguing for broad new federal jurisdiction and authority to police voting rights throughout the nation. Mitchell proposed a bill that would ban literacy tests nationwide. It included new authority for the Justice Department to send voting examiners and observers anywhere in the country, and similar new nationwide authority for the Attorney General to initiate suits in federal courts and ask for a freeze on discriminatory voting laws.

Mitchell pursued the historical logic of *Gaston County* to explain to Celler why Congress should ban literacy tests in Brooklyn as well as Birmingham. Four million poorly educated blacks had fled the South since 1940, Mitchell said. They had spread themselves throughout those 14 non-southern states, like New York and California, where literacy tests were also required and where the migrants' inferior education would continue to deny them an equal chance to pass the tests. The formula of 1965 no longer made much sense in the South, Mitchell said, where all seven covered states already exceeded the 1965 law's 50 percent triggering level of eligible blacks registered. Indeed, "a higher percentage of voting-age Negroes went to the polls in the Deep South," Mitchell said, "than in Watts or Washington."[48] "Little more than one-third of the voting-age Negro population cast 1968 ballots in Manhattan, the Bronx, or Brooklyn, New York City," Mitchell explained to the Brooklyn-based committee chairman, "and this amounted to only one-half the local white turnout." "A higher percentage of Negroes voted in South Carolina and Mississippi," Mitchell added, "where literacy tests are suspended, than in Watts or Harlem, where literacy tests are enforced." The four million southern blacks had carried their history with them, and deposited its burden on Mr. Celler's doorstep.

The Tar Baby Logic Preclearance

Celler and his Democratic colleagues were not amused by Mitchell's lectures about the poor voting participation of Democratic minorities in Los Angeles and New York. They objected not to the expansion of coverage nationwide, but rather to a Republican trade-off that would free the South from special scrutiny, especially from the preclearance requirements of section five. They

voiced the fears of the liberal voting-rights bar that without section five, southern officials would return to the bad habits of their past. As evidence they cited
the Civil Rights Commission's 1968 report, *Political Participation*.[49]

Most of *Political Participation* described willful violations of both the letter
and the spirit of the Voting Rights Act by Black Belt counties, where blacks
typically outnumbered whites, especially in Mississippi and Alabama. A burst
of diehard legislative creativity in 1966 had produced nakedly racist attempts
to nullify the effect of the Voting Rights Act. These included many of the
shopworn devices that prevented black registration and voting itself. But most
of these only hastened the arrival of federal observers and examiners, and
hence were self-defeating. More creative, and somewhat more subtle, were
attempts to minimize or prevent the election of blacks to office. Such racially
motivated manipulation of otherwise permissible changes included switching
from district elections to at-large elections, where the larger pool of white
voters could prevent the election of blacks, and switching offices like superin-
tendent of schools from elective to appointive status. Other tactics included
extending the terms of elective offices and even abolishing the offices, increasing the minimum qualifications and filing fees for office, and preventing newly
elected officials from obtaining required bonds. It was, over-all, a shabby
parade of racist trickery, if a fairly obvious one.

It was also a highly localized counter-revolution, one that was closely
watched and sharply challenged. The Civil Rights Commission's report acknowledged that the "dramatic increase" in black political participation in
such a short period represented "unprecedented progress."[50] White officehold-
ers and candidates in the South were manifesting a greater responsiveness to
black needs and concerns, the commission agreed. There had been a decline in
open appeals to racism by candidates and officials, and "contrary to the dire
predictions of violent reaction," progress had taken place quietly and without
major conflict. The report described a vigorous network of civil rights watch-
dogs whose challenges had generated a wave of test cases that were welling up
toward a sympathetic Supreme Court.

The report was dominated, however, by a catalogue of offenses, especially
in Mississippi and Alabama. These were not the old-fashioned barriers to
Negro voting, which were largely abandoned, but rather attempts to dilute the
impact of the new black vote. The Civil Rights Commission singled out 38
counties as the prime offenders, three-quarters of them in Alabama and Mississippi. But the Voting Rights Act covered 593 southern counties or equivalent
jurisdictions. Thus *Political Participation* attacked abuses found in only 6 percent of the covered counties, while nine out of ten jurisdictions were described
as responding well to the new law.

Congressman Richard H. Poff of Virginia, the second-ranking Republican
on the Judiciary Committee, voiced the complaints of southern elected officials.
Virginia was covered by the 1965 law, Poff observed. Yet the Civil Rights
Commission itself had concluded as early as 1961 that blacks encountered "no
significant racially motivated impediments to voting" in Virginia. Since 1965
the Justice Department had sent not a single federal examiner or observer into

any precinct in Virginia.[51] Yet none of Virginia's more than 2000 precincts could even switch from paper ballots to machine voting without applying for permission from a Washington agency.

Poff's complaints, however, were unavailing. His fellow Republican on the Judiciary Committee, ranking minority member William McCulloch, felt pride of co-authorship in the 1965 law. McCulloch had exercised leadership in 1965, like Dirksen in the Senate, to ensure that the sanctions of the Voting Rights Act applied mainly to southern Democrats, not northern Republicans. In 1969 he shared in a growing congressional consensus that the liberal voting reforms of 1965 had worked and didn't need fixing. McCulloch attacked the Nixon bill for "sweep[ing] broadly into those areas where the need is least and retreat[ing] from those areas where the need is greatest."[52] The administration's bill would repeal the preclearance provision "in the face of spellbinding evidence of unflagging Southern dedication to the cause of creating an ever-more sophisticated legal machinery for discriminating against the black voter." It had only been a year since Martin Luther King's assassination in Memphis, and McCulloch's reference to the "unflagging Southern dedication" to perpetuating racial oppression captured a persisting mood in Congress. Republicans were badly outnumbered on the Hill, and southern Republicans were rarer still.

The Voting Rights Act of 1970

The resolution of the debate of 1969–70 over extending the Voting Rights Act demonstrated the Nixon administration's strategic weakness in a Congress dominated by the opposition party. Bryce Harlow had early concluded that the lack of a partisan majority in either chamber dictated a strategy of seeking ad hoc "floating coalitions" in Congress. This meant building upon a core bloc of Republican loyalists, then searching for allies either by reaching to the left or to the right, depending upon the issues.[53] Such coalition-building worked best in the House, as in January 1970 when Nixon rallied traditionalist Democrats to help sustain his veto of a HEW appropriation he called budget-busting and inflationary, or when he forged an alliance with liberal Democrats the following April to pass his radical Family Assistance Plan.

But the floating coalition strategy was most vulnerable in the Senate. There Nixon's problem was the substantial bloc of Republican senators from urban-industrial states whose moderate-to-liberal politics blunted their party loyalty. They constituted a third of the GOP's 43 senators—men like Edward Brooke of Massachusetts, Clifford Case of New Jersey, Jacob Javits and Charles Goodell of New York, Mark Hatfield and Robert Packwood of Oregon, John Sherman Cooper of Kentucky, Charles Mathias of Maryland, Charles Percy of Illinois, and Hugh Scott and Richard Schweiker of Pennsylvania. It was this bloc of mostly eastern Republican "progressives" whose independence had pushed Dirksen in 1968 to reverse himself on the fair housing bill. Nixon's leverage in the Senate was further reduced when Dirksen suddenly died in September 1969. The Republican senators selected as their new minority leader

Hugh Scott, himself up for re-election in 1970, and Scott's support for the legislative agenda of the Nixon White House was at best episodic. As a result of these cumulative forces in the Senate, Bryce Harlow's floating coalitions often floated in reverse, with the not very loyal Republican bloc joining the liberal Democrats. Such a bipartisan coalition on the left had defeated the administration in November 1969 by rejecting Nixon's nominee to the Supreme Court, Clement Haynsworth.[54] Because Celler's Judiciary Committee had forced a House-first strategy on the administration by beginning hearings on voting-rights extension early in 1969, the contest over whose voting-law coalition would "float" was first joined in the House.

In mid-July 1969 a bipartisan Celler-McCulloch coalition in House Judiciary voted 28 to 7 to extend the 1965 law for five years with no amendments. In the fall, however, the White House rallied the conservative coalition of midwestern Republicans and southern Democrats behind the administration's bill, and on December 11 this coalition of the right substituted the Nixon bill for the Judiciary Committee bill by a slim margin, 208 to 204.[55] The Nixon bill's common national standard drew the support of 129 Republicans and 79 Democrats, most of the latter from the southern and border states. NAACP lobbyist Clarence Mitchell called the vote "a cataclysmic defeat for civil rights engineered by the President."[56] "The Klan was on the floor of Congress today," Mitchell said, "waiting to lynch Negroes at the polls." The House then voted 234-179 to pass the amended bill, H.R. 4249, and send it to the Senate to consider in the second session of the 91st Congress in 1970.[57]

When H.R. 4249 came over to the Senate in the spring of 1970, however, a bipartisan majority of Scott-led Republicans and norther Democrats reversed the House action and resubstituted the five-year extension of the 1965 law. They then added Majority Leader Mike Mansfield's controversial provision to enfranchise 18-year-olds, a move that Nixon opposed as a statutory enfranchisement that was constitutionally impermissible. On March 13, 1970, the Senate's radically revised voting rights bill was returned to the House.[58] The 18-year-old provision was difficult for politicians to oppose while so many young draftees were dying in Vietnam, and this helped change the political arithmetic on voting-rights extension in the House. On June 17 the House voted 224-183 to accept the Senate bill, thereby avoiding a conference in which Senator Eastland's Judiciary Committee would have been strongly represented. Despite warnings by Nixon's advisers that enfranchising 18-year-olds required a constitutional amendment, and that the youth vote, like the southern black vote, would go overwhelmingly to his Democratic opponent in 1972, Nixon signed the bill into law on June 22.[59] His voting-rights strategy had backfired. But signing the bill seemed preferable to vetoing it and handing the Democrats the double-barreled issue that Nixon opposed voting rights for blacks and youth.

The new law not only retained the original, regionally targeted, 1964-based formulas for preclearance and triggering that the Nixon administration had sought to remove. It also added a new triggering formula for the rest of the country that identified jurisdictions in which less than half of the minority voting-age populations were registered on November 1, 1968, or had voted in the 1968 elections. This extended coverage to electoral districts in Alaska, Arizona, California, Idaho, and Oregon, and also to Bronx, Kings (Brooklyn), and New York (Manhattan) counties in New York. It also suspended the use of literacy tests in *all* states until August 1975. Congress had bought the Nixon-Mitchell nationalizing rationale, but had rejected the trade-offs behind the rationale that would have removed the regional stigma from the South. The civil rights coalition had defeated Nixon's voting-rights bill, much as they had defeated his nominees Haynsworth and Carswell. And the voting-rights bar had won a watershed victory: section five had been transformed from a regionalized, emergency backstop for section four into an expanding national charter for federal regulation of local electoral systems.

CHAPTER 9

The Philadelphia Plan and the Politics of Minority Preference

The Enigma of Richard Nixon

During his first year in the White House, Richard Nixon led his government in three different directions in an ill-coordinated attempt to construct a coherent civil rights policy. Nixon's Supreme Court nominations of Haynsworth and Carswell reached rightward toward the Middle American constituencies of George Wallace and the Southern Strategy. His voting-rights proposal by contrast was centrist, replacing regional formulas with a common national standard that would minimize federal intrusion. In both efforts Nixon was defeated by the Democrats controlling Congress. Nixon's third initiative in civil rights policy, the leftward-leaning Philadelphia Plan, would astonish Republican regulars and confound normal political alignments on the Hill. It would lead to a congressional showdown won by the Nixon administration, and produce Nixon's most lasting—and paradoxical—contribution to American civil rights policy.[1]

Ideologically, Nixon was ambidextrous. This doctrinal flexibility permitted him as President to abandon the crusading anti-communism that had brought him political success during his formative political years, 1946–60, and replace it with the nimble internationalism that led in the 1970s to détente with Communist China and the Soviet Union. In domestic policy, Nixon's odd streak of "Tory socialism" puzzled and often irritated congressional Republicans, who expected a more consistently conservative agenda from their Republican President. The Nixon administration was most successful in domestic policy when it pursued the procedural agenda of centrist Republican prudence, as initially sketched out by the post-election task forces led by Arthur Burns. This was the "new federalism," an attempt to streamline the programmatic sprawl of the Great Society, reorganize the executive structure, consolidate agency-driven programs into bloc grants to the states, transform the green-eyeshaded Budget Bureau into a policy-planning Office of Management and Budget.[2] On substantive domestic programs, Nixon began his administration with no coherent agenda, and the confused structure of domestic policy advice in the White House produced more bickering than consensus—until Haldeman and Ehrlichman took charge in the fall of 1969. Nixon's lasting achievements in domestic policy represented somewhat grudging accommodations with Democratic majorities in Congress—for example, the rapid growth of environmental programs, such as the creation of the Environmental Protection Agency in 1970, and the major expansion of college student aid in 1972.[3]

On civil rights policy, however, Nixon's problems with policy coherence in the White House and with Democratic control in Congress were compounded by the development of an old pattern in American political life that was taking on a new form. The old pattern was interest-group politics: the log-rolling process of legislative lobbying and bureaucratic bargaining that historically had entrenched powerful coalitions around the government's benefit programs. The traditional beneficiary groups were successful because they were highly organized. They included commercial farmers, veterans, home-owners, doctors, railroads and airlines, timber and grazing interests, tobacco-growers, makers of shoes and textiles, and many others. Groups that were weakly organized generally won few benefits—small farmers, minorities, consumers. During the 1960s the new form of interest-group politics came from new players in the competition for government benefits. These were the clients of the Great Society's redistributive social programs—the elderly, blacks, women, Hispanics, the disabled, the rural poor, and soon many others. They were learning the organize-or-perish rules of the high-stakes game of pluralist group-based politics. They were a new clientele, armed with powerful claims on the national conscience for historic discrimination, forming the constituent base of new "iron triangles."[4]

"Iron Triangles" and the New Civil Rights Bureaucracy

In the folklore of Washington politics and power, "iron triangles" was a metaphor that originated with the classic, pork-barrel politics of rivers-and-harbors and agricultural subsidy programs. Typically the three points or institutional bases of the triangle were: (1) congressional committees, which authorized new spending programs; (2) executive agencies, which controlled the flow of benefits in the new programs (dams, harbor-dredging, sugar and peanut subsidies); and organized clientele groups (port authorities, shipping interests, commodity growers). The beneficiary groups closed the triangle by directing campaign contributions and votes back to key members of Congress. These triangular arrangements of mutual back-scratching were neither illegal nor necessarily undesirable. Indeed, they were a staple of pluralist politics in America, where the myriad associations of civil society in the United States (union workers, schoolteachers, professional associations, private colleges, dairy farmers, stamp collectors) lobbied on behalf of their memberships. The standard pork-barrel model, however, was tainted by a history of corruption and public waste. American liberals had long complained that iron-triangle bargaining typically produced public give-aways for cattle and timber barons, agribusiness, strip-miners, insurance companies, medical schools—programs of public assistance that amounted to "socialism for the rich and free enterprise for the poor."[5]

In the aftermath of the Great Society, however, the proliferation of new social programs began quite naturally to produce new triangular coalitions. Lyndon Johnson's aid-to-education programs of 1965 nurtured the growth of a beehive of education associations on Dupont Circle in Washington, where triangular ties reached deeply into mission agencies like HEW and the Education committees of the House and Senate. Similarly, Medicare accelerated the triangular networking among senior citizen groups and health care providers. In civil rights policy, black Americans constituted the chief constituency. The NAACP claimed pride of place among civil rights organizations, joined by the less visible National Urban League, and the fading SCLC (during the late 1960s internal chaos destroyed SNCC and left a decimated CORE in the control of West Indian black nationalists). Following the legislative triumph of 1964–65, the Leadership Conference presided over a broad coalition of minority, labor, and religious organizations, backed by major private foundations like Ford and Rockefeller, with international prestige and formidable potential for constituency-based bargaining.[6]

The civil rights coalition provided the natural constituency of clients for the second point of the civil rights triangle, the federal agencies that ran the regulatory and benefit programs. The institutional base of civil rights agencies had begun timidly in 1957, but accelerated after 1964. These organizations included the U.S. Commission on Civil Rights and the Civil Rights Division of the Department of Justice, both created by the Civil Rights Act of 1957. The Civil Rights Act of 1964 created the EEOC to enforce Title 7 in private employment. Less visible to the public eye than the EEOC, but potentially more muscular, were the sub-agencies spawned by Title 6 to monitor contract compliance. These sub-departmental offices were established first in HEW (the Office of Civil Rights), then in the departments of Labor (the Office of Federal Contract Compliance Programs), Defense, HUD, and Transportation, and soon in all eleven cabinet-level departments. In 1969 the Nixon administration created the OMBE, and also a new Voting Rights Section within the Justice Department. This expanding civil rights network of Washington-based sub-bureaucracies was also reaching out to parallel networks in state and local government, as for example in the EEOC's state-grant liaison with state and municipal EEO agencies. In the 1970s the network would include parallel structures in state and local governments, higher education, and in the larger houses of private commerce and industry. The defeat of Nixon's voting-rights proposal in 1970 signaled the arrival of the voting-rights bar as a new and forceful component of the civil rights triangles.[7]

The congressional base of the civil rights triangles, however, was initially a weak point. Historically, the South's one-party system had combined with congressional seniority to lodge southern Democrats in the chairs of most standing committees in Congress. Few congressional committees had shown much solicitude for minority interests (three exceptions were the House committees on the

Judiciary and on Education and Labor and the Senate Committee on Labor and Public Welfare), and two of the most powerful committees, Senate Judiciary and House Rules, remained openly hostile until the late 1960s. Emanuel Celler's liberal-dominated House Judiciary Committee had been a prominent exception since 1955, and by the late 1960s James Eastland's conservative grip as chairman of Senate Judiciary had effectively been broken by a bipartisan coalition of Senate liberals. By 1970 the civil rights coalition was winning strong backing throughout the congressional committee structure, and this new strength was reinforced by a proliferation of new subcommittees that Congress created to service and monitor the legacy of expanding programs and constituencies from the 1960s. The most important new subcommittee for the civil rights coalition was Judiciary Committee No. 4 on Civil Rights Oversight, chaired by a liberal Democrat from California, Representative Donald Edwards.[8]

Moreover, the early weakness of the civil rights coalition's third institutional base, the congressional committees, was partially compensated for by the increasing intercession of the federal courts. Increasingly in the 1960s, the federal judiciary, led by the Warren Court, ruled in favor of minority interests in policy disputes. This trend was most noticeable in the Court's growing impatience in the school desegregation cases. Similarly, the Supreme Court's *Gaston* decision in June of 1969 had destroyed the assumptions upon which the White House had based the sixth-grade strategy for voting-rights revision. All these ingredients of triangular, interest-group politics were present in 1969 when President Nixon, at the urging of his new Secretary of Labor, George C. Shultz, breathed new life into a collapsed program of the Johnson administration, the Philadelphia Plan for minority hiring in construction. Its resurrection promised to radicalize the meaning of affirmative action and fan the flames of debate over racial quotas.

The Peculiar Problem of the Construction Industry

The Philadelphia Plan was an unlikely instrument for Richard Nixon to revive. It was developed during 1965–68 under the aegis of a tiny and awkwardly named new office in the Labor Department, the Office of Federal Contract Compliance (OFCC), and was designed to attack one of the most intractable problems in fair employment policy: the construction industry. The heart of the problem was historic job discrimination against minorities, especially in the skilled and well-paid construction trades. The craft unions of the old AFL were rooted in guild traditions in which the master-apprentice role approximated a father-son relationship. This produced tightly knit, often all-white locals that controlled the work assignments for such highly skilled construction trades as electrical and sheetmetal workers, plumbers, steamfitters, structural iron workers. The Great Society had pumped billions of dollars into urban renewal projects, where the whiteness of the skilled craftsmen on the jobsite stood in dramatic relief against the surge of black rioting in the 1960s. By 1967, when the Detroit riot prompted President Johnson to appoint the Kerner Commission, black leaders across the nation were demanding access to the white-dominated skilled trades and threatening violence if their demands were not met. What leverage could federal officials use to hasten integration on the construction sites?[9]

In the fall of 1965, Johnson had rejected proposals that he appoint a czar for civil rights enforcement, and instead through Executive Order 11246 he created a decentralized mechanism for enforcing the Civil Rights Act. Primary enforcement responsibilities were assigned by area to several agencies. The Civil Service Commission would police equal employment in federal jobs. The new EEOC would police private employers under Title 7. The Justice Department would coordinate EEO enforcement under Title 6 in "federally assisted" grant programs, such as federal aid to local schools. Finally, to enforce EEO in federal contracts, each mission agency would take the "lead" with employers it mainly dealt with. For example, Defense would police EEO for builders of warships, bombers, tanks; Agriculture would enforce EEO in foodstuff contracts; the General Service Administration had EEO jurisdiction over suppliers of government office equipment, and so forth.[10]

The "lead" agency approach was a prudent formula from the viewpoint of public administration and the politics of bureaucracy, because it reflected the decentralized and turf-sensitive reality of the executive agencies. But for the same reasons it tended to produce weak enforcement efforts. The major federal departments were called *mission* agencies for good reason. Their ties to client groups and contractual suppliers were governed by a mutual interest in accomplishing the mission, and superimposing a policeman's role tended to upset these traditional relationships. Pentagon supply officials, for example, were rewarded or punished according to their ability to sustain the flow of provisions to the troops in Vietnam, and this primary goal was threatened by contract holdups over the workforce composition of their suppliers. The Pentagon was willing to impose desegregation on vulnerable, major-target offenders like Lockheed-Marietta or the Newport News shipbuilders. But because most of the federal government's two million annual contracts were of the workaday variety, EEO enforcement did not rank high in most agency priorities.[11]

In construction, moreover, the lead-agency formula was least promising of all. Federally aided construction was spread widely across the spectrum of mission agencies, financially "assisting" the local construction of hospitals, airports, libraries, college dormitories, roads and bridges, urban renewal projects, federal courthouses, military bases. Because there was no dominant contractual "lead" agency for such a sea of building projects, Johnson in 1965 assigned contract compliance in construction to the Labor Department.[12]

Labor's prospects for effective enforcement, however, were dim. Construction was a fluid, ad hoc, contract-chasing enterprise where construction companies bid competitively for projects, and the winning low bidders then obtained their workers from hiring-halls bound by union contracts. Thus unlike most employers, the contractors didn't really control their own hiring. Instead, the AFL-CIO craft locals made the specific assignments, based primarily on union seniority. Title 6 and Executive Order 11246 gave the Labor Department authority over contractors, not over unions. Discrimination by labor unions was covered by the EEOC under Title 7, but the EEOC had little enforcement power. Moreover, Labor's compliance authority over construction contracts was filtered downward through many levels. For example, Johnson's executive order of 1965 directed the Labor Department (through the OFCC) to "coordinate" EEO enforcement with contract compliance staffs in HEW or HUD or the Department of Transportation. Mission agencies—HEW, for example—would award a construction grant-in-aid to a state or municipal entity, such as Cuyahoga County, Ohio, or the city of Cleveland, to build a pediatrics wing onto the general hospital or a classroom building for a community college. The construction company that won the bidding competition would then notify the craft locals in the Cleveland area who were certified as collective bargaining agents that the company needed specific numbers of craftsmen—such as 27 electricians, 48 sheetmetal workers, 18 bricklayers, 20 plumbers, and so forth. Each craft local in Cleveland would then select its tradesmen—the plumbers and pipefitters local, for example, would pick the 20 plumbers. By the time the taxpayers' dollar reached the plumber in hourly wages, the chain of EEO enforcement was so remote and fragmented that even maximum good will on all sides could scarcely reconstruct it as an instrument of public accountability.[13]

For all these reasons, the Labor Department seemed to face a near-impossible task for exercising influence. Given the decentralized nature of the construction industry and the traditional structure of collective bargaining agreements, Labor's control problem was inherently frustrating, like pushing on a piece of string. Yet the stakes were high. In 1967, some 225,000 contractors throughout the United States were building $30 billion worth of federally assisted construction projects, and directly or indirectly employing 20 million workers on contracts and subcontracts. What could the Labor Department do to bring black Americans into this employment mainstream and help avert a future characterized by Detroit in flames?

The First Philadelphia Plan

In the fall of 1965, Labor secretary Willard Wirtz placed the OFCC under the direction of a highly regarded black administrator, Edward Sylvester. During 1966–67, Sylvester attempted without much success to find metropolitan-based solutions, first in St. Louis, then in San Francisco and Cleveland. His method was to hold up the awards of federal construction funds to successful low bidders and demand that winning contractors submit evidence that would persuade the OFCC to issue a finding that the low bidders were "in compliance" with the Labor Department's affirmative action standards. The required evidence took the form of "manning table" schedules for construction jobs. These were work-assignment charts that identified the number of minority workers the builder would hire in every job category for the full construction project.

The contractors, however, objected. They pointed to their union contracts, certified and enforced by the NLRB, which bound them to employ only the workers sent from the hiring halls of the craft locals. The construction trades unions emphatically agreed. As a result of these disputes, local squabbles erupted, construction was interrupted, delays produced cost over-runs, and lawsuits proliferated. Sylvester needed a better model. He found his new model in Philadelphia.[14]

Despite its Quaker roots, the "City of Brotherly Love" had a troubled racial history, especially in the area of job discrimination. During World War II, 5000 army troops were required to put down a transit strike, when white workers closed down the streetcar lines in 1943 to protest the hiring of black conductors. Twenty years later Philadelphia's AFL-CIO Council, in an attempt to integrate the area's construction locals, negotiated with builders and city officials an agreement on a school construction project that would add only *six* Negro workers—one steamfitter, one plumber, two sheet metal journeymen, and two electrical apprentices. In protest at this breach of standard hiring-hall assignments, the 2200-member Steamfitters Local 420 withdrew from Philadelphia's Building and Construction Trades Council. When the Philadelphia NAACP counterprotested by picketing a school construction site, thirty-nine people were injured in the turmoil.[15]

When the Detroit riot exploded in the summer of 1967, civil rights leaders in Philadelphia warned that job discrimination would trigger similar violence. The black population of metropolitan Philadelphia had grown from 18.3 percent of the total in 1950 to 26.7 percent in 1960 and to 33.5 percent in 1970. The U.S. government was funding $550 million in school construction in Philadelphia's five-county area, where blacks constituted approximately 30 percent of the population of two million. Within the city itself, $250 million in U.S. funds were earmarked in the fiscal 1968 budget for construction. Most of this was federal grant money for projects built by local agencies, like libraries and college dormitories, but it included the Treasury Department's new U.S. Mint, going up on the mall of Independence National Historical Park at Franklin Square. There the skilled construction crews were disproportionately (and very visibly) white, and local black leaders were threatening demonstrations to close down the work sites. In this volatile environment the regional administrator for HUD, Warren P. Phelan, led his fellow federal officials on Philadelphia's regional coordinating panel (the Federal Executive Board or FEB) in a drive to break the lily-white grip of the skilled construction trades.[16]

Phelan surveyed the patterns of union membership in the Philadelphia area and identified seven of 22 building trades locals that remained virtually all-white. The targeted craft locals were the electrical and sheetmetal workers, plumbers, structural ironworkers, roofers, steamfitters, and elevator constructors. Their combined membership was estimated at 8500, but included only 25 to 30 minority workers. The ironworkers had the best record, yet this meant only 5 to 10 minority workers out of a membership of 800. The sheetmetal and elevator locals had no minority workers at all, nor any minority apprentices being trained to join the journeymen. Armed with this fresh evidence of racial exclusion, the Philadelphia FEB coordinated its planning with Sylvester in Washington and moved toward a fall announcement of their aggressive new affirmative action plan.

Sylvester, Phelan, and their determined colleagues in the federal enforcement effort in 1967 were racing the flames of Detroit, and they viewed the resistance of lily-white locals like the sheetmetal workers in Philadelphia as a gauntlet hurled at their feet. The atmosphere of national racial crisis in the late 1960s created a "policy window" that invited sharp breaks with the past, much as had the southern crisis of the early 1960s.[17] Social emergency permitted extraordinary interventions. In hindsight, the evidence shows that organized labor in Philadelphia was making large strides toward workforce integration in the 1960s. The merger of the AFL and CIO in 1955 had produced a weak confederation with little authority over local unions. But George Meany and Walter Reuther had made substantial progress in integrating the union movement, working with federal officials and local civil rights organizations, and meanwhile contributing heavily to the national lobbying of the Leadership Conference. By 1967 their national desegregation drive had reduced the number of all-black locals (such as rail porters and musicians) from approximately 500 in 1960 to fewer than 170 in 1967.[18]

In Philadelphia, Phelan's FEB survey found 225,000 union members in the five-county area, with 75,000 working in construction, and 28,000 of these belonged to the 22 building trades locals. Union segregation by then had essentially been reduced to the construction trades. Phelan's target list had originally included an eighth union, Local 542 of the Operating Engineers. But the FEB survey revealed that the 5000-member engineers union, which was all-white in 1960, had made rapid progress in response to desegregation pressures. By the summer of 1967 the operating engineers included 800 to 900 minority workers and 150 minority apprentices. So Phelan dropped them from the hit list. Thus Phelan's offending seven locals represented less than 4 percent of the Philadelphia area's union membership. In the politics of civil rights during the crisis-ridden late 1960s, however, new standards of policy for the nation's building industry were shaped by the exigencies of a refractory 4 percent of construction craftsmen—much as voting-rights policy in 1969–70 would be shaped by the defiance of racist officials in approximately 6 percent of the southern counties covered by the Voting Rights Act.

The mechanics of the Philadelphia Plan were simple. They closely resembled the Cleveland approach, and the chief differences between the two were political and organizational. Cleveland represented a one-shot feeler that quickly got entangled in local complexities and litigation. But the Philadelphia Plan represented a tightly coordinated federal phalanx. The local FEB, representing policy solidarity on behalf of *all* federal agencies in a metropolitan area, would set no firm target numbers for minorities that builders must promise to hire. To do so would amount to assigning racial quotas that the Civil Rights Act prohibited. Instead, builders who emerged as low bidders were held in a new limbo status called "apparent low bidder," while the FEB and the OFCC examined their compliance posture. To be declared in compliance, contractors were themselves required to produce manning tables that assigned minority hiring numbers high enough to satisfy the OFCC.

In September 1967 the Labor Department informed all federal agencies of the new Philadelphia Plan requirements.[19] Sylvester called it a "pre-award" plan. His purpose was to position the manning-table negotiations *prior* to the final, formal award of contract. But the pre-award label could not obscure the fact that negotiations over the acceptable numbers of projected minority hires occurred *after* the bids were opened. The distinction was not lost on the contractors, who had long played the high-stakes game of competitive bidding according to the basic ground rule of procurement practice: government contract work required that all potential bidders receive the same pre-bid specifications on the work to be done.

Counterattack 1968

The announcement of the Philadelphia Plan requirements brought cries of betrayal from organized labor as well as from the contractors. The manning-table negotiation between contractors and federal officials threatened labor's bedrock achievements, dating back to the 1930s, in collective bargaining and seniority rights. Secretary Wirtz explained to an angry AFL-CIO conference in the fall of 1967 that the Labor Department rulings in Cleveland and Philadelphia were exceptional because of the EEO problems in those two cities were uniquely severe. "But it isn't right as a general policy," Wirtz agreed, "and it won't work."[20] Similarly John Macy, chairman of the U.S. Civil Rights Commission, told complaining members of Congress in January 1968: "There are no intentions to implement such a plan on a nationwide scale."[21]

In addition to alienating the AFL-CIO, a traditional Democratic constituency, the Philadelphia Plan angered the employers represented by the U.S. Chamber of Commerce and the National Association of Manufacturers—a traditional Republican constituency. Early in 1968 the director of the Associated Contractors of America, William E. Dunn, summoned a war council in Washington. The contractors concentrated their appeal for help on Representative William Cramer of Florida, the ranking Republican on the House Public Works Committee. Cramer in turn sent objections to the novel bidding arrangements in Cleveland and Philadelphia to the Comptroller General of the United States, Elmer Staats. "In order for the bidding to be truly competitive," Cramer reminded Staats, "all bidders must compete on the same basis with no allowance for negotiation on particular aspects of the program after the bids are opened."[22]

In response, Staats sent Wirtz in May 1968 a ruling on the Cleveland procedures (where the contracting process was further advanced than in Philadelphia) that reaffirmed the General Accounting Office's standard protocols for competitive bidding. Agencies will make awards "only on the basis of a low bid," Staats ruled, "*including* any additional specific and definite requirements set forth in the invitation, and [stipulating] that the award will not thereafter be dependent upon the low bidder's ability to successfully negotiate matters mentioned only vaguely before the bidding."[23] In mid-November 1968 the Comptroller General extended his ruling on Cleveland to the Philadelphia Plan. Agency awards "may not properly be witheld pursuant to the [Philadelphia] Plan from the lowest responsive and otherwise responsible bidder on the basis of an unacceptable affirmative action program," Staats held, "until provision is made for informing prospective bidders of definitive minimum requirements to be met."[24]

Wirtz and Sylvester were caught up in a classic dilemma, like Joseph Heller's Catch-22. If their affirmative action plans required explicit numbers of minorities to be hired, they ran afoul of the prohibitions of Dirksen's section 703(j) of Title 7 of the Civil Rights Act of 1964, which prohibited preferential treatment on account of race, sex, and ethnicity. If on the other hand the OFCC's model for affirmative action remained carefully vague, as in Phelan's FEB plan for Philadelphia, then they ran afoul of the GAO's insistence that bidders be specifically informed in advance of all job requirements. No rational planner, to be sure, would design a system of public bidding that included anything like the coy guessing game fashioned by the OFCC in Cleveland or the FEB in Philadelphia. But the Philadelphia Plan was less a public works construction document than a political document, forged in the subpresidency for social purposes that had little directly to do with building college dormitories and hospital wings. Lacking any backing from the wounded, lame-duck President Johnson on the eve of a presidential election, the sponsors of the Philadelphia Plan looked defeated. Two weeks after the election of Richard Nixon in November 1968, the Labor Department quietly announced that the Philadelphia Plan was rescinded.[25]

Nixon, Shultz, and the Resurrection of the Philadelphia Plan

The surprising revival of the Philadelphia Plan during Nixon's first year as President was primarily the handiwork of Secretary of Labor George Shultz. A Marine veteran of World War II who earned a doctorate in labor economics at MIT, Shultz became dean of the University of Chicago's business school in 1962, and in 1968 he assisted his fellow academic economist, Arthur Burns, in Nixon's presidential transition by directing the task force on manpower. Because organized labor was a Democratic constituency, the post of Labor secretary in Republican cabinets had been something of a stepchild, and Nixon was happy to appoint Burns' nominee Shultz—a man Nixon scarcely knew. Shultz brought to the cabinet a free-market, Chicago-school brand of economics that was as comfortably Republican as its leading exponent, Milton Friedman. For Shultz this included a special hostility toward the kind of inflationary, noncompetitive hammerlock that the construction unions had fastened on the nation's building industry.[26] A fiscal conservative, Shultz like many highly educated Republicans held more liberal views on social issues like civil liberties and racial integration. This pattern of political beliefs reversed the values of typical white Democrats in union ranks, where economic liberalism was balanced by "hard-hat" social conservatism.

During the early months of 1969, Shultz told Nixon's Budget director, Robert Mayo, that he agreed with recommendations to transfer the functions of the OFCC out of Labor and into the EEOC or perhaps the Justice Department.[27] But the early attacks by Democrats on Nixon's civil rights stance, including Clifford Alexander's blast of March 1969 in resigning as chairman of the EEOC, persuaded Shultz to make a public claim that fighting job discrimination was a "top priority" of the Nixon administration.[28] Accordingly, Shultz decided to strengthen rather than transfer the OFCC, and to convince the White House of the virtues of reviving the Philadelphia Plan.

Shultz pressed his argument on Nixon, Ehrlichman recalled, by appealing to the Quaker virtue of honest toil and to the prospect of creating black conservatives by giving them a stake in the middle class. Not lost on Nixon, however, was the delicious prospect of setting organized labor and the civil rights establishment at each other's Democratic throats. Ehrlichman recalled Nixon's rather rapid conversion by Shultz to the Philadelphia Plan: "Nixon thought that Secretary of Labor George Shultz had shown great style in constructing a political dilemma for the labor union leaders and civil rights groups."[29] Shultz's major reason for reviving the Philadelphia Plan flowed in part from professional and personal convictions about the social irresponsibility of the construction trades unions and the economic irrationality of racism in the American political economy. But Ehrlichman conceded that Shultz was not above appreciating, with a twinkle in his Republican eye, the partisan virtues as well as the moral splendor of linking the Democratic-voting black laborers and the lily-white construction craft unions in intimate dialogue by "tying their tails together." "The NAACP wanted a tougher requirement," Ehrlichman said, and "the unions hated the whole thing." "Before long, the AFL-CIO and the NAACP were locked in combat over one of the passionate issues of the day and the Nixon Administration was located in the sweet and reasonable middle."[30]

Philadelphia Plan Redux: Proportional Representation for Whom?

To revise the moribund Philadelphia Plan, Shultz appointed as assistant Labor secretary a black Republican, Arthur A. Fletcher, who had lost a race for lieutenant governor in Washington the previous year. Fletcher and the OFCC staff took three steps over the summer of 1969 to retool the Philadelphia Plan. First, on June 27, Fletcher sent an administrative order to the heads of all agencies, signed at a public ceremony in Philadelphia, announcing that a new Philadelphia-style plan "will be put into effect in all the major cities across the Nation as soon as possible."[31] He explained that specific "goals or standards for percentages of minority employees" were necessary because America's history of segregation had been forcefully imposed upon her minorities. In that historic experience, Fletcher said, "quotas, limits, boundaries were set." He agreed that "it might be better, admittedly, if specific goals were not required—certainly the black people of America understood taboos." But the brute fact of historic discrimination meant that "Visible, measurable goals to correct obvious imbalances are essential."

What Fletcher meant by "imbalances" was clarified by the revised plan itself.[32] At its heart was a model of proportional representation. This had been a vaguely implicit model ever since Roosevelt's FEPC in 1941, and Vice President Lyndon Johnson had seemed to imply as much when he had complained during the early 1960s, as head of the PCEEO, of minority "underutilization." The notion of underutilization implied an unfair shortfall in the representation of certain groups, whose presence under normal circumstances presumably would reflect their proportion in the total population of the relevant worker pool, absent invidious discrimination. The storm over racial quotas and "reverse discrimination" that raged through the 1970s often lost sight of the model of demographic proportionality that provided the logic and generated the numbers for the compensatory remedies.

Fletcher's June plan, however, seemed in direct conflict with the Civil Rights Act of 1964, which prohibited in Title 7 any government requirement that would coerce employers toward proportional representation. So Fletcher sought to avoid this conflict in the revised Philadelphia Plan by providing for the OFCC area coordinators in all cities to assess local conditions, and then establish for each designated construction trade not a specific numerical target, but rather a target *range*. The range in turn was expressed as a percentage rather than as a numerical goal, although the percentage translated into a number whenever it was applied. Fletcher's second step was to provide a model with real numbers for the seven mechanical trades originally targeted in the Philadelphia Plan. To do this the Labor Department held hearings in Philadelphia during August 26–28 to gather information for setting the new standards.

Then, on September 23, Fletcher took his third step by publishing a 20-page memorandum of implementation, based on the "findings" from the August hearings, that set five-year target ranges for Philadelphia. The plumbers and pipefitters, for example, with what Fletcher's figures claimed were only 12 minority workers among 2,335 union members in Philadelphia (or 0.5 percent), were set a minority goal for 1970 that ranged from 5 to 8 percent. This escalated annually to reach a range of 22–26 percent for 1973. Similarly escalating ranges were set for the other trades. These target ranges in turn represented a rough splitting of the difference between Philadelphia's 30 percent black population in the metropolitan population (and by presumption, also in the workforce) and its 12 percent black representation in the skilled construction trades in 1969.[33]

Fletcher thus sought to finesse what Hubert Humphrey had referred to as the "bugaboo" of quotas by establishing, in the invitation for bids, suggested ranges of minority employment within which bidding contractors could presumably choose targets. As a disarming gesture toward the anti-quota language of section 703(j) in Title 7, the revised plan also contained a formal disclaimer of uncertain import: the requirement of specific goals "is not intended and shall not be used to discriminate against any qualified applicant or employee." Fletcher insisted in 1969, as did Republican spokesmen thereafter, that the goals were not "fixed and rigid quotas," and that employers who subsequently failed to meet them would be given a chance to demonstrate that they had made "every good faith effort" to meet their goals.[34] On the other hand, putting the blame for discrimination on the unions was ruled an unacceptable excuse for contractors.

But which groups qualified as minorities for the purpose of proportional representation? Obviously blacks did. Fletcher's "Revised Philadelphia Plan" defined the covered minority groups as "Negro, Oriental, American Indian and Spanish Surnamed American."[35] Oriental was not further defined. Spanish Surnamed American was defined merely as "all persons of Mexican, Puerto Rican, Cuban or Spanish origin or ancestry." This rather casual enumeration of protected groups, which was buried in an appendix, essentially repeated the enumeration contained in the old PCEEO's Standard Form 40, which had since evolved into form EEO-1.[36] There was no reference to any prior hearings or findings over the years, whether by administrative agencies or congressional committees, where a public forum or deliberative process had been provided for making such a momentous policy determination. The Revised Philadelphia Plan's list of protected classes instead was inherited from the boilerplate of earlier bureaucratic forms, themselves the product of drafting by anonymous staff.

Consistent with this tradition, Fletcher's policy announcement of September 1969 made no attempt to explain why some groups were listed for special treatment and others were not. It is understandable why administrative officials would be reluctant to hold such hearings, for the number of groups seeking special advantage might escalate in problematical and embarrassing ways. Nor had Congress held such hearings or made such difficult determinations—indeed, Congress had reached much the opposite conclusion in the Civil Rights Act of 1964. During the summer of 1969 the Labor Department's bureaucratic maneuvering over contract-compliance in Philadelphia had scarcely been noticed by the media. Yet by September 23, the list of protected classes in America was virtually set.

There was one significant omission, however, and also one revealing addition. The omission was the nation's largest bloc of workers with a history (probably the world's longest) of job discrimination: women. Like the Johnson administration, Richard Nixon's administration simply forgot about women when they contemplated EEO enforcement in contract compliance. Johnson had forgotten women in 1965 in his enforcement order for the Civil Rights Act, and they were tacked back on only in 1967 (that revealing oversight will be discussed in Chapter 11). The OFCC's *addition* to the approved list of minorities in 1969, on the other hand, was also intriguing, and like the omission of women it went essentially unnoticed by the press. This was the inclusion of Cuban-Americans.

Adding Cubans made some immediate political sense for a Republican administration, in that the large bloc of Cuban-Americans who had fled Castro's revolution was overwhelmingly Republican.[37] And the Cubans were indubitably of Spanish heritage. But the Cuban émigrés had fled Castro's violent revolution in 1959 largely because they represented the propertied, professional, conservative classes who had the most to lose. Hence as an American ethnic group of quite recent origin, they had found economic success with unusual speed.[38] If the chief rationale for affirmative action was to compensate for historic discrimination against a disadvantaged minority, then the Cubans' had little credible claim—except perhaps against Fidel Castro's government—and it is not clear that the proud and upwardly mobile Cubans ever pressed such a claim.[39] Thus the mere possession of a Spanish surname seemed a fanciful reason to single out for special protection such a relatively prosperous, Republican group. If the rationale of the Philadelphia Plan was to remedy past discrimination against minority groups, then the Cuban inclusion raised troublesome questions about the relationship between ends and means, about the linkage between actual disadvantage and mere group membership, and about the relative primacy of individual and group rights in the American constitutional order.

For America in the summer of 1969, "minorities" essentially meant blacks, especially in cities like Philadelphia. It certainly did not seem to mean women, although the snowballing feminist movement was beginning to press the question. It logically seemed to include Asians, who were indubitably a racial minority with a history of severe discrimination and deprivation in America, especially in the West. Yet Asian-Americans, like Cuban-Americans, did not seem to be organizing to press the matter.[40] Hispanic-Americans were specifically listed as ethinic minorities, although confusion over their appropriate rubric (Spanish-speaking, Spanish-surnamed, Hispanic "heritage," Chicano) reflected a larger conceptual muddle over the relative roles of language, race, and religion in defining Hispanic heritage as an affirmative action category. Such difficult questions of definition, rationale, and consistency would surface later, when the basic black-based mold was pretty much set according to a proportional model. But by the summer recess of Congress in 1969, Shultz had revised the Philadelphia Plan and with his President's backing, the Labor secretary was ready to do battle to defend it. He did not have long to wait.

The Confused Proxy War of 1969: The White House vs. the Hill

Beginning in August 1969, the Shultz-led offensive over the revised Philadelphia Plan escalated into a proxy war over government powers. In the process it confused and overwhelmed the original issue of desegregating the construction industry, or even enforcing the Civil Rights Act. But its conclusion on the eve of Christmas, 1969, while not resolving the larger questions involving separation of powers, left an opening that the civil rights establishment adeptly exploited.

The contest heated up during the summer of 1969 against the too-familiar background crackle of urban violence. By 1969 the spontaneous and self-destructive race riots that had characterized the summers of 1965 through

1968 had given way to a more purposive pattern of bargaining, where the threat of violence backed specific black demands. In Chicago, job protests launched by a coalition of black neighborhood organizations shut down twenty-three South Side construction projects involving $85 million in contracts and idled 1200 construction workers (half of them black). In Pittsburgh, where 20 percent of the city residents were black but only four of the twenty-five building trades locals had black membership exceeding 2 percent, job-site violence in August injured fifty demonstrators and twelve policemen.[41] In Philadelphia, black protest leaders acknowledged with approval that the Philadelphia Plan was "in effect, a quota system," and predicted a race riot if the plan was not quickly reinstated.[42]

To defend Fletcher's plan from the expected GAO attack, the Labor Department's solicitor general, Laurence Silberman, issued a 44-page supporting brief in mid-July. The Labor brief attempted to trump Staats' statutory authority by citing the superior constitutional powers of the President as exercised through his executive orders and his cabinet departments. In reply, Staats on August 5 wrote that the new Philadelphia Plan still violated Title 7. He quoted Hubert Humphrey's pledge of 1964: "Contrary to the allegations of some opponents of this title, there is nothing in it that will give any power to the Commission or to any court to require hiring, firing, or promotion of employees in order to meet a racial 'quota' or to achieve a certain racial balance."[43]

This is turn drew a sharp attack from Shultz at a press conference the following day. Shultz lectured Staats that the GAO was an agent of Congress, not of the executive branch. The Comptroller's opinion, Shultz said, was neither solicited by the Labor Department nor supported by the Justice Department, and was based on interpreting a law (Title 7) unrelated to the Comptroller's proper field of procurement. Two days later, Nixon issued an executive order of his own directing all federal agencies to maintain a "continuing affirmative program" of equal opportunity for civilian federal employees. Then, on September 22, Attorney General Mitchell weighed in against Staats with a 20-page brief that argued, like Shultz, that the President's constitutional authority overrode the GAO's statutory mandate.[44]

Staats, however, was not without powerful allies. He could count on strong support from two normal adversaries, federal contractors and organized labor. Staats' most powerful allies, however, were in Congress itself. Congress had created the GAO in 1921 to be its watchdog on federal expenditures, and generally to act as a congressionally loyal counterbalance to the Bureau of the Budget, which Congress created at the same time to serve the President. In the intervening years the barons of Congress were generally displeased when executive departments attempted to circumvent or ignore the rulings of the Comptroller General. As an astute veteran of bureaucratic politics, Staats was eager to use the disputed Philadelphia Plan as leverage in a larger contest of power. Over the years attorneys general under both Democratic and Republican administrations had jousted with comptrollers general over final authority in contract disputes. Since his appointment in 1966, Staats had battled the Justice Department over contract work for agencies ranging from the air force and the

Atomic Energy Commission to HEW and HUD, crossing swords with attorneys general Katzenbach and Clark as well as with Mitchell. Now Staats had powerful congressmen rallying to his defense. In August no lesser a senatorial baron than Everett Dirksen himself warned Shultz that the new Philadelphia Plan violated the intent of Congress in 1964. Dirksen said he would ask the chairs of the Senate and House Appropriations committees to block funds for contracts "issued or conditioned upon any minority labor plan which is in violation of the 1964 Act."[45]

The Showdown in Congress

The instrument of congressional challenge was a Senate Judiciary subcommittee chaired by North Carolina's Sam Ervin. When Dirksen died in September his replacement as Senate Republican leader, Hugh Scott, was a liberal Republican from Pennsylvania who was campaigning for re-election and who supported the Philadelphia Plan. Thus Dirksen's mantle as defender of nondiscrimination ironically fell to Ervin, a southern Democrat who could not match Dirksen's credentials as leader of the principled opposition—in region, party, prestige, or political saavy. Ervin's purpose in the two-day hearings in late October was not to report a bill out of committee. Rather, it was to expose the racial quotas of the revised Philadelphia Plan.

Most of the eleven persons testifying before Ervin's committee, including spokesmen for the AFL-CIO, contractor associations, and Comptroller Staats, attacked the Philadelphia Plan. Union spokesmen pointed out that the Labor Department had held the hearings in Philadelphia only *after* it had first announced the policy the hearings would ratify *ex post facto*.[46] Fletcher had announced the new order on June 27, then held hearings in Philadelphia on August 26 and 27, where testimony was virtually unanimous in support of the plan that the Labor Department had already announced. As one critic wryly observed, "The Department of Labor decreed discrimination first and found it later."[47] Spokesmen for the contractors argued that the plan's minority "ranges" were thinly disguised minority quotas. The director of the Philadelphia contractors association pounced on the plan's curious device of a *maximum* range for minority hiring. "Except for camouflage," he asked, "what purpose is served by establishing a range with a maximum figure?" "If an employer's efforts to recruit minority workers should bear such fruit as to exceed the maximum figure in the range, will the employer be declared in noncompliance for recruiting too many minority workers?"[48]

Ervin made little dent in the testimony of Shultz, who carried a bulldog tenacity beneath what the press called his Buddha-like exterior. Ervin was more successful, however, in flustering Jerris Leonard, who struggled unconvincingly with the contradiction between Dirksen's anti-quota language in Title 7 and the minority preferences of the Philadelphia Plan. Over-all, Ervin demonstrated remarkable devotion and fidelity to the text and spirit of a civil rights act that he had done his utmost in 1963 and 1964 to destroy.

Following the softening-up exercise by Ervin's committee, Staats asked senior members of the two Appropriations committees, West Virginia's Robert C. Byrd in the Senate and George H. Mahon of Texas in the House, to attach some language to their current bills that would clarify the authority of the GAO over the mission agencies in procurement contract disputes. Staats sent both chairmen a model sentence that served his broader purpose splendidly. Drafted by the GAO's general counsel, it asserted that no congressional appropriation "shall be available to finance, either directly or indirectly or through any Federal aid or grant, any contract or agreement which the Comptroller General of the U.S. holds to be in contravention of any Federal statute."[49] On December 15, Byrd obtained unanimous consent from his subcommittee to attach the GAO rider to a minor supplemental appropriation for damage caused by Hurricane Camille.

The Byrd rider had surfaced so quickly, with Congress rushing its crowded agenda toward the Christmas adjournment, that its supporters were able to cast the issue as essentially a contest between the statutory authority of Congress and an overreaching Executive. The Nixon administration rallied its Republican minority to defend a Republican presidency. The alarmed White House held a news briefing at which Shultz attacked the rider as potentially "a great tragedy." The showdown in the Senate unified the northern and southern Democrats behind their leadership, and on December 18 Byrd's rider passed by a vote of 52 to 37. Nixon moved quickly to block the rider in the House. Meeting with Republican congressional leaders on December 22, Nixon urged them to use the Philadelphia Plan to split the Democrats' core constituency by driving a wedge between civil rights groups and organized labor. The Philadelphia Plan would even the score against labor, Nixon said, for the administration's humiliating defeat over Judge Haynsworth.[50]

The contest confounded normal alignments, as labor joined the southern Democrats in opposition, and the Nixon administration joined the civil rights liberals. House Republican leader Gerald R. Ford made the vote a litmus test of party loyalty, one soured by traditional conservative scruples, but considerably sweetened by the enraged opposition of organized labor. The result was a major victory for Nixon—and especially for Shultz. On December 22, the Senate rider failed in the House by a vote of 156 to 208. A majority of Democrats supported the Byrd rider (115 to 84), with the core supporters being southern Democrats (61 to 6). The deciding votes that killed the rider came from Republicans supporting their President by a solid vote of 124 to 41. In response to the House vote, the Senate later that day decided, on a roll-call vote, 39 to 29 to drop its now hopeless proposal, and both houses quickly adjourned until January 19, 1970.[51]

A Philadelphia Plan for All Contractors

Nixon's stand behind Shultz and the Philadelphia Plan was effective in splitting the Democrats' core coalition of labor and civil rights groups, at least temporarily. But the President's satisfaction at dividing his enemies and protecting executive prerogatives was purchased at the high price of splitting the Southern Strategy's core coalition of Republicans and conservative Democrats. The legislative battle had ended in a stand-off. In the new era of divided government, the two elective branches would continue their perennial battles over authority and turf, intensifying them in partisan disputes over the Vietnam war and Watergate. The defeat of the Byrd rider left the standing law intact, including the anti-quota provisions of Title 7. Critics of affirmative action quotas would emphasize this technically correct interpretation.[52] But the opponents of minority preferences had been bloodied. Dirksen was dead, the unusual coalition of organized labor and government contractors had been defeated, and the Comptroller General had lost his bid for veto authority over agency contracts.

The defeat left a power vacuum and the civil rights coalition moved quickly to fill it. Despite assurances from the Labor Department during the summer and fall of 1969 that the Philadelphia Plan's controversial requirements for minority percentages in hiring was uniquely tailored to the construction industry, the OFCC was planning to apply the Philadelphia model of proportional representation to *all* federal contractors. Jerris Leonard had explained to the Ervin committee that the Philadelphia Plan was construction-specific. It was narrowly tailored by hearings and findings to correct local pockets of segregation, Leonard explained, such as the six skilled crafts in Philadelphia. In emphasizing the Philadelphia Plan's limited reach, Leonard stressed the uniquely intermittent and hiring-hall nature of construction employment, as opposed to "the usual industrial situation, where the employer has a more or less fixed group or complement of employees." For nonconstruction employers, Leonard said, "the requirements of the Executive order ordinarily can be met if that employer engages in an affirmative recruiting program," such as "going into the minority areas in an attempt to seek out qualified minority group employees as new hires."[53]

On January 15, however, Ervin announced that the Labor Department had lied to him. He had discovered that at the same time the department was assuring Congress that its Philadelphia Plan would require only "good faith efforts" by construction contractors and would not set minority quotas, it had secretly issued a new order extending racial quotas to *all* federal contractors. Ervin quoted from the text of the Labor Department's Order No. 4 of November 20, 1969, signed by OFCC director John Wilks. Its language seemed to apply to all government contracts the Philadelphia Plan's model of proportional representation: "The rate of minority applicants recruited should approximate or equal the ratio of minorities to the applicant population in each location."[54] Order No. 4 required contractors to set their own hiring goals and objectives, Wilks explained, but these goals "would have to equal the minority ratio of the local applicant population." Like the revised Philadelphia Plan that Fletcher announced the previous June, Order No. 4 had been preceded by no hearings. Furthermore, Wilks had neglected to have it published in the *Federal Register* in the government's customary notice-and-comment fashion for administrative rule-making. "Unrevealed to the Congress or the public until now," Ervin charged, Order No. 4 "requires the imposition of flat quotas. It was an integral part of the Philadelphia Plan. In its scope, it makes the announced Philadelphia Plan look like small potatoes."[55]

Shultz knew that the defeat of the Byrd rider had defanged the congressional critics led by Ervin. The presidency was united, Congress was divided, and the federal courts increasingly were ruling in favor of stronger executive authority and remedial measures in civil rights disputes. The importance of political battles like the war over the Byrd rider was well understood within the Washington beltway, but such battles generally bored voters beyond the beltway. On February 3, Shultz issued a reworked Order No. 4 to a scarcely breathless public. It required all contractors, not just builders, to file an affirmative action program within 120 days of signing a contract. An acceptable program first required an analysis of all major job categories to identify any "underutilization" of blacks, Spanish Surnamed Americans, American Indians, and Orientals within each category. Underutilization was defined as "having fewer minorities in a particular job class than would reasonably be expected by their availability," and could be determined by comparing "the percentage of the minority work force as compared with the total work force in the immediate labor area." The contractor would then submit "specific goals and timetables" to "correct any identifiable deficiencies." Failing correction satisfactory to the OFCC, the contractor would cease to do business with the federal government.[56]

In the past the shock of an exposé like Ervin's trump against the red-faced OFCC would have sent the overreaching agency into retreat before congressional umbrage. But the turn of the decade into 1970 seemed to mark a sociopolitical watershed. Despite the fragmenting impact of Black Power and ghetto riots and the election of Nixon, the civil rights constituency was emerging from the 1960s with a momentum that increasingly was generated from within as well as outside the citadels of government. The civil rights coalition during the 1960s had achieved success in three areas that were mutually reinforcing. First, the breakthrough laws of 1964–65 had produced implementing structures staffed by a growing civil rights network in the federal agencies. Second, the coalition had mobilized grass-roots electoral power that swelled the ranks of its friends in Congress and neutralized its enemies. Third, the moral power of civil rights protest had provided the federal courts with a rationale for intervening in the formulation of social policy.

When Attorney General John Mitchell challenged the Comptroller's ruling against the Philadelphia Plan in September 1969, he cited the Supreme Court's recent *Gaston County* decision on voting discrimination to argue, as Earl Warren had done in *Gaston,* that the need to remedy past discrimination might require race-conscious forms of relief. "The obligation of nondiscrimination, whether imposed by statute or by the Constitution," Warren had written, "does not require and, *in some circumstances may not permit* obliviousness or indifference to the racial consequences of alternative courses of action which involve the application of outwardly neutral criteria [emphasis added]."[57] It was indeed striking to hear Richard Nixon's former law partner, Republican presidential campaign manager, putative designer of the Southern Strategy, and now Attorney General sounding like Joseph Rauh of the Leadership Conference on Civil Rights. But Mitchell was responding to accumulating hints that the Supreme Court might no longer agree with the famous dissent, in the segregation decision of *Plessy v. Ferguson* in 1896, of Justice John Marshall Harlan: the Constitution of the United States is color-blind.

CHAPTER 10

The "Color-Blind" Constitution
and the Federal Courts

The Strange Career of the Two Brown Decisions

In 1964, when the President and Congress joined the Supreme Court in pro-
claiming that racial discrimination violated national policy, the majority coalition supporting the Civil Rights Act seemed to share two broad conclusions
about the decade since *Brown v. Board of Education*. One was that the *Brown*
decision had overturned the separate-but-equal doctrine of *Plessy*, and had
adopted in its place Justice John Marshall Harlan's ringing dissent—that the
American Constitution is "color-blind" and "neither knows nor tolerates
classes among its citizens."[1] In 1954 the *New York Times* greeted Earl Warren's ruling in *Brown* by observing that Harlan's lonely dissent in *Plessy*, which
for half a century had been "a voice crying into the wilderness," had at last
been transformed by *Brown* into "the law of the land."[2]

A second staple of consensus in 1964, more firmly held by liberals than
moderates, was that *Brown* II, the Supreme Court's implementing decision of
1955, had been a shameful retreat from the moral grandeur of *Brown* I in
1954. The Warren Court's charge to the lower federal judges in *Brown* II to
pursue school desegregation "with all deliberate speed" had led to a decade of
southern tokenism. If the *New York Times* represented a fair barometer of
cosmopolitan convictions about such matters, then enlightened opinion in
1964 agreed that *Brown* I had struck a mighty blow for the color-blind Constitution and that *Brown* II had wilted from the challenge. Time and events,
however, have since turned this interpretation on its head.

The first assumption, that *Brown* I had overruled *Plessy*, was correct to the
extent that *Brown* in 1954 held unconstitutional the racially segregated caste
system that *Plessy* in 1896 had approved. Warren's opinion in *Brown*, however,
left Harlan's famous dissent in *Plessy* curiously unmentioned. It seemed a missed
historical opportunity that the *Times* should celebrate Harlan's sweet vindication but that the Supreme Court itself in *Brown* did not.[3] The justices in 1954 did
not disagree on whether school segregation should be ruled unconstitutional.

170

Indeed, the Court was unanimous on that in 1954, and it maintained unanimity on its school desegregation decisions until the busing controversy nationalized the issue in the early 1970s.[4] The disagreement came over how to enforce desegregation. The Court in 1954 feared the social chaos and judicial humiliation that might follow widespread southern defiance of a desegregation order from the bench. By remaining silent on Harlan's principle of color-blindness, the Court in *Brown* I had determined what was *not* constitutional (racially dual school systems), but had not explained what *was* constitutional. Thus the Court in 1954 temporized, held another year of hearings on how best to implement *Brown* I, and in May of 1955 issued its implementing decree in *Brown* II. The NAACP's Thurgood Marshall, when arguing before the Supreme Court in 1955 for relief for his victorious plaintiffs, put the point with elegant simplicity: "The only thing that the Court is dealing with," Marshall explained, is "whether or not race can be used."[5] "What we want from the Court," he said, "is the striking down of race." But having won *Brown* I, Marshall's plaintiffs would win no direct relief from the court in *Brown* II. Oliver Brown's daughter, Linda, would graduate from an all-black school in Topeka. The dismaying story of tokenism under a decade of *Brown* II is familiar, but the obvious ironies of Linda Brown's fate are compounded by more hidden ironies.

When the Court's implementation decision was announced on May 31, 1955, the white South responded with a sigh of relief that the NAACP's call for "majestic instancy" had been rejected, and instead the five cases were remanded to the local federal district courts. In a cautious gesture that was designed in part to forestall a violent southern reaction against the Court's call for a social revolution in *Brown* I, the Court in *Brown* II asked not for admission to public schools on a nondiscriminatory basis, but only for a "prompt and reasonable start toward full compliance."[6] Warren's opinion borrowed the phrase "all deliberate speed" from an obscure opinion by Justice Holmes. But the enigmatic modifier (if not, indeed, the oxymoron) was inserted at the insistence of Felix Frankfurter, who feared a disastrous southern backlash against a Court that could not enforce its decree. This sealed the bargain between Warren and the more conservative justices, with the unanimous decision in *Brown* I balanced by a constitutionally novel remedy in *Brown* II that would deny Linda Brown her individual relief, but would buy time for a gradual enforcement by local federal judges who would be provided no clear judicial guidelines or deadlines.[7]

Brown II, then, *was* a conservative decision, as the relieved white South and the disappointed civil rights community immediately perceived. Or at least it so appeared in 1955 and for a decade thereafter. Looking back from 1963, Columbia law professor Louis Lusky concluded that "Conceptually, the 'deliberate speed' formula is impossible to justify."[8] Since its beginning judicial review was grounded in the judge's duty to give a litigant his rights under the Constitution, Lusky said. "But the apparently successful plaintiff in the *Brown* case [Linda Brown's father] got no more than a promise that, some time in the indefinite future, other people would be given the rights which the Court said he had." Legal scholar Lino Graglia, a conservative critic who regarded the ambiguity of the twin *Brown* decisions as a prelude to "disaster," called *Brown* II's denial of relief to Linda Brown and her co-plaintiffs "the racist element of *Brown* II."[9]

By imbedding in its implementation decree in *Brown* II a presumption against Harlan's color-blind Constitution, however, the court ironically linked enforcement to class actions that would ultimately require *more,* not less, government classification by race. Warren had warned in the school desegregation cases that "Classifications based solely on race must be scrutinized with particular care, since they are contrary to our traditions and hence constitutionally suspect."[10] By the late 1960s the Warren Court had firmed up a doctrine of constitutionally "suspect" classifications.[11] Racial distinctions in statute or policy were at the forefront, and when challenged they automatically triggered a "strict" judicial scrutiny that was virtually certain to invalidate the challenged provision. This was consistent with the liberal rule of equal treatment and nondiscrimination, which lay at the heart of Harlan's dictum that the Constitution was color-blind. But it was not consistent with the compensatory theory that also flowered in the late 1960s, and that increasingly required preferential policies for "protected classes."

The Supreme Court's new postwar doctrines of strict judicial scrutiny for suspect classifications and compensatory relief for protected classes, despite their tension, shared a common origin in the nation's historical discrimination against minorities. Racial and ethnic classifications were suspect because they had historically been used to discriminate against minorities; similarly, affirmative action was designed to compensate for past discrimination. The remedies required by the two doctrines, however, were contradictory. The remedy for suspect classifications, like racial segregation laws or Jewish quotas in state medical schools, was to invalidate them. In the classic liberal formulation, the remedy for discrimination was nondiscrimination. But the remedy for compensating protected classes was minority preferences.

During the first decade of desegregation under *Brown* II, the Warren Court showed amazing tolerance toward continued use of racial classifications in the school desegregation cases (although not in other areas of state policy, such as access to libraries, government offices, transit systems, and recreational facilities). Southern school officials were allowed to institute "freedom of choice" plans that produced only token desegregation because they were keyed to race. Often parents were permitted to transfer their children out of schools where they would be in the racial minority—an option exercised by virtually all white parents, and also by some black parents who sought to protect their children from racial hostility and violence.[12]

Brown II thus had the conservative effect of remanding the enforcement of the school desegregation cases back to the federal district and circuit judges in the South. These jurists included the *Fifty-eight Lonely Men* in the Fourth and Fifth judicial circuits (none was female), pillars of their local civic establishments, whose cautious decisions during the subsequent decade were described by J.W. Peltason in 1961 as virtual socio-legal inevitabilities.[13] The lamentable but not surprising result was that after a full decade of court-ordered desegregation, only *2.3 percent* of southern black schoolchildren were enrolled with white children in desegregated schools. In light of high black birthrates, this meant that more black schoolchildren were attending segregated southern schools in 1964 than in 1954. Many federal judges in the South showed exceptional courage in the face of repeated threats to their persons and families. But over-all the extraordinary deference of the federal courts to white southern sensitivities amounted essentially to a decade of default.[14]

From Brown II to Busing

With the passage of the Civil Rights Act of 1964, however, the federal courts began to abandon their caution. Within the next few years the courts transformed the ambiguously enforced duty of local governments to desegregate their schools into an ill-defined duty to integrate them. The transition began most notably with *United States v. Jefferson County Board of Education* in 1966, in the Fifth Circuit Court in New Orleans under the leadership of Judge John Minor Wisdom.[15] A Republican appointed by Eisenhower, Wisdom was exasperated with a decade-long pattern of compliance through pupil-placement and freedom-of-choice plans that had often taken race into account in order to guarantee the barest tokenism. In *Jefferson*, Wisdom ordered the school districts not merely to desegregate by abandoning the racially triggered transfers of the free-choice plans, but also to "undo the harm" of their Jim Crow past by racially balancing their school populations according to the new HEW guidelines. For Wisdom, the remedy must speak not just to individual black plaintiffs but to the entire race, and the courts were required to hold citizens of the present accountable for the sins of the distant past, even when they were yet unborn. This would require, Wisdom said, "the organized undoing of the effects of past segregation."[16]

Jefferson signified the transition in 1966 from the piecemeal approach of *Brown* II to a positive obligation imposed by the courts on school boards to plan affirmatively and comprehensively for school integration. Far from being blind to color, school superintendents would henceforth be required to use race as a lodestar for educational decision-making—not only in student assignment but also in teacher training and placement, transportation policy, school finance, and student testing and remediation. J. Harvie Wilkinson called *Jefferson* the crucial turning point which transformed the face of desegregation law: "To speak thus is to thrust law to the forefront of social change, to adopt an admirable, if impossible, goal."[17] "Relief to the class, as opposed to the individual relief practiced heretofore," Wilkinson said, "initiated the idea of compensatory justice, which later would influence the Supreme Court on such imposing issues as student busing and affirmative action programs." It was a radical change. Yet the courts slipped into it while inching their way along a frustrating spectrum of implementation, without apparent awareness of the indefinable burdens it would eventually place both on the courts and on society. By requiring society to "undo" the effects of that past, the courts were requiring a remedy for which they provided no definition and hence no principled point of termination.

In the spring of 1968, the Supreme Court itself rose above the circuit court fray to reject a freedom of choice plan. The dispute arose in New Kent County in rural eastern Virginia, where traditional county-wide school busing had produced no white students at all in the county's all-black Watkins school, which enrolled 85 percent of the county's black students. Justice Department attorneys scoffed at the county's elaborate freedom-of-choice plan as a transparent apparatus to avoid sending white children to predominantly black schools (which it was) and to minimize black attendance at predominantly white shools (which it did). The U.S. Solicitor argued for an "old-fashioned, traditional concept of neighborhood schools." In the traditionally bussed and residentially integrated rural South, this would produce immediate and significant school integration. In *Green* the Supreme Court shifted the burden of achieving integration from the backs of black children and their parents to the southern school systems. *Green* charged school boards with the responsibility to develop affirmative plans that, in the words of Justice William Brennan, promise "realistically to work *now.*"[18]

Jefferson and *Green* represented a leap in enforcement requirements that reflected more than accumulating dissatisfaction with the glacial creep of school desegregation. It reflected in addition the positive incentive provided by the Civil Rights Act of 1964, and especially by the guidelines developed by HEW in response to Title 4 on school segregation and Title 6 on contract compliance. These guidelines seemed to promise a basis for order, uniformity, and specificity in school desegregation that had been missing from *Brown* II. They offered as well the sanction of alleged educational expertise to back the writ of mere judges. So in affirming *Jefferson* the Fifth Circuit Court insisted that "courts in this circuit should give great weight to future HEW guidelines."[19] By the late 1960s the federal courts were finding support for the Warren Court's compensatory policies in the civil rights agencies—the EEOC, OFCC, and Voting Rights Section in Justice, as well as the Office of Civil Rights in HEW. This alliance of agency and bench was effective in overcoming the bias of Congress toward racial neutrality. Legislative bargaining required compromises, and the common ground for the great civil rights compromises of the 1960s was nondiscrimination. The Civil Rights Act, the Voting Rights Act, and the Fair Housing Act were all rooted in classic liberalism's command to do no harm on account of any citizen's race, sex, national origin, or religion. For courts impatient to balance the scales of history, this often placed the judge at odds with legislative intent. But the post-hoc nature of judicial review allowed the judges to interpret legislative intent for themselves.

Judicial Activism and Congressional Intent: Affirmative Action in Voting Rights

History had its selective uses in judicial construction, as the Supreme Court demonstrated in 1968 when it announced, to a startled Capitol Hill, that racial discrimination in housing had been banned by Congress in 1866.[20] History could thus occasionally be the friend of social justice, especially when the courts of the Second Reconstruction mined the legislative lode of the original Reconstruction following the Civil War. But in the eyes of the Warren Court, history was for the most part the custodian of our legacy of inequality, and hence the enemy of social justice. Particularly in the school desegregation cases, the federal courts had begun to view history as an unfair legacy of accumulated inequities that mere nondiscrimination was insufficient to correct. A history of de jure segregation seemed to establish not only the geographic distribution of the problem, but also the nature and extent of the Court-imposed remedy.

In litigation over the Voting Rights Act, the Supreme Court found in *Gaston County* in June 1969 that the blameless conduct of public officials was overwhelmed by the accumulated sins of the past. The hands of government in Gaston County, North Carolina, were procedurally clean in 1969. But historically they were deeply stained by traditions and institutions of racial discrimination. *Gaston* meant that after June 1969, no jurisdiction with a Jim Crow past (which conceivably could also include the Bedford-Stuyvesants of America with their southern black immigrants, and perhaps the Hispanic barrios and the western Chinatowns with their own unique versions of Jim Crow) could escape the critical scrutiny of the Civil Rights Division of the Justice Department. Although the Voting Rights Act appeared on its face to be premised on classic nondiscrimination theory, compensatory theory was implicit in *Gaston* in the general sense that black voters from segregated schools would require special federal protection until the harmful effects of historical discrimination had somehow been undone. But the Voting Rights Act's seeds of compensatory theory lay less in the triggering provision in section four, which had been the focus of *Gaston*, than in the preclearance provision in section five.

Gaston had been preceded in the spring of 1969 by another crucial voting-rights decision, one in which ironically the author of *Gaston*, Justice Harlan, found himself in sharp dissent. The case was *Allen v. State Board of Elections*, decided by the Court that March.[21] The focus of *Allen* was the meaning and reach of section five. The case came to the Court in the form of four appeals, the three important ones coming from Mississippi as challenges to a batch of laws passed by Mississippi's legislature in 1966. The new laws were designed to blunt the impact of the previous year's Voting Rights Act on the political power of black Mississippians by switching from district to at-large elections for county supervisors, moving from elected to appointed superintendents of education in eleven heavily black counties, and making more burdensome the requirements for independent candidates to qualify for public office. A three-judge federal trial court in Mississippi had dismissed the complaints on the grounds that they did not come within the purview of section five, which dealt only with voter registration procedures and equal access to the voting booth.

The main substantive question in *Allen* was whether section five reached beyond the voting booth to include such broad electoral policies as forms of districting and whether offices were appointive or elective—questions that bore not on access to the voting booth but on the relative political power reflected in the outcome. The Mississippi cases carried the naked imprint of racial discrimination. They thus offered the Warren Court an opportunity to expand the scope of federal anti-discrimination statutes from the bench, even though Congress in 1965 had declined to do so. The Voting Rights Act defined "voting" to mean "all action necessary to make a vote effective in any primary, special, or general election." This included registration, casting a ballot, and "having such ballot counted properly and included in the appropriate totals of votes cast."[22] Warren read the broadest possible meaning into the language of 1965, arguing that it was aimed at the "subtle as well as the obvious state regulations which have the effect of denying citizens their right to vote because of race."

In his broad interpretation of "the basic purposes of the act," as distinct from its specific language, Warren leaned heavily on the equal protection logic of the reapportionment cases. In *Reynolds v. Sims,* the "one-man, one-vote" decision of 1964, the Court propounded a new requirement of mathematical equality in the population of legislative districts, and Warren defended the new doctrine by alluding to the unfairness of voter "dilution." "The fact that an individual lives here or there," Warren observed, "is not a legitimate reason for overweighting or diluting the efficacy of his vote."[23] The concept of the dilution of power was inherently relative and enormously complex, in that all apportionment and districting decisions necessarily favored some groups over others. But *Reynolds* posited the concept of voter dilution without defining it. The reapportionment cases had been decided on Fourteenth amendment grounds, with the equal protection clause providing the rationale for the federal courts to command state legislators and local governments to create mathematically equal voting districts. Then, in *Allen,* Warren extended the "dilution" logic of the reapportionment cases to apply to voting-rights law and racial discrimination. "The right to vote can be affected by a dilution of voting power as well as by an absolute prohibition on casting a ballot," Warren said.[24] "Voters who are members of a racial minority might well be in the majority in one district, but in a decided minority in the county as a whole. This type of change could therefore nullify their ability to elect the candidate of their choice just as would prohibiting some of them from voting."

Warren's majority decisions were challenged by John Marshall Harlan, namesake grandson of the famous dissenter in *Plessy.* Like Felix Frankfurter, Harlan placed great value on adherence to precedent, maintaining the balance of federalism, and on judicial deference to the legislative branch as the proper source of social policy. Unlike Earl Warren, who was described by his biographer, G. Edward White, as "openly humanitarian and just as openly anti-professional, almost contemptuous of the niceties of a legal argument when fundamental American beliefs called out to be affirmed," Harlen adhered to the methodological canons of "process liberalism."[25] Harlan valued the unanimity that had marked the Warren Court's desegregation decisions. But his commitment to self-restraint for the elitist judiciary established Harlan as the chief critic of the Warren majority's impatient egalitarianism.[26] Harlan supported section five, but unlike Warren, he understood its function as part of a complex regulatory scheme that the majority was ignoring.

To Harlan, the heart of the Voting Rights Act was section four's triggering formula, which suspended all literacy tests and opened the door to federal referees to enfranchise voteless black citizens. Thus section five's requirement for preclearance, Harlan said, "was designed solely to implement" and "assure the effectiveness of the dramatic step that Congress had taken in [section] 4's substantive commands." A state might consistently violate section five and still escape it, so long as it complied with section four—but not vice versa. In prescribing relief, Harlan noted, section five stated that "no person shall be denied the right to vote *for failure to comply* with such qualification, prerequisite, standard, practice, or procedure." Congress thus was concerned with changes in electoral procedure with which voters could *comply*. But changing from a district to an at-large election did not require voters to comply with anything at all. All the stages of the electoral process enumerated in section five concerned the *procedures* by which voters were processed and finally counted, Harlan said, not the amount of political power that blacks or other groups might subsequently derive from exercising the franchise.

Harlan's view of the Voting Rights Act's regulatory context was reinforced by its legislative history. In hearings before the House Judiciary subcommittee in 1965, Burke Marshall was asked whether the administration's bill should reach beyond the question of who can vote and "address itself to the qualifications for running for public office as well as the problem of registration?" "The problem that the bill was aimed at," Marshall had replied, "was the problem of registration, Congressman. If there is a problem of another sort, I would like to see it corrected, but that is not what we were trying to deal with in the bill."[27] To Harlan, the majority decision, then, was permitting the "tail to wag the dog" by construing section five in isolation "to require a revolutionary innovation in American government that goes far beyond" the congressional premise in section four that "once Negroes had gained free access to the ballot box, state governments would then be suitably responsive to their voice, and federal intervention would not be justified." The new ruling would require prior federal approval of all state laws "that could arguably have an impact on Negro voting power, even though the manner in which the election is conducted remains unchanged." This would require the federal courts in the future "to determine whether various systems of representation favor or disfavor the Negro voter."

How would judges determine this? How was a court to decide, Harlan asked, whether an at-large system was to be preferred over a district system? "Under one system, Negroes have *some* influence in the election of *all* officers; under the other, minority groups have *more* influence in the selection of *fewer* officers." "If courts cannot intelligently compare such alternatives," Harlan said, "it should not be readily inferred that Congress has required them to undertake the task." Moreover, such a construction would logically extend well beyond states and counties triggered by section four, to encompass areas "which in the past permitted Negroes to vote freely, but which arguably have limited minority voting power by adopting a system in which various legislative bodies are elected on an at-large basis." Thus the statute, Harlan wrote, as newly interpreted by the Court "deals with a problem that is national in scope. I find it especially difficult to believe that Congress would single out a handful of states as requiring stricter federal supervision concerning their treatment of a problem that may well be just as serious in parts of the North as it is in the South."[28]

Warren's majority opinion had avoided the vulnerable areas that Harlan attacked. Relying instead on his own interpretation of "the basic purpose of the Act" beyond its text, Warren stretched section five to include all electoral arrangements which might dilute the future impact of black voting power.[29] In his dissent Harlan lectured Warren for grounding his opinion in the reapportionment cases and in the Fourteenth amendment's equal protection clause. "This is a statute we are interpreting, not a broad constitutional provision whose contours must be defined by this court," Harlan replied. "And the fact is that Congress consciously *refused* to base [section] 5 of the Voting Rights Act on its powers under the Fourteenth Amendment, upon which the reapportionment cases are grounded."[30] The proper corrective for the racist defiance of the scattered Black Belt counties in the South was for Congress to amend the Voting Rights Act, under its authority to enforce the 15th Amendment. This would require hearings and committee reports and risk the normal bargaining and delays of the legislative process. The mood of the Democratic Congress of 1969–70 was quite congenial to this task. But by then the Supreme Court had generated a momentum in shaping social policy that continued unabated beyond the departure in 1969 of Earl Warren himself.

Harlan's suggestion in *Allen* that the application of section five was inherently national in scope was reinforced by his own majority opinion in *Gaston* three months later, when Harlan had in effect ruled for the Court that the South's history of Jim Crow could not be logically quarantined either in space or in time. Thus Congress might continue to believe that it was passing or renewing regional laws with specified time limits, but the expansionist logic of the Warren Court was shaping legislative policy far beyond the confines either of statutory language or of the will of congressional majorities. Even Harlan in his *Allen* dissent, holding aloft the tattered banner of Felix Frankfurter and judicial restraint, was swept along by the Warren Court's sea change of judicial intervention in social policy. By 1970, the Supreme Court lacked Earl Warren. But the momentum of its judicial logic was accelerating. When Nixon appointed Warren Burger Chief Justice in the fall of 1969, the salient civil rights issues of school desegregation, housing discrimination, and voting rights had already reached the high bench and had been similarly decided. Only the major area of job discrimination and equal employment law remained unclarified by the Supreme Court.

Swann, Griggs, and Racial Proportionality

The voting-rights suits received little public attention—unlike the school desegregation cases, which tended to be closely watched for signs of judicial trends.

The national media devoted inordinate attention to Nixon's "Southern Strategy," even though his posturing over school desegregation and busing disguised a pattern of quiet and effective cooperation by executive agencies with the toughening judicial mandate in the South. When in the fall of 1969 Nixon's Justice Department and HEW petitioned the federal courts for further delay in desegregating 33 Mississippi school districts, the Supreme Court in *Alexander v. Holmes County* issued a sharply worded, two-page per curiam order that *all* school districts must abandon dual school systems "at once" and operate "now and hereafter" only unitary systems.[31] Virtually all commentaries on the inside workings of the Nixon administration on civil rights policy, from Ehrlichman's *Witness to Power* to Woodward and Armstrong's *The Brethren,* agree that the President and his strategists were content with *Alexander.* The Nixon administration had asked for "reasonable" delay, but the Supreme Court had insisted on immediate integration, and thus the courts and not the White House should be held responsible for the consequences.[32]

By 1971 the Supreme Court had built its equitable powers of remedy into a plenary instrument. When that year in the *Swann* case the Supreme Court upheld federal district judge James B. McMillan's order for a massive program of busing in North Carolina's 550-square-mile Charlotte-Mecklenburg school system, the Nixon administration distanced itself from the racial balancing. Solicitor General Erwin Griswold argued that total integration was not a constitutional mandate, so the remedy required only the disestablishment of dual school systems, not "racial balance or integration of every all-white, all-Negro, or predominantly Negro school."[33] Griswold pointed out that Congress in Title 4 had carefully defined what desegregation was and what it was not. According to the law, Griswold said, desegregation meant "the assignment of students to public schools and within such schools without regard to their race, color, religion, or national origin," but it "shall not mean the assignment of students to public schools in order to overcome racial imbalance." Title 4 had further stipulated that in authorizing the attorney general to file desegregation suits,

> nothing herein shall empower any official or court of the United States to issue any order seeking to achieve a racial balance in any school by requiring transportation of pupils or students from one school to another or from one school district to another in order to achieve such racial balance, or otherwise enlarge the existing power of the court to insure compliance with constitutional standards.[34]

Speaking for a unanimous Court, Chief Justice Burger found the federal courts remarkably unrestrained by this language—or at least unrestrained by its prohibitions when dealing with public schools in the South. Burger explained in *Swann* that because the courts' equitable powers of remedy were historic as well as broad, Congress could not have intended to *reduce* them in 1964. Rather it had intended to restrict their expansion to affect de facto segregation *outside* the South. Burger's notion that Congress did not intend its definition of desegregation in Title 4 to apply to southern schools was bizarre.[35] But with the troublesome statutory language of 1964 thus dismissed, the Supreme Court in *Swann* approved Judge McMillan's order that the school system bus an additional 13,300 children to achieve racial balance. As a practical matter the plan ordered in *Swann* was sensible and worked well. This was chiefly because Charlotte's city-county school system was merged in an unusual form of metropolitan consolidation, and because only 29 percent of the system's 84,000 pupils were black.[36] But as a matter of statutory interpretation *Swann*, like *Allen,* demonstrated that the Court's new claims to remedial powers through equity were virtually unlimited. Burger himself expressed it with unconscious irony: "in seeking to define the scope of remedial power or the limits on remedial power of courts in an area as sensitive as we deal with here, words are poor instruments to convey the sense of basic fairness inherent in equity."[37] Or more precisely, the words of Congress were poor instruments when pitted against the Supreme Court's newly asserted powers of historic equity.

By comparison with the high public visibility of the courts' school desegregation cases, however, the judicial evolution of equal employment law remained obscure. Court challenges over the new equal employment provisions of 1964, whether contained in or administratively spawned by titles 6 and 7, tended to hinge on arcane technicalities of labor and contract law, like seniority and bumping rights and bidding protocols. These early tests cases often involved Title 6 and the bureaucratic intricacies of contract compliance rather than Title 7. On March 13, 1970, a federal district judge in Pennsylvania granted a motion by Nixon's Justice Department to dismiss a suit against the Philadelphia Plan filed two months earlier by an association of eighty contractors. In *Contractors Association of Eastern Pennsylvania v. Secretary of Labor* the judge threw out the contractors' suit because in his view the Philadelphia Plan was needed to end an employment practice that was "repugnant, unworthy, and contrary to national policy."[38] In 1971 the Third Circuit Court of Appeals upheld the Philadelphia Plan as a permissible policy under Johnson's executive order of 1965. Despite the intense controversy over racial quotas surrounding the Philadelphia Plan, the Supreme Court declined to review the case.[39] As the job discrimination suits bubbled up from the state circuits and the federal districts, they basically did not command the public attention that their importance warranted. This changed dramatically, however, when the Supreme Court's *Griggs* decision was announced in 1971. *Griggs v. Duke Power Co.* signified the Supreme Court's transition from the equal treatment standards of employment discrimination that underpinned the Civil Rights Act of 1964, to the equal results standards of a new body of "disparate impact" case law that rested normatively on a model of proportional representation in the workplace.[40]

Griggs was a class action brought by thirteen of the fourteen black workers among the 95 employees at the Duke Power Company's Dan River steam station near Draper, North Carolina. Prior to 1965 the company had restricted blacks to the plant's labor department, where the highest paying jobs paid less than the lower paying jobs in the four all-white operating departments. In

1955, Duke Power had sought to upgrade the quality of its workforce by requiring a high school education for initial assignment to any department except labor (which therefore meant for all "white" departments). On July 2, 1965, the day Title 7 became effective, the company ceased restricting blacks to the labor department, and extended to that department a high school requirement for transfer into better job categories, but not for initial employment.

Also in July 1965, the company began requiring that for placement in any department other than labor, all new employees must achieve acceptable scores on two professionally developed general aptitude tests. Then, in September 1965, Duke Power began to permit incumbent employees, white or black, who lacked a high school education to qualify for upward transfer by passing the two tests. At trial the company conceded that the pencil-and-paper tests did not measure the ability to learn to perform a particular job or category of job. But the Duke Power management explained that the new higher standards were evenly applied to both races in an attempt to upgrade the workforce in a dangerous workplace. Thus the company had practiced systematic racial discrimination prior to the effective date of Title 7, but thereafter had applied all requirements equally, with the exception of the diploma requirement for the grandfathered employees hired prior to 1955—all of whom were white.

The results, however, were far from equal. The 1960 census showed that only 34 percent of white males in North Carolina had graduated from high school. Worse, the graduation rate for black males was only 12 percent. The EEOC in its amicus brief cited test results in a similar case in which 58 percent of whites had passed the tests compared with only 6 percent of blacks. Moreover, although the new requirements were racially neutral on their face, Duke Power's Jim Crow past meant that the only employees exempted were white. When Griggs and his twelve black colleagues sought relief in the federal district court, they lost. The trial court found that although Duke Power had followed a policy of overt racial discrimination prior to 1965, such conduct had since ceased. Because Title 7 was intended to be prospective only in its application (beginning on July 2, 1965), the trial court ruled, the impact of prior inequities was beyond the reach of remedies authorized by the Civil Rights Act.[41]

Griggs' NAACP lawyers then appealed to the Fourth Circuit Court of Appeals in Richmond. In 1970 the appeals court agreed with the trial court that because there was no showing of discriminatory purpose on the part of Duke Power in adopting the diploma and test requirements, and because the new standards had been applied evenly to blacks and whites alike, there was no violation of Title 7. But the appeals court rejected the district court's finding that residual discrimination arising from employment practices prior to the Civil Rights Act was insulated from remedial action. This retroactive view was consistent with the logic of the historical theory as applied in voting rights cases like *Gaston,* although it was not consistent with the language of Title 7. The appeals court limited its retroactivity to an equal treatment basis, however. It ruled that only those plaintiffs hired before 1965 had been discriminated against, because similarly situated whites had not been subject to the same requirement.[42]

After reading the appeals court decision, John Pemberton, deputy general counsel for the EEOC, drafted a letter of collegial advice to Jack Greenberg, who as director-counsel of the NAACP Legal Defense Fund was the chief lawyer of the *Griggs* plaintiffs. Pemberton urged Greenberg to accept the limited victory from the Fourth Circuit and not risk appealing to the Supreme Court. Pemberton read the appeals court decision to say that Title 7 prohibits an employment test "only if it is adopted with an affirmative desire to discriminate or is administered in a discriminatory fashion." According to Title 7, the job-relatedness of a professionally developed test did not matter, but only the intentions surrounding its use. This struck Pemberton as an articulation of the traditionally narrow, "bad motive" approach, and hence as "tragic insofar as it will allow all sorts of totally invalid tests and educational requirements to screen out blacks."[43]

But Pemberton found *Griggs* to be a vulnerable case on several counts for the plaintiffs to press on the new Burger Court. The tests given by Duke Power (the Wonderlic and Otis) were widely used in industrial and commercial employment, were selected by a professional psychologist who had testified at trial on their behalf, and were precisely the kinds of tests Congress had sought to protect when adopting the Tower amendment in 1964. Also, the decision as it stood would affect only four of the thirteen plaintiffs, since the remainder could either avoid the tests under the Fourth Circuit ruling, or had since been promoted by Duke Power anyway (including all plaintiffs with high school diplomas). Finally, the steam plant jobs sounded fairly complex and dangerous to Pemberton, thus indicating legitimate business needs for high standards. Moreover, Duke Power had agreed to waive the tests for any employee who could earn a high school diploma or its equivalent, and the company had begun a program to subsidize such efforts through adult education. "All of this means," Pemberton reluctantly concluded, "that the record in the case presents a most unappealing situation for finding tests unlawful. We are therefore reduced to making hypothetical arguments about what might happen in other cases—which is simply not a powerful litigating posture."[44]

Greenberg applied to the Supreme Court for a writ of certiorari in *Griggs* anyway, and Pemberton produced a strong amicus brief from the EEOC—to join supporting briefs from the United Steelworkers (which balanced an opposing brief from U.S. Chamber of Commerce) and also from Solicitor General Griswold and Assistant Attorney General Jerris Leonard. The plaintiffs' chief leverage before the Supreme Court was the dissent of Judge Simon Sobeloff of the Fourth Circuit, himself a former U.S. Solicitor General, who had argued the original *Brown* case before the Warren Court in 1954. Sobeloff's dissent had argued for a disparate impact standard that would disregard intent, and in doing so he quoted the district language of *Quarles v. Phillip Morris, Inc.* in 1968 that "Congress did not intend to freeze an entire generation of Negro employees into discriminatory patterns that existed before the act."[45] Sobeloff also cited the guidelines on employment testing issued by the EEOC in August 1966 and argued that the federal courts should give deference to the agency with administering the act, much as the courts had come to defer customarily to the more expert policy rulings of the other federal regulatory agencies.[46]

The EEOC's 1966 guidelines required that any test that rejected blacks at a higher rate than whites must be statistically validated with full documentation by employers. Moreover, this must be done separately for blacks and whites ("differentially validated"). In August 1970 the EEOC issued a more comprehensive set of guidelines, the professed goal of which was identical rejection rates for minority and non-minority job applicants.[47] Thus the NAACP and the U.S. Solicitor General could argue before the Supreme Court that modern psychometric science informed the guidelines of the agency established by Congress to administer Title 7, and that Judge Sobeloff had called for the customary judicial deference to the EEOC's rules and regulations. Moreover, the logic of the historical theory, as demonstrated in *Gaston*, suggested that a history of inferior segregated schooling had made fair competition impossible between blacks and whites on voting literacy and employment tests alike. Thus while discriminatory motives on the part of the Duke Power Company were not only historically demonstrable and subsequently probable, they were also irrelevant. What mattered was not discriminatory motive but the racial *effect* of employment provisions—whether their impact fell disparately upon blacks and whites, whether their results were racially proportionate. Clearly, the diploma and test requirements at Duke Power did not produce racially proportionate results.

Chief Justice Burger and the Legacy of Earl Warren: The Supreme Court as Historical Revisionist

When Chief Justice Burger first received the *Griggs* petition for certiorari, he saw no merit in it and placed it on the "dead list." A law-and-order conservative who disapproved of his predecessor's liberal crusade on behalf of the rights of the accused, Burger nevertheless had a moderate record in civil rights cases. Hugo Black, himself a passionate proponent of school desegregation, called Burger's civil rights record "decent."[48] The new Chief Justice thought the Fourth Circuit court's compromise in *Griggs* was sensible. But Justice Brennan, who had recused himself from *Griggs* because he had once represented the Duke Power Company, thought his former client ought to lose the case. So Brennan persuaded Justice Stewart to request its full discussion at the judicial conference. The conference then voted to grant review, and oral arguments were heard in December 1970. The Chief Justice, after several failed efforts either to derail the case or to build a coalition that would affirm the Fourth Circuit decision, eventually decided to vote with the majority. As the new Chief Justice he was anxious to appear to be the Court's leader, like his strong-willed predecessor, and voting with the majority would allow him to assign the decision to himself.[49]

Writing for a unanimous Court on March 8, 1971, and reversing the Fourth

Circuit, Burger sought to soften the decision's impact by inserting disclamatory dicta. He insisted that the Civil Righs Act "does not command that any person be hired simply because he was formerly the subject of discrimination, or because he is a member of a minority group."⁵⁰ "Discriminatory preference for any group, minority or majority," Burger proclaimed, "is precisely and only what Congress has proscribed." But Burger acknowledged the power of the historical theory, which once again was presented by the segregated history of North Carolina, as it had been in *Gaston*. This train of judicial logic, Burger explained, required the Court to take into account "the posture and condition of the job-seeker." *Griggs*, like *Gaston*, was a case requiring statutory rather than constitutional interpretation. So Burger claimed that the Supreme Court's decision was mandated by Congress. "Under the [1964 Civil Rights] Act," Burger said, "practices, procedures, or tests neutral on their face, and even neutral in terms of intent, cannot be maintained if they operate to 'freeze' the status quo of prior discriminatory employment practices." The Chief Justice thus borrowed from Judge Soboloff's 1970 dissent in *Griggs*, which in turn had borrowed from the trial judge's 1968 opinion in *Quarles*. "The Act proscribes not only overt discrimination," Burger paraphrased, "but also practices that are fair in form, but discriminatory in operation." Burger agreed with the lower courts in finding no discriminatory intent on the part of the power company. "[B]ut good intent or absence of discriminatory intent," Burger said, "does not redeem employment procedures or testing mechanisms that operate as 'built-in headwinds' for minority groups and are unrelated to measuring job capability." Burger even acknowledged that Duke Power had indicated some measure of benign intent by offering to finance two-thirds of the cost of tuition for high school training for its workers. "But Congress directed the thrust of the Act to the *consequences* of employment practices," Burger explained, "not simply the motivation."⁵¹

Burger's interpretation in 1971 of the legislative intent of Congress in the Civil Rights Act would have been greeted with disbelief in 1964. As the bill's floor co-manager that spring with Joseph Clark, Clifford Case had told the Senate that "Title 7 clearly would not permit even a Federal court to rule out the use of particular tests by employers," and that "no court could read title VII as requiring an employer to lower or change the occupational qualifications he sets for his employees simply because fewer Negroes than whites are able to meet them."⁵² The subsequent Clark-Case memorandum had assured the Senate that Title 7 required no employers to abandon bona fide qualification tests where, "because of differences in background and education, members of some groups are able to perform better on these tests than members of other groups. An employer may set his qualifications as high as he likes, he may test to determine which applicants have these qualifications, and he may hire, assign, and promote on the basis of test performance."⁵³ Clark told the Senate that he personally disagreed with Title 7's intent approach and equal-treatment criterion, and preferred instead a results-centered definition. But Clark's job was to explain and defend the bill's language and meaning, which the administration and the congressional leadership wanted passed.

The Duke Power Company in its defense had appealed to the protection of Title 7's section 703(h), Senator Tower's amendment to protect the employee tests used by Motorola, and the district and appeals courts had agreed. Burger's opinion, however, emphasized a codicil in the Tower amendment's language—that such tests, including their administration or action upon their results, must not be "designed, intended or used to discriminate because of race, color, religion, sex or national origin." Burger interpreted this to mean unintentional as well as intentional discrimination. He then turned to the EEOC guidelines on testing, as updated and elaborated in August 1970, after the district and appeals courts had already acted on *Griggs*.[54] The "touch-stone" of the case, Burger said, was "business necessity." This was a term that Congress had never used and Burger did not define. Burger concluded for the Court that the administrative interpretation of Title 7 by "the enforcing agency is entitled to great deference." "Since the Act and its legislative history support the Commission's construction," Burger reasoned, "this affords good reason to treat the [EEOC] guidelines as expressing the will of Congress."[55]

In 1964, Senator Dirksen had anticipated such broader readings of the scope of government's power over business in Title 7. So he offered an amendment to stipulate in section 706(g) that violation required a finding that "respondent had intentionally engaged in or is intentionally engaged in an unlawful employment practice." This would avoid, Dirksen explained, a situation wherein "[a]ccidental, inadvertent, heedless, unintended acts could subject an employer to charges under the present language."[56] Five years later, the EEOC explained in its official *Administrative History* of 1969 that the record of Congress in passing the Civil Rights Act "establishes that the use of professionally developed ability tests would not be considered discriminatory."[57] The EEOC acknowledged that under the "traditional meaning" which was the "common definition of Title VII," and act of discrimination "must be one of intent in the state of mind of the actor." But by 1969 the agency's rapidly evolving enforcement policy had come to "disregard intent as crucial to the finding of an unlawful employment practice," and instead to emphasize forms of employer behavior "which prove to have a demonstrable racial effect without clear and convincing business motive." Because "the courts cannot assume as a matter of statutory construction that Congress meant to accomplish an empty act by the [Dirksen] amendment," the EEOC *Administrative History* explained, then "the Commission and the courts will be in disagreement." "Eventually this will call for reconsideration of the amendment by Congress," the text conceded, "or the reconsideration of its interpretation by the Commission." In the aftermath of *Griggs*, however, neither reconsideration had to occur, because the Supreme Court itself had interpreted the Tower amendment on tests and the Dirksen amendment on intent into nullities.

By 1971, Dirksen was dead, Congress remained paralyzed over revising Title 7, and the historical logic of the Warren Court had achieved a snowballing momentum that swept the reluctant Chief Justice Burger before it. As Gary Bryner observed in the *Political Science Quarterly*, "[w]hile the court's *Griggs* ruling is in agreement with the EEOC and OFCCP guidelines, it conflicts with the working and legislative history of title VII."[58] "Here, the court seems to be primarily concerned with consistency in discrimination cases rather than adherence to legislative intent," Bryner concluded. In *Griggs* the Court extended the logic of discriminatory effect that *Gaston* had inferred from the historical theory, while largely dismissing, as it did in *Swann*, the statutory restrictions of the Civil Rights Act.[59] "The effect of [Burger's] opinion," the *New York Times* reported, "was to approve the guidelines issued by the Equal Employment Opportunity Commission."[60] By calling for "great deference" to the EEOC's policy guidelines, *Griggs* lent blanket judicial approval to the agency's reinterpretation of its legislative charter. Alfred Blumrosen, who took leave from Rutgers law school in 1965 to help start the EEOC, reflected the agency's delight in the broad triumph that Burger's opinion had brought them: "*Griggs* redefines discrimination in terms of consequences rather than motive, effect rather than purpose."[61] It was a tour de force of administrative ingenuity, determination, and luck for the EEOC. The "poor enfeebled thing," in growing partnership with the federal courts, had come a long way from its defanged origins in the legislative compromise of 1964.

The Logic of Compensatory Theory in the "Rights Revolution"

The NAACP and the EEOC had a strong moral case in *Griggs,* and Duke Power made a highly vulnerable target. Duke had long coexisted amicably and profitably with racist regimes in North Carolina. When finally forced by Congress to end its Jim Crow policies, it had immediately slapped on high school diploma requirements and intelligence and ability tests. The region's poor black workers had been taught for generations in miserable segregated schools and confined to the dirtiest and lowest-paying job category at the power utility. Then when the old system was destroyed by federal law, Duke Power greeted the new spirit of equal access by creating new hiring and promotions criteria in the form of educational attainments that the vast majority of black workers in North Carolina lacked, and written tests that half of the high school graduates in the country would fail (the *New York Times* reported that no black laborers at Duke Power had passed the tests).[62]

Lawyers at the NAACP and the EEOC also advanced a challenging legal theory to transform a judicial legacy of "mere" nondiscrimination that they saw as ineffective. The evolving historical theory had logical underpinnings that permitted its partisans both on and before the bench to draw at least plausible inferences from the "broad purpose" and historical context of Title 7. Thus Burger reasoned in *Griggs* that the "markedly disproportionate" rates of black and white advancement at Duke Power must have occurred "because of" the inferior education received by segregated blacks.[63] This casual linkage by historical inference allowed the *Griggs* holding to be reduced to a shorthand formula: "If sufficient disparate impact is present, intention to discriminate need not be proved."[64] Such historical logic reinterpreted statutory law according to the vision of the plaintiffs' lawyers and the judges as to what the legislators *should* have intended, or *might* well have intended in the broadest construction. In light of what the legislators of 1964 had *said* they meant, however, the *Griggs* decision contravened the twofold legislative intention, which was to forbid preferential hiring on a racial basis, and to allow "an employer's bona fide use of professionally developed tests despite their disparate impact on culturally disadvantaged minorities."[65]

The historical or compensatory theory, on which the Supreme Court under both Warren and Burger was basing its increasing judicial activism in ever widening fields of social policy, had evolved out of *Brown*'s original concern for black schoolchildren. As long as the desegregation campaign was based on the classic liberal model of nondiscrimination—that government must do no harm to citizens because of immutable characteristics like race, and should not permit most private organizations to do so either—the particular constituency of the victim group seemed to matter little. When such equal-treatment protection was extended from schools to voting rights, the nondiscrimination logic extended to Hispanics, Asians, and American Indians, whose claims of unfair treatment at the polls were matters of historical record. American women had been nationally enfranchised in 1920, and unlike racial and ethnic groups, women did not live in identifiable residential areas. As the historical logic of compensatory theory spread to the employment field, however, the model of proportional representation on which it was based increasingly ran afoul in the 1970s of three new problematical areas that the original *Brown* model, based as it was on black schoolchildren, was ill-designed to accommodate.

The first problem area was illustrated by the tensions within *Griggs*, where an implicit model of proportional representation in the workplace clashed with Burger's assurance that discriminatory preference for any group, minority or majority, was "precisely and only what Congress had proscribed." The proportional interpretation of Title 7, together with the Philadelphia Plan approach to Title 6, led rather quickly to cries of "reverse discrimination" and to counterclaims by white workers which in turn produced the controversial *Weber* decision of 1979.[66] The second problem area also involved claims of reverse discrimination, but in the white-collar field of admission to professional schools. There the blue-collar origins of *Griggs* and the Philadelphia Plan collided with the complex cultural variables that governed paths to professional success. The American Jewish community, with its long historical memory of the evils of racial and ethnic quotas, and its more recent memory of vindication through the virtues of classically liberal nondiscrimination, divided sharply over the logic of proportional representation by race and ethnicity. These developments fueled a "neoconservative" movement that strained the historic black-Jewish alliance, and in the 1970s focused a national debate on the *DeFunis* and *Bakke* cases.[67]

The third problem area involved the role of women in the burgeoning "rights revolution." The anti-ERA wing of the women's movement, which dominated the feminist reform impulses of the victorious Democratic party as it entered the 1960s, was challenged at mid-decade by the "second-wave feminists" led by NOW, who pressed a race-sex analogy in their drive for the ERA.

The defensive battalions of Esther Peterson sought to disarm the growing ERA challenge by claiming that women were equally protected by the Fifth and Fourteenth amendments, and that the federal courts needed only to look to find them there. As sound as this presumption was in theory, however, in practice the courts remained blind—even as they were making wholesale discoveries of new black rights in the Constitution and in a century of congressional statutes.

By March 1971, when the Supreme Court announced the *Griggs* decision, the federal courts had found precious little in the way of equal protection for women. In *Goesaert v. Cleary* (1948), the first U.S. Supreme Court case to consider the constitutionality of discrimination against women under the equal protection clause, the Court had upheld a Michigan law prohibiting any woman except the wife or daughter of the male owner of a licensed liquor establishment from working as a bartender.[68] In 1961 in *Hoyt v. Florida,* the Suprme Court searched the Fourteenth amendment again, this time to determine whether a woman convicted of killing her husband with a baseball bat in an altercation could claim protection from an all-male jury.[69] Florida law protected women from being pulled by jury duty away from home and maternal obligations by providing that they could not be called unless they voluntarily registered for jury duty—which, not surprisingly, few did. The Warren Court upheld the Florida law as a rational state classification, explaining that "[d]espite the enlightened emancipation of women from the restrictions and protections of bygone years, and their entry into many parts of community life formerly considered to be reserved to men, woman is still regarded as the center of home and family life." However lightly the Warren Court may have treated legislative intent in statutory cases concerning race relations, it showed a conservative respect for the strict construction of constitutional precedents where women's rights were concerned. Faced with such a sustained judicial disregard for women's claims to the same constitutional protections that blacks enjoyed—and especially black males—the feminists forged within their own ranks a new bipartisan consensus for the ERA. Then they descended on the new Nixon administration in a phalanx.

CHAPTER 11

Women, the Nixon Administration, and the Equal Rights Amendment

The Semi-feminist Legacy of the Democratic Party

When Richard Nixon was sworn in as President in January 1969 there seemed to be little reason to expect that women's rights would be a major issue of public policy in his administration. Nixon had routinely endorsed the Equal Rights Amendment as a presidential candidate in 1968, as he had previously done in 1960. The ERA's chief historic constituency lay among the Republican-inclined women's professional and business clubs, and Republican presidential platforms had regularly endorsed the ERA since 1940. By the early 1950s, however, when it had become clear that the ERA stood virtually no chance of passing the House and could only pass the Senate with the nullifying Hayden rider attached, the ERA cause rather quietly lapsed into the status of a routine political abstraction.[1]

Moreover, the Democrats remained badly divided over the issue, or at least by 1968 they appeared to be. John F. Kennedy as representative and senator had faithfully mirrored his labor constituency's opposition to the ERA (or support of it with the Hayden rider, which amounted to the same thing), and only the release by Democratic committeewoman Emma Guffey Miller of a selectively edited letter she received from Kennedy in 1960 had made him appear to accept the ERA.[2] The AFL-CIO Democrats and the Women's Bureau coalition had kept the ERA out of the Democratic platforms in both 1960 and 1964.[3] In response to urgings by Esther Peterson and Arthur Goldberg, Kennedy in December 1961 appointed his President's Council on the Status of Women. In its final report of October 1963, *American Women,* the commission concluded that the ERA "need not now be sought" because a more immediate source of constitutional protection for women lay in the Fifth and Fourteenth amendments.[4]

Because the Kennedy administration could legitimately claim credit for the Equal Pay Act of 1963, and the Johnson administration could claim credit for the Civil Rights Act, which included sex within Title 7's ban on employment discrimination, the ERA seemed safely defused, at least as a divisive issue that might split the Democratic coalition. But beneath the surface of policy continuity, tensions were building within the ranks of Democratic women. A new national network of feminist women was being created, one that by 1968 would surround and enfold Peterson and her ERA-resisters.[5]

Initially, the Kennedy-Johnson administration's national panel on women's issues, the Citizen Advisory Council on the Status of Women, was steered away from the divisive ERA issue by Esther Peterson. When President Johnson early in 1965 appointed Peterson as his special assistant for consumer affairs, she retained her assistant secretaryship in Labor but relinquished her directorship of the Women's Bureau. Peterson's replacement at the bureau, Mary Dublin Keyserling, was an economist with strong anti-ERA convictions. Peterson and Keyserling were able to focus the council's early efforts on such matters of traditional Women's Bureau concern as the minimum wage, unemployment compensation, and defense of state protective labor laws.

In June 1966 the original chairwoman of the council, editor Margaret Hickey of the *Ladies' Home Journal,* resigned and was replaced by retiring Democratic senator Maurine Neuberger of Oregon. A veteran politician, Neuberger concentrated on creating an active women's commission in every state, aiming to build a national network. The Women's Bureau had encouraged this drive, which had originated in 1962 with Virginia R. Allan, a Republican and then president of the National Federation of Business and Professional Women's Clubs. By February 1967 the drive had created commissions in all fifty states—including Texas, the last holdout.[6] Conferences of state commissions were held in Washington in the summers of 1964 and 1965, with the Women's Bureau in essential control of the agenda. But the watershed conference was in 1966, when debate was heating up over the EEOC's retreat on single-sex classified ads, and NOW was formed under the radicalizing whip of Betty Friedan. By the fourth conference, held in Washington in late June 1968 and presided over by Neuberger, the U.S. Government's semi-official women's agenda had been strongly liberalized, but in a Democratic direction that still excluded the troublesome ERA. At that meeting the council adopted the reports of four task forces, the most notable of which was Marguerite Rawalt's task force on family law and policy. Its recommendations embraced an expansive liberal feminism, including the "basic human right of a woman to determine her own reproductive life."[7] The report also called for repeal of all laws penalizing abortion; for egalitarian revisions in marriage law, including alimony and custody rights, no-fault divorce, and equal property settlements; for liberal provision of birth control information and services; and for public funding of day care for children and equal rights for illegitimate children. Three of the task forces called for various government guarantees of income maintenance. Not one mentioned the ERA.

During 1966–68 the Women's Bureau had tried to hold its traditional line in defense of protective legislation, and the result was a compromise. The council's task forces had produced egalitarian recommendations that states repeal or amend special protective laws that set maximum hours and weight-lifting limits for women, and excluded them from certain occupations. By the end of the Johnson regime, the younger, liberal feminists had quietly overcome, through a combination of persuasion and displacement, the protectionist dominance among the Democratic women. But the Democrats had exacted their traditional price, paid in the coinage of philosophical inconsistency, by avoiding the divisiveness of the ERA itself.

Five months later, Richard Nixon was elected President. Republican women, who long had nurtured the ERA tradition, now had access to the presidency. But they lacked the continuity and momentum associated with the dominant Democrats in the women's movement. The transition in domestic policy was being presided over by Dr. Arthur Burns—no feminist, he.

A Republican Brand of Feminism

In the 117-page report on domestic policy that Arthur Burns sent President-elect Nixon in January 1969, civil rights issues were mentioned only twice. One recommendation attacked union discrimination against minority workers, and the other opposed cease-and-desist authority for the EEOC. The Burns report did not altogether ignore other minority or special "problem" groups. It called for early fulfillment of Nixon's campaign promises to call conferences on the needs of Mexican-Americans, on the problems of the aging (including the appointment of a White House assistant on the aging), and on new programs to employ veterans, "particularly Negroes," when the war in Vietnam was concluded. But there was not one word about women. Nor was there any mention of the ERA.[8]

This was a crucial juncture. The feminist agenda of the Democrats, with its radicalizing commitment to abortion rights, wholesale changes in family law, and class-based programs for income redistribution, but with its internally imposed silence on ERA, had been swept aside by Nixon's victory. But the regime change created a vacuum that seemed unlikely to be filled by the Republican women's leadership. They had traditionally embraced the ERA, to be sure, but with a quaintly feckless fervor, and their elite origins had historically proved unsympathetic to the class-based demands of the Democratic coalition. Judging from the Burns report, the newly empowered establishment of Republican males perceived no vacuum at all. There, in limbo, the "woman question" was poised. But not for long.

The previously eclipsed Republican and pro-ERA wing of the feminist movement was immediately heard from. And they had caught the virus. At Nixon's press conference on February 6, 1969, the President was challenged by Vera R. Glaser, the Washington bureau chief for the North American Newspaper Alliance. Glaser noted that only three of the administration's first 200 top-level appointments were women, and asked whether this meant that women were "going to remain a lost sex?" In light of Glaser's subsequent role both in shaping the agenda of the Republican feminists and in flushing the administration out when it attempted to duck the issues, Nixon's reply proved ironical: "Would you be interested in coming into the government?" [*Laughter*][9]

Unlike most newspaper reporters (on both counts), Glaser was a woman and also a Republican. Indeed, she had been director of public relations for the women's division of the Republican National Committee when Vice President Nixon had kicked off his 1960 presidential campaign. On the heels of the 1969 press conference she wrote a story that focused on the President's seeming inability, as symbolized by his all-male cabinet (unlike President Eisenhower's), to locate qualified women for senior appointments. Catherine East, who had directed staff support in the Women's Bureau for the women's council during the Kennedy-Johnson years, saw Glaser's story and sent her a packet of material on women's issues and feminist proposals from the Democratic status-of-women groups. East's strategic position at the nerve center of the Democratic women's network provided a kind of informal transition task force, an institutional source of continuity for the Republican women who historically had carried little weight in party or policy councils, and whose role in the Democrat-dominated panels of the Kennedy-Johnson years had been minimal.[10]

Newly armed with East's wealth of data, Glaser wrote a five-part series on the new women's movement which was syndicated in the spring of 1969 in many of the nation's daily newspapers. In April, Glaser and East secured an appointment with Burns and persuaded him to meet with a group of mostly women correspondents. At the news briefing on May 15, Burns was asked whether the administration was planning any initiative to open up opportunities for blacks and women, who seemed to be boxed into the lower federal jobs. "Not as a matter of policy," Burns replied. "On the contrary, we've been trying very hard to place Negroes in government positions, and I'm not aware of any discrimination against the better half of mankind." This answer prompted the following colloquy:

Q. You're not?
A. No, I'm not.
Q. Are you really serious about that?
A. Oh yes. I'm speaking only for myself, and I may be blind.
Q. There isn't anybody in this room among the veteran women correspondents who hasn't run up against real hard-core discrimination.
A. You ought to make more noise about that because to some of us, the idea is abhorrent.

When asked why a country with more than half its population female should be "run practically by a male enclave," Burns conceded that "we don't have very many" women making policy. "If there is a prejudice against women, if there is discrimination against women," Burns said, "it is of the unconscious variety, and that may be so."[11]

In response to Burns' off-hand invitation to women to "make more noise about" discrimination, Glaser wrote him on May 23 to catalogue the sex discrimination that Burns and his colleagues had failed to notice. Glaser cited the customary data documenting the nation's persistent gender disparities in income, unemployment, and education. But she leaned hardest on the failed federal response. The Supreme Court had *never* held that a state law discriminated on the basis of sex, Glaser said. One-third of the federal workforce was female, but less than 2 percent of the top jobs were held by women. Of more than a thousand political appointments to be filled by the new administration, fewer than a dozen had thus far gone to women. The Justice Department to date had initiated *no* sex discrimination cases, although they had prosecuted at least forty-five suits charging racial bias.

What should be done? Glaser provided a catalogue. The President should honor his campaign pledge and ask Congress to pass the ERA. He should recommend that Congress provide cease-and-desist authority for the EEOC; add sex to Title 6 for OFCC enforcement, especially concerning education; and add sex discrimination to the formal jurisdiction of the Civil Rights Commission. On presidential authority alone, Glaser said, Nixon should appoint a White House assistant for women's issues, direct the Attorney General to begin filing sex discrimination suits under Title 7, and direct Labor secretary Shultz to issue the OFCC guidelines on sex discrimination that were blocked in October 1968 by organized labor under the Johnson administration.[12]

By the summer of 1969, the momentum of the women's movement among elite whites had raised the public consciousness of a feminist agenda that could not easily be dismissed as radical "bra-burning."[13] But the invisibility of women leaders and women's issues in the Nixon administration was noticed and resented by Republican women who denied being feminists themselves. Representative Florence Dwyer of New Jersey, the ranking Republican on the House Government Operations Committee, had written the President on February 26 to ask that he appoint a White House adviser on women, or create "an independent agency to strengthen women's rights and responsibilities." Dwyer's letter, however, had produced only a routine acknowledgment from the White House. Nixon's only visible early gesture toward women was to invite the cabinet wives—there being no cabinet husbands—to sit in on a cabinet meeting. Glaser told Burns that Republican career women and party workers resented the President's gesture, which symbolized the role of women as loyal but silent, wifely observers to male shapers of policy.[14]

On July 8, Congresswoman Dwyer, impatient with the administration's inaction and angered at Nixon's "empty gesture" with the cabinet wives, released a sharp memo to the President that was co-signed by three Republican colleagues in the House: Representatives Margaret M. Heckler of Massachusetts, Catherine D. May of Washington, and Charlotte T. Reid of Illinois. "None of us are feminists," Dwyer explained. In her litany of complaints and her list of recommendations Dwyer reflected the Republican women's traditional class-based resentment against sex discrimination in business and the professions and increasingly in government as well. Of women college graduates, Dwyer said, 20 percent could find "no better employment than clerical, sales or factory jobs." Women accounted for only 7 percent of America's physicians, 1 percent of engineers, 3 percent of lawyers, and 8 percent of scientists. Law and medical schools typically held women to a 7 percent quota, despite women's higher scores on entrance examinations. The Republican congresswomen's blast at their President included a list of seventeen recommendations, with presidential support for ERA hearings listed ninth, still well behind demands for more presidential appointments.[15]

Nixon's Unplanned Task Force on Women

The upshot of these growing pressures was a White House decision, by time-honored instinct, to study the matter. So in September a new task force on women's issues was added to the Burns portfolio. A new study group on women's issues would offer the virtues of being White House-picked and Republican controlled. The deliberations and recommendations of the women's task force would thus be filtered during the fall of 1969, along with the other twenty planning groups for the 1970 agenda, through the cautious Burns.

The eleventh-hour creation of the women's task force, together with the White House men's relative ignorance about both women's issues and the identity and capability of women leaders, meant that Vera Glaser and Catherine East would enjoy unusual freedom in shaping the task force's membership and agenda. Burns asked Virginia Allan to chair the task force, and Allan appointed East as staff director. Allan's credentials as a vice president of the Calahan drug store chain in Michigan, and as a former president of the Business and Professional Women's Club of America, made her a strong choice as chairwoman. Glaser herself was an obvious candidate for the task force, and given her unique leverage with the media, she proved to be a crucial member.[16]

By mid-September, Burns had selected the 13-member task force, appointed Allan to the chair, and assigned a broad mission of policy review and recommendation that gave ample running room. Politically, Burns could scarcely do less. Nixon in 1969 had no women's rights agenda at all, and he could not ignore the rising cry of the Republican women. So visible was the issue and so important was the need to appear to be responding sympathetically to it that, on October 1, Nixon elevated the women's task force to a presidential operation. The title he chose—President's Task Force on Women's Rights and Responsibilities—was in character for Nixon's uncertain domestic agenda. It was balanced, prudently Republican, and carried an odd ring of nervous condescension. It was difficult to envision parallel task forces on the responsibilities as well as the rights of Negroes, Hispanics, and the handicapped.[17]

The women's task force was functionally similar to the outside task forces appointed by Lyndon Johnson in 1964. But the eleven women and two men on Nixon's panel were far less familiar with the corridors of power in Washington than had been Johnson's task forcers. In October briefings from senior agency officials, the members learned how weakly attuned official Washington was to the issues that most concerned the feminist movement. Outside of the Women's Bureau coalition, which had never been hospitable to Republicans or ERA supporters, American women had never generated the kind of clientele base of pressure groups with their iron-triangle connections that commanded attention from the power structure. Justice and Labor department officials explained that their agencies were concentrating on racial issues, especially in job discrimination. Since 1964 the Justice Department had filed 47 pattern-or-practice suits under Title 7 to combat race discrimination, but none had been filed against sex discrimination. The OFCC in 1969 was devoting most of its energy to battling for the Philadelphia Plan, in which women were invisible. So consuming had been the racial issue that the OFCC's contract-compliance guidelines for women under Title 6, promised after President Johnson in 1967 got around to correcting the omission of sex discrimination in his 1965 executive order, had been shelved since 1968.

At the EEOC, a lonely feminist bright spot in 1969 among federal agencies, enforcement strategies on behalf of blacks and women were headed in opposite directions. For blacks the EEOC was pressing an equal-results standard based on proportional representation, while for women the agency was demanding equal treatment and attacking sex-segregated job listings and broad BFOQ interpretations that kept women in pink-collar ghettos. The task force members, most of them ERA partisans, approved of the EEOC's nondiscrimination strategy for women. These were highly educated and affluent women (and two men, one of whom was president of Vassar College) drawn from the Republican party's historic equal rights wing, with its emphasis on nondiscrimination—on open access to the male-dominated world of business and the professions. By the end of November the task force had reached a remarkably firm consensus.

On December 15, Allan sent Nixon, through Burns, the task force's 40-page final report. It contained two sets of recommendations. The first set was concerned less with substance than with visibility and symbolism. The President should establish an Office of Women's Rights and Responsibilities, whose director would serve as a special assistant reporting directly to the President. The President should also call a White House conference on women's rights and responsibilities in 1970, the fiftieth anniversary of the ratification of the suffrage amendment and the founding of the Women's Bureau. The substantive recommendations called for a presidential message asking Congress for several legislative actions, the first one being passage of a joint resolution sending the ERA to the states for ratification. Next, Congress should amend Title 7 to transform the private right of 1964 into a public right by empowering the EEOC to enforce the law (the recommendation did not choose between the administration's prosecutorial approach and the cease-and-desist approach favored by the Democratic leadership of Congress). Congress should also extend Title 7 coverage to employees in state and local governments and educational institutions, and add gender protection to titles of the 1964 act other than Title 7.[18]

The priorities in the women's task force report are instructive. The ERA was seen as a universal, one-swoop corrective, much as the suffrage amendment had been regarded by 1920. But the panel was aware of the record of congressional resistance, and beyond congressional approval of an ERA resolution lay the formidable requirement of ratification by three-fourths of the states. In the meantime, therefore, priority went to two areas. One was to extend EEOC authority under Title 7 to cover state and local governments, including their schools, where millions of women languished in pink-collar entrapment. The task force report listed evidence of "gross discrimination" against women in education, where women predominated in the low-paying teaching positions and men dominated the administrative posts. In the public schools, 75 percent of elementary school principals were men, as were 96 percent of the junior high principals and 90 percent of the senior high principals.[19]

Second, existing contract-compliance authority under Title 6 should be used to protect women against discrimination in institutions of higher education, where colleges and universities controlled access to the world of business and government, science and technology, and the learned professions. In 1968 only 5.9 percent of law students and 8.3 percent of medical students were women. Vera Glaser, noting at a briefing by Labor Department officials that the EEOC was helpless to pursue more than 100 complaints filed by women "against colleges like Harvard, the University of Michigan" and others that received more than $3 billion in federal grants, asked: "[I]s the Department of Labor going to pursue this and will those contracts be cut off?"[20] To the Labor Department, rooted in a blue-collar world, the question was alien to the agency's mission and experience. To the EEOC, it was off-limits.

Over-all the women's task force report reflected a feminist vision that was elite in its social origins, yet persistently egalitarian in its demand for equal treatment. In 1969 a feminist constituency that was highly educated, predominantly white, and careerist was competing for attention from a Nixon administration that was locked in battle with Congress over minority job preferences for plumbers and structural steelworkers. The ERA feminists were demanding equal opportunity for women in business, the professions, and public service. They were competing at some political disadvantage, with the specter of unemployed or underemployed black males threatening the cities. But the questions they were raising were persistent and troublesome: why were American women, who were protected from sex discrimination by the Civil Rights Act, finding so little relief from their government?

After receiving the women's task force report in mid-December, Burns wrote Virginia Allan on January 9, 1970, that he hoped she was enjoying some leisure, now that the report "has been filed."[21] Burns thanked Allan and her task force colleagues for completing their difficult task in such good order. But he made no comment on the substance of the report's far-ranging recommendations. The report was "now being reviewed here at the White House," Burns said. But "filed" was the better term, after all.

Flushing Nixon Out on Women's Issues

Not only did the White House not release or comment on the task force report of December 1969, the staff did not even get around to the routine task of sending its recommendations to the relevant agencies for comment until April. By then, however, the new feminist consensus for ERA was gaining too much momentum and publicity for the administration to sit much longer on the report and the issues it raised. In late 1969 the League of Women Voters reversed almost a half-century of opposition and endorsed the ERA. On February 7, 1970, the Citizens Advisory Council on the Status of Women, which since its appointment by Kennedy in 1963 had avoided the ERA issue, officially embraced the amendment.[22] The council also "borrowed" attorney Mary Eastwood from the Justice Department and published her legal brief supporting the ERA. In March, Martha Griffiths entered Eastwood's brief into the *Congressional Record,* and then launched her successful 1970 campaign to force the ERA from Celler's Judiciary Committee through a discharge petition. Also that spring, women from NOW began to disrupt the hearings on 18-year-old voting by Senator Birch Bayh's subcommittee of judiciary on constitutional amendments by shouting demands for a hearing on the ERA.[23] Inside the administration, Republican women like Rita E. Hauser at the U.N. and Patricia Reilly Hitt in HEW began to pepper the White House with memoes warning that Democrats like Griffiths and Bayh were beginning to take the lead on the ERA. Glaser supplied a copy of the task force report, which was titled *A Matter of Simple Justice,* to Marie Anderson, editor of the women's page of the *Miami Herald,* which published it in tabloid form.[24] The bootlegged publishing of an embargoed report to the President on such a hot topic attracted unusual attention to the document, and left the White House with little practical recourse but to release the report.[25]

The senior White House aides, however, did not want to release the report without first getting from Nixon a clear position on the ERA. For Leonard Garment, whom the press often identified as the staff's resident liberal Republican, that clearly meant Nixon's timely *re*-endorsement. On May 25, Garment sent to Ehrlichman a decision paper for the President, arguing the pros and cons of the ERA and urging an early presidential decision to release with the report. The position paper first summarized the arguments in favor of endorsement, and did so pretty much as the women's task force had presented them. The arguments listed against the amendment were chiefly three. First, it was impossible to predict how the federal courts would interpret the amendment, and the increased litigation could flood the courts with novel constitutional challenges to a vast and intricate body of state statutes on family relationships, property and contract law, education and health and safety. Second, the ERA would almost certainly make unconstitutional the state protective laws. Garment added that the AFL-CIO had opposed the amendment earlier that month in hearings before Senator Birch Bayh's subcommittee, arguing that losing such historic protection would lead to "wholesale exploitation of women workers."[26]

Third, the ERA, with all of its potentially radical and unpredictable implications, might not even be necessary. This was the position taken in 1963 by Kennedy's commission on women—that the courts should more actively discover the principle of gender equality that is implicit in the Fifth and Fourteenth amendments. Garment pointed out that federal courts and the EEOC had already reduced the effect of state protective laws, and federal district courts had recently held that state laws exempting women from jury service and discrimination against women applying to state colleges were unconstitutional under the Fourteenth amendment. The first federal court decision under Title 7 against a state protective law had come in Los Angeles in 1968, and that same year a federal district court in South Carolina had struck down a private company's rule that the travel and physical duties of its sales representatives limited such jobs to men only. Curiously, Garment's draft made no mention at all of the commonplace argument that the ERA would require the military conscription of young women and force them into combat.

Indeed, Garment clearly favored the ERA and his decision paper was so slanted. Despite the efforts of Garment and the Republican feminists and their allies within the higher councils, Nixon made no endorsement, or rather re-endorsement. Like Br'er Fox, he lay low—while the ERA debate shifted in 1970 to the congressional committees and, thanks to Griffiths' triumph in August with her discharge petition, even to the floor of the House.[27] The nearness of the congressional elections of 1970 would preclude any real chance for ERA in the 91st Congress. But its momentum could carry over strongly into 1971. Opposition to the ERA seemed to be weakening. The core of the opposition, the Women's Bureau coalition of labor Democrats, was losing its main argument as the EEOC and the federal courts whittled down the state protective laws under Title 7. Meanwhile the White House, muzzled by Nixon on the ERA question, was fastening on any positive action it could safely take to rally the aroused women's support. And once again, Secretary Shultz was prepared to take the initiative on behalf of civil rights. As he had done with the Philadelphia Plan, Shultz would revive an initiative that had died in the late hours of the Johnson administration.

A Philadelphia Plan for Women?

Shultz was fighting his major public battles over equal employment opportunity one at a time. First priority went to cracking the refractory construction unions with the Philadelphia Plan, a high-risk contest that was narrowly won only in the closing days of 1969. But meanwhile Shultz was preparing for Round Two on women. He appointed to head the Women's Bureau a Democrat, Elizabeth Koontz, whose professional role with the National Education Association had kept her largely free of the Democrats' ancient wars over protective legislation. Koontz shared Shultz's view that the federal courts and the EEOC were rapidly rendering the question moot by trumping state protective laws with Title 7. This trend helped her neutralize opposition in the Women's Bureau to the proposed OFCC guidelines on sex discrimination that had been blocked in 1968. Meanwhile the EEOC further weakened the protectionist opposition to ERA with two initiatives in 1969. In March the commission published the results of its national survey on women in the workforce. This showed that women constituted 40 percent of white-collar workers, but only held one of every ten management positions and one of every seven professional positions. Then, on August 19, the EEOC issued a guideline formally asserting the primacy of Title 7 over state protective laws.[28]

By early 1970, Shultz's victory with the Philadelphia Plan allowed him to extend its logic of proportional representation beyond construction to cover *all* areas of government contracting by issuing Order No. 4 on February 3. In the process the compensatory remedies that Labor had originally sought mainly for blacks in Philadelphia were officially and nationally extended to Spanish Surnamed Americans, American Indians, and Orientals. But what about women? The key to the Philadelphia Plan's de facto quota system for racial and ethnic minorities was geographic. The residences of these minorities were unevenly distributed by neighborhood and region. Where their concentration contrasted with their relative invisibility in the workforce, the arithmetic difference provided both evidence of unfairness and an implicit, proportional goal for a federally coerced remedy. Women, however, were evenly distributed everywhere. As the more radical liberationists phrased it, women cohabited with "the enemy." And unlike men, virtually all of whom were assumed as adults to be entering the labor force, the majority of women (60 percent in 1970) were *not* in the paid labor force.[29]

The Philadelphia Plan's constitutional and statutory legitimacy caused a storm of controversy. But the plan's normative assumptions for men working in blue-collar jobs was not attacked as unreasonable per se. If 30 percent of the Philadelphia area's population was black, the plan's proponents asked, was it not fair to assume that, absent discrimination, the craftsmen working in the well-paid structural steel jobs would similarly reflect the area's racial demographics? Even in the absence of controversy, however, would such a male-biased model work for women? The Philadelphia Plan implicitly assumed that construction workers were men, that basically all working-age men were in the workforce, and that interest in performing different jobs and ability to perform them were equally distributed in that workforce. Most American women, however, were not in the full-time, paid workforce, and the interest and ability of those who were varied greatly among jobs as schoolteachers, fire fighters, secretaries, and structural steelworkers. What percentage of women should the OFCC require contractors to hire as pipefitters and sheet metal workers? The OFCC, having no answer, had buried the question in 1968.

By early 1970 the feminist movement had united under the banner of the ERA. Its dominant voices came not from the Eleanor Roosevelt and Esther Peterson wing of the Democratic party, but rather from the upper-middle-class and professional women of NOW and the Women's Equity Action League (WEAL), from Republicans like Virginia Allan, Vera Glaser, and Democrats like Edith Green and Martha Griffiths. In the color-coded world of occupational mobility, these women saw women's liberation as escape from the pink-collar ghetto into the white-collar world of business and the professions, not into the blue-collar world of craft unions. Their main targets were the ERA and, until that battle was won, strict egalitarianism under the Civil Rights Act. This included lobbying to extend the jurisdiction of the EEOC, now that the agency was supporting the feminist agenda, and new pressure to use contract-compliance leverage against colleges and universities. The latter effort was a special focus of WEAL, and it engaged the attention of two WEAL board members who were strategically placed in Congress: Edith Green and Martha Griffiths.[30]

Faced with these pressures, Shultz on June 2 provided his grateful President with a measured response to the rising clamor of his Republican women by signing and sending to the White House the OFCC's proposed new guidelines on sex discrimination. Garment forwarded them to the Oval Office with the recommendation that their prompt release along with the hot-potato task force report could "put the President in the best possible light" by placing the emphasis on "what the President *has done* rather than on what he is being urged to do."[31] The new guidelines were a model of nondiscrimination. They demanded equal treatment for both sexes in recruitment and advertising, job opportunities and fringe benefits, pay and seniority, and physical facilities. They required equal treatment of married and unmarried persons, and barred penalties for childbearing. They stipulated that "An employer must not deny a female employee the right to any job that she is qualified to perform in reliance upon a State 'protective' law."[32]

Thus, in June 1970, Secretary Shultz signed and the President approved a Magna Carta commanding equal treatment for women in the workforce. Compared with Title 7 as enforced by the puny EEOC, the dimly understood Title 6 as enforced by the obscure OFCC reached directly to a third of the U.S. workforce, and set the tone for the rest. Now the visible but weak EEOC and the muscular but obscure OFCC had joined in a bracing, one-two punch for non-discrimination by gender—including men, who also could suffer (but rarely did) from sex discrimination. The hoary, crippling feud over protective legislation was over. And the entire Republican package was consistent with the feminist steamroller that was gathering momentum for the ERA. There was no mention at all of the goals and timetables that had put the sharp teeth into Order No. 4 for men. The OFCC guidelines' brief section on Affirmative Action for women was limited to urging extra efforts in recruitment, such as including women's colleges in itineraries of recruiting trips, and in recruiting women for training and management trainee programs.[33]

On June 9 the White House announced the guidelines and formally released the women's task force report, *A Matter of Simple Justice*, now embargoed for half a year (yet widely available commercially for the previous two months). Nixon thus rested most of his case for responding to the women's constituency on Schultz's sex discrimination guidelines, and quietly stood pat on his pre-presidential endorsements of ERA, content to allow Congress to absorb most of the controversy.

Passing the Equal Rights Amendment

The dramatic story of congressional approval of the ERA has not been fully told. We have far better studies on how and why the ERA failed in ratification than on why and how it was approved by Congress.[34] Yet the two questions are closely linked. So committed were ERA partisans to the purity and simplicity of the amendment's classically anti-discriminatory text—"Equality of rights under the law shall not be denied by the United States or by any State on account of sex"—

that they rejected a range of compromise that, in hindsight's speculative light, might have avoided the ERA's ultimate defeat. In the fall and winter of 1970 the feminist organizations rejected the bipartisan compromise suggested by the amendment's Senate co-sponsors, Democrat Birch Bayh of Indiana and Republican Marlow W. Cook of Kentucky, with the weighty support of senators Dole, Griffin, Javits, and Kennedy, to add "sex" to the equal protection clause of the 14th Amendment.[35] When Martha Griffiths reintroduced the ERA into the new 92nd Congress in January 1971 as H.J. Res. 208, hearings were scheduled for late March and early April by Judiciary Subcommittee No. 4, the new committee on civil rights oversight chaired by ERA-supporter Don Edwards of California. Only two of the subcommittee's eighteen witnesses opposed the ERA resolution. One was Sam Ervin, who continued to propose amendments exempting women from military conscription and permitting state protective legislation and privacy laws (Griffiths referred to the latter contemptuously as Ervin's "potty argument"). The other was Mary Dublin Keyserling, testifying for the National Consumers League and the National Council of Catholic Women. Testifying in favor of ERA were Griffiths, Virginia Allan, Marguerite Rawalt, Aileen Hernandez, Bernice Sandler, Olga M. Madar of the United Auto Workers, Norman Dorsen of the American Civil Liberties Union, and Thomas I. Emerson of the Yale Law School.[36]

The surprise witness of the hearings, however, was Assistant Attorney General William Rehnquist. Testifying on April 1 for the Justice Department, Rehnquist agreed that the problems the ERA addressed were serious, but a constitutional amendment was both unnecessary and dangerous. The ERA was problematical, Rehnquist said, because its ambiguity would require protracted litigation to dispel, as the convoluted interpretations of the Fourteenth amendment had demonstrated. Politically, Rehnquist conceded, the post-Civil War Congress had no realistic alternative to the constitutional amendment process. But the legislative history to date on the ERA already demonstrated broad disagreement on the meaning of its sweeping language even among its supporters, and to this ambiguous record would then be added the complex ratifying debates of three-fourths of the states. Moreover, Rehnquist said, recent decisions in the lower federal courts indicated a new willingness to extend Fourteenth amendment protections to the field of sex discrimination. Furthermore, many of the inequalities suffered by women occurred in the area of private rather than public conduct, and could therefore only be reached by statute.[37]

Such a statute, Rehnquist said, was offered by H.R. 916, sponsored by Democrat Albert J. Mikva of Chicago and reported by the House Education and Labor Committee. The fourteen sections of the Mikva bill responded in detail to the recommendations of the presidential task force on women. They would amend the Civil Rights Act of 1964 by adding protections against sex discrimination in most of the titles—Title 7 of course already contained it. H.R. 916 would also similarly amend the Open Housing Act of 1968 and the Fair Labor Standards Act of 1938. Rehnquist supported the basic statutory approach and many of the specific provisions of H.R. 916. He opposed, however, simply adding sex to the categories protected by Title 6 in all federally assisted programs. Such a blanket approach could have a confusing impact on the Nixon administration's complex new proposals for revenue sharing and family assistance, he said, and the complications should first be carefully explored by the mission agencies, especially HEW and Treasury. Rehnquist agreed that it was time to include state and local governments and educational institutions under Civil Rights Act coverage, and also to beef up the enforcement power of the EEOC. But the administration was willing to support this, he insisted, *only* if the EEOC were given prosecutorial authority, *not* the cease-and-desist powers proposed in H.R. 916.

The feminist leaders were astounded by this demonstration of the Nixon administration's "support" for the ERA. Jacueline Gutwillig, Republican chairwoman of the Citizens Advisory Council on the Status of Women, scrawled across the top of Rehnquist's written statement: "This is incredible—to both proponents and opponents. That as fine a lawyer as Mr. Rehnquist could give such testimony is most curious. With friends like this we don't need enemies."[38] She sent her editorialized copy of Rehnquist's testimony to President Nixon the next morning, politely suggesting how puzzled her council colleagues were by such ambiguous support and internally contradictory testimony. But Gutwillig needn't have worried. Despite Ervin's Spanish proverb that "An ounce of mother is worth a pound of priest," and Celler's insistence that "the Fallopian tube has not become vestigial," and also despite the more serious problem of Ervin's waving a 1971 Roper poll showing wide disagreement among American women over the meaning and desirability of the ERA, the feminist drive in Congress was superbly organized and appeared unstoppable. Celler's Judiciary Committee reported the ERA resolution out after voting 19 to 16 to attach a Hayden-like rider, sponsored by Republican Charles E. Wiggins of California, that exempted military conscription and state protective laws. The full House, however, stripped the Wiggins amendment away by a resounding vote of 265 to 87. On October 12, the extraordinary vote 354 to 23, the House sent the ERA resolution to the Senate.[39]

One month after Rehnquist testified that the lower federal courts were beginning to extend the Fourteenth amendment's equal protection clause to women, the Supreme Court for the first time struck down a state's gender classification under the Fourteenth amendment. In *Reed v. Reed,* the unanimous Court overturned an Idaho statute preferring a man over a woman as executor of an intestate estate.[40] This seemed to support, at long last, the arguments of the special-protection Democrats, and also Rehnquist's caution, that the federal courts might obviate the need for ERA by discovering women in the Fifth and Fourteenth amendments. Griffiths, however, dismissed the *Reed* ruling as merely a narrow technicality that would leave the Court unchanged as a "bottleneck" for women's rights. "They're just nine old idiots," Griffiths told the *Washington Post.*[41]

Griffiths and her allies sensed imminent victory in Congress, and they were right. On February 29, 1972, the Senate Judiciary Committee, a former bastion of conservatism, steamrollered over Ervin's objections by a vote of 15 to 1.[42] The symbolism of feminist triumph was rich, for in 1963, Marguerite Rawalt had stood alone on President Kennedy's status-of-women commission in calling for the ERA. In mid-March the full Senate easily rejected all nine of Ervin's qualifying floor amendments and, on March 22, voted to send the ERA to the states for ratification with a lop-sided tally of 84 to 8.[43] Only four days earlier President Nixon had finally weighed in, timidly and late, by sending Hugh Scott a letter reminding the Senate minority leader, not very credibly, that "as a Senator in 1951 I co-sponsored a Resolution incorporating the original amendment," and "in July of 1968 I reaffirmed my support for it as a candidate for the Presidency." "Throughout twenty-one years," Nixon's letter continued, "I have not altered my belief that equal rights for women warrant a Constitutional guarantee—and I therefore continue to favor the enactment of the Constitutional Amendment to achieve this goal." Nixon's timing cast doubts on the sincerity of his conviction—just two months earlier his State of the Union address had devoted three paragraphs to "Equal Rights for Women" without mentioning the Equal Rights Amendment at all.[44]

The rest, as journalists and politicians (but not historians) say, is history. By the end of 1972, 23 states has rushed through ratification of ERA, only 15 short of the required 38. The Supreme Court rather quickly followed *Reed* with a series of decisions that stopped just short of categorizing women, like blacks, as a class whose suspect classification in statutes merited "strict judicial scrutiny." Instead the Court fashioned a middle range of judicial scrutiny to test classification by sex.[45] Subsequent constitutional litigation over gender distinctions is filled with efforts to define the dimensions of the Court's middle-way scheme.[46] But it is not filled with clarifying litigation to define the precise meaning of the Constitution's new Equal Rights Amendment. In 1973, the Supreme Court's abortion decision of *Roe v. Wade* galvanized an anti-ERA coalition of conservatives and traditionalist women led by Phyllis Schlafly, and the resulting stalemate ultimately doomed the feminists' congressional triumph of 1972.[47] In the euphoria of victory in 1971–72, however, feminists turned their energies and momentum to the parallel battle over revising the Civil Rights Act of 1964 and related laws in order to end discrimination against women. By adding their formidable new weight to the civil rights coalition during a presidential election year, feminists promised to tip the balance of power decisively against the conservative coalition in Congress. But the dominant feminist commitment to egalitarian principles also promised to complicate the politics of the civil rights coalition, reinforcing class-based distinctions that the race-sex analogy had blurred.

CHAPTER 12

The Consolidation of 1972

The Feminist Movement and the Sex-blind Constitution

By 1970 the two great liberation movements of the 1960s, the black freedom movement and the new feminist movement, were lobbying Congress and the executive agencies with similar appeals to liberation rhetoric, but with diverging goals in public policy. In the wake of the urban riots and assassinations, racial politics had grown increasingly acrimonious. Nixon's revival of the Philadelphia Plan, together with parallel developments in the EEO enforcement agencies and the federal courts, ushered in a decade of controversy over racial quotas and reverse discrimination. By 1970 the EEOC had adopted an equal-results standard under Title 7, and the OFCC was requiring minority preferences under Title 6. The feminist movement, however, was abandoning the tradition of special protection for women. Feminists were pressing enforcement policies under titles 7 and 6 that reflected the bedrock principle of the ERA: the Constitution of the United States was properly sex-blind.

By 1970 the feminists had won their battle with the EEOC. Title 7 was interpreted as requiring equal treatment of the sexes in every realm of employment opportunity (including the classified ads and most labor-standards laws) except in the *narrowest* range of BFOQ cases (including ladies' restroom attendants but not including airline stewardesses or "firemen"). The feminist victory in Title 7, however, had produced limited dividends. The EEOC was a relatively weak enforcement agency, and Title 7 excluded coverage of state and local governments and educational institutions. Somewhat similarly, the Equal Pay Act of 1963 covered most blue-collar and pink-collar jobs, but excluded executive, administrative, and professional employees. For feminists determined to break down traditional barriers against women in business, government, and the professions, the most promising weapon was Title 6. That title's contract-compliance leverage, little noticed in the great congressional debate of 1964 and even less understood by the public, covered *all* federally assisted programs, from university research and corporate contracts through grants to state and local governments. Title 6 offered unique possibilities for women's groups to bring government pressure on the overwhelmingly male worlds of corporate and government executives, university faculties, school administrators, scientific laboratories, law firms, and medical institutions.

When the Senate by a vote of 84 to 8, in March 1972 sent the ERA to the states for ratification, the triumph of feminist nondiscrimination could scarcely have been more complete. Judged by the barometer of congressional support, so overwhelming was the consensus for the ERA that the national opinion surveys did not even begin to poll public attitudes toward the ERA until 1974! The story of the discovery and exploitation of Title 6 by feminist groups is a study in contrast: feminists lobbied with increasing effectiveness in an environment almost devoid of opposition. In the fall of 1966, NOW took the lead in persuading first the Labor Department and then the Johnson White House to issue Executive Order 11375, which amended Johnson's 1965 order by formally adding sex discrimination to the federal government's enforcement responsibilities under Title 6. Then in 1970 two Democratic congresswomen, both members of the advisory board of the Women's Equity Action League, used their strategic positions to turn nondiscrimination policy into enforcement practice. Edith Green, chairwoman of the House Special Subcommittee on Education, began extensive hearings on discrimination against women in January 1970. Later that spring Martha Griffiths used the forum of the House floor to chide HEW for failing to use its contract-compliance leverage to attack sex discrimination in institutions of higher education. By June, when the Labor Department released its OFCC guidelines on sex discrimination under Title 6, HEW added sex discrimination as a responsibility of its Office of Contract Compliance.[1]

Not content to rely on executive orders and agency guidelines alone, Edith Green teamed up with Birch Bayh in the Senate to bar sex discrimination in federally assisted programs by act of Congress. The instrument chosen was an obscure addition to the Educational Amendments of 1972, which Congress passed on July 1, 1972. Title 9 of the act prohibited sex discrimination in all federally aided education programs. Similar protections for women had been included in the 1971 training acts for health manpower and nursing, and also in a widening range of authorizations and appropriations including revenue sharing, public works, economic development, Appalachian redevelopment, and water pollution control. The Revenue Act of 1971 included a new provision for child care deductions (although Nixon vetoed a child development bill that would have funded day care for poor families). In the same year Congress equalized benefits for married women who were federal employees. Such initiatives were usually sponsored in Congress by feminists and their allies, but the Nixon administration generally supported them.

So noncontroversial was Title 9 that in order to avoid attracting attention and stirring controversy, Green asked women's groups not to testify in its favor. The tactic was effective, and the broad feminist agenda moved smartly through the 92nd Congress. A rare grumble of dissent came, ironically, from the Civil Rights Commission, which objected to adding sex discrimination to its monitoring responsibilities. An investigative agency whose agenda by the 1970s had grown almost indistinguishable from that of the NAACP and Hispanic lobbying groups, the commission was ordered by Congress to begin monitoring gender discrimination in 1974. By the mid-1970s, Title 9 would embroil Congress and the White House in high-stakes controversies over the male-dominated priorities of collegiate athletics. By the late 1970s the counterattack of conservative groups against the ERA would plunge the ratification debate into acrimony. But in 1972, at least in the world of Washington politics, the feminist tide against sex discrimination seemed unstoppable.[2]

Rationalizing Enforcement Policy in the 92nd Congress

In Congress the feminist surge carried four implications for civil rights policy. The first was that voting against the agenda of the united feminists was perilous for elected politicians. Second, the new combination of black and feminist pressures seemed potent enough to expand the coverage of the Civil Rights Act. The compromise of 1964 had excluded employees of state and local governments and educational institutions as a political price of enactment. In 1964, the notion of giving the new EEOC blanket authority to desegregate all the state houses and courthouses and schools in the South seemed fanciful indeed. But not by 1970. Politics aside, there seemed little reason in logic why the rights against discrimination that Congress guaranteed for American workers should apply to Lockheed-Marietta but not to the county clerks or schoolteachers in Marietta—or to the Boeing workers and schoolteachers in Seattle, for that matter. At stake were the rights of 10.1 million employees working in 81,000 units of state and local government, most of them clerical and service workers, and 4.3 million employees of 130,000 educational institutions, most of them teachers. Blacks and women had long memories of anchoring the bottom rung in these nonfederal layers of America's public bureaucracy.

Third, Congress shared a consensus that the Dirksen compromise in 1964 left the EEOC too impotent to accomplish even its original mission. If the EEOC were charged with protecting the rights of minorities and women in new jurisdictions, then its authority must surely be increased. This was not a problem for the OFCC and the contract-compliance offices in the mission agencies, because Title 6 armed the enforcers with the ultimate weapons of cutting off federal funds and debarring contractors. But Title 7 remained ambiguous, creating a social regulatory agency in the EEOC but denying it the authority to enforce its determinations.

Finally, there was the thorny issue of reverse discrimination. This was perceived as a problem of minority preferences, not gender preferences. Public opinion polls showed a rising resentment against "racial quotas," with majorities disapproving of racial and ethnic preferences even among black survey samples.[3] Here the interests of organized black and feminist groups seemed to diverge. During the 1960s the black-activist definition of affirmative action had evolved from the special recruiting of Kennedy's 1961 order to the racial preferences of the Philadelphia Plan. The feminists of the 1970s, on the other hand, were demanding open access, rigorous nondiscrimination—affirmative action that broke up the old boy networks, that advertised all employment and promotional opportunities, specified job criteria, and applied them with strict gender neutrality.

These distinctions were not so clear to the participants themselves in the early 1970s. Leaders of African-American and feminist organizations claimed solidarity on important matters of common advantage, such as strengthening the EEOC, and they avoided public disagreements. But the two movement constituencies were distinctive; the minority organizations were dominated by black and Hispanic men, and the feminist movement was led by highly educated white women. The political instincts of Congress shied away from areas of tension between the two movements, and Congress was anxious to avoid the snares of a "racial quota" debate. The congressional solution to this problem was to leave the substantive definitions of the Civil Rights Act alone, and to concentrate instead on procedural questions of coverage, jurisdiction, and authority.

The 92nd Congress, elected in November 1970, began its first session in January 1971 with a strengthened Democratic majority. The Republicans had gained two Senate seats, but remained outnumbered in that chamber 45 to 55. In the House the Democrats picked up nine seats and stretched their margin to 255 to 180, thus leaving the dispirited Republicans beyond reasonable striking distance for regaining control of the House. So the Democrats had strengthened both their congressional control and their determination to force the Nixon administration to accept their civil rights bill.

In the 91st Congress the Democratic leadership had pushed a bill through the Senate that would confer cease-and-desist authority on the EEOC and would also extend Title 7 to cover state and local governments and educational institutions. The Nixon administration had objected on the traditional Republican grounds that cease-and-desist authority would make the EEOC both prosecutor and judge, and that giving Washington officials authority over the personnel practices of state and local governments violated the principles of federalism. The Nixon administration, however, agreed that some revisions were needed in the civil rights enforcement structure. So the White House sponsored a Senate bill of its own that would empower the EEOC to bring suit in federal trial courts. This would give defendants the full range of legal protections afforded by the adversary process, and upon a finding of guilty the courts rather than an administrative agency would enforce the law.

Senate Democrats had little difficulty shelving the Nixon bill, which was sponsored by Vermont's Winston L. Prouty, and passing their own, sponsored by Harrison Williams of New Jersey. But the Democrats' companion bill in the House, sponsored out of the Education and Labor Committee by its chairman, Augustus Hawkins, was bottled up in the Rules Committee by a coalition of Republicans and southern Democrats, and died there when the 91st Congress expired in December 1970. The Democrats were ready, however, when the gavel opened the 92nd Congress in January 1971.[4]

Surprise Reversal in the House: 1971

In the 92nd Congress the Democratic leadership switched to a House-first strategy and proceeded at a forced-march pace. Hawkins re-introduced his cease-and-desist bill (H.R. 1746) before the Labor and Education Committee in early January, the labor subcommittee held hearings on it in March, and on April 7 the subcommittee recommended the bill to the full committee.[5] On June 4 the bill was sent to the Rules Committee, which no longer was in a position to block the determination of both party leaderships that *some* form of EEO enforcement bill must be sent to the Senate before the end of the first session.[6] The Hawkins bill would give cease-and-desist power to the EEOC and extend its Title 7 coverage to employees of state and local governments and educational institutions. Lobbyists for the U.S. Chamber of Commerce and the National Association of Manufacturers weighed in on the side of the Nixon administration's court-enforced substitute bill (H.R. 9247), which was offered on the House floor by Representative John T. Erlenborn of Illinois.[7]

The heart of Erlenborn's bill was the provision for enforcement through EEOC suits in federal trial courts. The EEOC would be given the prosecutorial authority that Dirksen had stripped away in the spring of 1964, but it would be denied the judge-like power, long wielded by established regulatory bodies like the NLRB or the FTC, to issue cease-and-desist orders. The Erlenborn bill made no additions to the coverage provided by the 1964 law. It provided for the President to appoint an independent general counsel for the EEOC, and it prohibited class action suits. It also stipulated that only the Attorney General could intervene in private suits or conduct appeals in the federal circuit courts and the Supreme Court. Erlenborn's substitute bill had earlier been rejected by a vote of 19-14 in the Education and Labor Committee. But the membership of that committee, like its Senate counterpart, the Labor and Public Welfare Committee, was considerably more liberal than the full chamber, and for this reason both committees suffered reversals on floor votes more often than most standing committees. When the floor vote on the Hawkins bill came due in mid-September, the Nixon administration rallied the southern Democrats to the classic conservative coalition, aiming to substitute the Erlenborn for the Hawkins bill.[8]

The ensuing debate, however, was unusually confused. It was no longer clear which was the more aggressive enforcement policy, cease-and-desist or court trials, since both sides were making strong arguments based on institutional arrangements that had never been tried. Even more confusing was the anomaly that the Republicans found themselves wooing conservative Democrats with the cowbird's egg of the Philadelphia Plan's racial quotas. The southern Democrats wanted no enforcement bill at all. So they tended to back the Erlenborn substitute, whose judicial approach appeared less immediately threatening than an EEOC armed with cease-and-desist authority. But the Republican leadership responded by making three basic arguments for their bill, only the first of which the southern conservatives found very appealing, and the last of which the southerners, and many conservative Republicans as well, found most unappealing indeed. The Republicans' first and most unifying argument was to oppose extending coverage to employees in state and local governments. House Republicans generally shared the view of Arthur Burns that this represented an unprecedented and unacceptable intrusion by a federal agency into state and local affairs. This objection easily rallied the Republicans' traditional coalition partners among the southern Democrats. But it did not deal with the heart of the Hawkins bill.[9]

The second argument did. It held that court enforcement provided *more* effective EEO protection than the cease-and-desist approach. It would be more effective, the Republican leaders claimed, partly because it was faster (by 1971 the EEOC already had a 21-month backlog of approximately 25,000 complaints; and NLRB cases, even under cease-and-desist authority, were averaging 630 days to resolve). Court enforcement was also more effective, the Republicans said, because it was fairer and more thorough. This was because the rules of civil procedure in federal trials, where a *preponderance* of evidence was necessary to convict, provided broad discovery of evidence backed by the judges' contempt power. The more limited and cumbersome use of subpoena authority by regulatory boards with cease-and-desist power, on the other hand, was narrowly designed to provide only enough "substantial" evidence to find reasonable cause for administrative relief, not the "preponderance" of judicial evidence that was traditionally necessary to convict. These arguments, however, stirred little enthusiasm among the southerner congressmen, whose fondness for the federal judiciary was notoriously weak.

The Republicans' third argument against the Hawkins bill was that it would transfer the OFCC to the EEOC, and thereby threaten the Nixon-Shultz Philadelphia Plan. The Democratic leadership in Congress had agreed to this provision at the insistence of organized labor, which wanted to purge the hated Philadelphia Plan from the Labor Department. But the "bugaboo" of racial quotas raised by the proposed OFCC transfer only added to the confusion of the debate. On the central question of enforcement power, the Republicans were rallying to a judicial strategy that liberals were beginning to support. In the aftermath of the Supreme Court's *Griggs* decision of 1971, the EEOC stood armed by the federal courts with broad rule-making authority that was potentially far more powerful than retail, cease-and-desist orders. The Republicans, clinging to old habits of thought, were relying on the deliberative traditions of the judicial process to put the brakes on runaway regulatory agencies. But as the southerners in Congress too-well knew, the conservative jurists during the 1960s had been disappearing from the federal bench. Hence the Republicans' judicial strategy elicited little enthusiasm among the southerners.[10]

On September 15, with the House vote scheduled for the following day, the floor manager for the Hawkins bill, Democrat John H. Dent of Pennsylvania, sensed danger. Fearing defeat by the conservative coalition, Dent offered a package of sweetener compromises that included an amendment to bar the EEOC from imposing quotas or requiring preferential treatment of minority group citizens. Hawkins himself said he would accept such an amendment to get his bill passed. But he declared that the anti-quota ban was redundant because it was already in the federal civil rights laws. Erlenborn, however, attacked the anti-quota amendment, with which Dent was wooing Edith Green and her centrist Democratic allies, as "a blatant attempt to undercut the authority of the OFCC for the Philadelphia Plan." Thus the politics of civil rights had gone topsy-turvy: the Democratic floor leader of the liberal Hawkins bill was proposing anti-quota amendments that were opposed by the Republican bill's floor leader, whose stance accomplished the rare trick of offending both organized labor and southern Democrats. In such confused circumstances, a consensus seemed impossible, and a decisive resolution seemed improbable.[11]

On September 16, the House by a vote of 202 to 197 narrowly rejected the Hawkins bill and substituted for it the Erlenborn bill—which was to say, the Nixon bill. Thus the Nixon bill suddenly became H.R. 1746 and was sent to the Senate.

The Senate Debate and the Leadership Compromise of 1972

The second session of the 92nd Congress, when it convened in January 1972, shared a bipartisan consensus that the equal employment principles of 1964 were sound but the enforcement mechanism was not. Congress was weary of seven years of debate on rationalizing the means of enforcement. The *New York Times* captured that consensus when it observed that "[t]he question of giving enforcement teeth to the commission is one of the last of the pure civil rights issues in Congress that began with the Civil Rights Act of 1964 and continued through the Voting Rights Act of 1965 and the Open Housing Act of 1968."[12] Between January 16 and February 15, the debate on the Senate floor concentrated on whether to adopt the congressional leadership's Williams-Hawkins model of cease-and-desist authority, or the Nixon administration's court-enforced model as embodied in the Dominick-Erlenborn bill. In 1969 the new Nixon administration had enjoyed using the Philadelphia Plan to split the liberal coalition of blacks and labor. But this strategy had also split the conservative coalition by driving a wedge between the moderate Republicans and conservative southern Democrats. The trick for the administration in 1972 was to enlist southern support to prevent passage of the cease-and-desist bill, and then to obtain liberal Democratic acquiescence in a court-enforced bill that would leave the contract compliance program intact in the Labor Department.

In this delicate task the administration was ultimately successful.[13] During the January 16–February 15 debate in the Senate the administration's Dominick–Erlenborn bill was thrice rejected. But the Senate's Democratic leadership was unable to close debate and force through the cease-and-desist bill. The administration profited from such a stalemate, for time sweetened the congressional leadership's appetite for compromise. In 1972, however, unlike 1964, the bipartisan coalition of conservatives was so split by Republican loyalty to the Nixon-Shultz Philadelphia Plan that southern attempts to reassert the comprehensiveness of Title 7's ban on racial quotas and ratios—in effect, to reverse legislatively the *Contractors Association* decision that had upheld the Philadelphia Plan—were blocked by the Nixon administration. Sam Ervin was still there and leading his battalion. But Everett Dirksen was not.

Ervin was an ideologue who lacked the late minority leader's sense of timing and instinct for negotiation. The North Carolinian fired his blunderbuss early, often, and usually ineffectively, rushing forward amendments that had not been thought through, hoping to attract supporters who had not been courted and counted in advance. Such skills were little necessary on the Watergate committee of 1973, where Ervin's constitutional scruples were essential, and his constitutional homilies were the stuff of folk heroism. Temperamentally unsuited to play Dirksen's role as conservative broker and moderator in the second half of the second phase of the great civil rights reform of 1960–72, Ervin squandered his opportunities in the showdown on the Senate floor in 1972. But the Nixon forces did not.

In the floor battle over amendments that began on January 20, Nixon and his congressional allies demonstrated that they narrowly lacked the strength to substitute their Dominick-Erlenborn bill for the Williams-Hawkins bill. On January 24 the Senate for the first time considered the Dominick-Erlenborn substitution and rejected it by a roll-call vote of 41–43. On the same day the Senate agreed 40-37 to permit the EEOC to try its own cases in the federal appeals courts as well as in the district trial courts. Although the administration had lost on both votes, the close margin provided a bedrock of strength with which to wear the Democratic leadership down. Thereafter, loyalist Republicans generally provided the margins to pass compromises acceptable to the administration while rejecting the southern forces under Ervin and James B. Allen of Alabama. Thus on January 26, the Senate agreed that in exchange for the administration's support for extending Title 7 coverage to state and local governments, the Attorney General rather than the EEOC would conduct all litigation in suits brought against state and local governments. Then on January 31, when Ervin sought to undo that compromise by excluding coverage of state and local governments altogether, only 16 senators supported his motion, and 59 opposed. A subsequent attempt by Ervin to exclude coverage of educational and religious institutions failed by a similarly decisive vote of 25–55 on February 1 (although Ervin was later able to win an amendment excluding religious institutions alone).

The proposal to expand federal power over state and local governments in job discrimination was the main target of southern opposition in 1972.[14] This position, like opposition to lunch counter desegregation in 1964, was theoretically defensible on principled grounds of federalism. But its public relations were similarly atrocious, for images of defending George Wallace's lily-white Alabama state patrol were conjured up. If northern blacks provoked images of arsonists and rioters, southern blacks had not been part of the mass ghetto rioting, and they remained demonstrably excluded from any fair vision of public service in the Deep South—certainly including Ervin's North Carolina and Allen's Alabama. Nevertheless Senator Ervin, still smarting from his defeat over the Philadelphia Plan in 1969, launched a series of amendments that he argued with a sense of moral outrage that seemed ill-suited to the evil practices they would appear to defend. The result was a boomerang effect that rallied the Republicans around their President.

On January 28, Ervin warmed to his task by denouncing the Williams-Hawkins bill as a "ridiculous" bill designed "to rob all American citizens of basic liberties."[15] It represented, he said, nothing less than "the greatest threat of tyrannical power ever presented to the American Congress throughout the history of this Nation." Like H.L. Mencken, Ervin was a master of hyperbolic overkill, whose broadsides at his prime target managed to insult and alienate numerous secondary targets. For Mencken, this was a fine strategy for selling his deliciously outrageous opinions. But in 1972 Ervin needed to attract allies in a Congress that was intent on bringing its seven-year debate to a close by finding a reasonable middle ground for compromise. Ervin refused to acknowledge this manifest reasonableness. He had already alienated feminist leaders, many of whom were prominent Republicans, by leading the attack on the ERA in a similar mocking spirit. Thus he produced a double-barreled slur, although probably unintentionally, when he told the Senate that the history of the EEOC "down to this date shows that virtually all the men who have been appointed to serve on this Commission were men who were psychologically incapable of holding the scales of justice evenly"—men who were so biased that "they would be disqualified to serve on a jury passing merely on questions of fact, and who certainly should never sit jointly as the prosecutor and the judge."[16] Commissioners Aileen Hernandez, Elizabeth Kuck, and, by 1972, Ethel Bent Walsh thus failed to qualify even for Ervin's wholesale psychological disqualification.

In response to Ervin's string of assaults, Republican Jacob Javits of New York, a veteran tormentor of southern Democrats on civil rights issues, responded with reasoned moderation. In explaining one of his amendments Ervin charged, for example, that requiring merely "substantial" rather than "a preponderance" of evidence to make a judgment of discrimination was a "crowning prostitution" because "substantial" meant merely "a scintilla, a percentage point beyond being purely imaginary." In reply Javits politely devastated this legally indefensible argument—which Ervin, the simple country lawyer from the Harvard law school, well knew was nonsense—by citing a half-century of regulatory law, including opinions by that apostle of judicial restraint, Felix Frankfurter, and also by recounting his own experience as New York attorney general in dealing with its highly regarded and prudent State Commission on Anti-Discrimination. Ervin stubbornly pressed his amendment on evidence to a vote, and was badly beaten, 22–43.

Having fired too many of his volleys in scattershot fashion, Ervin (together with Alabama's Allen) pressed ahead undaunted with an amendment to bar reverse discrimination. The amendment, which Ervin cobbled together hastily (and twice changed in the process of merely introducing it on the Senate floor), stipulated that "No department, agency, or officer of the United States shall require an employer to practice discrimination in reverse by employing persons of a particular race, or a particular religion, or a particular national origin, or a particular sex in either fixed or variable numbers, proportions, percentages, quotas, goals, or ranges."[17] Ervin made it plain that his target was not only the

EEOC, which was already bound by the 1964 ban but was beginning to ignore it. Ervin was mainly gunning for the racial quotas of the Philadelphia Plan.

In his haste to ban all agents of reverse discrimination, however, Ervin had included any "officer" of the United States. But *any* officer would necessarily seem to include federal judges or officials implementing judicial decrees. Javits was quick to attack this vulnerability in Ervin's hastily designed attack. Javits pointed out that Ervin's amendment threatened not only to destroy the Philadelphia Plan. Worse, it threatened to undo the entire corpus of federal court decisions reaching back to 1967, including *Quarles v. Philip Morris* in 1968 and *Contractors Association* in 1970. *Quarles* had ruled that the history of segregation in the South's tobacco industry had stripped the *bona fides* from its white-dominated seniority system.[18] The *Quarles* dictum had held that Congress in 1964 could not have intended to freeze blacks in a permanent historical lag of disadvantage, and Javits placed Ervin and his supporters in the posture of heartless freezers, most of them with southern accents. Ervin's amendment was therefore not conservative but radical, Javits implied, because "it would torpedo orders of courts to correct a history of unjust discrimination in employment on racial or color grounds." Ervin's amendment, Williams said, would therefore "deprive even the federal courts of any power to remedy clearly proven cases of discrimination."[19]

When the votes were tallied, a familiar pattern emerged. Ervin could count on the support of only three small groups: his own hard core of southern Democrats; a corporal's guard of like-minded southern Republicans like Strom Thurmond of South Carolina, John Tower of Texas, and Edward J. Gurney of Florida; and a fringe of nonsouthern Republican conservatives like Barry Goldwater and Paul Fannin of Arizona, Nebraska's Roman Hruska and Carl T. Curtis, Norris Cotton of New Hampshire, and Milton R. Young of South Dakota. With most Republicans staying loyal to their own minority leadership and their President, and the nonsouthern Democrats remaining solid behind the majority leadership, Ervin's battalion was reduced to a platoon. His amendment lost 22–44.

Thus the Nixon administration used Ervin's intransigent bloc to hold off the cease-and-desist bill (Nixon told Haldeman "I will veto the EEOC. Not appealable. Won't discuss it."),[20] while successfully fending off Ervin's threats to the Philadelphia Plan. This tactic ultimately forced the congressional leadership to settle for a court-enforced bill that left the liberal coalition disappointed but nevertheless "moderately pleased" with the final result. Clarence Mitchell told Tom Wicker of the *New York Times* that he was "completely satisfied with the outcome."[21]

The EEO Act of 1972 and the Legacy of "Reverse Discrimination"

The shape of that final result, the Equal Employment Opportunity Act of 1972, was largely determined as early as February 8, when the Democratic leadership admitted defeat on the Williams-Hawkins bill. By February 22 the amendment battles had sorted out the essential compromises, and the Senate voted 73-21 to close debate and send the bill to the House. The House called for a conference and the conferees filed their reports on March 2, which the Senate accepted on March 6 and the House on March 8. In conference the House basically accepted the Senate version. To do otherwise would invite reopening the debate in the Senate, and therefore risk having to watch the bill die as time ran out in an election year—as had happened in 1970.[22] The Senate accepted the more conservative House language requiring courts to find that respondents "intentionally" engaged in unlawful employment practices, and the House accepted the Senate stipulation that judicial relief may include "any other equitable relief [in addition to reinstatement or hiring with back pay] as the court deems appropriate."[23]

In the end the administration's court-enforced approach had prevailed, and the White House was comfortable with the law's other main compromises. These included extending coverage to (1) employers and unions with 15 or more full-time workers (rather than the original Williams-Hawkins bill's 8, but down from the existing threshhold of 25); (2) employees in state and local government (but exempting elected officials and their policy advisers, and requiring the Attorney General rather than the EEOC to bring suits against government units); and (3) employees of educational (but not religious) institutions. Also, the Attorney General's pattern-or-practice authority would be transferred over a two-year period to the EEOC. But the President would appoint the commission's general counsel, and the Attorney General would control EEOC appeals to the Supreme Court (but not to the circuit courts of appeal).

As for reverse discrimination, direct attacks by congressional conservatives on the Philadelphia Plan in 1969 and 1972 had failed. But Dirksen's prohibition against "preferential treatment" by race or sex "on account of any imbalance" was still embedded in the heart of the Civil Rights Act of 1964. Under the doctrine of the separation of powers, the defeat of a legislative proposal does not accomplish the statutory enactment of an executive program with which the proposal may deal.[24] The lower federal courts, however, had begun to reason their way around Title 7's prohibitions against discrimination, whether invidious or compensatory. In most cases the Supreme Court had quietly acquiesced, as in *Contractors Association* on the Philadelphia Plan. In *Griggs* the Supreme Court had accelerated the shift of standards from the equal-treatment model stipulated by the Civil Rights Act toward the equal-results test preferred by the EEO enforcement agencies.

Legal scholars have debated whether the 1972 law fundamentally altered the anti-discriminatory core of the Civil Rights Act of 1964. Supporters of race-conscious remedies have argued that the rejection of the Ervin amendments in 1972 signified tacit acceptance by Congress of the OFCC's nationwide imposition of numerical hiring requirements.[25] Critics of compensatory preferences for minorities have countered that historically the Supreme Court has resisted inferences of congressional intent from *nonaction*, whether in appropriating funds for otherwise unauthorized activity or in acquiescing in unauthorized executive conduct. The Court has been reluctant "to discover in congressional silence an implicit delegation of power," one critic concluded, "particularly where such delegation would effectively upset some explicit statutory scheme or vest the delegatee with extraordinary authority."[26] The Supreme Court, in *Bakke* and *Weber* during the Burger years and through the 1980s under Chief Justice Rehnquist, continued to split indecisively when interpreting the hard, zero-sum questions that lie at the heart of civil rights disputes.

In 1972, as in 1969, President Nixon had thrown the full weight of the White House against the congressional conservatives in a successful defense of the system of minority preferences that his administration had embedded in national policy. This was especially ironical in light of Nixon's subsequent behavior in his campaign for re-election. For having fought so successfully to defend the Philadelphia Plan and to unleash the EEOC as a prosecutor in the courts, Nixon followed his victory in the Equal Employment Opportunity Act of 1972 by turning up his campaign rhetoric and directing it against the institutions he was empowering and the purposes they were furthering.

Richard Nixon and the Irony of Civil Rights

In the Watergate hearings Sam Ervin would become an American folk hero as defender of the Constitution against the abuse of executive power—a far nobler purpose than defending Jim Crow as a local option of federalism. But Richard Nixon, who had defeated Ervin in the civil rights battles of 1969 and 1972, knew that the American public showed little interest in debates over enforcement technicalities—over cease-and-desist authority, executive orders on contract compliance, mind-numbing descriptions in the *Federal Register* of Revised Order No. 4. But the American public cared about rising crime, deteriorating neighborhoods, ineffective schools. By deflecting civil rights initiatives toward the courts, Nixon's judicial strategy had sought to shift from the White House to the federal judiciary the popular discontent of the 1970s with the Great Society legacy of social experimentation. Thus Nixon's civil rights victories freed him to run for re-election by taking a stand against the school integration orders and minority quota requirements that he had done so much to further. The strategy worked magnificently, at least in the short run—much as Nixon's similarly unRepublican imposition of wage and price controls in 1971 had worked to stave off economic turmoil until after he was safely re-elected in 1972. Sam Ervin would have his revenge in the slightly longer run.

In mid-March 1972, one week following the administration's congressional victory in the EEOC debate and two days after George Wallace had won the Democratic presidential primary in Florida, Nixon made a televised address to the nation demanding immediate congressional action to stop school busing for racial balance.[27] He asked for a moratorium on such busing, coupled with an emergency appropriation of $2.5 billion for remedial education in the disadvantaged neighborhood schools where students would remain in the absence of busing. The following day Nixon sent Congress a special legislative message that concentrated on the abuses of busing, but did so in language that seemed equally applicable to his own OFCC and HEW. Objecting to such "arbitrary Federal requirement[s]—whether administrative or judicial"—Nixon insisted that "the remedies imposed must be limited to those needed to correct the particular violations that have been found."[28]

In early April, Nixon began sending Ehrlichman and Haldeman detailed memoranda on campaign politics and policy. He directed Ehrlichman to delegate domestic program and cabinet coordination to Shultz and various White House assistants, and thus free himself and a team of spokesmen to "sell our line" for the re-election campaign.[29] The "gut" issues of the campaign, Nixon said, would be crime, busing, drugs, welfare, inflation—"issues the Democrats hate." By mid-May, however, it was clear that the Democratic leadership in Congress would not act on Nixon's busing moratorium. Disturbed by Wallace's strong showing in the early polls and primaries,[30] Nixon directed Ehrlichman and his presidential surrogates to counter the Wallace appeal by exploiting tensions over busing orders in suburban communities like Pontiac, Michigan, a suburb of Detroit where a federal judge had ordered busing across the city school district line.[31] Ehrlichman led a cadre of hard-selling spokesmen and toured the television news circuits in such targeted communities as Detroit, Fort Worth, Rochester, Grand Rapids, Buffalo, and Wilmington. Like Nixon's proposed busing moratorium, which was dying in a congressional committee, Ehrlichman's team called for federal intervention in suits involving court-ordered busing. So widespread was Nixon's proposed intervention that Ehrlichman aid Ed Morgan asked why they must support school boards like the one in Augusta, Georgia, "which even my most conservative southern friends admit is racist."[32] The keynote speaker at the NAACP's national convention, meeting in July in Detroit, declared that "the NAACP considers itself in a state of war against President Nixon and 'his Constitution wreckers.' "[33]

As the presidential campaign reached the party conventions in Miami, Nixon, the patron of the Philadelphia Plan, increased his attacks on quotas. In his acceptance speech in Miami on August 23, Nixon compared the Republicans' "open convention without dividing Americans into quotas" with the elaborate system of racial and sexual quotas that George McGovern had engineered and profited from at the Democratic convention. "[M]y fellow Americans," Nixon proclaimed, "the way to end discrimination against some is not to begin discrimination against others."[34] He told a radio audience in his Labor Day salute to the work ethic that "quotas are intended to be a short cut to equal opportunity, but in reality they are a dangerous detour away from the traditional value of measuring a person on the basis of ability."[35] The *Wall Street Journal* explained this as an "election year effort to woo the traditionally Democratic union and Jewish vote," and during the summer and fall the White House so dampened the enforcement efforts of the OFCC through an internal reorganization that its new (since the previous February) black director, George Holland, resigned in protest.[36]

In light of the poll results of October and the election returns of November, Nixon's rightward lunge seemed quite unnecessary. The McGovern-Shriver campaign had collapsed, the economy was thriving, and inflation had abated under the temporary impact of Nixon's wage and price controls. The opening to China, the arms control negotiations and atmosphere of détente with the Soviet Union, and Henry Kissinger's proclaimed triumph of peace in Indochina, all conspired to win the President a landslide re-election. Within two years, the "real" Richard Nixon would appear to the public to be the culpable architect of Watergate, driven from the presidency in disgrace. But in the long view of policy evolution in civil rights, the real Richard Nixon was not only the demagogue of busing and the hypocrite of quotas during the warm months of 1972. He was also the expedient and successful defender of the Philadelphia Plan, the careful but quiet enforcer of school desegregation in the South, the architect of judicial empowerment for the EEOC.

On February 15, 1972, the day after Nixon had invited the congressional foes of busing to the White House to promise a joint fight against it, an assistant to the White House communications director released a progress report on the administration's civil rights achievements. "We have nothing to be ashamed of," the assistant lamely announced.[37] Under the election-year circumstances of Nixon's anti-busing and anti-quota campaign, the communications assistant's task was understandably awkward. But in historical perspective, it provided a more revealing benchmark, as an indicator of continuity in direction and quiet acceleration in velocity, than the shrill headlines over busing and the artful codes of the quota debate. In its progress report the Nixon administration claimed credit for boosting the proportion of racial and ethnic minorities in the civilian federal workforce to 19.5 percent, for doubling aid to black colleges, and increasing minority business aid by 152 percent. The percentage of black children in all-black schools nationwide had decreased from 40 percent in 1969 to 12 percent in 1972. For Hispanics, Nixon had sweetened his special legislative message on busing by proposing an "educational bill of rights for Mexican-Americans, Puerto Ricans, Indians, and others who start under language handicaps." This initiative was quickly buried along with the busing moratorium, but it would be revived and enacted under President Ford.[38]

As for the EEOC, the symbol of the seven-year legislative debate that Nixon had shaped and concluded in 1972, the "poor enfeebled" agency had grown from a staff of 359 and a budget of $13.2 million in 1968 to a staff of 1,640 and a budget of $29.5 million in 1972.[39] For fiscal year 1973 the Nixon budget for civil rights enforcement increased from $49.9 million to $66.3 million, providing for a doubling of OFCC compliance checks from 22,500 in 1971 to 52,000 in 1973.[40] In March 1973, *Business Week* reported that despite "loud cries of anguish" from civil rights forces over Nixon's deep budget cuts in social action programs, his budget for fiscal 1974, "almost unnoticed," had doubled the 1972 allotments for civil rights enforcement agencies. The EEOC budget increased 107 percent, the contract compliance budget for all agencies rose by 66 percent, and the Justice Department's budget for the Office of Civil Rights increased by 67 percent.[41] As for encouraging blacks and Hispanics in business, despite the controversy and cynicism that had greeted Nixon's initiative with the Office of Minority Business Enterprise in 1969, the Republican effort to encourage minority entrepreneurship had started small but had grown like Topsy. The budget for minority procurement set-asides for all agencies had increased from a fledgling $8.2 million in fiscal 1972 to $242.2 million in fiscal 1974—an increase of almost 3000 percent. In the modern American administrative state, the future lay far more in the budget than in campaign speeches and newspaper headlines.

By 1972, the election rhetoric notwithstanding, the President and Congress had rounded out the basic structure of civil rights policy and enforcement machinery that John F. Kennedy had begun to erect in 1961 with Executive Order 10925. Lyndon Johnson and the congresses of 1964–68 had responded creatively to the moral crisis. The compromise between the Nixon administration and the 92nd Congress in 1972 had completed a rationalizing process. It was a legislative tidying up that reflected more than shaped a fundamental shift in authority and power since 1965—one that had been determined more in the federal courts and the agencies of the permanent government than in the White House or the halls of Congress.

CHAPTER 13

The Rights Revolution and the American Administrative State

The Storm Over Affirmative Action

For a generation following the consolidation of civil rights policy in 1972, Americans have debated the legitimacy and wisdom—and meaning—of affirmative action. During the 1970s public attention was fixed on the reverse discrimination cases in the federal courts, most notably the white-male challenges brought by Marco DeFunis, Allan Bakke, and Brian Weber.[1] During the 1980s the Reagan and Bush administrations sponsored counterattacks against policies of minority preference and "racial quotas."[2] Public opinion polls from the 1970s into the 1990s have continued to show widespread disapproval of minority preferences, especially among whites (including white women). Survey research during the 1970s showed considerable rejection of preferences even among minority respondents themselves, especially among Asians.[3] African-American and Hispanic organizations, however, have continued to coalesce around affirmative action programs and have generally formed effective alliances with elected leaders and agency officials to defend and expand preferential policies in employment, contract set-asides, university admissions, and electoral districting.

For a generation, since 1972, the persistent debate over affirmative action has remained remarkably bitter. Its capacity to polarize, to resist consensus-formation and policy resolution, has reinforced the paralysis in national domestic policy that has come with the divided government that is also a legacy of the 1960s. Indeed, the potent symbolism of minority preferences has played a leading role in defining the cleavage that seems to have willed the presidency to the Republicans and the Congress to the Democrats.[4] This debate cannot be resolved by evidence drawn from the period 1960–72. The storm over reverse discrimination is at bottom a philosophical dispute, and the main arguments long ago grew familiar and repetitive.[5]

The first task of policy history is to clarify policy origins. And clarification is sorely needed, for the civil rights era confronts us with a puzzle. The reforms of 1960–72 came in two phases, roughly dividing at the watershed year 1965. Phase II was essentially the implementing stage for Phase I. Yet the equal-results thrust of Phase II appears to contradict the equal-treatment assumptions that anchored Phase I. In trying to understand how this contradiction developed, we discover something even more important. This strange evolution of civil rights policy was part of a larger process that transformed the nature of the American administrative state itself during the 1960s.

Phase I of the civil rights era, the belated triumph of nondiscrimination for blacks and women, is less difficult to explain. Its philosophical basis was relatively simple and coherent. Equal protection of the laws meant that government must shield all citizens from harm due to immutable characteristics like race, sex, and national origin. Everyone could grasp the meaning of the NAACP's long quest for a color-blind Constitution. It was Phase II's rapid development of minority preferences that was more difficult to comprehend. Its rationale was politically vulnerable and philosophically awkward. Yet the practical and historical arguments for driving civil rights policy beyond "mere" nondiscrimination carried considerable force. From its origin in the Wagner Act to President Kennedy's borrowing for his executive order of 1961, the term "affirmative action" had always required something more than mere even-handedness. The "something" remained ambiguous, to be sure. It ranged from the NLRB's opposition to unfair labor practices, within a larger presumption that labor unions were a desirable norm in modern industrial society, to the insistence of Vice President Johnson's committee that employers make special recruiting efforts to hire "underrepresented" minorities. The notion of underrepresentation, with its implicit, ethno-racial standard of proportional distribution, provided the key for the transition from the "soft" affirmative action of the Kennedy approach to the "hard" or equal-results affirmative action developed under Nixon. In between, the Johnson administration courageously won the great campaigns of the Second Reconstruction, then struggled inconclusively with the complexities of implementation while the Vietnam war consumed its energy and its future.

Johnson's footrace metaphor in the Howard University speech of 1965 captured the historical core of the compensatory argument: innocent minorities had inherited a crippling legacy, and social justice therefore required a period of affirmative or preferential discrimination. Johnson never followed through on his speechwriter's rhetoric. The compensatory theory that undergirded the anti-poverty programs of the Great Society, such as Head Start and Model Cities, was class-based, not race-conscious. During Phase II, however, the non-labor wing of the civil rights coalition rather quietly fashioned a results-centered rationale that was keyed primarily to racial and ethnic identity rather than to economic disadvantage. The equal-results rationale countered the equal-treatment creed with an essentially historical argument about institutions and culture. Equality must mean more than the equal right of the rich and the poor to sleep under the public bridges. Liberalism's historic command not to discriminate could not achieve its goal of a color-blind society because the racism of the past had become too deeply institutionalized. Current institutions thus might perpetuate discrimination even if no one in those institutions remained personally prejudiced.[6]

The camel's-nose logic of affirmative action, and the historical argument that past discrimination required race-specific remedies, struck a resonant chord on the federal bench. To judges, the doctrine of make-whole relief provided a familiar rationale for compensatory remedies, even in the absence of statutory provisions. The traditional concept of make-whole relief, as expressed for example in judicial orders to stop the offending practice or in the award of money damages for suffering, was being driven by civil rights litigation during the 1960s toward a new norm of equitable remedy. Traditional make-whole relief had typically involved a dispute between private parties leading to a judge-ordered, one-time, one-way transfer that retrospectively righted a wrong. A judge would order a discriminating employer to stop refusing to promote blacks to supervisory positions, for example, and to promote a vindicated plaintiff and award her back pay. But the new equitable remedies sought to balance the class-action interests of multiple parties (some of them absent) rather than to declare specific winners and losers in a bipolar dispute. The school desegregation cases had invited the rapid expansion of the logic of equitable remedy, and the defiance of southern die-hard regimes provided public legitimacy for the federal courts' growing assertiveness in social policy during Phase II.

In *Contractors Association, Allen, Gaston, Swann, Griggs,* and similar test cases the federal courts embraced the compensatory argument to justify as equitable relief a preferential treatment for minorities in fields as varying as voting and electoral districting, employee and union seniority, education and training, hiring and promotions, and job testing. Increasingly the judicial decree sought less to judge past behavior than to adjust future behavior. As the courts declared that Congress's overarching substantive purpose in the Civil Rights Act (more jobs for minorities) was more compelling than its specific procedural prohibitions (no discrimination in a color-blind society), sympathetic legal scholars argued that the Warren-era judges were correcting a formalist bias of the late nineteenth century.[7] Anglo-American law had then defined punitive damages in tort and criminal prohibitions in terms of malicious "intent," and held that courts properly interpreted statutes only by divining and applying their legislative intentions.[8] Thus in Phase II the intent test in statutory interpretation, which had been stipulated in Phase I, was replaced by statistical demonstrations of disparate impact or disproportionate results. "Hard" affirmative action through preferential remedies was transforming nondiscrimination into modern, no-fault civil rights.

Looked at from this longer and wider perspective, the two-phase transformation of civil rights policy takes on an importance and meaning that transcends its salience as a morality play over principles that were either betrayed or fully matured. Instead, from the perspective of the 1990s the Phase-II shift of civil rights policy appears to have been the unwitting cutting edge of a vast but quiet revolution in the nature of the American state itself.

The Quiet Revolution in the American Regulatory State

The civil rights revolution of the 1960s was part of a larger regulatory shift that lacked a blueprint or planned direction. This was a deep, national shift in the American administrative state, beginning around 1960, away from the consolidation that followed the New Deal and World War II, and toward a regulatory apparatus that paradoxically combined disaggregation with growth and even greater intrusiveness by government.

The shift was massive, unanticipated, and largely unperceived. Its components were unconnected by conscious design, yet together they ushered in a new era of social regulation with profound consequences for civil rights policy. The federal budget, which had grown to $92 billion by 1960 but was almost half-consumed by defense outlays, doubled by 1970 to reach $195 billion. During the same period, however, the defense share of the budget dropped by one-fifth, even in the face of the Vietnam war. This was the Great Society's "welfare shift." It endowed an enlarged array of social agencies with new domestic programs and funds and provided them with unprecedented discretion in distributing these funds to new constituencies.[9] The political need to avoid an explosion of Washington bureaucrats produced a federal bureaucracy that added only 400,000 employees during the 1960s, and then remained relatively static during the 1970s. But this coincided with a genuine bureaucratic explosion in state and local government, where employment increased during the 1960s by 4 million or 40 percent. During the 1960s the amount of federal financial aid received by the sub-national governments increased by 230 percent, from $7 billion in 1960 to more than $23 billion in 1970.[10]

The relative freeze in federal personnel led to a pattern not only of farming out public services to state and local governments, but also of jobbing them out to a growing army of private contractors. These were the "beltway bandits," whose skill at winning federal contracts and grants extended far beyond the infamous Washington beltway and its spectacular repository of interest-group associations. Accompanying this process was an explosion in federal regulations. Between 1969 and 1974 the number of pages in the *Federal Register* sextupled. Finally, and most relevant to our civil rights focus, there occurred a vast mobilization of constituencies, as the Great Society programs and the surprising initiatives of the Nixon administration in environmental and consumer protection and safety spun a web of new "iron triangle" networks across the realm of government.[11]

The convergence of these trends had created by the end of the 1960s an administrative apparatus that was sprawling, complex, and disjointed. It linked not only federal, state, and local governments but also a host of private organizations. These were the nongovernment organizations of "civil society." They constituted the pluralist mosaic of membership organizations, lobbying groups, public interest law firms, think tanks, and business and professional organizations whose prosperity or suffering depended increasingly on their ability to influence public policy. In the new era of expansive government rule-making, success required elbowing a place at an expanding bargaining table, where new ranks of regulators dealt with new arrays of client and supplicant groups—black, feminist, and Hispanic groups, consumer organizations, environmentalists, public-interest lobbies for highway and worker safety, even anti-war groups challenging the equity of selective service policy. The rapid growth of the new regulatory apparatus coincided with the grass-roots, decentralizing, citizen-participation movement of the 1960s. The combination created a new and potent linkage in government: "the explicit adoption of citizen participation as an adjunct to bureaucratic decision-making. It signified that administrative agencies were now mobilizing and organizing political constituencies on their own."[12] Students of public administration have called the regulatory results of this marked shift of the 1960s the "new social regulation."[13]

Paradigm Shift of the 1960s: The New Social Regulation

The new social regulation emerged from an unplanned confluence of the distinctive grass-roots and citizen-lobby movements of the 1960s—the civil rights, anti-war, environmental, consumer protection, and worker health and safety movements. Its common denominator was a demand that citizens be protected from being harmed by private or government behavior. Its means were a combination of executive and legislative guarantees and new social programs that emphasized the rights of consumers and employees over the needs of producers. These new programs were to be policed or run either by the established mission agencies, such as the Office of Education in HEW, the OFCC in Labor, and the OMBE in Commerce, or more characteristically by the establishment of independent new agencies, like the EEOC or the Environmental Protection Agency. A chief advantage of new agencies was their freedom from the constraints imposed by established clientele relationships in the old line agencies. Between 1900 and 1964, only *one* such regulatory agency had been established at the federal level with such a primary responsibility: the Food and Drug Administration, created in 1938 out of the old Bureau of Food and Drugs. Between 1964 and 1972, however, *seven* new federal regulatory agencies were created by Congress with social regulation as their mandate. These were the EEOC (1964), the National Transportation Safety Board (1966), the Council on Environmental Quality (1969), the Environmental Protection Agency (1970), the National Highway Traffic Safety Administration (1970), the Occupational Safety and Health Administration (1970), and the Consumer Product Safety Commission (1972).

The new social regulation differed from the traditional norms of economic regulation in several fundamental respects. Economic regulation sought to control such evils as monopoly, collective restraint of trade, price-fixing, and labor abuses by regulating market entry and rates and prices. The quasi-judicial commissions and boards (ICC, FTC, SEC, CAB), created during the Progressive era and the New Deal, typically pursued their regulation through a relatively unified and vertical form of agency surveillance. They focused on coherent areas of market policy like railroads, the communications and power industries, the stock market, airlines, trucking. The impact of economic regulation on citizens was indirect and diffuse. Social regulation, however, confronted the reality or prospect of direct physical and economic harm to millions of employees, consumers, and citizens. Its form evolved through a common, three-step pattern that linked the civil rights movement to the movements for environmental, health, safety, and consumer protection and created for them a quite different model of regulation.[14]

The first step in the pattern was often a scandal or disaster that would command national and therefore congressional attention, such as the Thalidomide controversy in 1962, or the Santa Barbara oil spill of 1969—or the racial brutality in Birmingham in 1963 and Selma in 1965 (where television played the publicist role of a Rachel Carson or Ralph Nader). Second, Congress would respond to public urgency by creating a new agency and new programs. Typically, Congress would pattern the new agencies after existing commissions or boards like the FTC and the NLRB, and new program jurisdictions would be cannibalized out of the turf of existing administrative agencies, like HEW. But the congressional instinct for shaping the new agencies of social regulation according to the old economic model caused major problems. As the first of these new entities in the modern era, the "poor enfeebled" EEOC got caught up in crossfires over role and function that *no* one understood at the founding.

For Congress the standard model of regulation was an economic one. Its history reached back to the creation of the ICC in 1887—the founding of the regulatory era and its "headless fourth branch of government." The economic model of regulation generally dealt with the challenges that came before it on a retail, case-by-case basis, and it used court-like procedures that were basically adjudicatory. Agencies like the FTC and the FPC dealt typically with dichotomous variables, like approving or disapproving a challenged rate, price, merger, or unfair labor practice. For this reason the main club or sanction of existing regulatory agencies took the form of disapproval or cease-and-desist authority. Their trial-like hearing procedures were governed by the judicial model of the Administrative Procedures Act of 1946. Similarly their verdict, in the judicial mode, was essentially yes or no.[15]

Social regulation, on the other hand, tended to deal not with dichotomous variables but rather with a complex spectrum of risk. It addressed such questions as how much use or discharge of what chemical over what period of time would impermissibly pollute the food or air or water. This form of regulation, however, posed a dilemma for Congress. Pressed to act by a broadly based public outcry, Congress was nevertheless uncomfortable with the *re*distributive politics and the zero-sum implications of much of the new social regulation (clean air regulations could force millions of old cars off the roads and jack up the price of new ones). So Congress typically responded to the crisis by giving a contradictory set of charges to the new agencies of social regulation. They must make sure that the specific triggering offense never happen again. But they must at the same time cast a wide net to prevent a broad class of potential but still unspecified harms. The new agencies must move quickly and decisively. But they must also grant access in policy deliberations to the newly mobilized armies of citizen participants. Congress in its founding statutes therefore often spelled out elaborate procedural directives for the new agencies of social regulation. But Congress did not stipulate clear substantive policies with definitions and standards, because Congress lacked both the expertise and the will to do so.[16]

The result, in the third stage, was that the new agencies of social regulation developed implementing strategies which created a new model of regulation. Their mode of enforcement was wholesale rather than retail. Their administrative style was more legislative than adjudicatory. This therefore led not to cease-and-desist orders, but rather to a detailed process of "notice-and-comment" rule making. Proposed guidelines, regulations, and standards were published in the *Federal Register*. Comments were received, hearings were held, revised rules were promulgated—often in lengthy and technical detail. Given contradictory and ambiguous mandates from Congress, and given also a vast and horizontal, layer-cake structure of regulation (covering the entire nation's air, water, worker safety, consumer health), the new agencies of social regulation adopted notice-and-comment rule-making as a procedure for two good reasons: (1) it maximized their political freedom to respond to organized and insistent new constituencies; (2) it produced detailed standards with which producers must comply and which in turn proved to be a faster, less expensive, and farther-reaching method of enforcement than the retail, case-at-a-time approach of the adjudicatory model. The rule-making approach of the social regulators won ready approval from the federal courts, which had learned to defer to the expertise of the economic regulators when confronting highly technical questions of scientific import.[17]

The rule-making rather than the cease-and-desist model of enforcement provided legal advantages to the social regulators as well. Rule-making blocked noncompliance by complaining industries or employers by depriving them of legal defenses that had previously been sufficient. This was critical in undermining the importance of *intent,* the traditional standard in discrimination law that was stipulated in the Civil Rights Act. Under the intent standard, the burden of proof was on minority plaintiffs to provide evidence of intentional discrimination against them, irrespective of their statistical underrepresentation. But social regulation tended to disregard intent, and hence to disarm it as a defense. The promulgation by the EPA of a minimal pollution standard that had to be met, for example, severed the old common-law connections in tort that had tied harm to intent. Because evidence of damage caused by exceeding the standards was sufficient justification for the regulators to act, proof of the polluter's evil designs need not be adduced. The social regulators' main goal remained the reduction or prevention of future pollution, and hence was forward-looking, rather than retrospective as in the standard adjudicatory model. For this reason the standards of performance set by social regulators tended also to sever tort's old direct link between harm and relief. The agency's prescribed standards, as a forward-looking form of equitable relief, could be justified as preventing future environmental harm. Or, in the case of civil rights, agency standards could be justified to compensate for an accumulation of past harm that required no specific finger-pointing. Thus the relevance of intent was greatly weakened.

The Phase II Shift and the Upward Ratchet

The process of agency rule-making and judicial deference helps to explain the otherwise puzzling ability of enforcement agencies like the EEOC and the OFCC to appear to violate the requirements of the Civil Rights Act they were created to enforce. In 1971 in *Griggs v. Duke Power,* for example, the Burger Court deferred to the EEOC's new guidelines on employee testing, even though the Tower amendment in Title 7 had specifically exempted such tests. This ruling, which pushed the substantive result of *Griggs* far beyond the mere testing question at hand, granted broad approval to the "disparate impact" version of the equal-results test. Although Congress in the Civil Rights Act had required an intent test and had prohibited proportional ratios and quotas, Congress generally resisted reopening the debates of 1964 and rearguing on constant appeal the rulings and guidelines of the new civil rights agencies.

Similarly, when the federal courts ruled in the *Contractors Association* suit against the Philadelphia Plan that Title 7's ban on racial preferences could not override the President's constitutional authority to control government procurement policies through executive orders, Congress refused to re-enter the dispute. The same thing happened when the Warren Court essentially rewrote section five of the Voting Rights Act in the *Allen* decision, and rewrote the Open Housing Act of 1968 in *Jones v. Mayer.* Because congressional differences over civil rights issues remained deep, and passing such controversial laws was difficult and time-consuming, Congress had little stomach for re-entering these arenas. To handle complex disputes administratively was after all why Congress had created the quasi-judicial regulatory agencies in the first place.

This major shift in the rules of the game angered conservatives and split the ranks of liberals. During the 1970s "neoconservatives," most of them supporters of the civil rights breakthrough of Phase I, watched in dismay as their equal-treatment model was transformed by courts and agencies into an equal-results model. Elected legislators working with the elected President had constructed the policy, critics claimed, and appointed bureaucrats and judges had transformed it beyond recognition.[18] The civil rights regulators, working in tandem with the courts, had developed a one-way ratchet. At key points they jacked it sharply upward. They justified increased state control by pointing to evidence of obstructionism that offended the public's sense of fairness. The offending behavior was often localized, limited in scale, or declining under the assault of less expansive federal interventions. But in the wake of Birmingham and Selma, where the offending behavior was far more typical of a pervasive social problem, the tactic was politically effective.

Thus the racist behavior in 1966–67 of white electoral officials in roughly 6 percent of the counties covered by the Voting Rights Act was cited to justify requiring all covered counties to obtain prior approval from Washington officials for any changes in electoral procedures. Thus also, racist practices by building trades locals containing approximately 5 percent of metropolitan Philadelphia's union members in 1969 were used to create a system of proportional representation in minority employment to govern the nation's entire workforce. The OFCC's hearings and "findings" in Philadelphia's construction industry in 1969, not replicated in other cities, were used to extend the Philadelphia Plan to federally assisted programs everywhere. Even Laurence Silberman, the Labor Department solicitor who successfully defended the Philadelphia Plan during 1969–70, wrote several years later in the *Wall Street Journal* that the nationwide extension of the Philadelphia Plan had been legally indefensible.[19]

The critics of minority preferences drew their criteria of legitimacy from the traditional canons of liberal nondiscrimination, and by these standards the abrupt switch from Phase I to Phase II looked like a betrayal of principle. But the breakthrough legislation in civil rights of 1964–65 was both a culmination and a new beginning. The framers of the Civil Rights Act, none more instrumental than that quintessential centrist Everett McKinley Dirksen, had embedded their standards in the law just as the American regulatory state was about to explode into a new era. That did not represent a betrayal by willful men. Rather, it was part of a sea change in the role of the state that none of the architects of the civil rights laws had foreseen.

Civil Rights Policy and Social Regulation

The birth of the new civil rights agencies and offices of the 1960s, including especially the EEOC and the OFCC, thus marked the national transition to the new era of social regulation. Unknowingly, they provided the cutting edge. Prior to the 1960s, social regulation had remained largely a state and local responsibility in the decentralized scheme of American federalism. Cities and states might run welfare bureaucracies and school systems and even FEPCs, but it was impermissible for the central government in Washington to do so. Wide veto power against centralizing such functions under Washington bureaucrats was exercised by the political parties, by regional and business and professional groups, and by the congressional seniority system. So the new civil rights agencies of the 1960s had to cut the national path, caught up between the old forces and the new. Modeled after the NLRB, yet deprived of the quasi-judicial authority that typified the economic model of regulation, the wobbly EEOC turned for support to its constituency of newly mobilized minorities. Denied cease-and-desist power, it gravitated quickly toward the new model of wholesale rule-making. In hindsight, the stubborn opposition of Senator Dirksen and the congressional conservatives to cease-and-desist authority for the EEOC appears to have boomeranged on them. In seeking to prevent another New Dealish, regulatory runaway, like the CIO capture of the early NLRB, they accelerated a process they intended to curb.

It is one of the great ironies of the civil rights era that the time-tested judicial strategy of the congressional conservatives backfired on them so badly. History, however, cannot reveal whether a straight NLRB or FEPC model could have long insulated the EEOC from the powerful magnet of rule-making that was driving the new wave of social regulation. The power of this shift during the 1960s swept up not only the regulators themselves, but also the Congress. In 1960 a national FEPC was politically inconceivable, and a national Environmental Protection Agency was improbable. But only a decade later Congress created the EPA, and then strengthened weak federal pollution legislation through far-reaching amendments for air in 1970 and for water in 1972. Similar revisions of existing statutes in 1972 greatly extended the reach of federal EEO regulation by race and sex in the previously sacrosanct areas of education and state and local government.[20]

The common attributes of the new social regulation should not, however, be exaggerated. Everybody wanted breathable air, drinkable water, cars that did not explode, toys that did not maim, employers who did not discriminate against them. Yet fundamental differences distinguish civil rights policy to protect minorities from social regulation to protect consumers and the environment. In the 1960s both sources of regulation, civil rights enforcement on the one hand, and the consumer-environment-safety cluster on the other, built strongly motivated and politically organized constituent groups. The crucial difference lay in who benefited from the regulations and who was excluded. The civil rights groups sought to advance the interests of such discrete population subgroups as blacks, Hispanics, women, and the disabled. The consumer-environment groups, on the other hand, sought to protect all citizens equally from producer-induced harm. Consumer and environmental protection was thus increasingly a positive-sum game, where minimal standards of air and water pollution, worker and product safety, equally protected all citizens. Civil rights protection, on the other hand, was increasingly a zero-sum game. As protected classes proliferated in the "rights" revolution, the rights of citizens fragmented into a confusing variety of special claims—race, sex, ethnicity, religion, language, culture, age, physical and mental handicap, sexual orientation.[21]

The difference between civil rights regulation and social regulation of the consumer-environment-safety variety is most apparent when one compares the distribution of costs and benefits. In such a comparison, the two forms are opposites. Social regulation to protect consumers and the environment has found wide public approval because regulatory costs are *narrowly* distributed (auto manufacturers must invest billions to develop more efficient engines), while benefits are *widely* distributed (all citizens breathe cleaner air). Political scientist James Q. Wilson calls this the *entrepreneurial* pattern of regulatory politics. It has been common, for example, in regulation for air and water pollution, workplace and highway safety, and consumer protection. In an era of active public-interest groups, the cost-benefit ratio of this kind of regulation favors consumers over producers. Entrepreneurial regulation is generally resented by regulatees (power companies, extractive industries, motor vehicle manufacturers), but it has remained popular with voters and politicians.[22]

Conversely, civil rights regulation of the modern affirmative-action variety remains controversial because the cost-benefit ratio is reversed. Enforcement costs are *widely* distributed (all non-minority citizens compete for a proportionally reduced number of jobs, promotions, admissions), while benefits are *narrowly* distributed (the beneficiaries are designated "protected class" minorities). Popular with beneficiary groups, this pattern is resented by non-minorities, who feel penalized by the state for immutable characteristics even though they are accused of no wrong-doing. Wilson calls this pattern the *client* model, where costs are distributed widely and benefits are focused narrowly. Historically, the client model has represented the lobbyists' dream, and as a genre of federal regulation it antedates Phase II civil rights regulation by almost a century.[23]

The client model brought us, in the middle of the 20th century, the pessimistic literature of "regulatory decay." This was the sad story of the capture of the regulators by the enterprises they were created to regulate (the ICC by the railroads, the CAB by the airlines, the AEC by the nuclear energy industry). The "capture" metaphor reflects the conspiratorial assumptions of its populist origins, and in this crude form it can blur and distort the complex politics of regulatory relationships. But when used as a model that reflects the dominance of interests in the contest for advantage, the notion of capture is a useful general guide in charting the uses of power. Increasingly after the watershed of 1965 in civil rights policy, the client model with its capture corollary came to fit the minority preference requirements of the civil rights regulators (the Philadelphia Plan, minority contract set-asides, proportional requirements in appointments and admissions). Like economic capture by the regulated industries, the capture of civil rights regulatory agencies by the beneficiary groups raised the same questions of fairness in the client model of regulation. The many paid and the few benefited—not by dint of economic disadvantage per se, but because of immutable characteristics. And unlike the classic captures of iron-triangle lore, the new clientele capture had taken on a new geometry.

Clientele Capture, the Agencies, and the Courts: From Iron Triangles to Quadrilaterals

Liberal reformers had long deplored capture in the agencies of economic regulation, like the airline-dominated Civil Aeronautics Board (which was ultimately terminated by the deregulation movement during the Carter presidency). Capture was generally resisted, for the most part successfully, by the new agencies of social regulation for consumer protection, workplace and transit safety, and the environment. They lacked the vertical structure (airlines concentrating on the CAB) that made the economic regulators vulnerable. So many different enterprises created water or air pollution, for example, that they could form no coherent lobbying force.[24] The new agencies created in the 1960s for civil rights regulation, however, tended to be directed and staffed from the beginning by members of their beneficiary clientele groups. These included, in addition to the OFCC, the offices of civil rights within the mission agencies, especially Justice, HEW, Defense, and HUD, all deriving their authority from Title

6 on contract compliance. The EEOC between 1965 and 1968 followed the pattern established earlier by the Civil Rights Commission, and for the same reason of convergence of interest and function. In 1969 Nixon added the OMBE in Commerce.

The civil rights coalition then reached outward into the equivalent agencies in state and local governments and ultimately into the parallel echelons of personnel and management throughout the larger institutions of private industry and commerce.[25] In a sequential development, women and Hispanics in the latter 1960s followed the black initiatives. In the 1970s a snowballing effect adding Asians and American Indians, the elderly, and the physically and mentally disabled, and further claims to protection were made by lesbians and gays and other groups.[26] Interest-group lobbying for social regulation reached a new level of effectiveness in the mobilizing of the physically handicapped during the 1970s.[27] As the civil rights coalition accumulated new political power by adding coalition partners, it paid a price in diminished cohesion. Contract compliance agencies thus faced a trade-off, with constituent blocs of affected-class groups vying for a greater share of agency resources. The OMBE was torn by infighting between black and Hispanic claimants during the Nixon administration, for example. On the whole, however, the civil rights coalition by the early 1970s had learned to maximize the benefits of growing coalition while submerging the internal conflicts—as, for example, the EEOC had done by increasing attention to sex discrimination in the late 1960s. The political pay-off of this coalition-building in Congress was impressive.

The administration and regulatory agencies in the new fields of social and civil rights regulation thereby joined their organized constituent groups to form the base of triangular relationships with the appropriate congressional committees. But in social regulation the old iron-triangle paradigm, which historically had described the relatively closed policy worlds of the Army Corps of Engineers and the agricultural interests, no longer seemed to explain how policy was made. What was happening instead was that in the expanding programs of social entitlement, the old triangles were often reshaped into quadrilaterals. This new, fourth policy intersection represented the increasing intervention of the federal courts. Responding to the suits of the constituency groups as plaintiff-clients, the judges began to monitor and reverse the decisions of both the Congress and the administrative agencies in the expanding fields of social legislation.[28]

This new mode of public law litigation represented a radical shift in the role of the courts. The lawsuit was no longer a bilateral dispute between private parties, but rather a grievance about public policy involving multiple parties. The courts' fact-finding became predictive and legislative rather than retrospective and adjudicatory. The relief granted was typically an ongoing, affirmative decree by a participant-judge. In his enthusiastic analysis of this seismic legal shift, Abram Chayes conceded that the new public law litigation "inevitably becomes an explicitly political forum and the court a visible arm of the political process." In the new public law litigation, Chayes said, the trial judge has "passed beyond even the role of legislator and has become a policy planner and manager."[29]

Temporary Remedies and Political Permanence

The confusion over governing models between civil rights policy and social regulation was reflected in differences concerning the duration of remedies. In social regulation, the permanence of protective responsibilities for consumers and the environment was assumed, and only the standards varied for determining acceptable levels of air purity or vehicle safety. In civil rights policy, however, the only consensual standard of permanence was Phase I's commitment to nondiscrimination. In deference to this tradition, the creators of the Phase II policies, which required minority preferences to compensate for past discrimination, defended them as temporary measures. But no criteria were provided to govern the conditions and timing for returning to a norm of nondiscrimination. This tension was more difficult for judges to rationalize than for agency officials. The judiciary was grounded in the pairing of violation and remedy, with the judge serving as neutral third-party referee in adversary disputes. The violation-remedy model was biased toward settlement, and the judge was not supposed to participate as an ongoing policy entrepreneur.

For these reasons, when the federal courts in 1969 began approving numerical quotas and ratios as compensatory relief for past job discrimination, they generally did so with apologetic disclaimers. They described their compensatory remedies as temporary, looking toward the day when the historic discrimination had been balanced off, and the Constitution could properly assume its color-blind character. But as in the case of the school busing decrees, the courts provided no clear set of principles according to which compliance might be satisfied, and in response to which the judicially injoined institutions might be allowed to return to their normal independent operations. When Chief Justice Warren Burger struck down the Duke Power Company's employee tests in *Griggs* in 1971, for example, he explained that the Civil Rights Act "does not command that any person be hired simply because he was formerly the subject of discrimination, or because he is a member of a minority group." Burger insisted in dicta that "Discriminatory preference for any group, minority or majority, is precisely and only what Congress has proscribed."[30] But the long-run practical result of *Griggs* was to mock Burger's disclaimer.

Seven years later, Burger voted with the majority in the *Bakke* case to order the University of California to admit to the medical school at Davis a white applicant, Allan Bakke, whose race had excluded him from competing for seats set aside for minorities. Justice Harry Blackmun voted to uphold the university's minority quota, and thus to exclude Bakke because he was white. In doing so, however, Blackmun insisted that "I yield to no one in my earnest hope that the time will come when an 'affirmative action' program is unnecessary and is, in truth, only a relic of the past."[31] The U.S. was going through a regrettable but necessary stage of "transitional inequality," Blackmun explained. He hoped, however, that "within a decade at the most," American society "must and will reach a stage of maturity where acting along this line is no longer necessary." "Then persons will be regarded as persons," Blackmun said, "and discrimination of the type we address today will be an ugly feature of history that is instructive but that is behind us." That was in 1978. The following year Justice Blackmun in the *Weber* decision agreed that affirmative action quotas were a "temporary tool for remedying past discrimination without attempting to 'maintain' a previously achieved balance."[32]

Despite the repeated disclaimers from high authorities that the preferential policies were temporary, everything we know about the normal politics of the regulatory process and the workaday competition for government benefits points in the opposite direction. In pluralist America, interest groups have historically entrenched themsevles in the political infrastructure in defense of their claimed rights and entitlements. Middle-class and affluent Americans have been most adept at this practice, protecting government benefits that disproportionately favor the owners of mortgages, irrigated agricultural land, airplanes, yachts, private schools, country clubs. The organized beneficiaries of affirmative action programs have entrenched themselves with no less energy than have the beneficiaries of similar group-based entitlements among farmers, veterans, homeowners, rentiers, the elderly. It would be naïve to expect such self-denial.

Thus during Phase II of the civil rights era, two contradictory forces emerged under the rubric of one implementing strategy—affirmative action. One was an exceptional rationale that minority preferences were a temporary expedient, defensible only as a bridge to the color-blind Constitution of individual rights. The other was the normal pluralist process that embedded the new model of proportional representation, group rights, and equal results deeply within the social and political structure. But within these tensions lay another source of contradiction: the two dominant political blocs in the civil rights campaign, blacks and women, followed ostensibly similar paths that obscured fundamental differences.

Black Rights, Women's Rights, and the Race-Sex Analogy

Feminist leaders of the 1960s shared a belief, based on a historical analogy of shared victimhood from group discrimination, that the war against sex discrimination should be linked to the principles and methods of the black civil rights movement. This after all had been the original model of the nineteenth century's first-wave feminism, which had emerged from the abolitionist movement and demanded during Reconstruction that women's equality be linked to black equality. Excluded from the first Reconstruction, American feminists had continued to play catch-up. Their suffrage amendment followed the constitutional protection of black males by half a century. A full century following ratification of the Fourteenth amendment in 1868, the Supreme Court had still not extended the amendment's equal protection clause to women. The eleventh-hour inclusion of women in the civil rights bill designed for blacks in 1964 came from a surprising tactical coup on the House floor that was replete with its own ironies of strange and expedient political alliance. The flagship organization of second-wave feminism, the National Organization of Women, was created in 1966 to demand that the new EEOC fight sex discrimination with the same zeal and weapons the agency was devoting to racial discrimination.[33]

But in order for the second-wave feminist leaders to exploit the race-sex analogy by demanding the same remedies accorded to blacks, they had to resolve their historic internal dispute. For generations American feminism's historic fault line had separated cultural feminists who defended the special-protection legacy of the liberal Democratic establishment and egalitarian feminists who demanded the ERA. This class-based split had set the women's liberation model apart from the black model. In black America, generations of racial oppression had so flattened the class pyramid that the dominant stream of black protest had been clasically egalitarian. Women, however, were evenly distributed throughout the social pyramid and hence mirrored its class divisions. This had endowed American feminism with its pronounced dualism, and much of the feminist energy of the early and middle 1960s was devoted to defusing the ancient quarrel between the senior protectionists of the Women's Bureau coalition and the ERA coalition of the future. The ERA coalition itself represented a class fusion across party lines—the Rawalt-Friedan-Griffiths Democrats and the Glaser-Allan-Gutwillig Republicans, joined in a bipartisan battalion to embed gender equality in the Constitution. The second-wave feminist shift from protectionist dominance at the beginning of the 1960s to ERA dominance by 1970 was thus a class-related transition. Power had shifted from the Democrats' traditional blue-collar constituency to a bipartisan coalition of business and professional elites. The shift was fueled primarily by demographic and economic trends and by the self-selectivity of an affluent and highly educated national leadership.[34]

The federal courts, to be sure, played their role in providing incentives, as they had done with black civil rights. But they did so in an opposite direction. During Phase II the federal courts found greater reasons to treat the races differently and to treat the sexes similarly. Beginning in 1968 the lower courts began to strike down the state protection laws on Title 7 grounds, thereby undercutting the foundations of the Women's Bureau coalition. But the federal courts continued to fail to locate women in the Fifth and Fourteenth amendments until 1971. That year in *Reed v. Reed* the Supreme Court sustained a feminist challenge on Fourteenth amendment grounds. But by then it was too late to deflect the ERA juggernaut on Capitol Hill by arguments that a constitutional amendment was now unnecessary. By 1972 mention of the federal courts at a NAACP convention drew predictable and instinctive applause. But at NOW conventions during the first half-dozen years, mention of the federal bench drew hoots of derision.

The year 1965 was a watershed for women in a dual sense. It marked the opening for business of the EEOC and launched the implementation process for the liberal reforms of 1964–65. This in turn provided a catalyst for the egalitarians of NOW to rout the special protectionists and unify the second-wave feminists under the banner of the ERA. Thus, for egalitarian feminists, 1965 reversed the old momentum, sending special protectionists into decline and reviving the ERA for congressional passage after a half-century in protectionist limbo. Yet, at the same time, 1965 marked the beginning of the transition from Phase I to Phase II of the civil rights era, when the cutting edge of the black civil rights movement began to turn agianst the equal-treatment doctrine as a consistent, coherent, and sufficient theory of liberation. Just as the women's movement was at long last solidifying behind the equal-treatment creed of the ERA, the black civil rights movement was beginning to abandon it.

The rhetoric of feminist leaders continued throughout the decade to salute the logic of the race-sex analogy. Historian William Chafe has emphasized the similarities between the black and feminist movements, pointing to their different yet parallel tactics of mobilization (sin-ins, consciousness-raising groups).[35] The feminists supported affirmative action policies and demanded that women be included in the Title 6 goals and timetables. The race-sex analogy, however, has been made to carry too much weight. In 1960 the dominant feminist leadership was Democratic and ideologically rooted in a working-class constituency. They were determined on the one hand to preserve special legislation that protected group rights, and on the other to press for new advances through amendments to the New Deal's labor-standards formula that would enlarge the protections of this class. By 1972, however, when the ERA was sent by Congress to the states, the cutting edge of second-wave feminism was bipartisan, rooted in the middle- and upper-class culture of business and the professions, driven by classic liberalism's defense of individual rather than group rights, and united to attack barriers to women's advancement through Title 7 and Title 9 and the ERA. Midway through the era, the two great engines of the civil rights movement passed like two trains in the night. The women were finally moving in unity under elite leadership and the banner of the ERA toward a common standard of citizen rights, while the black movement, riven by ghetto riots and cries of Black Power, and caught up in the quadrilateral momentum for racial preferences, shifted its emphasis toward racial difference.

The Irony and the Triumph of the Civil Rights Era

Like all periods of profound social transformation, the civil rights era produced changes with unintended and ironical consequences. The strategic role reversal of the black civil rights movement and second-wave feminism was one of them. By 1972, classic liberalism's vision of the color-blind Constitution was fast receding, while the modern notion of a sex-blind Constitution, always opposed by the liberal establishment in twentieth-century America, was approved as a constitutional amendment by Congress with astounding majorities.

Another irony was the boomerang of the congressional conservatives' judicial strategy, which further empowered a federal judiciary that was abandoning the conservative instincts and judicial restraints upon which the strategy had been historically premised. Conservatives during the *Lochner* era, when progressive reformers had attacked the trusts, had invented judicial activism to protect liberty and property rights. In response, the liberals of the Holmes-Brandeis-Frankfurter tradition had countered with the doctrine of judicial restraint in order to protect the democratic freedom of the elected branches of government to regulate private property in the public interest. But during the 1960s the Warren Court used judicial activism to legislate liberal social policy from the bench. On both sides, judicial philosophy proved to be an amazingly flexible handmaiden to ideological preferences in social policy.

The civil rights era culminated under the putatively conservative regime of Richard Nixon. His administration was marked by public disputes over busing and Supreme Court nominations that increased racial polarization. Yet hidden beneath this divisive rhetoric was a quiet and surprisingly effective process of desegregating southern schools and public institutions. It was also under Nixon that the permanent government invented and consolidated the machinery that would nationally enforce Phase II's decrees of hard affirmative action. The Nixon irony is sharpened by the contrast between the relative moral indifference that characterized the political calculus of Nixon's domestic policy decisions, and the passion that drove President Johnson to strike at the jugular of America's caste system. If there is an unanticipated hero in this story about the entrepreneurs and manipulators of federal policy, it is the master manipulator himself, Lyndon Johnson.

The continuing debate over the legitimacy and effectiveness of affirmative action programs finds its origins in the civil rights era of 1960–72, but not its resolution. Its ironies abound. But ironists flirt dangerously with cynicism, because the ironic stance allows us to comment coyly, armed by hindsight, on the paradoxical contradictions that entrap historical actors and confound their best-laid plans. It is the *intended* consequences of the civil rights era's great social reforms, however, that mark its most fundamental and promising breaks with the continuities of history. In 1960, most American blacks still confronted the formal as well as informal symbols of daily humiliation that marked a caste society. Southern whites, the chief but not the exclusive offenders, were also—but unknowingly—victimized economically and brutalized psychologically by the daily corruptions of their own caste dominance. By 1972, the institutions of Jim Crow were everywhere shattered, broken by the most successful American social movement of the 20th century.

For American women in 1960, males dominated the worlds of power and status so overwhelmingly that most women and girls could realistically aspire to an independent status and achievement, beyond the rewards of housewifery and motherhood, little loftier than that of airline stewardess. Even that was reserved for young white women only. Most American men and boys took for granted a world of male norms in which women were auxiliaries, and in which the creative talents, beyond the acknowledged procreative capacities, of half of humankind remained largely untapped. It is possible—only time will tell—that the American feminists of the 1960s ignited a global movement that will change human life in ways not seen in recorded history. And not just for women. Feminism was ultimately about gender freedom—for everybody. Mar-

tin Luther King understood that the same principle obtained about racial freedom for all of God's children.

The civil rights era was a rare American epiphany. In only a dozen years its
two great social movements won astonishing achievements against the most
formidable odds. Its mixed legacy now defines the conditions of our civil life
and commands our best efforts to understand.

Further Reading

During the 1980s the publishing industry discovered a rich market for books on the 1960s. One of the earliest interpretations of that tumultous decade, William L. O'Neill's *Coming Apart: An Informal History of America in the 1960s* (New York: Random House, 1971), combines the freshness of an eyewitness account with a historian's perspective. For a second-generation assessment, see Irwin Unger and Debi Unger, *Turning Point: 1968* (New York: Scribner's, 1988). Allen J. Matusow, *The Unraveling of America: A History of Liberalism in the 1960s* (New York: Harper & Row, 1984), concentrates on the liberal (and mainly Democratic) reform impulse in politics and government. Most of the literature on civil rights focuses exclusively on the racial issue and tends to conclude with the Johnson administration. For a more detailed analysis that includes gender as well as racial issues and extends through the first Nixon administration, see Hugh Davis Graham, *The Civil Rights Era: Origins and Development of National Policy, 1960–1972* (New York: Oxford University Press, 1990). Paul Burnstein, *Discrimination, Jobs, and Politics: The Struggle for Equal Employment Opportunity in the United States since the New Deal* (Chicago: University of Chicago Press, 1985), compares the development and impact of federal EEO policy through the early 1980s in both race and gender categories.

The Twayne series on social movements has filled a large gap in the literature by reconstructing the development of grass-roots social movements and analyzing their effectiveness in politics and public policy. Stewart Burns, *Social Movements of the 1960s* (Boston: Twayne, 1990), provides a theory and definition of social movements and explores case studies in black civil rights, feminism, the anti-war movement, and the student-oriented New Left. Myra Marx Feree and Beth B. Hess, *Controversy and Coalition* (Boston: Twayne, 1985), studies the new feminist movement, and Rhoda Lois Blumberg, *Civil Rights: The 1960s Freedom Struggle* (Boston: Twayne, 1984), examines the black freedom movement. Similarly equating civil rights with the black freedom movement is Aldon D. Morris, *The Origins of the Civil Rights Movement: Black Communities Organize for Change* (New York: Free Press, 1984), which concentrates on the role of the black church prior to the 1960s. Jo Freeman, ed., *Social Movements of the 1960s and 1970s* (New York: Longman, 1983), is a useful anthology that provides a theoretical framework and case studies that extend beyond the black and feminist movements, including social movements with conservative orientations.

Not surprisingly, the literature of the 1960s is dominated by political and sociological studies of black civil rights. Two fresh recent syntheses are Steven F. Lawson, *Running for Freedom* (New York: McGraw-Hill, 1990) and Robert Weisbrot, *Freedom Bound: A History of America's Civil Rights Movement* (New York: Norton, 1990). But see also Harvard Sitkoff, *The Struggle for Black Equality 1954–1980* (New York: Hill and Wang, 1981). The standard account for the Kennedy years is Carl M. Brauer, *John F. Kennedy and the Second Reconstruction* (New York: Columbia University Press, 1977), and the standard legislative history of the Civil Rights Act of 1964 is Charles Whalen and Barbara Whalen, *The Longest Debate* (Cabin John, Md.: Seven Locks Press, 1985). The evolution of voting-rights law and its effect on black electoral politics is covered in two volumes by Steven F. Lawson: *Black Ballots: Voting Rights in the South, 1944–1969* (New York: Columbia University Press, 1976), and *In Pursuit of Power: Southern Blacks and Electoral Politics, 1965–1982* (New York: Columbia University Press, 1985).

The literature on black organizations and their leaders is rich. No full organizational studies have yet been published for the mainline NAACP and National Urban League in the 1960s, but good studies exist for the activist organizations involved in civil disobedience: August Meier and Elliott Rudwick, *CORE: A Study in the Civil Rights Movement, 1942–1968* (New York: Oxford University Press, 1973); Clayborne Carson, *In Struggle: SNCC and the Black Awakening of the 1960s* (Cambridge: Harvard University Press, 1981); David J. Garrow, *Bearing the Cross: Martin Luther King, Jr. and the Southern Christian Leadership Conference* (New York: Random House, 1986); Adam Fairclough, *To Redeem the Soul of America: The Southern Christian Leadership Conference and Martin Luther King, Jr.* (Athens, Ga.: University of Georgia Press, 1987); and Taylor Branch, *Parting the Waters: America in the King Years, 1954–1963* (New York: Simon & Schuster, 1988).

The most significant feminist book of the 1960s remains Betty Friedan's catalytic *The Feminine Mystique* (New York: Norton, 1963). One of the earliest books on the women's movement that spun out of the 1960s remains one of the most perceptive: Jo Freeman, *Politics of Women's Liberation: A Case Study of an Emerging Movement and Its Relation to the Policy Process* (New York: David McKay, 1975). The dual theme of Sara Evans' participant-memoir is indicated by its title and subtitle, *Personal Politics: The Roots of Women's Liberation in the Civil Rights Movement and the New Left* (New York: Random House, 1979). The Kennedy and Johnson presidential archives have been mined to produce two well-documented studies of the development of national policy on women's issues: Patricia Zelman, *Women, Work, and National Policy: The Kennedy-Johnson Years* (Ann Arbor, Mich.: UMI Research Press, 1980), and Cynthia Harrison, *On Account of Sex: The Politics of Women's Issues, 1945–1968* (Berkeley: University of California Press, 1988). Most studies of the ERA concentrate on the ratification process in the 1970s; we still await a thorough study of the congressional passage of the ERA, and we also lack full organizational studies of the National Organization of Women and the Women's Equity Action League. A policy-focused recent survey with bibliography is Susan M. Hartman, *From Margin to Mainstream: American Women and Policy Since 1960* (New York: Knopf, 1989).

The best analysis of racial desegregation and the courts is J. Harvie Wilkinson III, *From Brown to Bakke: The Supreme Court and School Desegregation: 1954–1978* (New York: Oxford University Press, 1979). Derrick A. Bell, Jr., *Race, Racism and American Law* (Boston: Little, Brown, 1980) is a standard text on race and legal issues. On women's issues and the law, see Karen O'Connor, *Women's Organizations Use the Courts* (Lexington, Mass.: Lexington Books, 1980), and David L. Kirp, Mark G. Yudof, and Marlene Strong Frank, *Gender Justice* (Chicago: University of Chicago Press,

1986). A comprehensive guide to the literature on equal employment and affirmative action issues is Floyd D. Weatherspoon, *Equal Employment Opportunity and Affirmative Action* (New York: Garland, 1985). For a critical view of judicial activism in civil rights policy, see Donald L. Horowitz, *The Courts and Social Policy* (Washington: Brookings, 1977).

Much of the literature on government regulation, administrative processes, and the politics of bureaucracy is specialized and technical, but Michael D. Reagan provides a clear introduction in *Regulation: The Politics of Policy* (Boston: Little, Brown, 1987). The politics of bureaucracy and public administration is examined in James Q. Wilson, *Bureaucracy: What Government Agencies Do and Why They Do It* (New York: Basic Books, 1989). Historical perspectives on the evolution of the modern American administrative state are collected in Louis Galambos, ed., *The New American State: Bureaucracies and Politics Since World War II* (Baltimore: Johns Hopkins University Press, 1987). For a recent interpretation of the development and problems of the regulatory state, see Cass R. Sunstein, *After the Rights Revolution: Reconsidering the Regulatory State* (Cambridge, Mass.: Harvard University Press, 1990).

Glossary of Organizations

AFL-CIO	American Federation of Labor–Congress of Industrial Organizations
ANPA	American Newspaper Publishers Association
BFOQ	Bona fide occupational qualification
BOB	Bureau of the Budget
CACSW	Citizen's Advisory Council on the Status of Women
COFO	Council of Federated Organizations
CORE	Congress of Racial Equality
CRD	Civil Rights Division [Department of Justice]
DDEL	Dwight D. Eisenhower Library
DOD	Department of Defense
DOL	Department of Labor
EEOC	Equal Employment Opportunity Commission
ERA	Equal Rights Amendment
FEB	Federal Executive Board
FLSA	Fair Labor Standards Act
FEPC	Fair Employment Practice Committee
GAO	Government Accounting Office
GRFL	Gerald R. Ford Library
HEW	[Department of] Health, Education and Welfare
HUD	[Department of] Housing and Urban Development
IAM	International Association of Machinists
ICSW	Interdepartmental Committee on the Status of Women
JFKL	John F. Kennedy Library
LBJL	Lydon B. Johnson Library
LCCR	Leadership Conference on Civil Rights
MIA	Montgomery Improvement Association
NAACP	National Association for the Advancement of Colored People
NARA	National Archives and Records Administration

NLRB	National Labor Relations Board
NOW	National Organization of Women
NWP	National Women's Party
NUL	National Urban League
OFCC	Office of Federal Contract Compliance
OMB	Office of Management and Budget
OMBE	Office of Minority Business Enterprise
PCEEO	President's Committee on Equal Employment Opportunity
PCSW	President's Commission on the Status of Women
RMNP	Richard M. Nixon Papers
SBA	Small Business Administration
SCAD	State Commission Against Discrimination
SCLC	Southern Christian Leadership Conference
SNCC	Student Nonviolent Coordinating Committee
WEAL	Women's Equity Action League

Notes

Introduction

1. During the 1970s, historical research shifted from the national civil rights movement, with its focus on politics and law, to local communities where the grass-roots mobilization of the social movements for black and women's liberation could be reconstructed. Social historian Stewart Burns provides a fresh synthesis in *Social Movements of the 1960s* (Boston: Twayne, 1990).

2. Paul Burstein, *Discrimination, Jobs, and Politics: The Struggle for Equal Employment Opportunity in the United States since the New Deal* (Chicago: University of Chicago Press, 1985), 15.

3. See Jeffrey L. Pressman and Aaron B. Wildavsky, *Implementation* (Berkeley: University of California Press, 1973); Erwin C. Hargrove, *The Missing Link: The Study of the Implementation of Public Policy* (Washington: Urban Institute, 1975); Eugene Bardach, *The Implementation Game: What Happens After a Bill Becomes a Law* (Cambridge: Massachusetts Institute of Technology Press, 1977); George C. Edwards III, *Implementing Public Policy* (Washington: Congressional Quarterly Press, 1980); Robert T. Nakamura and Frank Smallwood, *The Politics of Policy Implementation* (New York: St. Martin's, 1980); and Walter Williams et al., *Studying Implementation* (Chatham, N. J.: Chatham House, 1982).

4. *Public Papers of the Presidents: Lyndon B. Johnson, 1965* (Washington: U.S. Government Printing Office, 1966), I, 636.

5. The proliferation of modern social movements, following the model of black insurgency, is suggested by titles in the Twayne series on social movements published in Boston by G.K. Hall: Rhoda Lois Blumberg, *Civil Rights: The 1960s Freedom Struggle* (1984); Myra Marx Ferree and Beth Hess, *Controversy and Coalition: The New Feminist Movement* (1985); Barry D Adam, *The Rise of a Gay and Lesbian Movement* (1987); Robert N. Mayer, *The Consumer Movement* (1989); and Jerome Price, *The Antinuclear Movement* (1989).

6. Gunnar Myrdal, *An American Dilemma*, vol. 2 (New York: Harper & Bros., 1944), appendix 5.

7. See Carl M. Brauer, "Women Activists, Southern Conservatives, and the Prohibition of Sex Discrimination in Title VII of the 1964 Civil Rights Act," *Journal of Southern History* XLIV (February 1983): 37–56.

8. See generally Aileen Kraditor, *Ideas of the Woman Suffrage Movement, 1890–1920* (New York: Columbia University Press, 1965); William L. O'Neill, *Everyone Was Brave: The Rise and Fall of Feminism in America* (Chicago: Quadrangle, 1969); Wil-

liam H. Chafe, *The American Woman: Her Changing Social, Economic, and Political Role, 1920–1970* (New York: Oxford University Press, 1972); Jo Freeman, *The Politics of Women's Liberation: A Case Study of an Emerging Social Movement and Its Relation to the Policy Process* (New York: David McKay, 1975); Carl N. Degler, *At Odds; Women and the Family in America from the Revolution to the Present* (New York: Oxford University Press, 1980).

9. In the landmark study *The American Voter*, the authors dismiss the female role in voting as predictably dependent upon "her husband's partisan predispositions." See Angus Campbell, Philip E. Converse, Warren E. Miller, and Donald E. Stokes, *The American Voter* (New York: Wiley, 1964), 255–61. Since the typical male voter in this classic modern study appeared to be singularly ill-informed, the implications for the American woman voter were doubly depressing. During the 1980s, however, opinion surveys showed greater gender differences. See Robert S. Erikson et al., *American Public Opinion*, 3rd ed. (New York: Macmillan, 1988), 199–203.

Chapter 1

1. Richard Kluger, *Simple Justice* (New York: Knopf, 1976); Numan V. Bartley, *The Rise of Massive Resistance* (Baton Rouge: Louisiana State University Press, 1970); Robert Frederick Burk, *The Eisenhower Administration and Black Civil Rights* (Knoxville: University of Tennessee Press, 1984); Aldon D. Morris, *Origins of the Civil Rights Movement* (New York: Free Press, 1984).

2. Gerald Davis Jaynes and Robin M. Williams, Jr., eds., *A Common Destiny: Blacks and American Society* (Washington: National Academy Press, 1989), 269–328; U.S. Bureau of the Census, *Historical Statistics of the United States: Colonial Times to 1970* (Washington: U.S. Department of Commerce, 1975), chapters F, H.

3. *A Common Destiny*, 453–507; Marvin Wolfgang and Bernard Cohen, *Crime and Race* (New York: Institute of Human Relations Press, 1970); Michael J. Hindelang, "Race and Involvement in Crime," *American Sociological Review* 43 (February 1978): 93–109.

4. *Wall Street Journal*, 17 March 1960.

5. James C. Davies, "The J-Curve of Rising and Declining Satisfaction as a Cause of Some Great Revolutions and a Contained Rebellion," *Violence in America*, eds. Hugh Davis Graham and Ted Robert Gurr (New York: Praeger, 1969), 690–730; Ted Robert Gurr, *Why Men Rebel* (Princeton: Princeton University Press, 1970).

6. Quoted in Howard Schuman, Charlotte Steeh, and Lawrence Bobo, *Racial Attitudes in America* (Cambridge: Harvard University Press, 1985), 139. Sheatsley was referring to *An American Dilemma*, a 1944 study by Swedish sociologist Gunnar Myrdal of the contradictions between the democratic creed and racial discrimination in the United States.

7. Myra Marx Ferree and Beth B. Hess, *Controversy and Coalition: The New Feminist Movement* (Boston: Twayne, 1985), 78–84; Karen O. Mason, John L. Czajka, and Sara Arber, "Change in U.S. Sex-Role Attitudes, 1964–1974," *American Sociological Review* 41 (1976): 573–96.

8. William H. Chafe, *Women and Equality* (New York: Oxford University Press, 1977), 139.

9. Betty Friedan, *The Feminine Mystique* (New York: Norton, 1963).

10. Marynia Farnham and Ferdinand Lundberg, *Modern Woman: The Lost Sex* (New York: Universal Library, 1947). Farnham and Lundberg postulated the "psychosocial rule" that "the more educated the woman is, the greater chance there is of sexual disorder," and the fewer children such women would produce. See also Helene Deutsch, *Psychology of Women* (New York: Grune and Stratton, 1944).

11. Adlai E. Stevenson, "Purpose for Modern Woman," *The Woman's Home Com-*

panion 82 (September 1955): 29–31. See also Friedan, *Feminine Mystique*, 53–54, 111. Friedan had graduated summa cum laude from Smith in 1942.

12. Patricia A. Graham, "Expansion and Exclusion: A History of Women in American Higher Education," *Signs* 3 (1978): 759–73; Chafe, *Women and Equality*, 218–20, 234–35.

13. William H. Chafe, *The American Woman: Her Changing Social, Economic, and Political Roles, 1920–1970* (New York: Oxford University Press, 1972), 218–20.

14. Paul Burstein, *Discrimination, Jobs, and Politics* (Chicago: University of Chicago Press, 1985), 134–39.

15. The news beats covered by the three women reporters were music, society, and the United Nations.

16. Marya Mannes, "Female Intelligence: Who Wants It?" *New York Times Magazine*, 3 January 1960. During the 1930s Mannes had written for *Vogue* and *Glamour* magazines, and during World War II she served as an intelligence analyst for the Office of Strategic Services, the forerunner of the Central Intelligence Agency. Her subsequent career as a magazine journalist, like her sex, was atypical for staff officers of the OSS.

17. *New York Times*, 17 January 1960.

18. Morroe Berger, *Equality by Statute*, rev. ed. (New York: Farrar, Straus & Giroux, 1978), chap. 4; Hugh Davis Graham, *The Civil Rights Era: Origins and Development of National Policy 1960–1972* (New York: Oxford University Press, 1990), 19–22.

19. *New York Times*, 15 August 1960.

20. Neil J. Smelser, *Theory of Collective Behavior* (New York: Free Press, 1963); Richard Maxwell Brown, "Historical Patterns of American Violence," *Violence in America*, eds. Hugh Davis Graham and Ted Robert Gurr (Beverly Hills, Calif.: Sage, 1979), 19–48.

21. Hugh Davis Graham, "Violence, Social Theory, and the Historians: The Debate Over Consensus and Culture in America," *Violence in America: Protest, Rebellion, Reform*, ed. Ted Robert Gurr (Newbury Park, Calif.: Sage, 1989), 329–51.

22. Paul Wilkinson, *Social Movements* (New York: Praeger, 1971); Jo Freeman (ed.), *Social Movements of the Sixties and Seventies* (New York: Longman, 1983), 1–5.

23. Theodore J. Lowi, *The Politics of Disorder* (New York: Basic Books, 1971).

24. See Aileen Kraditor, *Ideas of the Woman Suffrage Movement, 1890–1920* (New York: Columbia University Press, 1965); William O'Neill, *Everyone Was Brave: The Rise and Fall of Feminism in America* (Chicago: Quadrangle, 1969).

25. Doug McAdam, *Political Process and the Development of Black Insurgency 1930–1970* (Chicago: University of Chicago Press, 1982), 117–45.

26. J. Mills Thornton III, "Challenge and Response in the Montgomery Bus Boycott of 1955–56," *Alabama Review* (July 1980): 181–204; Jack M. Bloom, *Class, Race, and the Civil Rights Movement* (Bloomington: Indiana University Press, 1987), 137–50.

27. Martin Luther King, Jr., *Stride Toward Freedom: The Montgomery Story* (New York: Harper & Row, 1958).

28. David J. Garrow, *Bearing the Cross: Martin Luther King, Jr. and the Southern Christian Leadership Conference* (New York: Random House, 1986), 83–126; Adam Fairclough, *To Redeem the Soul of America: The Southern Christian Leadership Conference and Martin Luther King, Jr.* (Athens: University of Georgia Press, 1987), 37–56.

29. Taylor Branch, *Parting the Waters: America in the King Years 1954–1963* (New York: Simon & Schuster, 1988), 451–91; Robert Weisbrot, *Freedom Bound* (New York: Norton, 1990), 18–44.

30. Miles Wolff, *Lunch at the Five and Ten: The Greensboro Sit-in* (New York: Stein & Day, 1970); William H. Chafe, *Civilities and Civil Rights: Greensboro, North Carolina, and the Black Struggle for Freedom* (New York: Oxford, 1980), 71–152; Harvard Sitkoff, *The Struggle for Black Equality 1954–1980* (New York: Hill & Wang, 1981), 69–96.

31. Weisbrot, *Freedom Bound*, 35; Sitkoff, *Struggle for Black Equality*, 69–72.

32. Clayborne Carson, *In Struggle: SNCC and the Black Awakening of the 1960s*

(Cambridge: Harvard University Press, 1981), 19–30; Rhoda Lois Blumberg, *Civil Rights: The 1960s Freedom Struggle* (Boston: Twayne, 1984), 65–74.

33. Garrow, *Bearing the Cross,* 131–34; Blumberg, *Civil Rights,* 69–70.

34. Hugh Davis Graham, *Crisis in Print* (Nashville: Vanderbilt University Press, 1967), 194–201.

35. McAdam, *Black Insurgency,* 138–45; Sitkoff, *Struggle for Black Equality,* 87–91.

36. Numan V. Bartley, *The Creation of Modern Georgia* (Athens: University of Georgia Press, 1983), 194–200.

37. *Atlanta Constitution,* 3 January 1960.

38. Garrow, *Bearing the Cross,* 143–49.

Chapter 2

1. Richard M. Nixon, *Six Crises* (New York: Doubleday, 1962), 391.

2. Stephen E. Ambrose, *Nixon: The Education of a Politician 1913–1963* (New York: Simon & Schuster, 1987), 597.

3. Donald E. Stokes, "Religion and Politics: The 1960 Elections," in Angus Campbell, Philip E. Converse, Warren E. Miller, and Donald E. Stokes, *Elections and the Political Order* (New York: Wiley, 1966), 96–124.

4. Alfred O. Hero, Jr., *The Southerner in World Affairs* (Baton Rouge: Louisiana State University Press, 1965), 369–73.

5. Angus Campbell, Philip E. Converse, Warren E. Miller, and Donald E. Stokes, *The American Voter* (New York: Wiley, 1960).

6. Edward G. Carmines and James A. Stimson, *Issue Evolution: Race and the Transformation of American Politics* (Princeton: Princeton University Press, 1989), 68–72.

7. Angus Campbell et al., *The American Voter,* 2nd ed. (New York: Wiley, 1964), 67–72.

8. The theory of critical elections and the party-systems model of partisan realignment, which were based on a combination of survey research and historical voting studies, were constructed during the 1960s. See Campbell et al., *The American Voter* and *Elections and the Political Order;* William Nesbit Chambers and Walter Dean Burnham, eds., *The American Party Systems* (New York: Oxford University Press, 1967); and Burnham, *Critical Elections and the Mainsprings of American Politics* (New York: Norton, 1970).

9. Numan V. Bartley and Hugh D. Graham, *Southern Politics and the Second Reconstruction* (Baltimore: Johns Hopkins University Press, 1975), 81–110.

10. Richard M. Scammon and Ben J. Wattenberg, *The Real Majority* (New York: Coward-McCann, 1970), 72–81.

11. See generally Nelson W. Polsby and Aaron B. Wildavsky, *Presidential Elections: Strategies of American Electoral Politics,* 3rd ed. (New York: Scribner's, 1971).

12. Carl M. Brauer, *John F. Kennedy and the Second Reconstruction* (New York: Columbia University Press, 1977), 300.

13. Ibid., 33; Hugh Davis Graham, "John F. Kennedy, 1961–1963," *The American Presidents,* Vol. III (Pasadena, Calif.: Salem Press, 1986), 691–711.

14. Donald B. Johnson and Kirk H. Porter, *National Party Platforms* (Urbana: University of Illinois Press, 1966), 599–600.

15. Hugh Davis Graham, *The Civil Rights Era* (New York: Oxford University Press, 1990), 16–19.

16. David J. Garrow, *Bearing the Cross* (New York: Random House, 1986), 118–19.

17. Earl Mazo, *Richard Nixon* (New York: Harper & Row, 1959); 257; Steven F. Lawson, *Black Ballots* (New York: Columbia University Press, 1976), 252.

18. Ambrose, *Nixon,* 614–15.

19. James M. Sundquist, *Politics and Policy: The Eisenhower, Kennedy, and Johnson Years* (Washington: Brookings Institution, 1968), 250–53.

20. Theodore H. White, *The Making of the President 1960* (New York: Atheneum, 1961), 201–8.

21. Doug McAdam, *Political Process and the Development of Black Insurgency 1930–1970* (Chicago: University of Chicago Press, 1982), 117–45.

22. Robert Weisbrot, *Freedom Bound* (New York: Norton, 1990), 47.

23. Roy Wilkins and Tom Matthews, *Standing Fast: The Autobiography of Roy Wilkins* (New York: Viking, 1982), 277.

24. Ambrose reports that Nixon sought a way out of the dilemma by asking Attorney General William Rogers to approve a Justice Department inquiry on behalf of Dr. King's constitutional rights. Rogers sought approval from the White House, but Eisenhower refused to approve Justice Department intervention. Ambrose, *Nixon,* 596–97.

25. Brauer, *Second Reconstruction,* 48–51; Ambrose, *Nixon,* 596–97.

26. Kennedy's civil rights dilemma was politically well understood at the time. Subsequent scholarship has emphasized his intellectual and emotional distance from the liberal ideology of state intervention that drove the civil rights coalition, at least before the watershed events of 1963. See Brauer, *Kennedy,* chaps. 1–3; Herbert S. Parmet, *Jack: The Struggles of John F. Kennedy* (New York: Dial, 1980), 188–89, 409–14, 461–78; Parmet, *JFK: The Presidency of John F. Kennedy* (New York: Dial, 1983), 50–56, 249–76; and Allen J. Matusow, *The Unraveling of America: A History of Liberalism in the 1960s* (New York: Harper & Row, 1984), 20–25, 62–95.

27. Harris Wofford to John F. Kennedy, 30 December 1960, 1960 Campaign and Transition file, Robert F. Kennedy Papers, John F. Kennedy Library (hereafter JFKL).

28. Anthony Lewis, *Portrait of a Decade* (New York: Random House, 1964), 137–40.

29. See generally Adam Fairclough, *To Redeem the Soul of America* (Athens: University of Georgia Press, 1987), chaps. 3–5; Garrow, *Bearing the Cross,* chaps. 3–5; Taylor Branch, *Parting the Waters* (New York: Simon & Schuster, 1988), chaps. 17–18; Stephen Oates, *Let the Trumpet Sound* (New York: Harper & Row, 1982), part 5; Brauer, *Second Reconstruction,* chaps. 7–8.

30. The explanation lies in another paradox: social status in the South's biracial caste system was so rigidly prescribed by skin color that residential mixing was both historically familiar and socially nonthreatening to whites. In the North, however, social and economic competition in a more fluid and ethnically mixed environment made residential integration a greater threat to the group status, neighborhood cohesion, and financial investment of whites.

31. Graham, *The Civil Rights Era,* 16–19, 27–32.

32. Robert A. Caro, *The Years of Lyndon Johnson: The Path to Power* (New York: Knopf, 1982), interprets Johnson's career as driven by a raw ambition uncluttered by principle and unredeemed by ideology. See also Ronnie Dugger, *The Politician* (New York: Norton, 1982); and Robert Dallek, *Lone Star Rising* (New York: Oxford, 1991).

33. Arthur M. Schlesinger, Jr., *A Thousand Days* (Boston: Houghton Mifflin, 1965), 933; Theodore White, *The Professional: Lyndon Johnson* (Boston: Houghton Mifflin, 1964); George Reedy, *Lyndon Johnson: A Memoir* (New York: Andrews & McMeel, 1982).

34. Transcript, George Reedy oral history interview, 12 December 1968, Tape 3, 8, Lyndon Baines Johnson Library (hereafter LBJL).

35. Theordore C. Sorensen, *Kennedy* (New York: Harper & Row, 1965), 265–67; Schlesinger, *A Thousand Days,* 702–7.

36. In his biography of Johnson's congressional years, Ronnie Dugger called this period of Johnson's Red-baiting and reaction after 1948 the "most cynical period of his career," when "his radicalism [was] suppressed or well hidden." See Dugger, *The Politician,* 310.

37. Leonard Baker, *The Johnson Eclipse: A President's Vice Presidency* (New York: Macmillan, 1966), chap. 2; Rowland Evans and Robert Novak, *Lyndon B. Johnson: The Exercise of Power* (New York: New American Library, 1966), 305–8; Reedy oral history, Tape 5, 22–28, LBJL.

38. Graham, *The Civil Rights Era*, 19–24, 27–29.

39. "Statement by the President Upon Signing Order Establishing the President's Committee on Equal Employment Opportunity," 7 March 1961, *Public Papers of the Presidents of the United States: John F. Kennedy, 1961* (Washington: U.S. Government Printing Office, 1962), 150.

40. The National Labor Relations Act, 5 July 1935, *U.S. Statutes at Large*, vol. XLIX, Sec. 9(c), 454.

41. Section 297.2(c) of the New York Law Against Discrimination provided for the state commission, upon a written finding of unlawful discrimination, to order the respondent to "cease and desist from such unlawful discriminatory practice and to take such *affirmative action* [emphasis added], including (but not limited to) hiring, reinstatement or upgrading of employees, with or without back pay, restoration to membership in any respondent labor organization, admission to or participation in a guidance program, apprenticeship training program, on-the-job training program or other occupational training or retraining program, the extension of full, equal and unsegregated accommodations, advantages, facilities and privileges to all persons, payment of compensatory damages to the person aggrieved by such practice as, in the judgment of the commission, will effectuate the purposes of this article, and including a requirement for report of the manner of compliance." Texts of the state EEO laws may be found in *State Fair Employment Laws and Their Administration* (Washington: Bureau of National Affairs, 1964).

42. Michael I. Sovern, *Legal Restraints on Racial Discrimination in Employment* (New York: Twentieth Century Fund, 1966), chap. 2; Morroe Berger, *Equality by Statute: The Revolution in Civil Rights*, rev. ed. (New York: Farrar, Straus & Giroux, 1978), chap. 4.

43. Johnson to the President, 14 February 1961; Katzenbach to Moyers, 20 February 1961, Vice Presidential Papers, Civil Rights File (hereafter VPP/CRF), LBJL.

44. Executive Order No. 10925, 26 *Federal Register* 1977 (1961), Part III, Subpart A, Section 301.

45. A study of employment at Lockheed-Marietta by the National Urban League in 1957 had revealed that the 1300 black employees (of a 1957 total of 18,000) were restricted to 30 of the plant's 450 job categories. See Ray Marshall, *The Negro and Organized Labor* (New York: Wiley, 1965), 226–31.

46. *New York Times*, 8 April 1961; Sovern, *Legal Restraints*, 108–11. Lockheed-Marietta's employment had peaked in 1955 with 20,000 workers producing the turbo-prop Hercules and the small executive JetStar, and only 1400 of these workers had been black. Lockheed's laid-off black workers were generally at the bottom of the seniority ladder for re-employment rights on new contracts.

47. *New York Times*, 14 May 1961, and editorial 20 May 1961.

48. "Plan for Equal Job Opportunity at Lockheed Aircraft Corporation," *Monthly Labor Review* (July 1961): 748–49.

49. *New York Times*, 5 June 1961, 15 June 1961.

50. Graham, *The Civil Rights Era*, 67–73; Arthur M. Schlesinger, Jr., *Robert Kennedy and His Times* (Boston: Houghton Mifflin, 1978), 334–35, 55–61.

51. *New York Times*, 27 July 1962.

51. *New York Times*, 18 April 1962; Sovern, *Legal Restraints*, 112–13.

52. *New York Times*, 21 August 1961.

53. "Report by President's Committee on Equal Employment Opportunity," *Monthly Labor Review* 85 (June 1962): 652–54; President's Committee on Equal Employment Opportunity, *Report to the President* (Washington: U.S. Government Printing Office, 1963).

Chapter 3

1. Cynthia Harrison, *On Account of Sex* (Berkeley: University of California Press, 1988), 89–105.

2. Hugh Davis Graham, *The Civil Rights Era* (New York: Oxford University Press, 1990), chap. V; Charles Whalen and Barbara Whalen, *The Longest Debate: Legislative History of the Civil Rights Act of 1964* (Cabin John, Md.: Seven Locks Press, 1985).

3. Hugh Davis Graham, "Civil Rights and the Irony of the Race-Sex Linkage, 1964–1972," paper presented at the annual meeting of the Southern Historical Association, New Orleans, 13 November 1987. See also William H. Chafe, *Women and Equality* (New York: Oxford University Press, 1977).

4. See generally Aileen Kraditor, *Ideas of the Woman Suffrage Movement, 1890–1920* (New York: Columbia University Press, 1965); William O'Neill, *Everyone Was Brave* (New York: Times Books, 1969); William H. Chafe, *The American Woman* (New York: Oxford University Press, 1972); Jo Freeman, *The Politics of Women's Liberation* (New York: David McKay, 1975); and Carl N. Degler, *At Odds: Women and the Family in America from the Revolution to the Present* (New York: Oxford University Press, 1980).

5. Susan D. Becker, *The Origins of the Equal Rights Amendment: American Feminism Between the Wars* (Westport, Conn.: Greenwood, 1981); Susan Ware, *Beyond Suffrage: Women in the New Deal* (Cambridge: Harvard University Press, 1981). On the postwar years, see Leila Rupp and Verta Taylor, *Survival in the Doldrums: The American Women's Rights Movement, 1945 to the 1960s* (New York: Oxford University Press, 1987).

6. Susan Deller Ross, "Sex Discrimination and 'Protective' Labor Legislation," in *The "Equal Rights" Amendment,* Hearings before the Subcommittee on Constitutional Amendments of the Committee on the Judiciary, U.S. Senate, 5–7 May 1970, 408 *passim.*

7. Susan Becker, "They Are Reformers—We Are Feminists," *Origins of ERA,* 197–234; Nancy Schron Dye, *As Equals and As Sisters: Feminism, the Labor Movement, and the Women's Trade Union League of New York* (Columbia: University of Missouri Press, 1980); Judith Sealander, *As Minority Becomes Majority: Federal Reaction to the Phenomenon of Women in the Workplace, 1920–1963* (Westport, Conn.: Greenwood Press, 1983).

8. Harrison, *On Account of Sex,* 19–23.

9. Marguerite Rawalt, "The Equal Rights Amendment," in *Women in Washington,* ed. Irene Tinker (Beverly Hills, Calif.: Sage, 1983), 49–78.

10. Patricia G. Zelman, *Women, Work, and National Policy: The Kennedy-Johnson Years* (Ann Arbor: UMI Research Press, 1980). See also Cynthia Harrison, "A 'New Frontier' for Women: The Public Policy of the Kennedy Administration," *Journal of American History* LXVII (December 1980): 630–46.

11. The Senate rider that accompanied the ERA was called the Hayden amendment, after its sponsor, Democrat Carl Hayden of Arizona. By exempting women's protective laws from the ERA, the Hayden rider allowed liberal, pro-labor Democrats to vote for it. Supporters of the ERA rejected the Hayden amendment as gutting the ERA.

12. *New York Times,* 13 October 1960.

13. Some business critics, citing war industries' experience, argued that female workers cost more than males because they were more frequently absent and their turnover was higher and therefore their training costs.

14. Harrison, *On Account of Sex,* 93–98.

15. Zelman, *Women: Kennedy-Johnson Years,* 30–32; Esther Peterson, "The Kennedy Commission," in *Women in Washington,* 21–34; Harrison, *On Account of Sex,* 89–105.

16. Freeman, *Politics of Women's Liberation,* 174–77.

17. Carl M. Brauer, *John F. Kennedy and the Second Reconstruction* (New York: Columbia University Press, 1977), 259–60.

18. Harvard Sitkoff, *The Struggle for Black Equality 1954–1980* (New York: Hill and Wang, 1981), 129–51; Robert Weisbrot, *Freedom Bound* (New York: Norton, 1990), 68–72.

19. On the role of Martin Luther King in revising his nonviolent strategy after the Albany collapse, and then inviting a violent confrontation in Birmingham, see David J. Garrow, *Protest at Selma* (New Haven: Yale University Press, 1978), 2–4, 220–27; Stephen B. Oates, *Let the Trumpet Sound* (New York: Harper & Row, 1982), 209–32; Garrow, *Bearing the Cross* (New York: Random House, 1986); Adam Fairclough, *To Redeem the Soul of America* (Athens: University of Georgia Press, 1987), 51–55, 86–90, 100–109, 118–39; and Taylor Branch, *Parting the Waters* (New York: Simon & Schuster, 1988), 688–92.

20. Brauer, *Kennedy*, 181–204.

21. John F. Kennedy, "Radio and Television Report to the American People on Civil Rights," June 11, 1963, *Public Papers of the Presidents: John F. Kennedy, 1963* (Washington: U.S. Government Printing Office, 1964), 468–71.

22. Brauer, *Kennedy*, 259–78; Arthur M. Schlesinger, Jr., *Robert Kennedy and His Times* (New York: Houghton Mifflin, 1978), 372–74; Robert Kennedy and Burke Marshall oral history, 4 December 1964, 773–94, JFKL; Lee White oral history, 28 September 1970, 10–11, LBJL; Theodore Sorensen oral history, 3 May 1964, Tape 5, 133–34, JFKL.

23. Transcript, Norbert Schlei oral history, 20–21 February 1968, 44, JFKL.

24. Sorensen to the Attorney General, 21 May and 3 June 1963, Attorney General file, JFKL.

25. Kennedy, *Public Papers*, 11 June 1963, pp. 468–69. The address was hurriedly drafted by Sorensen on the heels of the afternoon's successful resolution of crisis with Governor Wallace in Alabama. The urgency of its message was reinforced the evening it was delivered by the sniper murder of civil rights leader Medgar Evers in Mississippi.

26. Kennedy, "Special Message to the Congress on Civil Rights and Job Opportunities," *Public Papers*, 19 June 1963, p. 486. Kennedy also cited municipal ordinances barring segregated public accommodations in Washington, D.C.; Wilmington, Del.; Louisville, Ky.; El Paso, Tex.; Kansas City, Mo.; and St. Louis, Mo.

27. Schlei oral history, 20–21 February 1968, pp. 45–46, JFKL.

28. "Memorandum Concerning Administration's Civil Rights Bill as Background for Meeting, Hotel Roosevelt, July 2, 1963," National Office Headquarters File, National Urban League Papers, Library of Congress (hereafter NUL Papers, LC).

29. "Labor Views on Administration Civil Rights Package," attached to Andrew J. Biemiller to Kenneth O'Donnell, 10 June 1963, Civil Rights file, George Meany Archives, Washington, D.C.

30. Meany testimony before the Senate Labor and Public Welfare Committee, 25 July 1963, quoted in *AFL-CIO News* press release, n.d., Meany Archives.

31. Supported mainly by labor funds, the Leadership Conference opened its permanent Washington office in the summer of 1963 specifically to lobby for the bill's passage. Its bi-weekly reports to cooperating organizations began on July 25, 1963, and were sent by Arnold Aronson from the Industrial Union Department of the AFL-CIO in the Mills Building on 17th Street. See the LCCR Papers, LC.

32. Executive Committee Meeting, 10 June 1963; Minutes, Board of Directors Meeting, 9 September 1963, NAACP Papers, LC.

33. National Urban League, "Memorandum Concerning Administration's Civil Rights Bill," 2 July 1963, p. 8, NUL Papers, LC.

34. See Hugh Davis Graham, *The Uncertain Triumph: Federal Education Policy in the Kennedy and Johnson Years* (Chapel Hill: University of North Carolina Press, 1984), especially chaps. 1–2.

35. Kennedy to Secretaries Wirtz and Celebrezze, 4 June 1963, Sorensen file, JFKL.

36. Wirtz to the President, 10 June 1963, Sorensen file, 30, JFKL.

37. Mansfield to the President, 18 June 1963, Sorensen file, JFKL; Allen J. Matusow, *The Unraveling of America* (New York: Harper & Row, 1984), 91–92; Brauer, *Kennedy*, 265–66.

38. Whalens, *The Longest Debate*, 9–13.

39. Garrow, *Bearing the Cross*, 231–86; Branch, *Parting the Waters*, 846–87.

40. Paul R. Clancy, *Just a Country Lawyer: A Biography of Senator Sam Ervin* (Bloomington: Indiana University Press, 1974), 78–88, 142–55.

41. Hearing, Senate Judiciary Committee, 88th Cong., 1st sess., 23 August 1963, p. 380.

42. Powell's 31-member committee contained only two southerners, and Roosevelt's seven-member subcommittee contained none. As was the case with most such constituency-based authorization committees in Congress, most members of the Education and Labor Committee had requested the assignment because they were elected from urban, pro-labor constituencies and they supported liberal positions on civil rights and federal aid to education.

43. Hearings before the Special Subcommittee on Labor, House Committee on Education and Labor, 87th Cong., 1st sess., October 23 and 24 (Chicago), 26 and 27 (Los Angeles), and November 3 and 4 (New York), 1961.

44. H.R. 405, Sec. 5(a), in Hearings, General House Subcommittee on Labor, 88th Cong., 1st sess., 3–11.

45. Audiotape log 108.2, 28 August 1963, JFKL; Whalens, *The Longest Debate*, 22–28.

46. Katzenbach to Celler, 13 August 1963, Attorney General file, JFKL.

Chapter 4

1. For a sprightly account of the journey of H.R. 7152 through the House Judiciary Committee, see Charles and Barbara Whalen, *The Longest Debate* (Cabin John, Md.: Seven Locks Press, 1985), 29–70.

2. *Civil Rights*, 1963 Report of the U.S. Commission on Civil Rights, 71–92; *New York Times*, 1 October 1963.

3. Proceedings and *Minutes*, Subcommittee No. 5, 11–12 September 1963; *Longest Debate*, 31–34; *New York Times*, 30 October 1963.

4. Celler had been heavily lobbied by LCCR leaders Clarence Mitchell, Joseph Rauh, Andrew Biemiller, Walter Fauntroy, and Arnold Aronson, and he had pledged to a NAACP convention in Washington on August 7 that he would add a FEPC provision to H.R. 7152.

5. Quoted in the *Wall Street Journal*, 7 November 1963.

6. Arthur M. Schlesinger, Jr., *Robert Kennedy and His Times* (New York: Houghton Mifflin, 1978), 436.

7. Kennedy and Marshall oral history, 22 December 1964, vol. I, pp. 10–11, JFKL; Katzenbach oral history, 12 Novebmer 1968, pp. 17–19, LBJL.

8. Attorney General Robert F. Kennedy testimony, Hearings before the House Judiciary Committee, 88th Cong., 1st sess., on H.R. 7152, as Amended by Subcommittee No. 5, 15–16 October 1963, pp. 2656–58.

9. "Equal Employment Opportunity Act of 1962," H. Rept. No. 1370, 87th Cong., 2d sess., 21 February 1962, pp. 6–7.

10. Matthew A. Crenson and Francis E. Rourke, "By Way of Conclusion: American Bureaucracy since World War II," in *The American Administrative State*, ed. Louis Galambos (Baltimore: Johns Hopkins University Press, 1987), 139–46.

11. James O. Freedman, *Crisis and Legitimacy: The Administrative Process and American Government* (Cambridge: Cambridge University Press, 1978), 137–49.

12. Statement by Griffin and Frelinghuysen, "Equal Employment Opportunity Act of 1963," H. Rept. No. 570, 88th Cong., 1st sess., 22 July 1963, p. 15.

13. *Wall Street Journal,* 12 July, 26 October 1963.

14. *New York Times,* 29 October 1963.

15. Anthony Lewis, "Civil Rights Compact," *New York Times,* 30 October 1963; "Legislative History of H.R. 7152," Burke Marshall file, n.d., LBJL.

16. Quoted in *New York Times,* 17 October 1963.

17. The scholarly literature of 1963 was dominated by Morroe Berger, *Equality By Statute* (Garden City, N.Y.: Doubleday, 1952), which judged the pioneering New York commission to have been procedurally conservative and conciliatory, yet successful in protecting minorities from discriminatory acts. The following year two studies that were more critical were published: Paul H. Norgren and Samuel E. Hill, *Toward Fair Employment* (New York: Columbia University Press, 1964), especially pp. 93–113 on the state FEP experience; and Herbert Hill, "Twenty Years of State Employment Practice Commissions," 14 *Buffalo Law Review* (1964), 22–39, which condemned the ineffectiveness of the state commissions.

18. Lyndon B. Johnson, *Public Papers of the Presidents, 1963–64* (Washington: U.S. Government Printing Office, 1965), I, 8–10.

19. Hugh Davis Graham, *The Civil Rights Era* (New York: Oxford University Press, 1990), 125–39; Whalens, *The Longest Debate,* 84–86.

20. Colmer, quoted in *New York Times,* 10 January 1964; Smith, quoted in Whalens, *Longest Debate,* 110.

21. 110 *Congressional Record,* 7 February 1964, Pt. 2, pp. 2462–2513.

22. Donald Allen Robinson, "Two Movements in Pursuit of Equal Employment Opportunity," *Signs* 4 (1978–79): 413–17.

23. Carl M. Brauer, "Women Activists, Southern Conservatives, and the Prohibition of Sex Discrimination in Title VII of the 1964 Civil Rights Act," *Journal of Southern History* XLIX (February 1983): 37–56.

24. Cynthia Harrison, "A 'New Frontier' for Women: The Public Policy of the Kennedy Administration," *The Journal of American History* LXVII (December 1980): 630–46; Cynthia Harrison, *On Account of Sex* (Berkeley: University of California Press, 1988), 109–65.

25. Quoted in Brauer, "Women Activists," 43. See also Patricia G. Zelman, *Women, Work, and National Policy* (Ann Arbor: UMI Research Press, 1980).

26. Emily George, *Martha Griffiths* (Washington: University Press of America, 1982), 148–52; Harrison, *On Account of Sex,* 176–82.

27. Quoted in *Congressional Quarterly Almanac,* 1964, 348.

28. *New York Times,* 9 February 1964.

29. Lyndon Johnson as quoted by Robert Kennedy, Kennedy and Marshall oral history interview with Anthony Lewis, 22 December 1964, Vol. 7, Pt. II, 871, JFKL.

30. Kennedy oral history interview with John Bartlow Martin, 30 April 1964, Vol. 3, Tape VI-A, 470, JFKL.

31. Kennedy and Marshall oral history, 22 December 1964, Vol. 7, Pt. II, 873, JFKL.

32. *New York Times,* 2 February 1964; *Public Papers: Johnson, 1963–64,* Vol. I, 259.

33. See Rowland Evans and Robert Novak, *Lyndon Johnson: The Exercise of Power* (New York: New American Library, 1966), 376–84; Jim F. Heath, *Decade of Disillusionment: The Kennedy-Johnson Years* (Bloomington: University of Indiana Press, 1975), 169–76; Steven F. Lawson, "Civil Rights," in Robert A. Divine, ed., *Exploring the Johnson Years* (Austin: University of Texas Press, 1981), 100–103; Whalens, *The Longest Debate,* 149–57; Allen J. Matusow, *The Unraveling of America* (New York: Harper & Row, 1984), 209–12.

34. See generally Whalens, *Longest Debate,* 124–217; Matusow, *The Unraveling of*

America, 60–96; James L. Sundquist, *Politics and Policy* (Washington: Brookings Institution, 1968), 259–70.

35. August Meier and Elliott Rudwick, *CORE* (New York: Oxford University Press, 1973), 192–202; Robert Weisbrot, *Freedom Bound* (New York: Norton, 1990), 86–92.

36. Carl Solberg, *Hubert Humphrey: A Biography* (New York: Norton, 1984), 224.

37. Neil MacNeil, *Dirksen: Portrait of a Public Man* (New York: World, 1970), 223–38.

38. *New York Times,* 2 April 1964.

39. Quoted in *Congressional Quarterly Almanac,* 1951, 381.

40. *New York Times,* 21 March 1964; *Wall Street Journal,* 8 April 1964.

41. The Justice Department administrative history summarized the clarification Dirksen demanded in Title 6, which authorized cutting off federal funds to programs found to be discriminating, as follows: "The changes in Title VI are designed to clarify what has always been the intention of the bill: that is, to insure that only the part of a program or activity in which discrimination is found is curtailed and that discrimination in one program or part of a program cannot result in funds being withheld from other programs or from other parts of the same program within a state." In 1984 the Supreme Court reaffirmed this legislative intent and overturned an institution-wide application in the *Grove City College* decision; in 1988 Congress amended Title 6 to reverse *Grove City* and permit broad cut-off of federal funding.

42. On the national debate over racial quotas in 1964, see Graham, *The Civil Rights Era,* chap. 4.

43. *New York Times,* 8 May 1963.

44. Whalens, *Longest Debate,* 189.

45. *New York Times,* 21 April 1964.

46. Illinois FEPC Charge No. 63–127. On the Motorola case see Graham, *The Civil Rights Era,* 149–50.

47. *New York Times,* 13 March 1964.

48. 110 *Congressional Record,* Pt. 11, 13 June 1964, 13724. The Motorola case is published in the *Congressional Record* at 13492.

49. See *The Civil Rights Act of 1964* (Washington: Bureau of National Affairs, 1964), 335, 346.

50. See *Wall Street Journal,* 3 March 1965; *New York Times,* 22 November 1964, 25 March 1966; 57 *Labor Relations Report* (1964), 264; *Motorola, Inc. v. Illinois F.E.P.C.,* 51 CCH Lab. Cas. par. 51, 323 (Cook County Circuit Court, 1965). Motorola appealed the commission's decision to the Cook County circuit court, which in March 1965 upheld the FEPC finding of discrimination against Motorola, but reversed the commission's $1,000 order for punitive damages. In March 1966 the Illinois supreme court reversed the circuit court in favor of Motorola.

51. Humphrey, quoted in 110 *Congressional Record,* pt. 5, 30 March 1964, p. 6549.

52. Clark and Case, quoted in 110 *Congressional Record,* pt. 6, 8 April 1964, p. 7213.

53. Ibid. In 1964, state fair employment statutes specifically prohibited quota systems in Michigan, Ohio, Pennsylvania, and Rhode Island.

54. Humphrey, quoted in 110 *Congressional Record,* pt. 10, 4 June 1964, p. 12723.

55. *New York Times,* 8 May 1964. The congressional debates and editorial discussions of 1964 seldom mentioned sex discrimination, which seemed an afterthought in a great national debate about racial policy.

56. Humphrey, quoted in 110 *Congressional Record,* 30 March 1964, pp. 12723–24.

57. Matusow, *The Unraveling of America,* 96.

58. V.O. Key, Jr., *Southern Politics in State and Nation* (New York: Knopf, 1949); Numan V. Bartley and Hugh D. Graham, *Southern Politics and the Second Reconstruction* (Baltimore: Johns Hopkins University Press, 1975).

Chapter 5

1. Seth Cagin and Philip Dray, *We Are Not Afraid: The Story of Goodman, Schwerner, and Chaney and the Civil Rights Campaign for Mississippi* (New York: Macmillan, 1988); Mary A. Rothschild, *A Case of Black and White: Northern Volunteers and the Southern Freedom Summers, 1964–1965* (Westport, Conn.: Greenwood Press, 1982).

2. Clayborne Carson, *In Struggle* (Cambridge: Harvard University Press, 1981), 111–29.

3. Doug McAdam, *Freedom Summer* (New York: Oxford University Press, 1988), 161–85; Robert Weisbrot, *Freedom Bound* (New York: Norton, 1990), 92–114.

4. Edward G. Carmines and James A. Stimson, *Issue Evolution: Race and the Transformation of American Politics* (Princeton: Princeton University Press, 1989), 68–72.

5. Barry M. Goldwater, *The Conscience of a Conservative* (New York: Hillman Books, 1960), 38.

6. The popular vote for Johnson-Humphrey was 43,128,958 to 27,176,873 for Goldwater-Miller. This provided a Democratic margin of 61.4 percent of the two-party vote and approximated Franklin Roosevelt's landslide of 1936. See Bernard Cosman, *Five States for Goldwater* (University: University of Alabama Press, 1966); and Numan V. Bartley and Hugh D. Graham, *Southern Politics and the Second Reconstruction* (Baltimore: Johns Hopkins University Press, 1975), chap. 4.

7. Johnson, *The Vantage Point* (New York: Holt, Rinehart & Winston, 1971), 161.

8. J. Morgan Kousser, "The Undermining of the First Reconstruction: Lessons for the Second," in *Minority Vote Dilution*, ed. Chandler Davidson (Washington: Howard University Press, 1984), 27–46.

9. Katzenbach testimony, *Hearings on Voting Rights*, House Judiciary Committee, 89th Cong., 1st sess. (Washington: U.S. Government Printing Office, 1965), 9.

10. Katzenbach to the President, 18 December 1964, Administrative History of the Department of Justice, vol. VII, Civil Rights, 2, LBJL.

11. David J. Garrow, *Bearing the Cross* (New York: Random House, 1986), 357–430. See also Garrow, *Protest at Selma: Martin Luther King and the Voting Rights Act of 1965* (New Haven: Yale University Press, 1978).

12. More sympathetic interpretations of King's post-Albany strategy are offered in Adam Fairclough, *To Redeem the Soul of America* (Athens: University of Georgia Press, 1987), 225–52; and Taylor Branch, *Parting the Waters* (New York: Simon & Schuster, 1988), 688–92.

13. Black registration as a percentage of eligible voters in the other southern states in 1964, in ascending rank order, were Louisiana 32%, South Carolina 38.8%; Georgia 44%, Virginia 45.7%, North Carolina 46.8%, Arkansas 54.4%, Texas 57.7%, Florida 63.7%, and Tennessee 69.4%. For the eleven former Confederate states in 1964 the average level of registration for eligible blacks was 43.8%, whereas the average for whites was 73.2%.

14. King's carefully laid scenario was almost wrecked when shortly before his protest began, Selma's new mayor appointed a shrewd segregationist, Wilson Baker, as director of public safety. The cool Baker, however, could not duplicate Laurie Prichett's control in Albany because Baker could not control the volatile Sheriff Clark. But King's demonstrators could. As Baker later observed, the protesters voted Clark "an honorary member of SNCC, SCLC, CORE, the N-Double A-C-P. . . . And from then on they played him just like an expert playing a violin." Interview of Wilson Baker in Howell Raines, *My Soul Is Rested* (New York: Putnam, 1977), 200; Garrow, *Protest at Selma*, 220–24; Allen J. Matusow, *The Unraveling of America* (New York: Harper & Row, 1984), 180–87.

15. Steven F. Lawson, *Black Ballots* (New York: Columbia University Press, 1976), 308–22.

16. *Congressional Quarterly Almanac, 1965, 533–65.*

17. Howard Ball, Dale Krane, and Thomas P. Lauth, *Compromised Compliance: Implementation of the 1965 Voting Rights Act* (Westport, Conn.: Greenwood Press, 1982), 64–94; Abigail M. Thernstrom, *Whose Votes Count?* (Cambridge: Harvard University Press, 1987), 24–27.

18. Cox to the Attorney General, 23 March 1965, Justice Department Administrative History, Civil Rights Doc. Supp., LBJL.

19. Johnson, quoted in Thernstrom, *Whose Votes Count?*, 15.

20. *Heart of Atlanta Motel v. United States,* 379 U.S. 241 (1964).

21. *Louisiana v. United States,* 380 U.S. 145 (1965); *United States v. Mississippi,* 380 U.S. 128 (1965). The following year, in *Harper v. Virginia State Board of Elections,* 383 U.S. 663 (1966), the Supreme Court invalidated the state requirement of poll tax payment as a prerequisite for voting in state and local elections.

22. *Public Papers of the Presidents: Lyndon B. Johnson, 1965* (Washington: U.S. Government Printing Office, 1966), I, 282–83. Johnson entitled his speech "The American Promise," but it would be remembered by his invocation of the Freedom Movement song, "We Shall Overcome."

23. J. Morgan Kousser, *The Shaping of Southern Politics: Suffrage Restriction and the Establishment of the One-Party South, 1880–1910* (New Haven: Yale University Press, 1974).

24. Daniel P. Moynihan, *Family and Nation* (New York: Harcourt Brace Jovanovich, 1986), 30.

25. *Public Papers of the Presidents: Johnson, 1965,* I, 636.

26. Douglas Kiker, "Johnson Spoke for History," *New York Herald Tribune,* 6 June 1965.

27. Robert Conot, *Rivers of Blood, Years of Darkness* (New York: Morrow, 1968), 14–17.

28. Carson, *In Struggle,* 215–43; Doug McAdam, *Political Process and the Development of Black Insurgency, 1930–1970* (Chicago: University of Chicago Press, 1982), 181–216.

29. Garrow, *Bearing the Cross,* 491–525.

30. *Revolution in Civil Rights,* 3rd ed. (Washington: Congressional Quarterly Press, 1967), 62; *Congress and the Nation, 1965–1968* (Washington: Congressional Quarterly Press, 1969), 5; Hugh D. Graham, *The Civil Rights Era* (New York: Oxford University Press, 1990), 202–3.

Chapter 6

1. Richard K. Berg, "Equal Employment Opportunity Under the Civil Rights Act of 1964," 31 *Brooklyn Law Review* 62 (1964).

2. Ibid., 64–47, 85–88; Comment, "Enforcement of Fair Employment Under the Civil Rights Act of 1964," 32 *Chicago Law Review* 430, 470 (1965).

3. Michael I. Sovern, *Legal Restraints on Racial Discrimination in Employment Law* (New York: Twentieth Century Fund, 1966), 83.

4. *Wall Street Journal,* 28 May 1965.

5. *EEOC Administrative History,* LBJL, 1969, chap. IV; Richard P. Nathan, *Jobs and Civil Rights* (Washington: Brookings Institution, 1969), 13–32, 66–69.

6. Jack Buchanek to William Carey, 9 August 1966; Buchanek to the Director, 24 October 1966, EEOC 6806-15, series 60.26, Bureau of the Budget files (hereafter BOB), National Archives and Records Administration (herafter NARA).

7. Buchanek to the Director, 12 August 1966, BOB, NARA; Hugh D. Graham, *The Civil Rights Era* (New York: Oxford University Press, 1990), chap. VII.

8. Biemiller to Tom Harris, 19 January 1960, Equal Rights file, Meany Archives.

9. Edith Green, who opposed the ERA, led the House opposition to Howard Smith's sex amendment, and explained that "I do not consider myself a suffragette,"

nonetheless was angered by Shriver's all-male Job Corps, and demanded a Women's Job Corps. See Patricia Zellman, *Women, Work, and National Policy: The Kennedy-Johnson Years* (Ann Arbor: UMI Research Press, 1980), 73–108.

10. Humphrey to the President, 9 August 1965, Lee White files, LBJL.

11. Moynihan to Moyers, 21 January 1965, EX HU 2-1, WHCF, LBJL. See Zelman, *Women: Kennedy-Johnson,* 85–87.

12. Moynihan to Moyers, 21 January 1965, GEN HU 2-1, WHCF, LBJL.

13. Lee Rainwater and William L. Yancey, *The Moynihan Report and the Politics of Controversy* (Cambridge: MIT Press, 1967).

14. *Wall Street Journal,* 22 June 1965.

15. *New York Times,* 3 July 1965.

16. John Herbers, "For Instance, Can She Pitch for the Mets?" *New York Times,* 20 August 1965.

17. *New York Times,* 21 August 1965.

18. Powers to the Secretary [Wirtz], 7 September 1965, NN 370-108, RG 174, Records of the Secretary of Labor, NARA.

19. Frances Reissman Cousens, *Public Civil Rights Agencies and Fair Employment* (New York: Praeger, 1969), 13.

20. Aileen C. Hernandez, *E.E.O.C. and the Women's Movement 1965–1975* (Newark: Rutgers University Law School, 1975), 6–7.

21. *New York Times,* 27 July 1965.

22. In 1965, 43 states and the District of Columbia had laws setting maximum daily or weekly hours for women, and 24 of these plus the federal district set maximum hours of 8 hours a day, 48 hours a week, or both, for women in one or more occupations. Twenty-one states prohibited or regulated night work for women. The only states without such protectionist laws were Alabama, Alaska, Florida, Hawaii, Indiana, Iowa, Minnesota, and West Virginia.

23. *New York Times,* 2 July 1965.

24. *The Civil Rights Act of 1964* (Washington: Bureau of National Affairs, 1964), 59–60. Vermont's law against sex discrimination was limited to equal pay.

25. *Wall Street Journal,* 29 July 1965. The *Journal*'s reporter, Joseph D. Mathewson, identified the enforcement official at the Wisconsin Industrial Commission as "Virginia Huebner, the attractive, red-haired director of the commission's fair employment practices division."

26. Wirtz to Roosevelt, 9 August 1965, NN 370-108, Labor, NARA; Cynthia Harrison, *On Account of Sex* (Berkeley: University of California Press, 1988), 185–96.

27. *New York Times,* 20 August 1965.

28. *Wall Street Journal,* 17 September 1965.

29. EEOC Minutes, meeting #25, 21 September 1965, 2, EEOC Library, Washington, D.C.

30. *New York Times,* 19 August 1965. Thirteen of the study committee's 17 members were men, and ten represented newspapers or advertising agencies.

31. *Wall Street Journal,* 13 October 1965.

32. Title 29 CFR Sec. 1604.1–3, 22 November 1965; *EEOC Newsletter* (December 1965), 2; *EEOC Administrative History,* 238–40.

33. *EEOC Administrative History,* 243–45. In its first annual report, the EEOC observed that "At first glance Title VII appears to have the effect of superseding all state protective legislation. However, there is nothing in the legislative history of Title VII to indicate that Congress intended any such far-reaching result." EEOC, *First Annual Report* (Washington: U.S. Government Printing Office, 1966), 43.

34. *Wall Street Journal,* 23 November 1965.

35. 31 *Federal Register* 6414, 28 April 1966; *EEOC Administrative History,* 241–42; *Wall Street Journal,* 29 April 1966; Graham, *Civil Rights Era,* 214–21.

36. Peterson, letter to the editor, *New York Times,* 3 September 1965.

37. 110 *Congressional Record* Pt. 10, 89th Cong., 2nd sess. (20 June 1966), p.

13690; Emily George, *Martha Griffiths* (Washington: University Press of America, 1982), 152.

38. 110 *Congressional Record,* Pt. 10 (1966), p. 13689; Hernandez, *EEOC,* 10–13.

39. 110 *Congressional Record,* Pt. 10, (1966), pp. 13693, 13694.

40. Betty Friedan, *It Changed My Life: Writings on the Women's Movement* (New York: Random House, 1976), 75–86; author interview with Richard Graham, 12 June 1986, Washington, D.C.

41. Friedan, *It Changed My Life,* 80; author interview with Sonia Pressman Fuentes, 9 October 1986, Potomac, Md.; memorandum, Pressman to Friedan, n.d. (Summer 1967), courtesy of Sonia Pressman Fuentes.

42. Zelman, *Women: Kennedy-Johnson,* 104–7; Harrison, *On Account of Sex,* 192–96.

43. Jo Freeman, *The Politics of Women's Liberation* (New York: McKay, 1975), 177–90.

44. EEOC, *First Annual Report* (Washington: U.S. Government Printing Office, 1966), 6. Most sex discrimination complaints came from women, but 35 of 175 complaints on hiring came from men seeking to enter such traditionally female jobs as nursing. In subsequent years the women's share of EEOC complaints averaged 25 percent of all complaints.

45. Nathan, *Jobs and Civil Rights,* 51, Table 2-4.

46. Donald Allen Robinson, "Two Movements in Pursuit of Equal Employment Opportunity," *Signs* 4 (1978–79): 413–33.

47. *Wall Street Journal,* 22 May 1967. The *Journal* reporter, Wayne E. Green, began his story with the following lead: "Shades of the suffragettes! The ladies are up in arms again. They're demanding equal rights."

48. *EEOC Adminsitrative History,* 119–21; Shulman to the President, 4 May 1967, EEOC, WHCF, LBJL; Shulman testimony concerning S. 1308, Subcommittee on Labor and Public Welfare, Senate Committee on Employment, Manpower and Poverty, 4 May 1967.

49. For a discussion of court rulings on the EEOC guidelines of 1965, 1969, and 1972, see Kenneth M. Davidson, Ruth Bader Ginsburg, and Herma Hill Kay, *Texts, Cases and Materials on Sex-based Discrimination* (St. Paul: West, 1974), 1001–5.

50. EEOC, *Third Annual Report* (Washington: U.S. Government Printing Office, 1969), 14–16; *Fourth Annual Report,* 15–17.

51. *Wall Street Journal,* 6 August 1968.

52. EEOC Minutes, meeting #180, 13 February 1968.

53. James Q. Wilson, ed., *The Politics of Regulation* (New York: Basic Books, 1980), 357–94; Freeman, *Politics of Women's Liberation,* 236–37.

Chapter 7

1. See generally the report of the Kerner Commission, *Report of the National Advisory Commission on Civil Disorders* (Washington: U.S. Government Printing Office, 1968).

2. Hugh Davis Graham and Ted Robert Gurr, eds., *Violence in America* (New York: Praeger, 1969), 788–822; Graham and Gurr, eds., *Violence in America* (Beverly Hills, Calif.: Sage, 1979), 261–86, 475–90.

3. Hugh Davis Graham, "On Riots and Riot Commissions: Civil Disorders in the 1960s," *The Public Historian* 2 (Summer 1980): 7–27.

4. Shulman, quoted in the *Wall Street Journal,* 12 April 1967.

5. Richard P. Nathan, *Jobs and Civil Rights* (Washington: Brookings Institution, 1969), 13–32, 66–69; Alfred W. Blumrosen, *Black Employment and the Law* (New Brunswick: Rutgers University Press, 1971), 9–20.

6. Nathan Glazer, *Affirmative Discrimination* (New York: Basic Books, 1975), 33, 68–69.

7. See Hugh Davis Graham, *The Civil Rights Era* (New York: Oxford University Press, 1990), chaps. VII and IX; Derrick A. Bell, Jr., *Race, Racism and American Law*, 2d ed. (Boston: Little, Brown, 1980), 612–17, 637–52.

8. U.S. Equal Employment Opportunity Commission, *Legislative History of Titles VII and XI of Civil Rights Act of 1964* (Washington: U.S. Government Printing Office, n.d.), 306.

9. 110 *Congressional Record*, Pt. 6, 8 April 1964, p. 7213.

10. Sonia Pressman to Charles Duncan, 31 May 1966, provided to the author by Sonia Pressman Fuentes; A. Ranney, "Enforcement of Fair Employment Under the Civil Rights Act of 1964," 32 *University of Chicago Law Review* 430 (1965).

11. James Q. Wilson, *Bureaucracy: What Government Agencies Do and Why They Do It* (New York: Basic Books, 1989), 72–89, 179–95.

12. Jeremy Rabkin, "Office for Civil Rights," in James Q. Wilson, *The Politics of Regulation* (New York: Basic Books, 1980), 304–56; Graham, *Civil Rights Era*, 282–90.

13. John Macy to the President, 11 May 1967, Macy files, LBJL.

14. Graham, *The Civil Rights Era*, 237–38.

15. Blumrosen, "The Newport News Agreement," *Black Employment*, 328–77; *EEOC Administrative History*, 119–25.

16. *Wall Street Journal*, 13 January 1966.

17. Blumrosen, *Black Employment*, 102–37; *New York Times*, 7 August 1967.

18. *EEOC Administrative History*, 146–54.

19. EEOC Minutes, meeting #133, 16 November 1966, and meeting #134, 23 November 1966; *EEOC Adminstrative History*, 129–45; Nathan, *Jobs and Civil Rights*, 28–29.

20. Samuel C. Jackson, "EEOC vs. Discrimination, Inc.," *The Crisis* (January 1968): 16–17.

21. *EEOC Administrative History*, 248.

22. Donald L. Horowitz, *The Courts and Social Policy* (Washington: Brookings Institution, 1977); Graham, *Civil Rights Era*, chap. XV.

23. William B. Gould, *Black Workers in White Unions: Job Discrimination in the United States* (Ithaca: Cornell University Press, 1977), 67–98; *EEOC Administrative History*, 249–50.

24. *Congress and the Nation*, II, 1965–68, p. 378; *Wall Street Journal*, 25 January 1968.

25. *Public Papers of the Presidents: Johnson, 1968*, I, 24 January 1968, 55–62; *New York Times*, 25 January 1968.

26. *Wall Street Journal*, 19 February 1968.

27. Arlen J. Large, "Federal Power and 'Flexible' Senators," *Wall Street Journal*, 13 March 1968.

28. *Congressional Quarterly Almanac*, 1968, 159; 114 *Congressional Record*, Pt. 4 (26 February 1968), p. 4574.

29. 114 *Congressional Record*, Pt. 4 (28 February 1968), p. 4574.

30. Ibid.

31. In 1968 the outgoing Johnson administration requested $11.1 million for fiscal year 1969 to employ 850 HUD enforcement officers, but Congress appropriated only $2 million.

32. James W. Button, *Black Violence: Political Impact of the 1960s Riots* (Princeton: Princeton University Press, 1978), 78–79.

33. U.S. Commission on Civil Rights, *The Federal Fair Housing Enforcement Effort* (Washington: U.S. Government Printing Office, 1979), 70–73; John M. Goering, ed., *Housing Desegregation and Federal Policy* (Chapel Hill: University of North Carolina Press, 1986), 256–63; Douglas S. Massey and Nancy A. Denton, "Trends in the Residen-

tial Segregation of Blacks, Hispanics, and Asians: 1970–1980," *American Sociological Review* 52 (December 1987): 802–25.

Chapter 8

1. Herbert S. Parmet, *Richard Nixon and His America* (Boston: Little, Brown, 1990), 91–113, 186–200, 429–30.

2. Kevin P. Phillips, *The Emerging Republican Majority* (New Rochelle, N.Y.: Arlington House, 1969).

3. Richard M. Scammon and Ben J. Wattenberg, *The Real Majority* (New York: Coward-McCann, 1970).

4. Irwin Unger and Debi Unger, *Turning Point: 1968* (New York: Scribner, 1988), 475–99.

5. Jules Witcover, *The Resurrection of Richard Nixon* (New York: Putnam, 1970), 343–44.

6. Author interview with John D. Ehrlichman, 5 August 1986, Santa Fe, N.M.; Joe McGinnis, *The Selling of the President, 1968* (New York: Trident, 1969), 199–201; Lewis Chester, Godfrey Hodgson, and Bruce Page, *An American Melodrama: The Presidential Campaign of 1968* (New York: Viking, 1969), 462–63.

7. Quoted from Nixon's Lincoln Day speech in Cincinnati, in Witcover, *Resurrection*, 71–72.

8. A. James Reichley, *Conservatives in an Age of Change: The Nixon and Ford Administrations* (Washington: Brookings Institution, 1981), 175–76.

9. Reichley, *Conservatives*, 176. At the Miami convention in 1968 Nixon received 228 of the 310 votes cast by southern Republican delegates, with 60 of the remainder going to Reagan.

10. Stephen E. Ambrose, *Nixon: The Triumph of a Politician 1962–1972* (New York: Simon & Schuster, 1989), 161–63, 172–94.

11. Theo Lippman, Jr., *Spiro Agnew's America* (New York: Norton, 1972), 154–67.

12. Philip E. Converse, Warren E. Miller, et al., "Continuity and Change in American Politics: Parties and Issues in the 1968 Elections," *American Political Science Review* 63 (December 1969): 1091–92.

13. Edward G. Carmines and James A. Stimson, *Issue Evolution: Race and the Transformation of American Politics* (Princeton: Princeton University Press, 1989).

14. Roland Evans, Jr., and Robert D. Novak, *Nixon in the White House: The Frustrations of Power* (New York: Random House, 1971), 133–76.

15. Ehrlichman to Domestic Plans Group, 20 August 1969, Burns Papers, Gerald R. Ford Library (hereafter GRFL).

16. Hugh Davis Graham, "Short-circuiting the Bureaucracy in the Great Society: Policy Origins in Education," *Presidential Studies Quarterly* XII (Summer 1982): 237–41.

17. Ehrlichman, *Witness to Power*, 207–62; Evans and Novak, *Nixon in the White House*, 37–74; Henry Kissinger, *The White House Years* (Boston: Little, Brown, 1979), 73–111; Safire, *Before the Fall*, 112–17, 463–78; Reichley, *Conservatives*, 59–78.

18. *Public Papers of the Presidents: Richard M. Nixon, 1969* (Washington: U.S. Government Printing Office, 1971), 1–4.

19. *Public Papers: Nixon, 1969*, 284–88; *New York Times*, 15 April 1969; Carl M. Brauer, *Presidential Transitions: Eisenhower Through Reagan* (New York: Oxford University Press, 1986), 156–58.

20. Ambrose, *Nixon* (1989), 296.

21. Harlow to the President, 15 March 1969, Ehrlichman files, Nixon Presidential Materials Project, Alexandria, Virginia (hereafter RMNP).

22. On Nixon's initiatives in national planning, see Otis L. Graham, Jr., *Toward a*

Planned Society: From Roosevelt to Nixon (New York: Oxford University Press, 1976), 188–263; on Nixon's environmental programs, see John C. Whitaker, *Striking a Balance: Environment and Natural Resources Policy in the Nixon-Ford Years* (Washington: American Enterprise Institute, 1976).

23. *Public Papers: Nixon, 1969*, 197–98; *Wall Street Journal*, 6 March 1969.

24. *Wall Street Journal*, 10 July 1969; Garment to Ken Cole, 20 April 1970, EX HU-2, RMNP.

25. Quoted in the *Wall Street Journal*, 10 July 1969.

26. *New York Times*, 15 March 1969.

27. *New York Times*, 26 March 1969, 10 April 1969. On March 29 Nixon released a mollifying memorandum to all department heads, reaffirming "my own official and personal endorsement of a strong policy of equal opportunity within the Federal Government." On May 7 he replaced Alexander as EEOC chairman with William H. Brown III, a black Republican lawyer from Philadelphia whose appointment to the commission by Johnson was awaiting Senate confirmation.

28. *Wall Street Journal*, 2 May 1969. Nathan had chaired a Nixon transition task force on welfare, and had subsequently joined the Nixon administration as assistant director in the Budget Bureau for human resources programs. See Nathan's critical account of the Nixon years in *The Plot That Failed: Nixon and the Administrative Presidency* (New York: Wiley, 1975).

29. *Wall Street Journal*, 7 July 1969.

30. Ehrlichman interview, 5 August 1986.

31. Parmet, *Richard Nixon*, 605–7; Ambrose, *Nixon* (1989), 314–17.

32. Parmet, *Richard Nixon*, 608–10. Nixon subsequently nominated Harry Blackmun, a federal appeals judge from Minnesota, who was approved unanimously by the Senate—and who wrote the abortion-rights opinion in *Roe v. Wade* in 1973.

33. For accounts of the effective role of George Shultz, Nixon's secretary of Labor during 1969–70 and thereafter director of the new Office of Management and Budget, in establishing and coordinating the network of biracial citizen committees in seven southern states beginning in early 1970, see Nixon, *RN: The Memoirs of Richard Nixon* (New York: Grossett & Dunlap, 1978), 439–43; Ehrlichman, *Witness*, 230–35; Reichley, *Conservatives*, 187–89.

34. See Wilkinson, *From Brown to Bakke*, 193–249. The key decision was *Milliken v. Bradley*, 418 U.S. 717 (1974), in which a 5-4 Supreme Court majority overturned a district court ruling that joined 53 of Detroit's 85 outlying suburban school districts in a metropolitan busing plan to integrate Detroit's schools. Chief Justice Warren Burger wrote the majority opinion, joined by justices Harry Blackmun, Lewis Powell, and William Rehnquist—all Nixon appointees—and Eisenhower appointee Potter Stewart.

35. Reichley, *Conservatives*, 189–90.

36. In 1966 the Supreme Court upheld sections four and five of the Voting Rights Act in *South Carolina v. Katzenbach*, 383 U.S. 301, holding that "In acceptable legislative fashion, Congress chose to limit its attention to the geographic areas where immediate action seemed necessary."

37. House Report 89-439, 1 June 1965, p. 15.

38. House Report 91-397, 28 July 1969, p. 5.

39. Steven F. Lawson, *Black Ballots: Voting Rights in the South, 1944–1969* (New York: Columbia University Press, 1976), 334–39; Abigail M. Thernstrom, *Whose Votes Count?* (Cambridge: Harvard University Press, 1987), 17–18.

40. Gary Orfield, *Congressional Power: Congress and Social Change* (New York: Harcourt Brace Jovanovich, 1975), 96.

41. U.S. Commission on Civil Rights, *Political Participation* (Washington: U.S. Commission on Civil Rights, 1968), 21–84; Steven F. Lawson, *In Pursuit of Power: Southern Blacks and Electoral Politics, 1965–1982* (New York: Columbia University Press, 1985), 128–31.

42. Burns to the President, 17 June 1969, EX HU 2–4, RMNP. The nonsouthern

states requiring literacy tests in 1969 were Alaska, Arizona, California, Connecticut, Delaware, Hawaii, Maine, Massachusetts, New Hampshire, New York, Oregon, Washington, and Wyoming. The 14th state, Idaho, had a "good character" requirement which qualified as a "test or device" within the meaning of Section 4(c) of the Voting Rights Act. Literacy tests were first required in Connecticut in 1855 and in Massachusetts in 1857, and they reflected nativist reactions to heavy Irish immigration. Similarly, the West Coast literacy tests generally followed in the wake of heavy Asian immigration.

43. Burns to the President, 17 June 1969, 3.

44. *Gaston County v. United States,* 395 U.S. 285 (1969) at 289, 291.

45. Leonard to Ehrlichman, 9 June 1969, Ex Hu 2–4, RMNP.

46. Howard Ball, Dale Krane, and Thomas P. Lauth, *Compromised Compliance: Implementation of the 1965 Voting Rights Act* (Westport, Conn.: Greenwood Press, 1982), 74–75.

47. Lawson, *Pursuit of Power,* 162–63.

48. Mitchell testimony, *Hearings,* 26 June 1969, 227.

49. U.S. Commission on Civil Rights, *Political Participation* (Washington: U.S. Government Printing Office, 1968).

50. Ibid., 177.

51. "Separate Views of Hon. Richard H. Poff," House Report No. 91-397, 28 July 1969, pp. 14–15. Poff conceded that historically, Virginia "sorrowfully has not always been innocent of racial discrimination."

52. Statement of William McCulloch, *Hearings,* 1 July 1969, 269.

53. Reichley, *Conservatives,* 85–97.

54. In December 1970 a floating coalition of the right in the Senate rejected the Nixon-Moynihan bill on welfare reform that a left-coalition had passed in the House.

55. *Congress and the Nation, 1969–1972* (Washington: Congressional Quarterly Press, 1973), 494–99.

56. *Wall Street Journal,* 12 December 1969.

57. Lawson, *Pursuit of Power,* 139–57.

58. The Senate voted 51-22 to substitute the five-year extension, and 64-17 to add the 18-year-old vote. Then the revised bill was passed on a 64-12 roll-call vote. The consensus of constitutional scholars supported Nixon's view that the Constitution did not permit Congress to lower the voting age by statute.

59. Evans and Novak, *Nixon in the White House,* 129–31. Nixon's constitutional reservation about enfranchising 18-year-olds by statute was partially sustained by the Supreme Court in *Oregon v. Mitchell,* 400 U.S. 112 (1970), which narrowly held that the law's enfranchisement of 18-year-olds was valid for presidential and congressional elections but not for state and local ones. In response to the constitutional uncertainty, Congress rushed a constitutional amendment through both houses and sent it to the states in March 1971. On June 30 the Twenty-sixth amendment was ratified by the requisite 38th state in the record time of three months and seven days.

Chapter 9

1. Hugh Davis Graham, *The Civil Rights Era* (New York: Oxford University Press, 1990), 301–9, 318–21.

2. Otis L. Graham, Jr., *Toward A Planned Society: From Roosevelt to Nixon* (New York: Oxford University Press, 1976), 188–263.

3. Carl M. Brauer, *Presidential Transitions* (New York: Oxford University Press, 1986), 121–69; Paul C. Light, *The President's Agenda* (Baltimore: Johns Hopkins University Press, 1982), 40–45.

4. Political scientist J. Leiper Freeman published the first textbook analysis of triangular politics in *The Political Process* (New York: Random House, 1955). Douglass Cater, national affairs editor for *The Reporter* magazine in 1964 when Lyndon

Johnson appointed him White House aide for education, published a journalistic account in *Power in Washington* (New York: Vintage, 1964).

5. For a discussion of such triangular relationships in education policy during the Kennedy-Johnson years, see Hugh Davis Graham, "Short-circuiting the Bureaucracy in the Great Society: Policy Origins in Education," *Presidential Studies Quarterly* XII (Summer 1982): 407–20. Patterns of bureaucratic politics are perceptively explored in James Q. Wilson, *Bureaucracy* (New York: Basic Books, 1989).

6. For a critical view, see Thomas Sowell, *Civil Rights* (New York: Morrow, 1984), 37–60.

7. Hanes Walton, Jr., *When the Marching Stopped: The Politics of Civil Rights Regulatory Agencies* (Albany: State University of New York Press, 1988), 28–42.

8. By the 92nd Congress (1971–73) there were 57 standing and special committees and 288 subcommittees, which together provided a total of 345 committees with chairs and staffs (including minority as well as majority party staff), for only 535 legislators. See David E. Price, "Congressional Committees in the Policy Process," and Roger H. Davidson, "Two Avenues of Change: House and Senate Committee Reorganization," in *Congress Reconsidered,* Lawrence C. Dodd and Bruce I. Oppenheimer, eds. (Washington: Congressional Quarterly Press, 1981), 107–33, 156–85.

9. William B. Gould, *Black Workers in White Unions* (Ithaca: Cornell University Press, 1977), 172–88; Ray Marshall et al., *Employment Discrimination* (New York: Praeger, 1978), 28–34.

10. Graham, *Civil Rights Era,* 177–89.

11. Richard Nathan, *Jobs and Civil Rights* (Washington: Brookings Institution, 1969), 101–7.

12. Department of Labor, *Administrative History,* Vol. I, 1965–73, LBJL; *The Federal Civil Rights Enforcement Effort* (Washington: U.S. Commission on Civil Rights, 1970), 68–69.

13. The classic study of job discrimination and the law for the 1960s remains Michael Sovern, *Legal Restraints on Racial Discrimination in Employment* (New York: Twentieth Century Fund, 1966); see also David H. Rosenbloom, *Federal Equal Employment Opportunity: Politics and Public Personnel Administration* (New York: Praeger, 1977).

14. Sylvester to the Secretary, 24 March 1967, Labor Department files NN 371-20, NARA; Alfred Blumrosen, *Black Employment and the Law* (New Brunswick: Rutgers University Press, 1971), 337–407.

15. *New York Times,* 1 June 1963.

16. Phelan to Members, Federal Executive Board for Philadelphia, 27 October 1967, Reel 28, Labor Executive Records, LBJL. Represented on the Philadelphia FEB were the departments of Defense, Justice, Labor, and HUD; and the General Services Administration, Post Office, Community Relations Service, EEOC, and OFCC.

17. John W. Kingdon, *Agendas, Alternatives, and Public Policies* (Boston: Little, Brown, 1984), 173–204; Nelson W. Polsby, *Political Innovation in America* (New Haven: Yale University Press, 1984), 167–74.

18. *Wall Street Journal,* 19 September 1967.

19. Sylvester to Heads of All Agencies, 22 September 1967; Macy to Chairmen of Federal Executive Boards, 30 October 1967, Reel 28, Labor Executive Records, LBJL.

20. *Wall Street Journal,* 16 October 1967.

21. Macy to Representative Odin Langren and senators Quentin Burdick, George McGovern, and Milton Young, 22 January 1968, Reel 28, Labor Executive Records, LBJL.

22. Cramer to Staats, 8 April 1968, Philadelphia Plan file, General Accounting Office Library, Washington, D.C.; *Wall Street Journal,* 17 June 1968.

23. Comptroller General Opinion B-163026, Staats to Cramer, 22 May 1968, copy to Wirtz, Philadelphia Plan file, GAO.

24. Staats to Cramer, 18 November 1968, Philadelphia Plan Document #3, Labor Department Library.

25. Commission on Civil Rights, *Federal Civil Rights Enforcement Effort* (1970), 170–71; Peter G. Nash, "Affirmative Action Under Executive Order 11246," 46 *New York Law Review* 232 (1971); Robert P. Schuwerk, "The Philadelphia Plan: A Study of the Dynamics of Executive Power," 39 *University of Chicago Law Review* 739 (1972).

26. George P. Shultz, "Priorities in Policy and Research for Industrial Relations," *Proceedings of the Twenty-first Annual Winter Meeting*, ed. Gerald G. Somers (Madison, Wis.: Industrial Relations Research Association, 1969), 1–13. This is Shultz's presidential address to the association, delivered on 30 December 1968 in Chicago, when Shultz was Nixon's Secretary of Labor-designate.

27. Robert P. Mayo to Dr. Arthur Burns, 13 February 1969, Budget Bureau files, National Archives.

28. *Wall Street Journal*, 28 March 1928.

29. John D. Ehrlichman, *Witness to Power* (New York: Simon & Schuster, 1982), 228–29.

30. Ehrlichman interview, 5 August 1986; *Witness to Power*, 229.

31. "Remarks by Assistant Secretary of Labor Arthur Fletcher at Signing of Philadelphia Plan," Philadelphia, Pennsylvania, June 27, 1969; Department of Labor *News*, 27 June 1969, Philadelphia Plan Documents, Department of Labor Library.

32. Fletcher to Heads of All Agencies, 27 June 1969, Philadelphia Plan Documents, Department of Labor Library.

33. Department of Labor *News*, 16 August, 23 September 1969; Fletcher and [John] Wilks to Heads of All Agencies, 23 September 1969, Department of Labor Library. Originally the roofers and waterproofers were included among the seven trades targeted in the June 27 revised plan. But the August hearings revealed progress in minority hiring since 1967 and this led to the roofers being dropped from the September 23 list. Similarly, in the FEB's original Philadelphia Plan of 1967 the operating engineers had been first included and then dropped following Phelan's survey. Thus the six Philadelphia trades covered by the OFCC's implementation order of September 23, 1969 were the iron workers, steamfitters, sheetmetal workers, electricians, elevator construction workers, and plumbers and pipefitters.

34. Contractors could demonstrate good faith effort by notifying community organizations of their work needs, maintaining an active file of minority workers, and availing themselves of relevant training programs. But contractors whose efforts failed to satisfy the OFCC faced the immediate sanction of disqualification from the bidding, and the ultimate sanction of being struck from the procurement list of potential contractors.

35. Appendix to the June 27 plan, 3. The appendix was a sample affirmative action form for contractors to submit with their bids.

36. See Nathan Glazer, *Affirmative Discrimination* (New York: Basic Books, 1975), 46–51.

37. Thomas D. Boswell and James R. Curtis, *The Cuban-American Experience* (Totowa, N.J.: Rowman & Allanheld, 1983), 168–79.

38. Alesandro Portes and Robert L. Bach, *Latin Journey: Cuban and Mexican Immigrants in the United States* (Berkeley: University of California Press, 1985), 200–239; Boswell and Curtis, *Cuban-American Experience*, 112–13.

39. Patrick Lee Gallagher, *The Cuban Exile: A Socio-Political Analysis* (New York: Arno Press, 1980), 121–45, 167–74.

40. The Office of Management and Budget during the Nixon administration incorporated Indians, Pakistanis, and Pacific Islanders into the Asian category; Eskimos and Aleuts were included as American Indians.

41. *New York Times*, 7 August 1969; *Wall Street Journal*, 26 September 1969.

42. Melvin Miller to Office of Legislative Liaison, 2 May 1969; Clarence Farmer to Staats, 11 June 1969, Philadelphia Plan file, GAO; Hugh Davis Graham, "On Riots

Commissions: Civil Disorders in the 1960s," *The Public Historian* 2 (Summer 1980): 7–27; James W. Button, *Black Violence* (Princeton: Princeton University Press, 1978).

43. Staats to Secretary Shultz, 5 August 1969, p. 9, GAO; 49 Comp. Gen. 59 (1969).

44. "Statement by Secretary Shultz," Department of Labor *News*, 6 August 1969; Executive Order 11478, 8 August 1969; Mitchell to Shultz, 22 September 1969, Labor Department Library; *New York Times*, 24 September 1969.

45. Dirksen to Shultz, 7 August 1969, NN 372-119, National Archives.

46. Subcommittee on Separation of Powers of the Senate Committee on the Judiciary, *Hearings: The Philadelphia Plan and S. 931*, 91st Cong., 1st sess., Oct. 27–28, 1969.

47. Schuwerk, "The Philadelphia Plan," 741, n100.

48. Testimony of Harry P. Taylor, Executive Director of the General Building Contractors Association, Inc., of Philadelphia, Philadelphia Plan *Hearings*, 70.

49. Sec. 904, "The Philadelphia Plan," an amendment to H.R. 15209, Supplemental Appropriation for 1970, S. Rept. 91-616, 19.

50. *Wall Street Journal*, 19 December 1969; *Washington Evening Star*, 23 December 1969.

51. *Wall Street Journal*, 23 December 1969; *Congress and the Nation*, 1969–1972, p. 6a.

52. Herman Belz, *Affirmative Action from Kennedy to Reagan: Redefining American Equality* (Washington: Washington Legal Foundation, 1984), 5.

53. Leonard testimony, Philadelphia Plan *Hearings*, 92–93.

54. *New York Times*, 16 January 1970.

55. *New York Times*, 16 January 1970; *Wall Street Journal*, 16 January 1970. The *Journal* story reported that the OFCC had extended the Philadelphia system to all contractors to offset criticisms that the Labor Department had "singled out" the construction industry.

56. 41 C.F.R. Part 60-2 (1970); *Wall Street Journal*, 4 February 1970; *New York Times*, 4 February 1970; Nash, "Affirmative Action," 235.

57. *Gaston County v. United States*, 395 U.S. 285 (1969).

Chapter 10

1. *Plessy v. Ferguson*, 163 U.S. 537 (1896) at 559; Charles A. Lofgren, *The Plessy Case* (New York: Oxford University Press, 1987).

2. *New York Times*, 23 May 1954.

3. *Brown v. Board of Education of Topeka*, 347 U.S. 483 (1954); Richard Kluger, *Simple Justice* (New York: Knopf, 1976), 315–45.

4. J. Harvie Wilkinson III, *From Brown to Bakke: The Supreme Court and School Integration 1954–1978* (New York: Oxford University Press, 1979), 118–27.

5. 347 U.S. 483, Brief for Appellants on Reargument, 15.

6. *Brown v. Board of Education*, 349 U.S. 294 (1955).

7. Stephen L. Wasby, Anthony A. D'Amato, and Rosemary Metrailer, *Desegregation from Brown to Alexander* (Carbondale: Southern Illinois Press, 1977), 108–30; David M. O'Brien, *Storm Center: The Supreme Court in American Politics* (New York: Norton, 1986), 233–34.

8. Louis Lusky, "Racial Discrimination and the Federal Law: A Problem in Nullification," 63 *Columbia Law Review* 1172 (1963), n37.

9. Lino A. Graglia, *Disaster by Decree: The Supreme Court Decisions on Race in the Schools* (Ithaca: Cornell University Press, 1976), 26–32, 36.

10. *Bolling v. Sharpe*, 347 U.S. 499 (1954).

11. Traditionally the courts had applied a "rational-basis" test to state classifications, which required only that legislators and other policy-makers demonstrate a rational relationship between means and ends—for example, a law requiring firemen to

retire at age 55, which was premised upon rational assumptions about advancing age and the dangers of firefighting. The rational-basis test reflects traditions of judicial restraint, where appointed judges defer to elected officials in the shaping of public policy. Critics have attacked the subjective nature of many "rational" policy assumptions, as, for example, the historical exclusion of women from practicing the learned professions.

12. Wilkinson, *Brown to Bakke*, 108–18.

13. J.W. Peltason, *Fifty-eight Lonely Men* (New York: Harcourt, Brace & World, 1961).

14. Jack Bass, *Unlikely Heroes* (New York: Simon & Schuster, 1981).

15. *United States v. Jefferson County Board of Education*, 372 F.2d 836 (5th Cir. 1966); Wilkinson, *Brown to Bakke*, 78–192; Raymond Wolters, *The Burden of Brown: Thirty Years of School Desegregation* (Knoxville: University of Tennessee Press, 1984), 150–55.

16. *Jefferson*, 372 F. 2d at 866.

17. Wilkinson, *Brown to Bakke*, 112.

18. *Green v. County School Board of New Kent County*, 391 U.S. 430 (1968) at 439.

19. Wilkinson, *Brown to Bakke*, 107, 327 n.171.

20. *Jones v. Alfred H. Mayer Co.*, 392 U.S. 409 (1968).

21. *Allen v. State Board of Elections*, 393 U.S. 544 (1969). The lead case in *Allen* arose in Virginia; see Hugh Davis Graham, *The Civil Rights Era* (New York: Oxford University Press, 1990), 377–81.

22. *Allen v. Board of Elections*, 393 U.S. at 563–64.

23. *Reynolds v. Sims*, 377 U.S. 533 (1964). For discussions of vote dilution that generally support Warren's broad interpretation, see Chandler Davidson, ed., *Minority Vote Dilution* (Washington, D.C.: Howard University Press, 1985); and Howard Ball, "Racial Vote Dilution: Impact of the Reagan DOJ and the Burger Court on the Voting Rights Act," *Publius* 16 (Fall 1986): 29–48.

24. *Allen v. Board of Elections*, 393 U.S. at 569.

25. G. Edward White, *The American Judicial Tradition* (New York: Oxford University Press, 1988), 341.

26. J. Harvie Wilkinson, "Justice John Marshall Harlan and the Values of Federalism," 57 *Virginia Law Review* 1185 (1971).

27. *Allen v. Board of Elections*, 393 U.S. at 564.

28. Ibid., at 586.

29. As G. Edward White conceded in his admiring biography of Warren, the Chief Justice "equated judicial lawmaking with neither the dictates of reason, as embodied in established precedent or doctrine, nor the demands imposed by an institutional theory of the judge's role, nor the alleged 'command' of the constitutional text, but rather with his own reconstruction of the ethical structure of the Constitution." G. Edward White, *Earl Warren: A Public Life* (New York: Oxford University Press, 1982), 359.

30. The relevant precedent was not *Reynolds v. Sims*, Harlan said, but *Gomillion v. Lightfoot*, 364 U.S. 339 (1960), a Fifteenth amendment opinion by Justice Frankfurter (whose mantle of judicial restraint Harlan carried, often and in dwindling company, on the Warren Court of the 1960s) that had struck down a gerrymander against black voters in Tuskeegee, Alabama.

31. *Alexander v. Holmes County*, 396 U.S. 1218 (1969), 396 U.S. 19 (1969).

32. John Ehrlichman, *Witness to Power* (New York: Simon & Schuster, 1982); Ehrlichman interview with the author, 5 August 1986; Bob Woodward and Scott Armstrong, *The Brethren: Inside the Supreme Court* (New York: Simon & Schuster, 1979), 60.

33. Jonathan Spivak, "Supreme Court to Take Up Desegregation, Pitting Nixon Policies Against the Liberals," *New York Times*, 12 October 1970.

34. 42 U.S.C. 2000 (c).

35. Burger's political reading of the play of congressional motives during 1963–64 was in part correct, especially regarding the determination of key moderates like McCulloch and Dirksen to direct the Civil Rights Act mostly against racial segregation in the South. In 1974 in *Milliken v. Bradley,* 418 U.S. 717, Burger in speaking for a 5-4 majority reversed a lower court order for racial busing across school district lines in metropolitan Detroit.

36. Wilkinson, *Brown to Bakke,* 131–51.

37. *Swann v. Charlotte-Mecklenburg Board of Education,* 402 U.S. (1971) at 31.

38. *Contractors Association of Eastern Pennsylvania v. Secretary of Labor,* 311 F. Supp. 1002 (E.D. Pa. 1790); *Wall Street Journal,* 16 March 1970.

39. *Contractors Association of Eastern Pennsylvania v. Secretary of Labor,* 442 F.2d 159 (3rd Cir. 1971), *cert. denied,* 404 U.S. 854 (1971).

40. *Griggs, v. Duke Power Company,* 401 U.S. 424 (1971).

41. *Griggs v. Duke Power Co.,* 292 F. Supp. 243 (1968); Derrick A. Bell, Jr., *Race, Racism and American Law* (Boston: Little, Brown, 1980), 619–23.

42. *Griggs v. Duke Power Co.,* 420 F.2d 1225 (4th Cir. 1970); Alfred W. Blumrosen, "Strangers in Paradise: *Griggs v. Duke Power Co.* and the Concept of Employment Discrimination," 71 *Michigan Law Review* 59 (1972).

43. Author interview with John deJ. Pemberton, Jr., 3 March 1985, San Francisco.

44. Pemberton to Greenberg (not sent), 27 January 1970, supplied to the author by courtesy of John deJ. Pemberton, Jr.

45. *Quarles v. Phillip Morris, Inc.,* 279 F. Supp. 505 (E.D. Va. 1968).

46. *Griggs v. Duke Power,* 420 F.2d at 1239–44; *New York Times,* 18 June 1970.

47. Phil Lyons, "An Agency with a Mind of Its Own: The EEOC's Guidelines on Employment Testing," *New Perspectives* 17 (Fall 1985): 20–25; *Personnel Testing and Equal Employment Opportunity,* eds. Betty R. Anderson and Martha P. Rogers (Washington: U.S. Government Printing Office, 1970).

48. G. Edward White, "The Burger Court," *American Judicial Tradition,* 424–34.

49. Nina Totenberg, "Behind the Marble, Beneath the Robes," *New York Times Magazine,* 16 March 1975, especially 63–64; Woodward and Armstrong, *The Brethren,* 140–41. Woodward and Armstrong based their portrait of the inside workings of the Burger Court primarily on the anonymous evidence provided by former law clerks. Thus *The Brethren* is essentially undocumented and must be used with caution.

50. *Griggs v. Duke Power,* 401 U.S. at 430–31.

51. Ibid., at 432; *Wall Street Journal,* 9 March 1971.

52. 110 *Congressional Record* 6415 (1964).

53. Ibid., at 7213.

54. Equal Employment Opportunity Commission, "Guidelines on Employee Selection Procedures," 29 CFR @1607, 35 *Federal Register* 12333 (1 August 1970).

55. 110 *Congressional Record,* Pt. 7 (1964), 13492. For interpretations that support Burger's view, see George Cooper and Richard B. Sobel, "Seniority and Testing Under Fair Employment Laws: A General Approach to Objective Criteria of Hiring and Promotion," 82 *Harvard Law Review* 1598 (1969); Blumrosen, "Strangers in Paradise," 59–110. For a critical view see Donald L. Horowitz, *The Courts and Social Policy* (Washington: Brookings Institution, 1977), 15.

56. 110 *Congressional Record,* pt. 7 (1964), 8194.

57. EEOC *Administrative History,* Vol. I, LBJL, 1969, 17.

58. Gary Bryner, "Congress, Courts, and Agencies: Equal Employment and the Limits of Policy Implementation," *Political Science Quarterly* 96 (Fall 1981): 411–30.

59. Hugh Steven Wilson, "A Second Look at *Griggs v. Duke Power Company:* Ruminations on Testing, Discrimination, and the Role of the Federal Courts," 63 *Virginia Law Review* 844 (1972), especially 852–58. But see also William N. Eskridge, Jr., "Dynamic Statutory Interpretation," 135 *University of Pennsylvania Law Review* 1479 (1987), especially 1506–11, for criticism of the "intentionalist' doctrine as incoherent.

60. *New York Times,* 9 March 1971.

61. Blumrosen, "Strangers in Paradise," 62.

62. *New York Times,* 9 March 1971.

63. *Griggs v. Duke Power,* 401 U.S. at 429.

64. Michael Brody, "Congress, the President, and Federal Equal Employment Policy-making: A Problem in Separation of Powers," 60 *Boston University Law Review* 239 (1980), especially 260–63.

65. Note, "Business Necessity Under Title VII of the Civil Rights Act of 1964: A No-Alternative Approach," 84 *Yale Law Journal* 98 (1974); Horowitz, *Courts and Social Policy,* 15.

66. *United Steelworkers of America v. Weber,* 443 U.S. 193 (1979).

67. *DeFunis v. Odegard,* 416 U.S. 312 (1974); *Regents of the University of California v. Bakke,* 438 U.S. 265 (1978); Robert M. O'Neil, *Discrimination Against Discrimination: Preferential Admissions and the DeFunis Case* (Bloomington: Indiana University Press, 1975); Timothy J. O'Neill, *Bakke and the Politics of Equality* (Middletown, Conn.: Wesleyan University Press, 1985).

68. *Goesaert v. Cleary,* 335 U.S. 464 (1948).

69. *Hoyt v. Florida,* 368 U.S. 57 (1961).

Chapter 11

1. Janet K. Boles, *The Politics of the Equal Rights Amendment* (New York: Long-man, 1979), 37–40; Marguerite Rawalt, "The Equal Rights Amendment," *Women in Washington,* ed. Irene Tinker (Beverly Hills, Calif.: Sage, 1983), 49–78. The Hayden rider, by exempting women's protective legislation, so compromised the amendment that its supporters rejected an ERA with the Hayden rider attached.

2. Esther Peterson, "The Kennedy Commission," *Women in Washington,* 23; Cynthia Harrison, *On Account of Sex* (Berkeley: University of California Press, 1988), 182–83.

3. Throughout the 1950s Rep. Emanuel Celler regularly sponsored bills to establish a commission to study the legal status of women, while keeping ERA bills bottled up in his Judiciary Committee. In 1961 Celler's status-of-women bill carried his own version of the Hayden rider: it called for equal treatment of women "except such as reasonably justified by differences in physical structure, biological, or social function." Celler's proposed commission, which would report to Congress, was pre-empted by President Kennedy's own status-of-women commission. Rawalt, "The Equal Rights Amendment," *Women in Washington,* 52–58.

4. *American Women: Report of the President's Commission on the Status of Women* (Washington: U.S. Government Printing Office, 1963), 45.

5. Patricia G. Zelman, *Women, Work, and National Policy: The Kennedy-Johnson Years* (Ann Arbor: UMI Research Press, 1980); Harrison, *On Account of Sex,* 192–209.

6. Catherine East, "Newer Commissions," *Women in Washington,* 35–36.

7. Press release, Citizen's Advisory Council on the Status of Women, July 1968, Clapp file, RMNP.

8. Burns Report, 18 January 1969, 81, 82–83.

9. The President's News Conference of February 6, 1969, *Public Papers of the Presidents: Richard M. Nixon, 1969* (Washington: U.S. Government Printing Office, 1971), 75.

10. Jo Freeman, *The Politics of Women's Liberation* (New York: David McKay, 1975), 205–6.

11. Partial transcript, enclosed with Glaser to Burns, 23 May 1969, Clapp file, RMNP.

12. Glaser to Burns, 23 May 1969, Clapp file, RMNP.

13. Bra-burning as a media symbol for radical feminist kookiness was resented by feminists as symptomatic of a generalized sexist refusal to take the movement and its

social critique seriously. Feminists pointed out that unlike draft card burning, the bra-burning was largely a media concoction, drawn from the feminist demonstration against the 1968 Miss America Contest, where bras and girdles and false eyelashes were thrown into a "freedom trash can." In response, many women's liberation leaders refused to speak to male reporters. Freeman, *Politics of Women's Liberation*, 111–13; Joanna Foley Martin, "Confessions of a Non Bra-Burner," *Chicago Journalism Review* 4 (July 1971): 11–13.

14. Dwyer's letter to Nixon is attached to Glaser to Burns, 23 May 1969.

15. Dwyer to the President, 8 July 1969, Clapp file, RMNP.

16. Burns to Allan, 12 September 1969; Allan to Burns, 30 September 1969, Women's Rights, Task Forces file, Burns Papers, Gerald R. Ford Library (GRFL).

17. White House Press release, 1 October 1969, RMNP. For a more detailed discussion of the women's task force, see Hugh Davis Graham, *The Civil Rights Era* (New York: Oxford University Press, 1990), 400–406.

18. Report of the President's Task Force on Women's Rights and Responsibilities, December 1969, Task Force file, Burns Papers, GRFL.

19. *Report of the President's Task Force on Women's Rights and Responsibilities* (1970), 8, 30, Clapp file, RMNP.

20. Transcript, White House press conference, 9 June 1970, 4.

21. Burns to Allan, 9 January 1970, Burns file, GRFL.

22. Citizens Advisory Council on the Status of Women, *Women in 1970* (Washington: U.S. Government Printing Office, 1970), 2.

23. Freeman, *Politics of Women's Liberation*, 212–21.

24. Glaser, "Female Elite of U.S., " *Detroit Free Press*, 13 April 1970; *New York Times*, 23 April 1970; East, "Newer Commissions," *Women in Washington*, 38.

25. The President's Task Force on Women's Rights and Responsibilities, *A Matter of Simple Justice* (Washington: U.S. Government Printing Office, April 1970).

26. Garment to Ehrlichman, 25 May 1970, EX HU 2-5, WHCF, RMNP.

27. Rawalt, "The Equal Rights Amendment," *Women in Washington*, 62–65; Emily George, *Martha Griffiths* (Washington: University Press of America, 1982), 170–72. On 10 August 1970, having forced the ERA resolution out of Celler's Judiciary Committee with a discharge petition bearing the requisite 217 signatures, Griffiths joined 331 of her House colleagues in voting for ERA to only 22 opposed.

28. *Hearings* on the Utilization of Minority and Women Workers in Certain Major Industries, Los Angeles, March 12–14, 1969; Sonia Pressman, "Job Discrimination and the Black Woman," *The Crisis* (March 1970): 103–8; Freeman, *Politics of Women's Liberation*, 209.

29. According to subsequent surveys the proportion of women in blue-collar jobs has remained surprisingly constant since 1970. The Bureau of Labor Statistics reported in 1987 that between 1970 and 1986, the female percentage of operators, fabricators, and laborers declined from 25.9 to 25.4 percent, and the women's proportion of workers in precision production, craft, and repair increased from 7.3 to 8.6 percent. Substantial increases came in managerial and business specialties (33.9 to 43.4 percent) and professional specialties like law, teaching, and writing (44.3 to 49.4 percent). But the largest category for female participation remained that of administrative support, including clerical (73.2 to 80.4 percent) and service occupations (60.4 to 62.6 percent). *New York Times*, 17 July 1987.

30. For a discussion of WEAL's campaign to apply Title 6 and Executive Order 11375 (Johnson's order of 1967 adding sex discrimination to his 1965 order) to institutions of higher education, see Freeman, *Politics of Women's Liberation*, 191–99.

31. Garment to Cole, 3 June 1970, EX HU 2-5, WHCF, RMNP.

32. Title 41, Ch. 60, Part 60-20, "Sex Discrimination Guidelines," U.S. Department of Labor, attached to Garment to Cole, 3 June 1970.

33. *Washington Post*, 10 June 1970. In 1971 the OFCC with little publicity issued a "Revised Order No. 4" that added women to the goals-and-timetables formula for

federally assisted contractors. The new order finessed the problem of population proportionality for women by defining underutilization with flexible vagueness as "fewer minorities or women than would reasonably be expected by their availability." See Graham, *Civil Rights Era*, 412–15.

34. Boles, *The Politics of the Equal Rights Amendment*, concentrates on the ratification process in the state legislatures prior to 1979. Similarly, Gilbert Y. Steiner, *Constitutional Inequality: The Political Fortunes of the Equal Rights Amendment* (Washington: Brookings Institution, 1985), focuses on the critical role of such unanticipated complications as the abortion ruling and Watergate. See also Hoff-Wilson (ed.), *Rights of Passage*, 39–92; Jane J. Mansbridge, *Why We Lost the ERA* (Chicago: University of Chicago Press, 1986); and Mary Frances Berry, *Why ERA Failed* (Bloomington: Indiana University Press, 1986).

35. 116 *Congressional Record*, 18075–78, 91st Cong., 2nd sess., 17 October 1970; George, *Griffiths*, 173–81; *Congressional Quarterly Almanac*, 1970, 706–10.

36. *Equal Rights for Men and Women*, Hearings Before Subcommittee No. 4 of the House Judiciary Committee, 92nd Cong., 1st sess., March 24, 25, 31 and April 1, 2, and 5, 1971. See Thomas I. Emerson, Barbara A. Brown, Gail Falk, and Ann E. Freedman, "The Equal Rights Amendment: A Constitutional Basis for Equal Rights for Women," 80 *Yale Law Journal* 871 (April 1971); Paul A. Freud, "The Equal Rights Amendment Is Not the Way," 6 *Harvard Civil Rights—Civil Liberties Law Review* 234 (March 1971); and Philip B. Kurland, "The Equal Rights Amendment: Some Problems of Construction," 6 *Harvard Civil Rights—Civil Liberties Law Review* 242 (March 1971).

37. Transcript, Statement of William H. Rehnquist, Assistant Attorney General, Office of Legal Counsel, on H.J. Res. 208, 1 April 1971, EX HU 2-5, WHCF, RMNP.

38. Gutwillig to the President, 2 April 1971, Ex Hu 2-5, WHCF, RMNP.

39. *Congressional Quarterly Almanac*, 1971, 656–59; Boles, *Politics of the Equal Rights Amendment*, 103, 139; Gary Orfield, *Congressional Power* (New York: Harcourt Brace Jovanovich, 1975), 298–306.

40. *Reed v. Reed*, 404 U.S. 71 (1971). Chief Justice Burger's opinion held narrowly that states could not pass laws treating men and women differently unless some clear, rational-basis reason was given for doing so.

41. George, *Griffiths*, 179.

42. *Washington Post*, 28 February 1972.

43. *Congressional Quarterly Almanac*, 1972, 199–204.

44. White House press release, Nixon to Scott, 18 March 1972; *Public Papers: Nixon, 1972*, 61.

45. The guiding case is *Craig v. Boren*, 429 U.S. 190 (1976). For a critique of the Court's "confused" and "muddled" attempts in *Reed v. Reed, Frontiero v. Richardson, Craig v. Boren*, and subsequent decisions to sort out the race-sex analogy, see David L. Kirp, Mark G. Yudof, and Marlene Strong Franks, *Gender Justice* (Chicago: University of Chicago Press, 1986), 90–123.

46. See Ruth Ginsburg, "Sex Equality and the Constitution," *Tulane Law Review* 52 (1978): 451–66; Rex E. Lee, *A Lawyer Looks at the Equal Rights Amendment* (Provo: Brigham Young University Press, 1980); and Joan Hoff-Wilson, "The Unfinished Revolution: Changing Legal Status of U.S. Women," *Signs* 13 (Autumn 1987): 16–36.

47. *The Phyllis Schlafly Report*, "What's Wrong with 'Equal Rights' for Women?," February 1972, and "The Right To Be a Woman," November 1972.

Chapter 12

1. Bernice Sandler, "A Little Help from Our Government: WEAL and Contract Compliance," in *Academic Women on the Move*, ed. Alice Rossi and Anne Calderwood

(New York: Russell Sage Foundation, 1973), 440–41; Freeman, *Politics of Women's Liberation* (New York: David McKay, 1975), 191–202.

2. Joyce Gelb and Marian Lief Palley, *Women and Public Policies* (Princeton: Princeton University Press, 1982), 93–128; Myra Marx Feree and Beth B. Hess, *Controversy and Coalition* (Boston: Twayne, 1985), 116–21; Susan M. Hartman, *From Margin to Mainstream* (New York: Knopf, 1989), 108–13.

3. Howard Schuman, Charlotte Steeh, and Lawrence Bobo, *Racial Attitudes in America* (Cambridge: Harvard University Press, 1985), 86–104; Robert S. Erickson et al., *American Public Opinion* (New York: Macmillan, 1988), 180–81.

4. *Congress and the Nation 1969–1972* (Washington: Congressional Quarterly Press, 1973), 505–9.

5. *New York Times,* 8 April 1971. H.R. 1746 was co-sponsored by New York Republican Ogden Reid, thus lending it the appearance of bipartisan support. But Reid was the only Republican on the Education and Labor Committee to vote for it.

6. *Wall Street Journal,* 4 May 1971; *New York Times,* 2 June 1971. Nineteen of 20 Democrats on the House Education and Labor Committee supported the Hawkins bill, and 11 of 13 Republicans opposed it.

7. House Report 238, 92nd Cong., 1st sess., 2 June 1971.

8. *Congressional Quarterly Almanac: 1971* (Washington: Congressional Quarterly Press, 1972), 644–49.

9. "Minority Views on H.R. 1746," House Report 238, 58–67. The only Democrat on the committee to vote against the Hawkins bill was Romano L. Mazzoli of Kentucky. Thus the Erlenborn-Mazzoli bill, like the Hawkins- Reid bill, was bipartisan in formal co-sponsorship only.

10. *New York Times,* 9 May 1971; *Wall Street Journal,* 15 September 1971.

11. *Congressional Quarterly Almanac: 1971,* 648.

12. *New York Times,* 27 January 1972.

13. George P. Sape and Thomas J. Hart, "Title VII Reconsidered: The Equal Employment Opportunity Act of 1972," 40 *George Washington Law Review* 824 (1971–72).

14. Ibid., 847.

15. 118 *Congressional Record,* Pt. 2, 92nd Cong., 2nd sess., 28 January 1972, p. 1656.

16. Ibid., 1657–58.

17. Ibid., 1661–62.

18. *Quarles v. Philip Morris, Inc.,* 279 F. Supp. 505 (E.D. Va. 1968). See William B. Gould, "Seniority and the Black Worker: Reflections on *Quarles* and Its Implications," 47 *Texas Law Review* 1039 (1969).

19. 118 *Congressional Record,* 28 January 1972, pp. 1675–76.

20. H[arry] R[obbins] Haldeman, Notes from Meetings with the President, 27 January 1972, Haldeman file, WHSF, RMNP.

21. *Congressional Quarterly Almanac: 1972,* 247; *New York Times,* 27 February 1972.

22. See generally *The Equal Employment Opportunity Act of 1972* (Washington: Bureau of National Affairs, 1973), a 415-page synopsis of the law's background, congressional evolution, and provisions.

23. Title VII of the Civil Rights Act, Sec. 706(g), as amended by P.L. 92-261.

24. Andrew Kahn Blumstein, "Doing Good the Wrong Way: The Case for Delimiting Presidential Power Under Executive Order No. 11246," 33 *Vanderbilt Law Review* 921 (1980), 946–61; Herman Belz, *Affirmative Action from Kennedy to Reagan* (Washington: Washington Legal Foundation, 1984), 5.

25. Robert P. Schuwerk, "The Philadelphia Plan: A Study in the Dynamics of Executive Power," 39 *University of Chicago Law Review* 723 (1972): 751–60.

26. Michael Brody, "Congress, the President, and Federal Equal Employment Policymaking: A Problem in Separation of Powers," 60 *Boston University Law Review* 239 (1980): 299.

27. "Address to the Nation on Equal Opportunity and School Busing," 16 March 1972, *Public Papers: Nixon, 1972,* 425–29; A. James Reichley, *Conservatives in an Age of Change* (Washington: Brookings Institution, 1981), 197–99.

28. *Public Papers: Nixon, 1972,* 436, 437.

29. Nixon to Ehrlichman, 8 April 1972, Haldeman files, WHSF, RMNP.

30. On March 14, Wallace by a plurality of 42 percent won the Democratic presidential primary in Florida, with more than double the vote of his nearest rival, Hubert Humphrey. Wallace placed second in the Wisconsin and Pennsylvania primaries in April and won more than 40 percent of the vote in Indiana in early May. He also easily won primaries in Alabama, North Carolina, and Tennessee. McGovern and Humphrey mounted last-minute "stop-Wallace" drives in Michigan and Maryland, where primaries were scheduled for May 16. Wallace was shot and permanently crippled while campaigning in Laurel, Md., on May 15. He won the Michigan and Maryland primaries the next day, but was forced by his injuries to drop out of the race.

31. In the Detroit school desegregation case, *Milliken v. Bradley,* 418 U.S. 717 (1974), the federal district court in 1972 had joined 53 of Detroit's 85 outlying suburban school districts with the city school system and ordered cross-district busing for 310,000 students. In 1973 the Sixth Circuit Court of Appeals affirmed the busing decree by a vote of six to three, but in 1974 the Supreme Court reversed by a vote of five to four, with Burger writing the majority opinion.

32. Ehrlichman to Nixon, 1 June 1972; Morgan to Ehrlichman, 18 May 1972, Ehrlichman files, WHSF, RMNP.

33. Transcript, Keynote Address by Bishop Stephen S. Spottswood, 5 July 1972, NAACP Papers, LC.

34. *Public Papers: Nixon, 1972,* 788.

35. Ibid., 852; *Wall Street Journal,* 5 September 1972.

36. *New York Times,* 14 June 1972.

37. *New York Times,* 16 February 1972.

38. In 1974 Congress would pass and President Ford would sign a $585-million authorization for bilingual education, and in 1975 Ford would propose and Congress would enact a revision of the Voting Rights Act to protect language minorities.

39. *Wall Street Journal,* 11 May 1971.

40. *Wall Street Journal,* 25 January 1972.

41. *Business Week,* 24 March 1973, pp. 74–75.

Chapter 13

1. See Barry R. Gross, ed., *Reverse Discrimination* (Buffalo: Prometheus Press, 1977); Timothy J. O'Neill, *Bakke and the Politics of Equality* (Middletown, Conn.: Wesleyan University Press, 1985); Robert Belton, "Discrimination and Affirmative Action: An Analysis of Competing Theories of Equality and *Weber,*" 59 *North Carolina Law Review* 531 (1981).

2. Criticizing the Reagan record from the left is Norman C. Amaker, *Civil Rights and the Reagan Administration* (Washington: Urban Institute, 1988); criticizing from the right is Robert Detlefsen, *Civil Rights Under Reagan* (San Francisco: ICS Press, 1990).

3. Howard Schuman, Charlotte Steeh, and Lawrence Bobo, *Racial Attitudes in America: Trends and Interpretations* (Cambridge: Harvard University Press, 1985), 86–104; Hugh Davis Graham, *The Civil Rights Era* (New York: Oxford University Press, 1990), 454–56. The survey data show growing polarization in the 1980s, as support for preferential policies increased among minorities.

4. Edward G. Carmines and James A. Stimson, *Issue Evolution: Race and the Transformation of American Politics* (Princeton: Princeton University Press, 1990).

5. A superior exploration of the legal, philosophical, and ethical dimensions is

Kent Greenawalt, *Discrimination and Reverse Discrimination* (New York: Knopf, 1983).

6. In 1971 John Rawls provided a philosophical treatise to justify contractarian obligations for compensating benefits to society's least advantaged members in *A Theory of Justice* (Cambridge, Mass.: Belknap Press, 1971). On the eve of the *Bakke* decision, Ronald Dworkin published a defense of preferential treatment in *Taking Rights Seriously* (Cambridge: Harvard University Press, 1977), 223–39.

7. Owen Fiss, "The Fate of an Idea Whose Time Has Come: Antidiscrimination Law in the Second Decade after *Brown v. Board of Education,*" 41 *University of Chicago Law Review* 742 (1974).

8. William N. Eskridge, Jr., "Dynamic Statutory Interpretation," 135 *University of Pennsylvania Law Review* 1479 (1987).

9. Samuel P. Huntington, "The Democratic Distemper," *The Public Interest* 41 (Fall 1971): 13.

10. Matthew A. Crenson and Francis E. Rourke, "By Way of Conclusion: American Bureaucracy Since World War II," in *The New American State: Bureaucracies and Policies Since World War II,* ed. Louis Galambos (Baltimore: Johns Hopkins University Press, 1987), 137–77.

11. For an elaboration of the oversimplified "iron triangle" model, see Hugh Heclo, "Issue Networks and the Executive Establishment," in *The New American Political System,* ed. Anthony King (Washington: American Enterprise Institute, 1978), 89–90.

12. Crenson and Rourke, "American Bureaucracy," 151.

13. David Vogel, "The 'New' Social Regulation in Historical and Comparative Perspective," in *Regulation in Perspective,* ed. Thomas K. McCraw (Cambridge: Harvard University Press, 1981), 155–86.

14. For a comparison of the new social regulation and the traditional economic regulation that does not include civil rights as a regulatory field, see Frederick R. Anderson, "Human Welfare and the Administered Society: Federal Regulation in the 1970s to Protect Health, Safety, and the Environment," in *Environmental and Occupational Medicine,* ed. W. Rom (Boston: Little, Brown, 1983), 835–64.

15. Michael D. Reagan, *Regulation* (Boston: Little, Brown, 1987), 45–71, 85–111.

16. Gary C. Bryner, *Bureaucratic Discretion: Law and Policy in Federal Regulatory Agencies* (New York: Permagon, 1987), 19–90.

17. It should be noted that in practice there was more overlap between the social and economic models of regulation than this bi-polar treatment suggests—i.e., all regulatory bodies exercised some measure of rule-making authority, and none performed in a purely zero-sum or redistributionist environment.

18. Nathan Glazer, *Affirmative Discrimination: Ethnic Inequality and Public Policy* (New York: Basic Books, 1975); Peter Steinfels, *The Neoconservatives* (New York: Simon & Schuster, 1979).

19. Laurence H. Silberman, "The Road to Racial Quotas," *Wall Street Journal,* 11 August 1977.

20. Graham, *The Civil Rights Era,* 460–68; John C. Whitaker, *Striking A Balance: Environmental and Natural Resources Policy in the Nixon-Ford Years* (Washington: American Enterprise Institute, 1976).

21. Donald L. Horowitz, *The Courts and Social Policy* (Washington: Brookings Institution, 1977). But see also Cass R. Sunstein, *After the Rights Revolution* (Cambridge: Harvard University Press, 1990).

22. James Q. Wilson, *Bureaucracy* (New York: Basic Books, 1989), 72–83.

23. The other two categories of regulation in Wilson's four-cell, cost-benefit analysis are *majoritarian* politics, where both costs and benefits are widely distributed (Social Security and highway safety programs), and *interest-group* politics (collective bargaining, shipper regulation), where both costs and benefits are narrowly distributed. Voting-rights enforcement in electoral districting, where selected minorities are advantaged in outcomes, follows the interest-group pattern and hence has been less controversial than

the client pattern of most affirmative action preferences. The costs are borne by a small number of white incumbent office-holders, and the benefits are enjoyed by a limited number of potential minority office-holders. Interest-group lobbying is intense, but most citizens do not feel directly affected. See James Q. Wilson, ed., *The Politics of Regulation* (New York: Basic Books, 1980), 364–72.

24. David M. Welborn, *Governance of Federal Regulatory Agencies* (Knoxville: University of Tennessee Press, 1977).

25. Paul Burstein, *Discrimination, Jobs, and Politics* (Chicago: University of Chicago Press, 1985), 97–124; Jeremy Rabkin, *Judicial Compulsions* (New York: Basic Books, 1989).

26. Samuel P. Hays, "The Politics of Choice in Regulatory Administrations," in *Regulation in Perspective*, 124–54.

27. Richard K. Scotch, *From Good Will to Civil Rights: Transforming Federal Disability Policy* (Philadelphia: Temple University Press, 1984); Edward D. Berkowitz, *Disabled Policy* (Cambridge: Cambridge University Press, 1987); Stephen L. Percy, *Disability, Civil Rights, and Public Policy* (Tuscaloosa: University of Alabama Press, 1989).

28. Francis E. Rourke, "Bureaucracy in the American Constitutional Order," *Political Science Quarterly* (Summer 1987), 25–28.

29. Abram Chayes, "The Role of the Judge in Public Law Litigation," 89 *Harvard Law Review* 1282 (May 1976).

30. *Griggs v. Duke Power Company*, 401 U.S. 424 (1971) at 430–31.

31. *Regents of the University of California v. Bakke*, 438 U.S. 265 (1978) at 403.

32. *United Steelworkers of America v. Weber*, 443 U.S. 193 (1979) at 216.

33. Cynthia Harrison, *On Account of Sex* (Berkeley: University of California Press, 1988).

34. Hugh Davis Graham, "Civil Rights and the Irony of the Race-Sex Linkage: 1964–1972," paper delivered at the annual meeting of the Southern Historical Association, New Orleans, 14 November 1987.

35. William H. Chafe, *Women and Equality* (New York: Oxford University Press, 1977).

Index